THE CAMBRIDGE COMPANION TO
VICTORIAN LITERATURE AND THE ENVIRONMENT

Today's environmental decimation and climate crises have arisen from our drive for individual material prosperity. We even appreciate nature primarily for its fulfilment of *our* interests, whether economic productivity, aesthetic pleasure, or personal well-being. And yet we still ask how we have reached this dire ecological condition and what it is that has kept us from acting effectively to maintain a thriving and diverse biosphere. This collection of chapters by major scholars from around the world analyzes how the industrial imperialist Victorian era gave rise to today's unwillingness to move beyond our acquisitive drive. But it also explores the Victorians' initiation of the modern environmentalist movement, formulation of the first legislation defending rights of non-human animals, and invention of literary forms for contesting environmental degradation. In this most unlikely of eras, the volume uncovers both valuable insights into the limitations of our own environmentalism and innovative suggestions for overcoming them.

Dennis Denisoff is the Ida Barnard McFarlin Chair of English at the University of Tulsa, Fellow of the Royal Society of Canada, and recipient of the President's Award from both the Nineteenth-Century Studies Association and the North American Victorian Studies Association. He held the position of Sarwan Sahota Distinguished Scholar at Toronto Metropolitan University and was recently Visiting Distinguished Researcher at Queen Mary University of London and the 2025 Ruth and Lillian Marino Chair of the Bread Loaf School of English at Middlebury College. He is the author of *Decadent Ecology in British Literature and Art, 1860–1910* (Cambridge University Press, 2021).

A complete list of books in the series is at the back of the book.

AF147925

THE CAMBRIDGE
COMPANION TO

VICTORIAN
LITERATURE AND
THE ENVIRONMENT

EDITED BY
DENNIS DENISOFF
University of Tulsa

CAMBRIDGE
UNIVERSITY PRESS

Shaftesbury Road, Cambridge CB2 8EA, United Kingdom

One Liberty Plaza, 20th Floor, New York, NY 10006, USA

477 Williamstown Road, Port Melbourne, VIC 3207, Australia

314–321, 3rd Floor, Plot 3, Splendor Forum, Jasola District Centre,
New Delhi – 110025, India

Cambridge University Press is part of Cambridge University Press & Assessment,
a department of the University of Cambridge.

We share the University's mission to contribute to society through the pursuit of
education, learning and research at the highest international levels of excellence.

www.cambridge.org
Information on this title: www.cambridge.org/9781009412810
DOI: 10.1017/9781009412865

First published 2026

Cover image: *Man Proposes, God Disposes*, 1864. Sir Edwin Landseer (1802–1873).
Oil on canvas. Purchased by Thomas Holloway, 1881; acc. no. THC 0032.

A catalogue record for this publication is available from the British Library

Library of Congress Cataloging-in-Publication Data
NAMES: Denisoff, Dennis, 1961– editor
TITLE: The Cambridge companion to Victorian literature and the environment /
edited by Dennis Denisoff.
DESCRIPTION: Cambridge ; New York, NY : Cambridge University Press, 2026. |
Series: Cambridge companions to literature | Includes bibliographical references.
IDENTIFIERS: LCCN 2025039296 (print) | LCCN 2025039297 (ebook) |
ISBN 9781009412841 hardback | ISBN 9781009412810 paperback |
ISBN 9781009412865 ebook
SUBJECTS: LCSH: English literature – 19th century – History and criticism | Ecology in
literature | Environmental literature – Great Britain – History and criticism |
LCGFT: Literary criticism
CLASSIFICATION: LCC PR468.E34 C36 2026 (print) | LCC PR468.E34 (ebook)
LC record available at https://lccn.loc.gov/2025039296
LC ebook record available at https://lccn.loc.gov/2025039297

ISBN 978-1-009-41284-1 Hardback
ISBN 978-1-009-41281-0 Paperback

For EU product safety concerns, contact us at Calle de José Abascal,
56, 1°, 28003 Madrid, Spain, or email eugpsr@cambridge.org.

To Morgan Holmes, who has been there for me throughout this project and all of my eco-life. Let me count the ways – concussed by a cliff in the Keystone Ancient Forest, drowned by a deluge on the Bannau Brycheiniog, among escaped snakes at the Accra Zoo, riding a rip current in the Gulf of Guinea, a little bit dead in Alba de Tormes. Way we go, way we go, way we go.

CONTENTS

vii

CONTENTS

FIGURES

CONTRIBUTORS

SUKANYA BANERJEE is Associate Professor of English at the University of California, Berkeley. She is the author of *Becoming Imperial Citizens: Indians in the Late-Victorian Empire* (Duke, 2010) and co-editor of *New Routes in Diaspora Studies* (Indiana, 2012). She is currently working on a book on loyalty and its relation to modernity in Victorian Britain and its empire.

ELIZABETH CHANG is an independent scholar and former Professor of English at the University of Missouri. Her publications include *Britain's Chinese Eye: Literature, Empire, and Aesthetics in the Nineteenth Century* (Stanford University Press, 2010), *Novel Cultivations: Plants in British Literature of the Global Nineteenth Century* (University of Virginia Press, 2019), and studies of British travel writing from China.

DENNIS DENISOFF is the Ida Barnard McFarlin Chair of English at the University of Tulsa and Fellow of the Royal Society of Canada. His recent publications include *Decadent Ecology in British Literature and Art, 1860–1910: Decay, Desire, and the Pagan Revival* (Cambridge University Press, 2022), *Arthur Machen: Decadent and Occult Works* (Modern Humanities Research Association, 2019), and, co-edited with Talia Schaffer, *The Routledge Companion to Victorian Literature* (Routledge, 2020).

KATE FLINT is Provost Professor of Art History and English at the University of Southern California. Her areas of specialization include Victorian and early twentieth-century cultural, literary, and visual history, and she has just completed writing *Habitatscapes: British and American Nineteenth Century Painting and Environmental Change.*

NATHAN K. HENSLEY is Professor of English at Georgetown University. He is the author of *Action without Hope: Victorian Literature after Climate Collapse* (University of Chicago Press, 2025) and *Forms of Empire: The Poetics of Victorian Sovereignty* (Oxford University Press, 2016). He is co-editor, with Philip Steer, of *Ecological Form: System and Aesthetics in the Age of Empire* (Fordham University Press, 2018) and, with Devin Garofalo, *The Barbara Johnson Collective* (Northwestern University Press, 2026).

ADELINE JOHNS-PUTRA is Professor of English Literature at Queen's University. Her books include *Climate Change and the Contemporary Novel* (Cambridge University Press, 2019). She edited *Climate and Literature* (2019) and co-edited with Kelly Sultzbach *The Cambridge Companion to Literature and Climate* (2022), both for Cambridge University Press, and co-edited with Axel Goodbody *Cli-Fi: A Companion* (Peter Lang, 2018).

BARBARA LECKIE is Professor in the Department of English and the Institute for the Comparative Study of Literature, Art, and Culture at Carleton University; and is the Academic Director of Re:Climate: Centre for Climate Communication and Public Engagement, Ottawa. She is the author of *Climate Change, Interrupted: Representation and the Remaking of Time* (Stanford University Press, 2022).

CAROLYN LESJAK is Professor of English at Simon Fraser University and Associate Member of the university's Labour Studies Program. Her publications include *Working Fictions: A Genealogy of the Victorian Novel* (Duke University Press, 2006) and *The Afterlife of Enclosure: British Realism, Character and the Commons* (Stanford University Press, 2021), as well as essays on Marxist theory, nineteenth-century culture, and contemporary criticism.

CAROLINE LEVINE is David and Kathleen Ryan Professor of the Humanities at Cornell University. She is the author of four books, most recently *The Activist Humanist: Form and Method in the Climate Crisis* (Princeton University Press, 2023). She helped to push Cornell University to divest its endowment of fossil fuels and works with the activist group TIAA-Divest.

ROGER LUCKHURST is the Geoffrey Tillotson Chair of Nineteenth-Century Studies at Birkbeck, University of London. He is the author, most recently, of *Gothic: An Illustrated History* (2021) and *Graveyards: A History of Living with the Dead* (2025), both published by Princeton University Press.

ALLEN MACDUFFIE is Associate Professor in the English Department at the University of Texas at Austin. He is the author of *Victorian Literature, Energy, and the Ecological Imagination* (Cambridge University Press, 2014) and *Climate of Denial: Darwin, Climate Change, and the Literature of the Long Nineteenth Century* (Stanford University Press, 2024).

MICHAEL MARDER is Ikerbasque Research Professor in Philosophy at the University of the Basque Country and Senior Fellow at the Institute for Global Reconstitution, Berlin. His recent books include *The Phoenix Complex* (MIT Press, 2023), *Time Is a Plant* (Brill, 2023), with Edward S. Casey, *Plants in Place* (Columbia University Press, 2024), and *Pyropolitics: Fire and the Political* (Rowman & Littlefield, 2025).

CATHERINE MAXWELL is Professor of Victorian Literature at Queen Mary University of London. The author of four monographs, including *Scents and Sensibility: Perfume in Victorian Literary Culture* (Oxford University Press, 2017), she was awarded the 2018 European Society for the Study of English Prize for Literatures in English and is completing a contracted book titled "The Flowers of Victorian Poetry" (Oxford University Press).

ELLA MERSHON is Lecturer in Victorian Literature and a co-founder of the Environmental Humanities Initiative at Newcastle University. Her work has appeared in *Victorian Studies*, *Victorian Literature and Culture*, *Modern Philology*, and elsewhere. She is currently working on a book tentatively entitled "Inorganicism: The Forms of Decay in the Age of Coal."

ELIZABETH CAROLYN MILLER is the Gwendolyn Bridges Needham Professor of English at the University of California, Davis. She is the author of three books, the most recent of which is *Extraction Ecologies and the Literature of the Long Exhaustion* (Princeton University Press, 2021). Her current project is titled "The Industrial Ocean: Water, Coal, and Culture 1830s–1930s."

GRACE MOORE teaches at the University of Otago. She is a Dickens scholar and ecocritic, and her books include *The Victorian Novel in Context* (Continuum, 2012) and *Dickens and Empire* (Routledge, 2017), and the collection *Victorian Environments* (Palgrave Macmillan, 2018), co-edited with Michelle J. Smith. She is the editor of the online *Literary Encyclopedia*.

BENJAMIN MORGAN is Associate Professor of English at the University of Chicago. He is the author of *The Outward Mind: Materialist Aesthetics in Victorian Science and Literature* (Chicago University Press, 2017) and is currently working on a project tentatively titled "In Human Scale: The Aesthetics of Climate Change."

WENDY PARKINS is former Professor of Victorian Literature at the University of Kent. She is now a writer/researcher affiliated with the University of Otago. Her publications include *Jane Morris: The Burden of History* (Edinburgh University Press, 2013) and *Mobility and Modernity in Women's Novels, 1850s–1930s* (Palgrave Macmillan, 2009). She is the editor of *Victorian Sustainability in Literature and Culture* (Routledge, 2018).

CANNON SCHMITT is Professor of English at the University of Toronto and President of the North American Victorian Studies Association. He is the author of *Alien Nation: Nineteenth-Century Gothic Fictions and English Nationality* (University of Pennsylvania Press, 1997) and *Darwin and the Memory of the Human: Evolution, Savages, and South America* (Cambridge University Press, 2009).

PHILIP STEER is Associate Professor of English at Massey University. He is author of *Settler Colonialism in Victorian Literature: Economics and Political Identity in the Networks of Empire* (Cambridge University Press, 2020), and co-editor, with Nathan K. Hensley, of *Ecological Form: System and Aesthetics in the Age of Empire* (Fordham University Press, 2019).

JESSE OAK TAYLOR is Professor of English at the University of Washington in Seattle. He is the author of *The Sky of Our Manufacture: The London Fog in British Fiction from Dickens to Woolf* (University of Virginia Press, 2016) and co-editor, with Tobias Menely, of *Anthropocene Reading: Literary History in Geologic Times* (Penn State University Press, 2017).

LINDSAY WELLS is an art historian and instructor in the Architecture and Interior Design Program at University of California, Los Angeles, Extension. Her research explores the visual culture of gardening, botany, and imperialism in nineteenth-century Britain and has appeared in the journals *Victorian Studies*, *Victorian Literature and Culture*, *Victorian Periodicals Review*, and *Literature Compass*.

ACKNOWLEDGMENTS

I thank Bethany Thomas and George Laver at Cambridge University Press for their support and thoughtful suggestions throughout the envisioning, compiling, and editing of this *Companion*. I also deeply appreciate the thoughtful and generous efforts of all the contributors, with whom it has been a real joy to work and who have taught me so much over the past few years.

I extend my gratitude to the following institutions for permission to reproduce the book's illustrations: Tate Britain, The Lloyd Library and Museum, Oak Spring Garden Foundation, the Alexander Turnbull Library, the Huntington Art Museum, the Royal Botanic Gardens (London), the Science Museum (London), and the Milwaukee Art Museum. I could not have conducted my research for the project without the help of the British Library, the Victoria and Albert Museum, and especially the McFarlin Library of the University of Tulsa. I gratefully acknowledge the University of Tulsa, where I hold the Ida Barnard McFarlin Chair of English, which has given me the time and resources to complete this project, as well as the University of London Queen Mary Institute for the Humanities and Social Sciences, where I was a Distinguished Visiting Research Fellow while conducting research on the *Companion*.

DENNIS DENISOFF

Introduction
Environments and Their Victorians

In our present time, we generally assume that a healthy economy is one marked by growth, rather than just sustained – let alone reduced – production. "The good life" is still characterized not by a thriving and diverse biosphere, but by individual material prosperity; the successful person (or nation) is, in so many eyes, the one displaying the most signs of wealth through conspicuous consumption and socioeconomic power. Even nature continues to be appreciated primarily for its fulfilment of human interests, such as our economic productivity, aesthetic pleasure, or improved personal health. And yet, despite the climate crises, resource-centered violence, and forced migrations of humans and other species arising from these self-centered, individualist views, we are still asking how we have reached such a dire situation and what it is that has kept us from acting effectively to improve it. With Britain one of the first among the most powerful, assertive, and technologically advanced nations to develop a culture reliant on self-worth defined by bourgeois affluence, the Victorian era marks the crucial historical period that gave rise to this current inability to see beyond our acquisitive drive or to act decisively as a collective in the face of global environmental destruction. But it also began the first local environmentalist groups, enacted the first legislation defending the rights of other-than-human species, and offered innovative literature aimed at shifting collective perspective and contesting environmental degradation. As such, the Victorian era holds not only valuable insights for understanding the limitations of our own environmentalist efforts, but also innovative suggestions for overcoming them.

Scholars to date have predominantly characterized the Victorian period's articulations of environmentalism as driven by models of stewardship and conservation, often rendering the organic world as a passive subject laid out for our appreciation and use. Human stewardship has been seen not simply as an ethical responsibility but also, by some, as an assumed right and privilege either given to us by a supernatural force or justified based on our perceived intellectual acumen. Consider, for example, the eco-sensitive rhetoric found in the 1897 *Spectator* essay "'Sixty Years' Change in Landscape,'" in which the anonymous author's articulation of environmental concern proves to function as a medium for a distinctly different ethical and economic investment than one might expect. Likely written by the journal's co-editor John St Loe Strachey, the piece proposes:

> It would have been a matter of deep regret had the Victorian Era witnessed a change in our rural scenery corresponding to that which has taken place near to the great towns. ... [S]ixty years have shown that the evil results even of these destructive agencies are not permanent. The coal is worked out, the scrap-iron foundries, collieries, and bottle-works are deserted, and the ground once more in process of being replanted with trees, and restocked with flowers, birds, and even game.[1]

To hear this author tell it, Britain's extraction industry had ended years earlier – and a good thing, too! The seeming respect for the organic ecology found in "'Sixty Years,'" however, does not reflect an appreciation for nature or for rewilding. Rather, it turns out, it speaks to an interest in the expansionist efficiencies of modern agribusiness. According to the author, the shift from the commons – the parcels of land left public for general use by people and other animals and plants – to enclosures and "the discovery of new crops and scientific farming" has

> fixed the character of our average rural scenery, and made it such as we love and desire to preserve to-day. It replaced much that was wild, and much more that was pastoral and not cultivated, with a tamer but richer outline. It brought its compensation by the increased wealth of colour with the golden corn crops, the rich greens of fields of imported plants like turnips, marigolds, rape, and mustard.

More than this, the profit available to landlords has led them "to plant woods, make lakes, add to parks, and contribute further to enhance the beauty of the country." The idea that landowners' profits from mass agriculture foster the construction of a better, more beautiful landscape is an utterly convoluted turn. What initially appears to be an essay on environmentalism proves to be a celebration of agro-industry where farmed crops are a vital improvement on what is seen as unconsumable vegetation and where landscapes heavily managed by humans are better than those left to ancient organic and community processes.

Shifting Terms and Terrains

In the title to my introduction, the awkward inversion of the seemingly more familiar phrase "Victorians and Their Environments" is intended to remind us that environments influence an individual's sense of themselves and their own potential agency. In other words, the world that we can now imagine was shaped in large part by the world that had been imagined and shaped for us. Perspectival and formal conventions create realities and so, if for the moment we can adopt a more biocentric outlook, we may recognize that ecology – the interactions among living organisms and the elements of their environments with and within which they coexist – also gave shape to what has become recognized as Victorian. Many who were neither British nor resident in its colonies contributed to the shaping of the Victorian Age, just as the current scholarly attention to the global anglophone is impacted and shaped in part by the nonglobal – the local and the regional, for example – and by non-English languages and cultures.

We can get a sense of these ecological and cultural interrelations from the first book written by an Indigenous author from the British colony of Upper Canada (Canada became a nation in 1867), the bestselling *Life History and Travels of Ka-ge-ga-gah-bowh, 1847* (1847). Written by Kahgegagahbowh (under the name George Copway), the autobiography demonstrates the complicated tangle behind our perceptions of both the environment and Victorians. The author describes being born

> in nature's wide domain! The trees were all that sheltered my infant limbs – the blue heavens all that covered me. I am one of nature's children ... and wherever I see her, emotions of pleasure roll in my breast, and swell and burst like waves on the shores of the ocean, in prayer to Him who has placed me in her hand.[2]

Kahgegagahbowh identified as Ojibwe, part of the Anishinaabe group of Indigenous peoples. At the same time, he readily acknowledged the influence of the English language and the Methodist religion on his values and self-identity. Born and raised near the mouth of the Trent River, he served as a Methodist missionary in the United States before being accepted as a preacher by the Wesleyan Methodist Canadian conference in 1842. He was elected vice president of the Ojibwe General Council but, in 1846, was accused of embezzlement by the Saugeen tribe and eventually defrocked.[3] Kahgegagahbowh then left Upper Canada for the US, where he published his autobiography. In 1850, he traveled to Europe, writing about the ocean crossing, "Fair winds, clear skies, and no rolling sea – calm as the waters of our dear 'Hudson,' that beloved river, which winds along (as Byron said of such scenery), 'In the wild power of mountain majesty.'"[4] Upon his arrival in Liverpool, he noted, "I am now in a strange place. The country, the people, and the places are strange. The sky is strange – indeed the waters before my window roll with strange rapidity."[5] Kahgegagahbowh's first impressions of Britain were mostly positive, as were, he tells us, those the

Victorians had of him. Notably, while the ocean is a calm mediation in which the Indigenous author turns to a Romantic poet to articulate his sense of a sublimity familiar to him, the colonizer is the alien and foreign, the people of Liverpool conflated with their organic environment in their strangeness.

It is an oversimplification to recognize Kahgegagahbowh as either Victorian or as *not* Victorian; his view of his ecological network reflects not only an Ojibwe worldview but also aesthetic and scientific developments in the nineteenth-century English-speaking world. In his description of his birthplace, in my first quotation from his autobiography above, he presents the natural environment as an all-consuming eco-spiritual force that permeates the human; however, it is simultaneously overridden by Christian authority. But then Kahgegagahbowh goes on to speculate on its transhistorical ineffability: "Nature will be nature still, while palaces shall decay and fall in ruins. Yes, Niagara will be Niagara a thousand years hence!"[6] He thus reconceptualizes the Christian promise of the eternal not as a *human* institution but, drawing on his First Nations cosmology, as a transhistorical organic force symbolized by an element of the precolonial landscape – the name "Niagara" likely deriving from an Iroquoian language and referring to the cataract connecting Lake Erie and Lake Ontario, as well as the falls and the surrounding land. While a global model of environmentalism did not become standard until the mid twentieth century, Kahgegagahbowh's work demonstrates that an all-encompassing or cosmological sense of the environment was active before any dominant national or Western concept took hold.

To effectively act on current formulations of our planet's environmental state requires an awareness of the diverse values, preferences, and limiting perspectives that gave shape to it, as well as those that were put aside. This has been a motivating factor in Victorian eco-studies over the past few decades. As *Life History and Travels of Ka-ge-ga-gah-bowh* suggests, the field benefits from a broad range of perspectives, as well as caution regarding understandings of history and activism that assume a unified field of opportunity. Appropriately, recent work on the subject has been characterized by myriad motivations and approaches. In 2002, John Parham asked, "Was there a Victorian Ecology?" and concluded that, indeed, there had been, albeit one distinct from the more coherent and thus familiar Romantic model. As he insightfully observes, "despite its attempts to re-write the canon, ecocriticism, to some extent, has only succeeded in creating a canon of its own," and one that gives short shrift to Victorian works.[7] Parham argues that, in the Victorian period, scientific writings on the subject were especially rich but contemporary scholars had not yet given this work the attention it warranted.

Since the time of Parham's argument, other scholars have addressed the same query, with the latest responses declaring that the study of Victorian literature and the environment has taken off. If there has been an absence of an especially coherent, dominant approach to the subject among academics, this does not signal a gap in Victorians' engagements with the environment or in today's engagements with Victorian eco-interests. Rather, gestures that undermine canonical and disciplinary cohesion reflect authors' and scholars' diverse modes of inquiry and representation, just as they did during Queen Victoria's reign. As the chapters in this collection illuminate, Victorian conceptions of the environment did not arise from a single source or history. Authors, artists, scientists, and others all offered different articulations rooted in their own experiences and sets of knowledge, including in works by – to suggest some of this diversity – Walter Lawry Buller, Charles Darwin, E. Pauline Johnson, Harriet Martineau, Susanna Moodie, John Ruskin, Henry Salt, Herbert Spencer, and Vernon Lee. These figures speak of the environment as, among other things, a planetary network of organic engagements, a source of resources for human use, a way of life and self-identification, the ecology in which one participates, an aesthetic force, and a spiritual responsibility. Scientists, primarily in Europe and the US, studied the environment through spatial and temporal scales ranging from the microscopic to the planetary to the otherworldly, from the transhistorical to the contemporary to the futuristic. Others, such as politicians, adventurers, local activists, farmers, Indigenous thinkers, and urban planners worked from other points of concern, while creative writers and visual artists used their media to imagine new themes, forms, and possibilities, often using the speculative to do so.

According to Ralph Jessop, Thomas Carlyle was the first to use the term "environment" in its current sense, "as a response to a large number of intersecting social, political, economic, and agrarian changes associated with the Industrial Revolution."[8] Carlyle's formulation, he argues, captures the "interrelation of literary, philosophical, and social critique [as] a paradigm-shifting challenge to the authority of mechanism." Victorian environmental studies takes into account the influence of not only the Industrial Revolution and imperialist and colonialist exploitation, but also Darwinian and Spencerian theory; fossil capitalism; new ideas around ecological justice, stewardship, and sustainability; the rise of Chartist, animal rights, and heritage and land preservation movements; and, not least, innovations in literature and other arts that all contributed to our current, complicated understanding of nature, environment, and environmentalism. Moreover, as I have remarked elsewhere, Victorians intentionally challenged dominant, economically driven frameworks and "often turned to a conveniently slippery notion of natural environments and identities in order to obscure normative dichotomies that were deeply invested in economic, political, and moral configurations of power and identity."[9] At the same time, as Allen MacDuffie observes, "racial, imperial, and economic ideologies blunted or even subverted the new conceptual possibilities for ecological thinking that the term *environment* both reflected and helped generate."[10] Just as certain especially influential individuals' ideas came to shape the Victorian environment, others that we might find useful today were erased from consideration, shifting into interstitial spaces of conceptual possibility.

Topical Crosscurrents

The twenty-two chapters in the *Cambridge Companion to Victorian Literature and the Environment* are divided into five parts that speak to these issues from interrelated perspectives: The Global Imaginary; Imperialism and Colonialism; Vegetal and Animal Correlations; Environmental Uses and Abuses; and Environmentalism. Written by scholars from around the world, each of the chapters addresses more than one of the five topics. The volume's structure is intended to encourage the decentering of the Western but also of the human in our consideration of the personal, local, global, and cosmological sense of the environment and environmentalism. Kahgegagahbowh's autobiography makes it apparent that many individuals who were technically defined as part of the British Empire and who contributed to the nineteenth-century conceptualization of the environment did not recognize themselves as particularly Victorian. Moreover, the multidirectional influences of imperialism and colonization troubled efforts by people at the time to define, manage, and use the planet. Kahgegagahbowh's *Life History* encourages us to consider who had a voice in the collective description of the environment.

As Part I of this collection suggests, while some Victorians celebrated the natural world on an intimate level, others turned to increasingly popular genres such as travel writing, science fiction, and the Gothic to consider expansive paradigms of ecological networking. In "Part I: The Global Imaginary," contributors consider generic and formal innovations that contributed to modeling a more coherent, less dispersed global environmental movement. Jesse Oak Taylor's chapter approaches literature as a geologic archive; with the "capacity to say more than it ought to properly know," this record unearths the catastrophism that belies the more familiar literary facade of fundamentally progressive order. Roger Luckhurst locates a comparable disturbance in the Gothic's frequent rupturing of scale. The Gothic sensibility, he argues, is tailormade for the eco-apocalyptic, often morphing into the subgenre of the eco-weird in its shift away from a human-centered perception as it allows for alternative framings of ecological crises in general. Benjamin Morgan situates the ecological impact of the Industrial

Revolution within paradigms of social excess and degeneration found in works of science fiction and decadence, while Cannon Schmitt turns to the study of blue ecology, arguing that, for Victorians, the ocean offered an illusion of infiniteness that fostered the creative conception of a vast realm beyond any notable human impact. In his contribution, Nathan K. Hensley considers notions of global systems of British Empire and economic development as, at bottom, ecological. As Hensley argues, Victorian literature molded imperialist exploitation into aesthetic shape.

This subject is developed further in "Part II: Imperialism and Colonialism," in which contributors speak to the intersectionality of individual and collective identities that impacted lives, practices, and cultures on an international scale. Grace Moore's chapter situates the analysis within the context of colonialist agriculture specifically, looking at the dysfunctional transposition of a British idyll of small-scale self-sufficiency onto the Australian landscape, along with Anthony Trollope's experience of and work on the subject. Meanwhile, Lindsay Wells demonstrates the competing models of colonial relations captured in the aesthetics of botanical illustrations by British and Indian artists. And Sukanya Banerjee explores the adaptation of the georgic in Indian literature as commentary on the agricultural interests of colonial power. Finally, Philip Steer addresses the crosscurrents among settler environments, Indigenous perspectives, and literature by drawing examples from New Zealand, Australia, and Canada.

"Part III: Vegetal and Animal Correlations" expands the inquiry into non-Western contributions to the shaping of what we know as the environment by complicating the very notion of human autonomy through consideration of the influence of other species. Innovations in the literature of the period – like more recent theories of trans-species communication, co-reliance, and cross-influence – problematized the more familiar human economic and capitalist framing. This part explores Victorians' own questioning of environmental (and environmentalist) models that present the human as central to an ecological understanding and yet independent from it. In 1866, German zoologist, marine biologist, and avid Darwinian Ernst Haeckel defined "ecology" as the science of "the *relationship* of the organism to the surrounding exterior world" (my emphasis).[11] Herbert Spencer likewise developed a model of human society as a single biological organism given cohesion and agency through the collective efforts of its micro-organisms. In a similar manner, various other Victorians asked where the human ends and other species begin and what the limits of human agency are or should be.

In her chapter, Catherine Maxwell turns attention to the intimate, personal, and specific through a rich survey of Victorian floral poetics. Maxwell observes the multiple ways in which the ecological saturates not only a

7

poetic tradition but the very idea of writing itself. Michael Marder extends this inquiry in his chapter, addressing the English tradition of the poetic herbarium, exploring Emily Dickinson's and other writers' engagements as defined in part by intimacies across species. Meanwhile, in my contribution to this part, I address trans-species intimacies as recognizing a queer animality that is not shaped by assumptions of sexuality and desire but by an inter-subjectivity rooted in an appreciation of co-reliance and co-identification. Elizabeth Chang then scales this subject of inquiry to a global level. Turning to the practice of plant miniaturization and invasion, Chang considers the relationship of species taxonomy to narrative form.

It is not surprising that our interest in the environment has always privileged those aspects recognized to have value to humans – whether as an aesthetic experience, something to be extracted, or a renewable resource. Visions of industrial development, imperial expansion, and political and scientific progress were often mutually reinforcing, brought together through a formulation that discredited anything that did not contribute to improving the lives of middle-class, Western people. In her chapter in "Part IV: Environmental Uses and Abuses," Elizabeth Carolyn Miller argues that the development of an extraction-based society often came with the sacrifice of the ecological networks from which coal and other resources were removed. Ella Mershon's chapter conceptualizes global exploitation through the model of the Capitalocene, as captured in Olive Schreiner's representation of the British South African Company in Rhodesia (modern Zimbabwe). In a particularly poignant chapter, Wendy Parkins looks at the way in which individuals concerned about the decimation of bird populations in New Zealand often seemed blind to their own contributions to the devastation. Moreover, as Parkins demonstrates, the displacement theory of natural history also then naturalized colonization and the disempowerment of the Māori population. And as Carolyn Lesjak argues in her chapter on Victorian approaches to land use, the question is "less whether they knew what was happening and more what they chose to do with that knowledge."

The collection's concluding chapters in "Part V: Environmentalism," extend the previous part's arguments into more explicitly environmentalist issues. The contributors explore ways in which literary and artistic renderings of the organic world were in a complicated relationship with concerns regarding the extraction industry, agricultural imperialism, and various other practices that damaged biospheric elements and interrelations. Allen MacDuffie notes in his chapter on pollution that, throughout the nineteenth century, debates continued around the actual nature and form of environmental change as crisis. The subject was explored through not only scientific discourses, but also those of aesthetics, activism, and others. In her chapter, Kate Flint asks not simply what it meant to look at environmental damage through an aesthetic eye, but what it would mean to look at nineteenth-century visual art through an ecological eye. As she emphasizes, this is never a question just about the arts but is always imbricated with other discursive fields vying for authority. Adeline Johns-Putra demonstrates in her piece that even the scientific conversion of weather into climate reflects rhetorical contributions to projects of empire. Eco-activism, in this light, occurs on the level of language and aesthetics, rather than that of conscious action. Meanwhile, Barbara Leckie tracks the sense of frustration to be found in fantastic works by Lewis Carroll and William Morris, where literary form and space are distended in transformative gestures as suggestions for real-world shifts in eco-perspective. In her contribution on activism, Caroline Levine speaks of the still persistent progress narrative that was both presented and critiqued within Victorian literature. As she notes, however, this earlier writing does not offer guidance in the form of activist strategies for undermining dominant economic systems. Levine proposes that, for such strategies, we should look to the form of past successful campaigns for action, outlining certain formal elements that contributed to positive environmental change in the Victorian Age and could do so today.

Collectively, these chapters offer examples from around the world that pay attention to complicated rhetorical maneuverings such as those found in "'Sixty Years Change,'" in which eco-friendly discourse serves unfriendly ends. At the same time, they bring forward the erasure of the perspectives of those – the non-Western, the nonhuman, and other disenfranchised lives – who did not have the privilege of being recognized as equal participants in their local and global ecologies. This new knowledge contributes to reformulations of our understanding of the Victorian environment and of the limits of our own capabilities as scholars in ever understanding it wholly. It is my hope, however, that this collection will also foster a dissident engagement with our sense of who the Victorians were, the factors that influenced the idea of environmentalism they developed, and what we might do to enhance environmentalist efficacy for all members of our ecologies today.

Notes

1. "'Sixty Years' Change in Landscape," *The Spectator* 3599 (June 19, 1897), 865–6 at 865, https://shorturl.at/uX133. A distinctly different understanding of the coal industry at the turn of the century can be found in Frances Molena, "Remarkable Weather of 1911: The Effect of the Combustion of Coal on the Climate – What Scientists Predict for the Future," *Popular Mechanics* (March 1912), 339–42.

2. George Copway, *The Life, History, and Travels of Ka-ge-ga-gah-bowh* (Albany: Weed and Parsons, 1847), 16. Library of Congress, https://shorturl.at/oP2qd.

3. Donald B. Smith, "Kahgegagahbowh," *Dictionary of Canadian Biography Online* ([1976] 2015), www.biographi.ca/en/bio.php?id_nbr=4517.

4. George Copway, *Running Sketches of Men and Places, in England, France, Germany, Belgium, and Scotland* (New York: J.C. Ricker, 1851), 45.

5. Copway, *Running Sketches*, 44.

6. Copway, *Life*, 18.

7. John Parham, "Was There a Victorian Ecology?," in John Parham, ed., *The Environmental Tradition in English Literature* (New York: Routledge, 2002), 156.

8. Ralph Jessop, "Coinage of the Term Environment: A Word Without Authority and Carlyle's Displacement of the Mechanical Metaphor," *Literature Compass* 9.11 (2012), 708–20 at 708.

9. Dennis Denisoff, "Fluid Margins: Natural Environments in Victorian Culture," *Victorian Review*, 36.2 (Fall 2010), 7–10 at 8.

10. Allen MacDuffie, "Environment," *Victorian Literature and Culture* 46.3/4 (Fall/Winter 2018), 681–4 at 681.

11. Cited in K. Friederichs, "A Definition of Ecology and Some Thoughts about Basic Concepts," *Ecology* 39.1 (January 1958), 154–9 at 154.

PART I

The Global Imaginary

I

JESSE OAK TAYLOR

Novel Geologies

Victorian Fiction in Catastrophic Times

The first shock of a great earthquake had, just at that period, rent the whole neighbourhood to its centre. Traces of its course were visible on every side.... There were a hundred thousand shapes and substances of incompleteness, wildly mingled out of their places, upside down, burrowing in the earth, aspiring in the air, mouldering in the water, and unintelligible as any dream. Hot springs and fiery eruptions, the usual attendants upon earthquakes, lent their contributions of confusion to the scene. Boiling water hissed and heaved within dilapidated walls; whence, also, the glare and roar of flames came issuing forth; and mounds of ashes blocked up rights of way, and wholly changed the law and custom of the neighbourhood.

    In short, the yet unfinished and unopened Railroad was in progress; and, from the very core of all this dire disorder, trailed smoothly away, upon its mighty course of civilisation and improvement.

Charles Dickens, Dombey and Son

For Charles Dickens, the coming of the railroad was a geological event: an earth-shaking, city-destroying rupture in the long history of human habitation through which the city had developed as an organic entity, the nooks and warrens of which he delighted in exploring and whose lifeways provided the warp and woof of his fiction. In short, a catastrophe. Reading Dickens now, in a rapidly overheating planet, the earthquake analogy anticipates the contested idea of the Anthropocene, a geological event defined by human impact on the Earth System, with "traces of its course visible on every side," in atmospheric carbon, oceanic acidity, ubiquitous plastics, chicken bones, radionuclides, and the palpable absence of earthlings doomed to oblivion. In turning to the language of geology to register the coming of the railroad, Dickens was more right than he knew: the "unfinished" fossil-fueled "progress" that emerged from the "dire disorder" of the nineteenth century continues to exert a determinative hold on all earthly life.

Dombey and Son is Dickens's most explicit meditation on the global reach of mercantile capitalism. The beginning of the novel satirizes Mr. Dombey's worldview, in which

> earth was made for Dombey and Son to trade in, and the sun and moon were made to give them light. Rivers and seas were formed to float their ships; rainbows gave them promise of fair weather; winds blew for or against their enterprises; stars and planets circled in their orbits, to preserve inviolate a system of which they were the centre.[1]

Dickens scorns this utilitarian view in which nature exists only to facilitate the extraction of profit and exposes the fragility of a world system that is ultimately dependent on natural systems that exceed it in scope and power. Neither the stars and planets nor the rivers, seas, and winds exist to "preserve inviolate" a system centered on human beings. To believe otherwise is to court disaster. Men like Dombey have brought the world to the calamitous threshold at which it is now poised through their mistaken, self-centered belief that Earth is nothing but a stock of natural resources for them to exploit. Hence, the railroad-as-earthquake appears in a novel framed within the nested spheres of the cosmos, in which Earth is one planet among many, and the belief that it exists only for one's own kind is a dangerous delusion.

Reading *Dombey and Son* in the Anthropocene is an uncanny experience, exemplifying what Nicholas Royle calls literature's "futurological power," its capacity to say more than it ought to be able to know.[2] The Anthropocene presents a particularly acute version of this dynamic because of the mismatch between geologic and human timescales. As historian Dipesh Chakrabarty explains, "the climate crisis reveals the sudden coming together – the enjambment, if you will – of the usually separated syntactic orders of recorded and deep histories of human kind, of species history and the history of Earth Systems, revealing the deep connections through which the planetary processes and the history of biological life interact with each other."[3] In geologic terms, that enjambment of human and natural history might be described as an *unconformity*, the term for folds and ruptures where strata laid down at different times intrude into one another and interrupt the nominally linear accumulation of time into clearly defined bands or layers. For Eric Gidal, unconformities offer "physical manifestations of heterogeneous time," providing the model for a kind of literary-historical analysis that he calls *biblio-stratigraphy*, "tracing the signatures of social and spatial changes" in order to perceive the "dynamic and protean nature of environmental and social conditions over wide scales of time."[4]

In this chapter, I examine Victorian fiction as a geological archive, a record not only of the transformative changes that industrial modernity has wrought within the Earth but also of the human encounter with those changes. Following critics like Gidal and Tobias Menely, who articulates a similarly "stratigraphic" approach to literary history, I demonstrate a reading practice adequate to thinking about Dickens's earthquake as a multilayered event in geologic time, asking not only what it *meant* when the novel was published but also how its implications continue to reverberate in our geological present.[5]

The Anthropocene unsettles received truths about Victorian science, literature, and the relationship between them. It marks a departure from the uniformitarianism associated with Victorian geologist Charles Lyell, whose *Principles of Geology* (1830–3) is widely credited with laying the foundations of modern geology by establishing the principle that Earth's deep history can be gleaned from the observation of traces and forces still visible in the present. For Lyell, the gradualism of geological change was an essential component of what made it comprehensible, an argument he frames in terms of literary genre. To illustrate the importance of deep time in geological thought, Lyell proposes an analogy, asking his readers to imagine studying the "civil and military transitions of a great nation" across 2,000 years under the mistaken belief that they had occurred in a century: "Such a portion of history would immediately assume the air of a romance; the events would seem devoid of credibility, and inconsistent with the present course of human affairs. A crowd of incidents would follow each other in thick succession … and the works effected during the years of disorder or tranquility would be alike superhuman in magnitude."[6] Expanding the timescale brings different kinds of causes into view, by allowing slow, incremental changes time to work (an insight that would, in turn, provide the basis for Charles Darwin's and Alfred Russel Wallace's understandings of evolution). Lyell then argues that those who "study the monuments of the natural world under the influence of a similar infatuation" as to the brevity of the timescale, "must draw no less exaggerated a picture of the energy and violence of the causes."[7] After pointing to the accumulation of earthquakes, volcanos, glaciers, erosion, and sedimentation known to have occurred over 5,000 years, he asks, "[w]ere an equal amount of change to pass before our eyes in the next year, could we avoid the conclusion that some great crisis of nature was at hand?"[8]

By describing prior geological theories as "romance," Lyell emphasizes their imaginative character and invites us to read his version as the more plausible explanation. In so doing, he presents his own book as kin to the realist novel, a genre that proceeds through the accumulation of everyday events carried out by unremarkable people rather than the "superhuman" agents of romance and myth. However, this passage lands differently when "a great crisis of nature" does appear to be at hand: one whose arrival is announced in part through the acceleration of geophysical processes. Hence, the Anthropocene appears as a direct inversion of Lyell's central claim. Indeed, many recent writers, such as historian of science David Sepkoski and journalist Elizabeth Kolbert, have presented Lyellian uniformitarianism as the paradigm that we must escape if we are to grasp the implications of this catastrophic event in Earth's history.[9]

A similar set of assumptions underpin recent discussions of the novel. In his indictment of the "modern novel" for rendering climate change "unthinkable," Amitav Ghosh argues that "the modern novel, *unlike geology*, has never been forced to confront the centrality of the improbable" (emphasis added), leading to what he calls the central "irony of the 'realist' novel: the very gestures with which it conjures up reality are actually a concealment of the real."[10] Ghosh further echoes Lyell's dismissal of romance in his own derision toward speculative genres such as science fiction and fantasy, arguing that treating the strange weather events sparked by global warming as "magical or surreal would be to rob them of precisely the quality that makes them so urgently compelling – which is that they are actually happening on this earth, at this time."[11] For Ghosh, then, the key challenge lies in describing planetary tumult in a way that renders it consistent with what Lyell called "the present course of human affairs."[12] Thus, whether in terms of Victorian geology, the dominant understandings of the novel genre, or the relationship between the two, the Anthropocene event seems to mark a radical departure from the norms established during the nineteenth century, especially the opposition between so-called uniformitarian and catastrophist understandings of geological change.[13]

This is not merely a question of the stories we tell about the past but of the kinds of work that we can ask nineteenth-century materials to do in the present, including the degree to which we allow subsequent scientific understandings to shape our conceptions of the historical archive, troubling longstanding opposition between historicism, which seeks to understand texts in relation to the context in which they were written, and presentism, which situates them in relation to contemporary concerns that might be unrecognizable to the work's author or original audience. The Anthropocene hypothesis complicates that distinction because the geologic timescale radically expands the scale within which historical events are to be defined. If your timescale spans billions of years, the difference between the mid-nineteenth and late-twentieth centuries becomes infinitesimal. And indeed, in 2024, the International Union of Geological Scientists voted not to establish the Anthropocene as a formal "epoch" within the Geologic Time Scale, categorizing it as a geological "event" instead, in part because geological events do not have a single defined scale: they can consist of anything from a few seconds to millions of years.

In this frame, the uncanny echoes that surround Dickens's earthquake register the historical compression occasioned by thinking about Victorian literature not at a historical remove but as part of a single expansive event that may well encompass all of human history. However, the historical distance still matters at the scale of lived experience. Dickens's lifeworld and worldview *are* long over and profoundly different from our own. Thus, if we want to situate this scene within the trans-scalar event of the Anthropocene, we have to think about it on at least two historical registers simultaneously, as *both* a historical artifact connected to a cultural and intellectual setting far removed from our own *and* a work composed within a single contemporaneous planetary event that is still unfolding around us. And we need to think about the relationship between those two, seemingly incommensurate, positions.

Once you start looking for them, traces of the Anthropocene are everywhere apparent in Victorian literature and science. Hence, in the remainder of this chapter, I attempt to point to a persistent catastrophism lurking just below the surface of Victorian fiction, an unconformity in this nominally staid and uniformitarian era. My goal is to destabilize the ground on which Victorian fiction rests, extending an invitation to rethink received notions aligning the period with stability, progress, and gradual change. In this view, Carolyn Lesjak's provocation that the Victorian era "was an age neither of equipoise nor of innocence" reverberates below ground, in the subsurface of both familiar texts and the Earth itself.[14] As Ian Duncan argues, the dual prospect of "an inhuman earth history and of a human conquest of earth history" constitute the "outside of the nineteenth-century novel, the horizon against which novels strive to think their reality."[15] The nineteenth-century novel mediates between two seemingly contradictory positions, taking shape in the push and pull between the inhuman depths of geologic time and the scaling up of human history as a disruptive force within the Earth.

When Dickens compares the coming of the railroad to an earthquake, or George Eliot ends *The Mill on the Floss* (1860) with a flood that seems to come out of nowhere, even though it has been forecast throughout the novel, or Thomas Hardy concludes a chapter in *A Pair of Blue Eyes* (1873) with a character stranded on the side of a cliff, face to face with a trilobite – suspended in both geologic and narrative time – they surely trouble the notion that geology was a stabilizing force in the Victorian imagination. Hardy's literal cliffhanger also concluded a periodical issue, thus leaving the reader similarly suspended while highlighting the distributed quality of Victorian publishing practices in ways that trouble the ostensible cohesion of the novel form. In these and many other examples, the intrusion of geological features serves to remake narrative possibility in ways that often bear a complex relationship to human agency, at once constraining (or killing) individual characters even as these features reflect the large-scale, systemic impact of human society.

This pattern recurs in both realism and more speculative genres, troubling the divisions between them. The ubiquitous energy "Vril" in Edward Bulwer-Lytton's hollow-Earth novel *The Coming Race* (1871), which is discovered in an abandoned coal mine, anticipates the advent of petroculture, in which oil would saturate all facets of life. Late in *Dracula* (1897), Van Helsing speculates that the Count's vampirism might be explained by "strangeness of the geologic and chemical world" in Transylvania: "There are deep caverns and fissures that reach none know whither. There have been volcanoes, some of whose openings still send out waters of strange properties, and gases that kill or make to vivify."[16] In both examples, Earthly elements reframe the bounds of possibility and species being, giving rise to supernatural and/or superhuman entities whose arrival threatens *Homo sapiens* with extinction.

This unease militates against the notion that the Anthropocene caught us unawares. Or rather, it speaks to the imaginative work required *not* to pay attention to the Earthly implications of industrialization, a phenomenon that Christophe Bonneuil and Jean Baptise Fressoz call the "modernizing unconscious."[17] As Allen MacDuffie has shown, that work of climate disavowal has frequently aided and abetted by the realist novel.[18] It is notable in this context that many of the landscapes in Victorian fiction are not so much industrial as *postindustrial* sites already defined by the footprints of extraction. The "Red Deeps" that offer Maggie Tulliver and Philip Wakem a temporary refuge in *The Mill on the Floss* are in fact an abandoned quarry, which is what makes their mud so distinctive and provides the clue that gives the lovers away.[19] Mr. Lockwood spends a fateful night at Wuthering Heights during a blizzard because the terrain is pitted with old mining sites, now hidden like crevasses beneath a blanket of snow, telling young Catherine that if he tries to find his way back to Thrushcross Grange, he will be "discovered dead in a bog or a pit full of snow." Lockwood may be incompetent, but the danger is real: Stephen Blackpool falls down an old mineshaft in Dickens's *Hard Times* (1854). The same fate awaits the villain Dunsey Cass in Eliot's *Silas Marner* (1861), who disappears early on and is later revealed to have stumbled into a quarry and drowned after stealing Silas's gold.

This latter example is particularly telling because of the way it illustrates the intersection of form and content. The quarry gives up its secrets only after sequestering them for long enough to produce the narrative's enabling condition by robbing Silas of his hoarded gold (itself extracted from the Earth) and creating space for Effie's arrival in his life. The big reveal then comes courtesy of another geological act: the emptying of the pit is a side effect of a drainage scheme in nearby fields, speaking to the subterranean interconnection of land and waterways. Thus, the conditions of possibility for *Silas Marner*'s narrative arc are established by the negative space of the old quarry, a hole in the ground that corresponds to the aftereffects of extracted resources. The narrative, in effect, flows into that the negative space in a formal correlate to the subterranean linkages between field drainage and the water in the old quarry. Such drainage projects were extensive in the Victorian era and integral to the introduction of the new industrial-farming techniques that would have a deleterious effect on both biodiversity and soil health. There is a very real environmental history buried just below the surface of the novel.

In each of these instances, the underground provides not a bedrock of stability but rather a porous space of sudden, unpredictable (and often dangerous) possibility. Though it is a natural feature, this formal pattern also fits one of the most memorably geological settings in Victorian fiction: the "shivering sand" in Wilkie Collins's *The Moonstone* (1868), which claims Rosanna Spearman's body, while also preserving – and then relinquishing – her secret, and with it one of several keys to the mystery of the missing diamond at the heart of the novel. Notably, these subsurface features are both literal features of the novels' settings and formal principles governing the conditions of possibility within the narratives. As such, they trouble the ostensible division between "surface" and "symptomatic" reading practices because the depths lie on the "surface" of the text, hidden in plain sight.

Several key points emerge from these examples: first, the ground upon which the Victorian novel rests is riddled with holes, befitting a society thoroughly (and self-consciously) dependent on mining. Second, these holes create negative spaces, in the sculptural sense of that term: constitutive absences that redefine the conditions of possibility in the narratives in which they appear, much the way that excavations around the world, whether archeological, mineralogical, or hydrological (and often some blend of the three), were remaking understandings of human history and its relation to the Earth.[20] The sudden disappearance of characters who are literally swallowed by the Earth and whose secrets are (at least sometimes) later disclosed must thus be recognized as a constitutive feature of Victorian narrative, and one that has the potential to trouble the conditions of possibility even in nominally "realist" novels. Third, at a formal level, the underground corresponds to another form of negative space, or constitutive absence, within the Victorian imagination, the "dark" spaces of empire into which characters can disappear for extended periods of time only to reappear (often bearing secrets) in ways that would otherwise defy narrative plausibility. The Sherlock Holmes stories are replete with examples of both tendencies, further illustrating the formal equivalence between the two. Moreover, this correlation between subterranean and imperial spaces is not just metaphorical, but rather corresponds to real conditions and derives from the same impulse: the extraction of resources, energy, and labor.

Elizabeth Carolyn Miller has demonstrated the strong conceptual alignment between the underground and the empire as sites of extraction, and hence the Victorian novel's mapping of extractivism as a formal structure, in her excellent book *Extraction Ecologies and the Literature of the Long Exhaustion*, published in 2021.[21] The argument I am pursuing here builds on Miller's, not least because geology has never been separable from mining. However, I want to extend Miller's argument as a way of thinking about the geological imaginary of Victorian fiction in terms not only of resource extraction but also of the absences that extraction leaves behind. These negative spaces, I propose, operate in ways akin to literary atmosphere, a quality that is notoriously hard to define but also works to establish the conditions of possibility for narrative, and which served as the repository for the waste produced by the combustion of Britain's most important subterranean resource: coal. I suggest that the underground operates similarly, underpinning the way that narratives work, and that it does so in ways that are often radically estranging rather than stabilizing.

Perhaps surprisingly, given the dominant narrative sketched earlier, a similar pattern holds true in Victorian geology. Adelene Buckland argues that the opposition between "uniformitarian" and "catastrophist" geology has been overemphasized, countering that Lyell's uniformitarianism was not a normative argument constraining Earth's potential for radical change, but rather a methodological one, made in the effort to understand changes that eluded direct perception because they operated on such vast timescales. As Buckland explains, "Lyell's uniformitarian geology did not suggest that all geological change took place by the accumulation of imperceptibly gradual processes."[22] Instead, *The Principles of Geology* offers up a litany of natural disasters: "From Pompeii to Lisbon to Calabria to Chili, thousands of people are shown to have died horrible deaths in a never-ending series of 'terrific catastrophes' that Lyell parades before us."[23] Moreover, at least some of those catastrophes are anthropocentric, most notably the genocide of Indigenous peoples following contact with Europeans, which Lyell describes as a "faint image" of species extinctions, including those exterminated by humans. Insofar as the opposition between "uniformitarian" and "catastrophist" schools of thought holds, it was less about whether geological catastrophes happen – as everyone agreed they do – and more about whether the underlying *causes* of geological change have changed.

Even there, Lyell hedges his bets. While he argued that "the general climate" would be unlikely to experience a "sensible change" in a mere few thousand years, Lyell conceded that there "must be exceptions to this rule" because "even the labours of man have, by the drainage of lakes and marshes, and the felling of extensive forests, caused such changes in the atmosphere as raise our conception of the important influence of those forces to which even the existence in certain latitudes of land or water, hill or valley, lake or sea, must be ascribed."[24] In this telling "exception," Lyell not only reveals an awareness that human terraforming has affected the climate, but also utilizes it to make the climate as *system* visible. Lyell ultimately downplayed the notion that human influence marks a distinct force in Earth's history, arguing that we "must command nature by obeying her laws ... and for this reason we can never materially interfere with any of the great changes which either the aqueous or igneous causes are bringing about on the face of the earth."[25] But you also cannot read his book without at least contemplating that possibility. Thus, as Devin Garofalo puts it, "Lyell chronicles humankind's rise to geologic power" while talking "out of both sides of his mouth" about the implications of that story.[26] The Anthropocene thus haunts both *The Principles of Geology* and Victorian fiction as a sublimated, disavowed shadow narrative, a hole that suddenly opens in what seemed like solid ground, threatening to unsettle the whole.

When Dickens described the coming of the railroad as an Earthly catastrophe, he was right. But he was right in ways that can only be fully understood in retrospect. In fact, Dickens himself was nearly killed in the Staplehurst train crash seventeen years later. This, in turn, suggests yet another aspect of stratigraphic reading, in which the novel is layered with authorial experience, both before and after its publication. The strata adjacent to many familiar narratives reveal traces of geological catastrophe. In her insightful study of the Brontës, Shawna Ross notes that, as a young girl, Emily was nearly killed (along with her siblings, Branwell and Anne, and their nanny) by a "bog burst," a "rare geological phenomenon ... in which tons of sand, rocks, or mud suddenly shift downslope," of which their father wrote one of the first published descriptions.[27] This literal geological event lies behind (or beneath, in stratigraphic terms) the Brontë sisters' later descriptions of the Yorkshire moors, including Lockwood's fears about dying in a pit. Meanwhile, Laura Eastlake points to a deleted scene from *Dracula*, where the vampire's death precipitates a volcanic eruption that consumes the castle, which Stoker took care to locate atop a dormant volcano, underscoring the geological dimension of the novel only hinted in the published version.[28] The more you look below the surface, the more catastrophic Victorian fiction becomes.

The unfinished railroad that emerges from the "core of all this dire disorder" in *Dombey and Son* operates as a synecdoche for the "mighty course of civilisation and improvement" that annihilates a coherent world.[29] The period in which this transformative impact takes place is, in turn, defined by it in retrospect. Moreover, the "first shock" that registers as an earthquake is one with which Dickens assumes his readers will already be familiar.[30] Hence, in the context of the novel, this passage works because both Dickens and his readers could already understand the transformations wrought by the railroad. Indeed, he will later return to this scene only to observe that there was "no such place as Staggs's Gardens," that it has "vanished from the earth" as if it had never existed, turning the book's early pages into a kind of fossil record in which the traces of vanished worlds remain inscribed.[31] Reading the passage now, from the perspective of the twenty-first century, the aftershocks of that earthquake continue to reverberate within the Earth. The real question is whether we can utilize its disruptive potential, amplifying those tremors to bust up the imaginative and physical infrastructure of fossilized modernity before it annihilates our world, too.

Notes

1. Charles Dickens, *Dombey and Son* (London: Macmillan, [1848] 1900), 2.
2. Nicholas Royle, "Reading Conrad: Episodes from the Coast," *Mosaic: A Journal for the Interdisciplinary Study of Literature* 47.1 (March 2014), 41–67 at 43.
3. Dipesh Chakrabarty, *The Climate of History in a Planetary Age* (Chicago: University of Chicago Press, 2021), 61.
4. Eric Gidal, *Ossianic Unconformities: Bardic Poetry in the Industrial Age* (Charlottesville: University of Virginia Press, 2015), 5, 183.
5. Tobias Menely, *Climate and the Making of Worlds: Toward a Geohistorical Poetics* (Chicago: University of Chicago Press, 2021).
6. Charles Lyell, *Principles of Geology*, James Secord, ed. (New York: Penguin, [1830–3] 1997), 29.
7. Lyell, *Principles of Geology*, 29.
8. Lyell, *Principles of Geology*, 31.
9. David Sepkoski, *Catastrophic Thinking: Extinction and the Value of Diversity from Darwin to the Anthropocene* (Chicago: University of Chicago Press, 2020); Elizabeth Kolbert, *The Sixth Extinction: An Unnatural History* (New York: Henry Holt, 2014).
10. Amitav Ghosh, *The Great Derangement: Climate Change and the Unthinkable* (Chicago: University of Chicago Press, 2016), 23.
11. Ghosh, *The Great Derangement*, 27.
12. Ghosh, *The Great Derangement*, 29.

13. I am thinking here not only of Ghosh but also of foundational work in literature and science by scholars like Gillian Beer and George Levine, both of whom link the expansive scale of the Victorian novel to uniformitarian geology. Gillian Beer, *Darwin's Plots: Evolutionary Narrative in Darwin, George Eliot, and Nineteenth-Century Fiction*, 2nd ed. (Cambridge: Cambridge University Press, [1983] 2000); George Levine, *Darwin and the Novelists: Patterns of Science in Victorian Fiction* (Cambridge: Harvard University Press, 1988).

14. Carolyn Lesjak, *The Afterlife of Enclosure: British Realism, Character, and the Commons* (Stanford: Stanford University Press, 2021), 1.

15. Ian Duncan, *Human Forms: The Novel in the Age of Evolution* (Princeton: Princeton University Press, 2019), 30.

16. Bram Stoker, *Dracula*, Maurice Hindle, ed. (New York: Penguin, [1896] 2003), 340.

17. Christophe Bonneuil and Jean-Baptiste Fessoz, *The Shock of the Anthropocene: The Earth, History, and Us*, trans. David Fernbach (New York: Verso, [2013] 2016), 199.

18. Allen MacDuffie, *Climate of Denial: Darwin, Climate Change, and the Literature of the Long Nineteenth Century* (Palo Alto: Stanford University Press, 2024).

19. Elizabeth Carolyn Miller, *Extraction Ecologies and the Literature of the Long Exhaustion* (Princeton: Princeton University Press, 2021).

20. See Pratik Chakrabarti, *Inscriptions of Nature: Geology and the Naturalization of Antiquity* (Baltimore: Johns Hopkins University Press, 2020).

21. Miller, *Extraction Ecologies*.

22. Adelene Buckland, *Novel Science: Fiction and the Invention of Nineteenth Century Geology* (Chicago: University of Chicago Press, 2013), 108.

23. Lyell, *Principles of Geology*, 108.

24. Lyell, *Principles of Geology*, 67.

25. Lyell, *Principles of Geology*, 312–13.

26. Devin M. Garofalo, "Victorian Lyric in the Anthropocene," *Victorian Literature and Culture* 47.4 (2019), 753–83 at 753.

27. Shawna Ross, *Charlotte Brontë at the Anthropocene* (Albany: SUNY Press, 2020), 38.

28. Laura Eastlake, "The Volcano and the Vampire: The Case for a Volcanic Gothic," *Gothic Studies* 26.3 (2024), 1–16. doi.org/10.3366/gothic.2024.0200.

29. Dickens, *Dombey and Son*, 60.

30. Dickens, *Dombey and Son*, 60.

31. Dickens, *Dombey and Son*, 205.

ROGER LUCKHURST

EcoGothic

Dislocations of Scale

How the Gothic intersects with the environment might seem integral to the study of the genre, given its penchant for dark and stormy nights, sublime landscapes, vengeful creature features, and wilderness terrors. Yet the awkward construction "EcoGothic" only first appeared in a 2013 collection edited by Andrew Smith and William Hughes and then in a 2014 special issue of *Gothic Studies* edited by David Del Principe, the same year that Stephen Rust and Carter Soles proposed "ecohorror" in the journal *Interdisciplinary Studies in Literature and the Environment*. There are other terms in circulation, such as Timothy Morton's "dark ecology," a set of lectures in 2016 that opens with a reflection on the weird – weird fiction and folk horror having notable revivals in this crisis, foregrounding these marginal forms of the Gothic.[1]

Like many areas of the humanities, Gothic Studies responds to the emergence of ecocriticism in the 1990s and the arrival of the term "Anthropocene," typically dated to the position paper published by Paul Crutzen and Eugene Stoermer in 2000.[2] Their paper argues that the term was needed to name a new geological epoch marking decisive human influence on the global ecosystem, and dated it from 1784, the beginning of the European Industrial Revolution driven by fossil fuels. The Anthropocene took off in the wider culture, Jeremy Davies argues, a decade later, around 2010.

The Gothic is as protean as the weather and accumulated diverse meanings in the course of the nineteenth century. But extreme affect is central to most definitions of the Gothic: expansive states of mental terror; contractive convulsions of body horror, as Ann Radcliffe's schema has it.[3] These heightened emotional states could be regarded as appropriate, even privileged, reactions to climate catastrophe. These are "Gothic times," "the realities of planetary destruction are disseminated in Gothic fictions."[4] Hence a Gothic sensibility saturates visions of apocalyptic environmental collapse or bare life in postapocalyptic scenarios both fictional – from the *Mad Max* franchise (1979–2024) to the literary earnestness of Cormac McCarthy's

The Road (2006) and nonfictional – such as David Wallace-Wells's *The Uninhabitable Earth: A Story of the Future* (2019). Global zombie hordes are quintessential Anthropocenic monsters, of course.

Simon Estok has insisted that the Gothic is "at core ecophobic," pitting man against a malignant "monstrous Nature," the raped and abused slave finally turning on its master.[5] This position is shaped as a counterreaction to more benign "Nature worship" perceived to color the initial emergence of ecocriticism in the 1990s. This ecophobic tendency has notably shaped some of the recent anthologies of Victorian and Edwardian Gothic stories in the British Library's "Library of the Weird" collection, for instance *Heavy Weather*, *Evil Roots*, and so on.[6] But genres rarely conform to confident generalizations such as Estok's stance, and the Gothic, driven by ambivalence and an oneiric tendency to transform opposites into each other (nature/culture, human/nonhuman, ecstasy/terror, and so on), is particularly resistant to such sweeping characterizations.

More persuasive is the idea that the realist literary novel, as it emerged in the eighteenth century and matured in the nineteenth century, does not operate on the appropriate scale to capture the climate crisis. The novel has been formulated as primarily a social typology, typically a characterological study in domestic and limited social settings, a product of the emergent "bourgeois public sphere" (to use Jürgen Habermas's formulation). If this is its primary function, then the scale of the novel is unable to pick up the slower movements of the wider ecologies that entangle the human and nonhuman. The climate crisis is what Timothy Morton calls a "hyperobject," "things that are massively distributed in time and space relative to humans."[7] This presents a challenge to human-centered perception and representation and demands at once a dethroning of the human and a recalibration of scale to much larger geological spatial and temporal extents. The classic *Bildungsroman*, so the argument goes, ill-fits this task. "The scale in which one reads a text drastically alters the kinds of significance attached to elements of it," Timothy Clark has observed, and the onset of a global climate crisis has resulted in "an implosion of intellectual competences," including in the art of the novel.[8] The novelist Amitav Ghosh has argued that "serious fiction" – by which he means the literary realist novel – is unable to work at this scale: the climate is "very rarely glimpsed within this horizon."[9] The question of the ecological scale of literary apprehension has become a critical one.

After Ghosh, this opens up a focus on literary forms that have been typically bracketed off from "serious fiction," most obviously the planetary and cosmic romances of science fiction or the insidious subversion of anthropocentrism found in Gothic and weird fiction. The experimental derangement of the novel form in, for instance, Kim Stanley Robinson's climate fictions *New York 2140* (2017) and *The Ministry of the Future* (2020) is exemplary in this regard.

The framing of horror fiction and film as part of the "nonhuman turn," a mode that tries to think outside human phenomenology to what philosopher Eugene Thacker calls the *"world-without-us"* (original emphasis), has given the Gothic a prominent place in what is sometimes called Object-Oriented Ontology.[10] The literatures of the fantastic, banished from the canon to those regions of "outer, unknown forces," to repurpose one of H. P. Lovecraft's famous phrases, is awash with vast, sublime scales, planetary dread and cosmic fear, and in this they can be regarded as privileged forms amidst this crisis of representation.[11] Horror is good to think (or unthink) the limits of the anthropocentric literary novel. The breakthrough success of Jeff VanderMeer's *Southern Reach* quartet of novels (a trilogy published in 2014 with an addendum in 2024) that thinks at this limit in a way directly influenced by the ideas of Morton and others is another symptom of the new value accrued by the interstitial genre of the weird within the Anthropocene.

Nineteenth-century Gothic in this account steps into the limelight, recast as an insistent climacteric record and counternarrative to the literary realism on the natural disorders produced by industrial modernity and fossil capital. That account can begin with Mary Shelley's *Frankenstein* (1818), a text engendered as part of a Gothic storytelling competition during a stay with Lord Byron's entourage at the Villa Diodati on Lake Geneva in June 1816. The group was compelled to stay sheltering inside, reading aloud from a French translation of the German collection *Fantasmagoriana*, because this was the "year without a summer." The torrid rains, dark skies, and constant storms of 1816 are often ascribed to the high levels of tephra blasted into the atmosphere by the eruption of the Tambora Volcano in Indonesia in 1815, an event that killed more than 50,000 people locally, while casting an atmospheric pall over the planetary weather system the next summer as its plume drifted through atmospheric systems. The true extent of the influence of this volcanic eruption on the composition of *Frankenstein* is contested, but Shelley was certainly attentive in her journal to the unusually violent winds, rain, and snowstorms of that summer, and folded these descriptions into her novel.

The association of Frankenstein's monster with lightning storms and the escape across Alpine mountains and into the wastes of the Arctic owes much to the landscape conventions of the Gothic set in place by Ann Radcliffe's *The Mysteries of Udolpho* (1794). Yet Frankenstein's creature can also be portrayed as emblematic of a new kind of human intervention into the natural order. The unnatural assemblage of the creature is no longer solely a transgression in conventional moral or theological terms but is the product of an epochal secular and scientific intervention that makes the monster emblematic of "the new nature of the Anthropocene, a nature no longer separate from culture."[12] The allegorical potential of the creature is capacious enough to be read as a catastrophic symbol of modernity's rapacious extractive reach into nature on a new scale at the start of the Industrial Revolution, or else, in stark contrast, as one of those "hopeful monsters" of hybridization embraced by the contemporary theorists Donna Haraway or Bruno Latour. In Latour's view, "monstrous" new entanglements might work actively to subvert modernity's violent hierarchy and separation of culture *over* nature and instead situate us inside a more co-implicated, networked being of human and nonhuman kinships. This is to read against Victor Frankenstein's rejection of his creature and the mutual urge to violent destruction. Latour's injunction in his essay "Love Your Monsters" opens with Shelley at Villa Diodati, and Latour often reaches for Frankenstein's creature as a symbol of networked or "compositionist" thinking in his other explorations of modernity.[13]

More abstractly, the monster's gigantic scale and its association with unmasterable landscapes of icy mountains and wilderness, the massiveness and obscurity of the terror typical of that which Edmund Burke described as sublime, can help figure the way the nineteenth-century Gothic registers the crisis of representation when it comes to the planetary or cosmic level. *Frankenstein* ends, in effect, in blank whiteness, at the limit of signification as the symbiotic couple of Frankenstein and his creature disappear into the Arctic, beyond the framing narrative. Shelley may have been influenced by the polar expeditions announced by John Barrow and William Scoresby to feverish excitement in London in the 1810s, part of the scientific and geopolitical push to render the globe a knowable grid as the Napoleonic wars came to their conclusion. The disappearance of Frankenstein and his double into the icy wastes is an influential trope, which is repeated by the enigmatic Antarctic end of Edgar Allan Poe's "Narrative of Arthur Gordon Pym of Nantucket" (1838), this impossible, unrepresentable space of the far south picked up in H. P. Lovecraft's "At the Mountains of Madness" (1936), which was composed just as America was trying to establish strategic bases on the Antarctic a hundred years later. Horror flashes up when figuration fails.

The summer residency at Villa Diodati in 1816 also resulted in Byron's remarkable apocalyptic poem "Darkness," composed that August, which begins with "The bright sun was extinguish'd" to unfold a full-scale vision of catastrophe, "The habitations of all things which dwell, / Were burnt for beacons; cities were consumed, / And men were gathered round their blazing homes." "Forests were set on fire ... / and all was black," its opening apocalyptic description continues.[14] Byron wrote the poem shortly after the visit of another Gothic writer to the Villa, Matthew "The Monk" Lewis, and is thought to have been influenced by Cousin de Grainville's *The Last Man* (1806). Some years later, Shelley would also contribute to this genre with her novel *The Last Man* (1826), the second book of which details the arrival of a plague from the East (as "Asiatic" cholera had done in 1823), a pandemic that annihilates the population of Europe. The novel is full of vivid descriptions of a desolate, plague-ridden and eventually depopulated London. Shelley's novel was initially vilified but it anticipated the catastrophic arrival of cholera in Europe in 1830 (contributing to the overthrow of the French government in 1830 and then arriving on English shores in 1832). Pandemics are another sign and symptom of accelerating climate crisis.

The imagination of disaster, visions of catastrophes figured on a planetary or cosmic scale, became an established subgenre by the late nineteenth century. The vast, nonhuman timescales required in both Charles Lyell's *Principles of Geology* (1830) and Charles Darwin's *On the Origin of Species* (1859) caused both scientists fundamental difficulties in evidential proof and in finding the language and analogy for conveying their arguments against the conventional calculations of biblical time. Since punctual catastrophism is easier to grasp than gradualist change over eons, a popular genre of the spectacular, sudden disaster developed, one aided at the beginning of the twentieth century by Hugo de Vries's theory of sudden mutation. It might be plague again (Guy Boothby's *Pharos the Egyptian* 1899), foreign or alien invasion (H. G. Wells's *The War of the Worlds*, 1898), time compression (Wells's *The Time Traveller*, 1895), planetary-scale punishment for humanity's Promethean hubris (M. P. Shiel's *The Purple Cloud*, 1901), accidental cosmic disaster (Arthur Conan Doyle's *The Poison Belt*, 1913). Catastrophism became embedded as a device in the scientific romance or Gothic mode to brood on the consequences of accelerating modernity. Even relatively benign postindustrial reversions to premodern pastoral states – such as Richard Jefferies *After London* (1885) or William Morris's *News from Nowhere* (1890) – had to engineer catastrophic change to bring a rapid end to the choking evils of industrial modernity.

For a long time, critics interpreted the British tradition of the disaster novel as allegories of various kinds of destabilizing social change (class, industry, war portents, imperial anxiety, and so on), but the emergence of the concept of the Anthropocene reframes a number of classic texts for more obvious surface readings. Maybe John Ruskin's eccentric 1884 lectures *The Storm-Cloud of the Nineteenth Century* were, after all, just about storm clouds.

The late Victorian Gothic revival could radically change scale and find these evolutionary spans of time compressed into the accumulated strata of a single human psyche, as in the biological degeneration of respectable Dr. Jekyll into simian Mr. Hyde in Robert Louis Stevenson's 1886 shocker. This catastrophic reversion – a biologized reworking of the central Gothic theme of inheritance – was rehearsed over and over after Stevenson's foundational *Strange Case* appeared. Most of the spectacular bodily devolutions or temporal collapses of ancient and modern in the fiction of Arthur Machen or William Hope Hodgson or the mental dissolution in Charlotte Perkins Gilman's "The Yellow Wallpaper" (1892) are unthinkable without Stevenson's account of biological reversion.

The affective valences of being exposed to the dislocating scales opened by nineteenth-century science can vary, though. Lovecraft typically regards these as moments of annihilation, as in the famous opening of "The Call of Cthulhu" (1928): "The most merciful thing in the world, I think, is the inability of the human mind to correlate all its contents. We live on a placid island of ignorance in the midst of black seas of infinity." "Some day," the narrator warns, "the piecing together of dissociated knowledge will open up such terrifying vistas of reality ... that we shall either go mad from the revelation or flee from the deadly light into the peace and safety of a new dark age."[15] This kind of affect horror, in John Clute's helpful formulation, leads the reader towards moments of *vastation*, "a laying waste to a land or a psyche; a physical or psychological devastation; desolation."[16]

Algernon Blackwood, much admired by Lovecraft for his weird atmospheres, was much more open to the mystical or occult revelations promised by these moments, on the other side of terror, whether in the wilderness of Canada in "The Wendigo" (1910) or amongst the trees in "The Willows" (1907) or the subsumption into a different spiritual order in "The Man Whom the Trees Loved" (1912). The last of these stories stages a debate between what Bruno Latour would deem the "modernist" insistence on separation of Nature and Culture in a logic of domination versus the "compositionist" position of a willing embrace of the intricate imbrication of human and nonhuman orders. For Blackwood, this was conceived through loosely pagan conceptions, although he also explored mystical Christianity, syncretic Theosophical writings and ritual magic in his restless career.

At a less sublime scale, the rise of urban Gothic in the nineteenth century focused on the depredations of modernity in more local ways. Charles Dickens's ghost story "No. 1 Branch Line: The Signalman" (1865) stages the tale in the grim, unnatural and abjected terrain of a railway cutting and registers a new kind of horror in its temporal dislocation. The signalman is haunting himself from the future, fractured in time and space by the tyranny of shift work and railway time, the principal vehicles for the reordering industrial modernity in the Victorian period.

Some have objected that the prefix *Anthropo-* makes for a universaliz-ing concept that offers no precise allocation of the human agents of climate change principally involved; that is, that this catastrophic transformation of the planetary ecology has been driven in the main by the Global North, while the earliest and worst effects have so far been encountered in the Global South. Andreas Malm and Jason Moore have been associated with the term "Capitalocene," the better to identify the agent of the climate crisis as capi-talism. Another term, the "Plantationocene," emerged in 2014 as a coinage to capture "the devastating transformation of diverse kinds of human-tended farms, pasture, and forests into extractive and enclosed plantations, relying on slave labour and other forms of exploited, alienated, and usually spatially transported labour."[17] Here the environmental impact of slavery and colo-nialism is foregrounded. "The horror! The horror!" that Kurtz names with his last words in Joseph Conrad's *Heart of Darkness* (1899) binds together in a conjuncture of associations the catastrophic slave labor system that killed millions in the Belgian Congo in the pursuit of maximum profits from rubber and ivory, Kurtz's exterminative relation to the native population, and the recognition of his (and Europe's) complicity in this atrocity.[18] The imperial or white settler horror fiction that precedes Conrad's work used the discourse of the supernatural to articulate the disturbance of the colonial encounter.

In this compressed account, the Gothic has moved from cultural margin to center in the nineteenth-century literary engagement with the environment. But some critics may well balk at this characterization because it suggests that we have to discard realism to find the right scale to render the environ-ment visible. The dominant literary form of the Victorian period can risk getting bracketed off as a mysteriously blinkered or cosseted default in this portrait. However, classic realist writers such as George Eliot and Elizabeth Gaskell might work to differentiate themselves from all those melodramatic sensation-seeking novelists, but they also find themselves dipping into the Gothic mode in a number of their key works, as if compelled to exceed real-ist containment for a more expansive affective register. Martin Willis has suggested that the reason the Gothic continually obtrudes into realist texts is to mark representational crisis or evoke the kind of interconnectedness that cannot otherwise be spoken.[19]

Realism is, of course, a contradictory and forever unstable form and it too constantly juggles different spatial scales and temporalities in a precar-ious coherence always on the verge of collapse. In a 2018 cluster of essays on climate change in *Victorian Studies*, Tina Young Choi and Barbara Leckie observe that the timescales required by Lyell's *Principles of Geology* or Darwin's *Origin of Species* need literary devices to be conceived on a human scale, while the "slow causality" of the serialized, three-volume novel assists an apprehension of these extended scientific temporalities to the reading public.[20] It might therefore be possible to discern the dislocated scales and exorbitant affects associated with the Gothic as being carried inside dominant realist forms, too. It does not require the brooding Gothic ruins of a Caspar David Friedrich painting in the 1810s or the planetary scale of Wells's apocalyptic visions in the 1890s to find the trace of the Anthropocenic representation.

A capsule reading to illustrate this: consider one of the most famous "realist" paintings of the mid Victorian period: William Holman Hunt's *The Awakening Conscience*, which gained notoriety as soon as it was shown at the Royal Academy Exhibition of 1854 (Figure 2.1). One of Hunt's inspirations was Charles Dickens's *David Copperfield* (1850), and the painting is a central instance of Victorian "literary" or narrative painting. It portrays the moment a "kept" woman, a mistress bouncing on her lover's knee as they play sentimental songs on the piano, is suddenly brought back into consciousness of her perilously fallen state. Her hands, clenched in agony, form the focal center of the painting in a very cluttered domestic space. Hunt obsessively researched every element of the interior, going as far as hiring rooms in a house in St. John's Wood in London, an area apparently known for its discretely installed mistresses. In his defense of the painting from the charge that it celebrated the immorality it depicted, Ruskin – consistent with his advocacy of absolute verisimilitude in art – proclaims that: "There is not a single object in all that room, common, modern, vulgar (in the vulgar sense, as it may be), but it becomes tragical if rightly read." He goes on to catalogue the rosewood furniture and its "fatal newness," the "embossed books, vain and useless," the loose threads of the tapestry strewn on the floor; even "the very hem of the poor girl's dress, at which the painter has laboured so closely, thread by thread, has story in it."[21] Every detail adds to the confrontation of "the moral evil of the age in which it is painted," Ruskin concludes. The critic Elizabeth Prettejohn agrees: each object is "pinpointed and displayed," and works to "convey the specificity, solidity and sheer abundance of the objects in the modern middle-class interior."[22]

This might be considered an exemplary scene of domestic realism, every element coded with signals of social class. But if we change scale, the objects also reveal a planetary reach located *inside* the domestic sphere. Rosewood was typically imported from the Brazilian Amazon basin; the ivory keys on the piano likely from Indian or African imports (piano makers in Europe and America imported tons of elephant tusks); the silk bow at her neck is likely from materials imported from Asia; the rings on her fingers (minus a wedding band), mined from sites across the world, such precious resources often central to the geopolitics of empire; the Cashmere shawl tied around

Figure 2.1 William Holman Hunt, *The Awakening Conscience*,
1853, oil on canvas, 76 × 56 cm.
Photo: Tate.

her waist, normally a signal of wealth and respectability, undoubtedly made from imported Indian fabric. The planetary scale of British imperial trade, celebrated three years before in the global reach of commodities at the Great Exhibition, here crams into this tiny domestic space. Walter Benjamin's micro-essay in *One-Way Street*, "Manorially Furnished Ten-Room Apartment," analyses "the horror of apartments" of the bourgeois of the second half of the nineteenth century. These rooms are "deadly traps," full of Persian carpets, ottomans and daggers, Orientalized spaces where the inhabitants are "tremulously awaiting the nameless murderer." No wonder, Benjamin suggests, these overstuffed rooms are the typical spaces of violent crime in the emergent genre of detective fiction.[23]

Holman Hunt painted *The Awakening Conscience* for Thomas Fairbairn, whose family fortune had come from Manchester iron foundries and ship building, the very engines of British expansionism. Holman Hunt recalled in his memoirs that Fairbairn had requested the face of the woman in the painting be substantially reworked in 1856, as he could not live with a face of the girl that Ruskin describes in its original version as "rent from its beauty into sudden horror."[24] That moral horror can be ascribed to the narrative of sexual transgression depicted in the scene, obviously. But if our reading of nineteenth-century culture is transformed by recognition of the emergent catastrophe of the Anthropocene as industrialism and global trade globally expanded, then the painting invites another way of reading horror and awakening conscience. The portents of that ecological disaster are telegraphed in many objects in the room. And what does she see as she starts up from her lover's lap? The spaces of nature outside, in bright sunlight, the trees reflected in the gaudy gilded mirror behind her. She is, as Lin Chang suggests, "stunned by the sunlight" that otherwise casts the room into deep shadow.[25] The cherry-tree blossom suggests rebirth, in contrast to the song the couple is singing ("Oft, in the Stilly Night," from Thomas Moore's 1817 poem), which speaks of joyous youth dying "like leaves in the wintry weather" and recalled amongst "garlands dead."[26] The white flowers that bloom beneath the tree, perhaps poppy or cosmos, symbolize purity. That we do not have direct access to the natural world, only see it via a complex set of mediations, reflected in the mirror or double-reflected in the windowpane, is emphasized again by the artifice of cut flowers sitting on the piano and in the borders of the gaudy wallpaper. The wall over her left shoulder schematically depicts grapes heavy on the vine, its guardian drunk and asleep, perhaps, in Bacchic abandon. The viewer is asked to compare an indirect, distant vision of nature with its secondary appearance inside this room. This is to say that the EcoGothic is not only about identifying a set of reframed textual objects or assembling a series of canonical texts identified as Gothic. It is a view askance, a *method* for disclosing the obtrusion of an ecohorror that has hitherto been painted out or painted over in some of the central cultural artefacts of the era.

Notes

1. Andrew Smith and William Hughes, eds., *EcoGothic* (Manchester: Manchester University Press, 2013); David Del Principe, "Introduction: The EcoGothic in the Long Nineteenth Century," *Gothic Studies* 16.1 (2014), 1–8; Stephen A. Rust and Carter Soles, "Ecohorror Special Cluster: 'Living in Fear, Living in Dread, Pretty Soon We'll All Be Dead,'" *ISLE* 21.3 (2014), 509–12; Timothy Morton, *Dark Ecology: For a Logic of Future Co-existence* (New York, Columbia University Press, 2016).

2. Paul Crutzen and Eugene Stoermer, "The 'Anthropocene,'" *Global Change Newsletter* 41 (2000), 17–18.

3. Ann Radcliffe, "On the Supernatural in Poetry" (1826), in E. J. Clery and R. Miles, eds., *Gothic Documents: A Sourcebook 1700–1820* (Manchester: Manchester University Press, 2000), 163–72.

4. Justin Edwards, Rune Grassland, and Johan Högland, "Introduction: Gothic in the Anthropocene," in Justin Edwards, Rune Grassland, and Johan Högland, eds., *Dark Scenes from Damaged Earth: The Gothic Anthropocene* (Minneapolis: University of Minnesota Press, 2022), ix–xxvi at ix.

5. S. C. Estok, "Theorizing the EcoGothic," *Gothic Nature* 1 (2019), 39.

6. Kevan Manwaring, ed., *Heavy Weather: Tempestuous Tales of Stranger Climes* (London: British Library, 2021); Daisy Butcher, ed., *Evil Roots: Killer Tales of the Botanical Gothic* (London: British Library, 2019).

7. Timothy Morton, *Hyperobjects: Philosophy and Ecology After the End of the World* (Minneapolis: University of Minnesota Press, 2013).

8. Timothy Clark, "Derangements of Scale," in Tom Cohen, ed., *Telemorphosis: Theory in the Era of Climate Change*, Vol. 1 (Ann Arbor: Open Humanities, 2012), 148–66.

9. Amitav Ghosh, *The Great Derangement: Climate Change and the Unthinkable* (Chicago: University of Chicago Press, 2016).

10. Eugene Thacker, *In the Dust of This Planet: Horror of Philosophy*, Vol. 1 (Winchester, UK: Zero Books, 2011), 5.

11. H. P. Lovecraft, *Supernatural Horror in Literature* (New York: Dover, 1973), 15.

12. Shalon Noble, "An Uncertain Spirit of an Unstable Place: *Frankenstein* in the Anthropocene," in D. W. Hall, ed., *Romantic Ecocriticism: Origins and Legacies* (Lanham: Lexington, 2016), 130.

13. Bruno Latour, "Love Your Monsters," *Breakthrough Journal* 2 (2011), https://libcom.org/article/love-your-monsters-bruno-latour.

14. Lord Byron, "Darkness," 1816, in Jerome J. McGann, ed., *The Complete Poetical Works of Lord Byron, Volume IV* (Oxford: Oxford University Press, 1986), 40–1.

15. H. P. Lovecraft, "The Call of Cthulhu," in R. Luckhurst, ed., *The Classic Horror Stories* (Oxford: Oxford University Press, 2013), 24.

16. John Clute, *The Darkening Garden: A Short Lexicon of Horror* (Seattle: Payseur & Schmidt, 2006), 147.

17. Donna Haraway, "Anthropocene, Capitalocene, Plantationocene, Chthulhucene: Making Kin," *Environmental Humanities* 6 (2015), 162 n. 5.

18. Joseph Conrad, *Heart of Darkness* (Harmondsworth: Penguin, 1983), 111.

19. Martin Willis, "Victorian Realism and the Gothic: Objects of Terror Transformed," in A. Smith and W. Hughes, eds., *The Victorian Gothic: An Edinburgh Companion* (Edinburgh: Edinburgh University Press, 2012), 15–28.

20. Tina Young Choi and Barbara Leckie, "Slow Causality: The Function of Narrative in an Age of Climate Change," *Victorian Studies* 60.4 (2018), 565–87.

21. John Ruskin, "The Prae-Raphaelites," *The Times* (May 25, 1854), 7.

22. Elizabeth Prettejohn, *The Art of the Pre-Raphaelites* (London: Tate, 2007), 98.

23. Walter Benjamin, *One-Way Street and Other Writings*, trans. E. Jephcott and K. Shorter (London: Verso, 1985), 48–9.

24. Ruskin, "The Prae-Raphaelites," 7.

25. Lin Chang, "Nature and Modernity in Édouard Manet's *Le déjeuner sur l'herbe* and William Holman Hunt's *The Awakening Conscience*: A Comparative and Critical Reading," *Journal of Visual Art and Design* 11.2 (2019), 119–34 at 119.

26. Thomas Moore, "Oft in the Stilly Night (Scotch Air)," 1817, www.poetryfoundation.org/poems/44782/oft-in-the-stilly-night-scotch-air.

3

BENJAMIN MORGAN

Entropy, Exhaustion, and Degeneration in Science Fiction and Decadence

What is an "environment"? Many scholars in the environmental humanities have challenged an everyday understanding of environment as the flora and fauna we encounter in nonurban spaces. Instead, they argue, we should think more broadly about the biological and geophysical earth systems which human society both depends upon and, increasingly, shapes. Jennifer Wenzel proposes that "rather than positing nature or environmental crisis as 'out there' in the world, available to and in need of literary representation," one ought to ask how literature has created an understanding of "what counts as 'nature,' 'environment,'" and so forth.[1] The environmental historian Jason Moore has contested a tendency within social theory to presume the "binary [of] Nature/Society," proposing instead the figure of the "web of life."[2] This web is "nature as us, as inside us, as around us. ... Put simply, humans make environments and environments make humans – and human organization."[3] Such interventions usefully undermine the dualism and givenness of the "environment" concept: the environment is neither conceptually distinct from humanity nor something that humanity acts upon as a singular external force.

This line of reasoning is not new. It has arisen in varying guises since the beginnings of industrial society. We now regard the environment as a site of crisis, but it would be wrong to think either that this crisis is a matter only of recent history or that the contemporary moment has a monopoly on rethinking binaries of environment/humanity or nature/society. In the Victorian period, new scientific findings – first, about the finitude of earth's history and second, about the evolutionary history of the human species – profoundly changed cultural understandings of the relation between human society and natural systems. These shifts not only produced famous crises of religious conscience, but they also raised existential questions about the future of humanity. If there had been a beginning of the earth and of the human species, then there was conceivably – inevitably? – also an end. To experience geological and evolutionary findings as crisis-inducing required understanding human history as embedded in environmental systems extending deep into the past and future. "Environment" was conceptualized not just as a static, unchanging place out there in nature, but as a relational network that was changing in ways that might render the existing conditions of human society unsustainable.

The chapter looks at two versions of this new, longer timescale of environmental consciousness. The first is centered on energy, including the formation of fossil energy and the thermodynamic qualities of solar energy. The second is centered on biology, including the possibility of human adaptation to changing environmental conditions. One important site where energy theory and evolutionary theory intersected was with the notion that both were tending toward decline: energy was being used up and dissipating on the one hand, and biological species were thought to be reverting to simpler forms on the other. With an eye toward these intersecting narratives of decline, this chapter draws a connection between two cultural domains, speculative fiction and decadent writing, in which this sense of decline was, paradoxically, a highly generative idea.

While it has been common to read nineteenth-century science fiction in relation to ecological issues, it has been less common to think of decadent or aestheticist writing as "ecological," since it is often associated with urbanity and artificiality. But as we will see, an intense concern with depletion and exhaustion links the two discourses. This chapter begins by addressing cultural and scientific context and then moves toward readings of a few key texts from science fiction and decadence that illuminate how they became especially fertile sites for sometimes purveying and sometimes interrogating an ideology of interconnected human and natural decline. These historical cultural formations are important predecessors of recent efforts to frame the "environment" as something more nuanced than the domain of nonhuman biological nature. They understand the environment in a broad and dialectical sense, as planetary systems, geology and geological time, energy systems, and the very long-term future of human life.

Exhaustion, Entropy, and Degeneration

The earth's geology was arguably the most important environment of Victorian society, whose wealth depended directly on the energy provided by coal. By the middle of the century, Victorians confronted the specter of energy exhaustion on two significant fronts, the first material and the second conceptual. In material terms, the manufacturing economy that sustained Britain's wealth and imperial dominance consumed a massive amount of coal. The historian E. A. Wrigley has described eighteenth- and nineteenth-century energy history in Britain as a shift from "organic" energy (peat, wood, animal fat) to "inorganic" energy (coal and later oil), with the important difference being that the latter could not be replenished on a timescale salient to human beings, who had inhabited the planet for a tiny fraction of the time it took for coal to develop. By the 1850s, 92 percent of total energy consumption in England, Wales, and Scotland came from coal, and it was clear that there would be no way to sustain factories, industry, and rail transport without it.[4]

The nonrenewability of coal became a matter of significant concern in the 1850s and 1860s. A parliamentary commission sought to reassure the public that over 70 million tons of unmined coal would last "upwards of a thousand years without exhaustion."[5] But the economist Stanley Jevons warned in his book *The Coal-Question* (1865) that, because demand could be expected to increase exponentially as machines became more efficient, in fact coal might be exhausted in just over 100 years.[6] While this was a moment of public crisis, the possibility of coal exhaustion had been discussed for many years. Nearly a half-century prior to the publication of Jevons's book, the geologists William Conybeare and William Phillips warned that "should our coal mines ever be exhausted, [our manufacturing industry] would melt away at once ...; we should lose many of the advantages of our high civilization."[7] Elizabeth Carolyn Miller has shown how, across scientific and literary domains, there was a growing sense that "extraction-based life entailed a diminished future."[8] Arising simultaneously with the transition to a coal-based economy were cultural and political fears about coal's eventual exhaustion.

A second related specter of energy exhaustion was even more existential, having to do with the sun–earth energy system, which operated at even a longer timescale than the formation of coal. Nineteenth-century physical sciences made advances in modeling thermodynamic energy systems that culminated in two principles. The first was that, within a "closed" energy system, energy cannot be destroyed; it can only be converted from one state to another (e.g., from motion to heat). The second was that, within such a system, energy will inevitably be converted into states that are less complex or useful for mechanical work; "there is," William Thompson (Lord Kelvin) wrote, "a universal tendency to [energy's] dissipation, which produces ... cessation of motion and exhaustion of potential energy."[9]

These principles are now known as the first and second laws of thermodynamics, and they accrued cultural meanings beyond their scientific import. The conservation of energy articulated by the first law, Tina Young Choi has argued, seemed consonant with natural theological "providentialism," in which nature was designed by God to be both stable and benefiting humanity.[10] But, Choi observes, the second law had a darker cultural tenor: the system described by the second law was in a state of ever-increasing disorder. When these laws were applied to the sun–earth energy system, the inevitable conclusion was that the energy arriving from the sun would eventually dissipate as the system tended toward equilibrium. The thermodynamic debate echoed the coal debate on two fronts. A providential ideology initially reassured readers that order was stable and permanent, that God had planned Britain's energy dominance in advance, and that he could be expected to reveal new sources of energy should coal run out. But this ideology sat in tension with the threat of depletion: the hard physical reality was that it would eventually take more energy to mine coal than the coal yielded, and that the sun would cool so much as to no longer be able to sustain life.

In the biological sciences, too, a conflict was taking place between progressivist and declensionist ideologies in the natural world, which led to a reconceptualization of the relation between society and environment. Charles Darwin ended *On the Origin of Species* (1859) on a note of wonder: "from the war of nature, from famine and death, the most exalted object which we are capable of conceiving, namely, the production of the higher animals, directly follows."[11] While Darwin eschewed a teleological account of evolution as a process of improvement, readers are here clearly meant to appreciate a distinction between "higher" and lower animals, and to be affectively uplifted ("exalted") by their contemplation of adaptation by natural selection. Herbert Spencer distinguished his evolutionary theory from Darwin's, coining the phrase the "survival of the fittest" to embrace a teleological version of natural selection in which "the death of the worst and multiplication of the best, must result in the maintenance of a constitution in harmony with surrounding circumstances."[12] Spencer's was a highly influential vision of nature tending toward ever more complex and "better" forms.

But the possibility that the direction of natural selection might be reversed was proposed by a number of writers who theorized "degeneration," or a type of natural selection that favored lesser complexity. Ray Lankester's 1880 pamphlet *Degeneration: A Chapter in Darwinism* seized on Darwin's distinction between higher and lower forms to elaborate "the possibility of a degeneration – a loss of organisation making the descendant far *simpler* or *lower* in structure."[13] Echoing fears about energy exhaustion and entropy, Lankester raised the possibility that "the white races of Europe" were showing symptoms of an incipient civilizational degeneration. The extrapolation of biological degeneration to culture found its most notorious expression in Max Nordau's *Degeneration* ([1892] 1895), which proposed that mental and physiological degeneration among certain individuals was responsible for the mood of dissipation and ennui in "the reddened light of the Dusk of Nations."[14]

Across these discursive domains we can see several common throughlines. Foremost is a sense of the interconnectedness of social and environmental systems, such that the principles of the biological and physical world are thoroughly interwoven with human society. Both geophysically and biologically, social change and organization were seen to be interdependent with energy systems and principles of evolution. Moreover, these systems were seen to be at an inflection point at the end of the nineteenth century, with the end of cheap fossil energy or the biological decline of civilization sitting just beyond the horizon. This fear of crisis speaks to the ideological tension built into the dominant teleologies: namely, a tension between a progressivist, providential view of ever-increasing complexity and a scarcity-based or degenerationist warning that progress might be at its end. Finally, these new ways of thinking about the relation between society and nature depended on a much expanded view of the place of human society within history: the individual is seen as the expression of millennia of biological natural selection; energy consumption in the present is recognized to be rapidly destroying coal that had taken eons to form. These scientific texts toggled between self-conscious modernity, on the one hand, and an awareness of a vast sweep of time, on the other. This trick of the scalar imagination was inaugurated by eighteenth-century theories of earth history, elaborated into biological and human history through Darwin and Spencer, and inverted near the end of the century to invoke fears of dissipation and decline.

The Time Machine and Speculative Fiction

Understanding the relation between human history and these much larger scales of evolutionary and geological history was from its origins a challenging undertaking for the human imagination. In her study of Darwin as a literary figure, Gillian Beer proposes that "evolutionary theory is first a form of imaginative history"; more recently, Adelene Buckland has argued that "geologists elaborated new *literary* forms."[15] Nineteenth-century science was public, imaginative, speculative, and spectacular. At the same time, the end of the century saw a rapidly expanding market for speculative genres such as utopian fiction, science fiction (or "scientific romance"), alternative histories, and the gothic. These ephemeral and popular genres invented future societies or undiscovered civilizations and then systematically explained to a fictional visitor how they functioned – all in order to comment on modern society. An increased appetite for didacticism and thinly fictionalized social theory meant that late century speculative fiction could explicitly address developing understandings of the interconnection of environment and society over long spans of time.

H. G. Wells's 1895 novel *The Time Machine* is both a culmination and self-reflexive treatment of this genre of speculative fiction grounded in scientific and social theory. The Time Traveller's journey addresses the competing models of providentialism and progress versus Malthusianism and degeneration by explaining and then revising the account of two species that are discovered in the year 802,701 CE. The basic thought experiment of *The Time Machine* is to imagine the long-term effects of human dominance over the natural world. As the Time Traveller begins to piece together how the world of the future is organized, his reasoning is based on evolutionary principles of artificial and natural selection. Meditating extensively on the relationship between organism and environment. The Traveller discovers that a world where "diseases had been stamped out" was also a world that did not favor the strong over the weak.[16]

Through his thought experiment, Wells shows Herbert Spencer's model of "the death of the worst and multiplication of the best" to be relative and mutable: if the natural conditions of survival are socially managed and the need for struggle is eliminated, then strength conveys no advantage.[17] The weakness of the creatures the Traveller first meets, the Eloi, leads him to reflect that "Humanity had been strong, energetic, and intelligent, and had used all its abundant vitality to alter the conditions under which it lived. And now came the reaction of the altered conditions. Under the new conditions of perfect comfort and security, that restless energy, that with us is strength, would become weakness."[18] Wells's language here depends on the portability of the metaphor of "energy" across geophysical, biological, and social domains: the individual "restless energy" that constitutes "strength" in the nineteenth century is an unfavorable trait when struggle is no longer needed – and adaptations to this situation favor a lack of energy leading to a general dissipation of humanity.

Upon discovering the underground race of toiling Morlocks, the Traveller revises his speculation. It is not only nature that the Eloi have dominated; rather they achieved "a triumph over nature and the fellow-man."[19] Here social relations are folded into natural conditions so as to become part of the environment that the human species controls and then slowly adapts to. Over a very long timescale, the distinction between artificial and natural comes undone; artificial changes to an environment become the context in which natural selection takes place. Or, more precisely, this distinction is revealed never to have been real in the first place. So, while the novel may at first seem to operate along a binary of natural/artificial, where the arcadian world of the Eloi is contrasted by the machinic world of the Morlocks, in fact both above and below ground we are meant to see artificial environments that have become so naturalized that they have exerted evolutionary pressures.

The novel's plot thus explores how the vast timescales of evolutionary theory alter the conception of the relation between human society and the environment. Nature is no longer conceivable as a stable and unchanging system, but one that is both in flux and highly reactive to human alterations of it. More than this, the distinction between the natural and the artificial cannot hold at the scale of evolutionary time. To describe an alteration as artificial can only make sense within the scale of human history; extrapolated far enough out and sustained over long enough time, artificial arrangements become the conditions to which organisms adapt.

After the Time Traveller escapes the encroaching Morlocks, the novel makes a leap forward millions of years into the future, appending a narrative of thermodynamic decline to the narrative of evolutionary decline. This thermodynamic plot has been foreshadowed within the evolutionary one in ways that link the two modes of decay. When the Traveller first arrives, he uses a solar metaphor to describe biological decline, noting that "the ruddy sunset set me thinking of the sunset of mankind."[20] To explain the hotter atmosphere of the future, the Traveller speculates that as the solar system has lost energy, a planet has fallen into the sun, providing it with "renewed energy."[21] The adventure narrative turns on the difference between a warm sunny daytime that keeps the Morlocks at bay and the night in which they can comfortably emerge from the ground. The Traveller gradually works out an account of an energy system: the metabolic system of the Eloi/Morlock world is one in which plants metabolize sunlight into fruit; Eloi metabolize fruit into their frail bodies; and Morlocks derive energy at a third remove from the sun by eating Eloi flesh.

The novel's second leap forward in time expands our view of the energy system that governs the systems and relations that have been previously described. In a world in which even the descendants of humans have gone extinct, the sun becomes the novel's main character. At first "it simply rose and fell in the west, and grew even broader and more red." It becomes "a vast dome glowing with a dull heat, and now and then suffering a momentary extinction."[22] It sits barely above the horizon, "red and motionless."[23] Then, "more than thirty million years hence, the huge red-hot dome of the sun had come to obscure nearly a tenth part of the darkling heavens."[24] The Traveller has previously speculated that the planets will fall into the sun and that the sun will lose its energy; as the earth follows suit, the sun grows dim and large. The time-travel narrative ends with an eclipse of this massive sun: "I saw the black central shadow of the eclipse sweeping towards me. In another moment the pale stars alone were visible. All else was rayless obscurity. The sky was absolutely black. A horror of this great darkness came on me. ... I shivered, and a deadly nausea seized me."[25] The structure of the narrative draws a parallel between degeneration and entropy.

The Time Machine treats this relationship with particular clarity, exposing not only that biological systems and energy systems are intertwined with human society but also how, at a long enough timescale, the very distinction between artificial and natural, between environment and society, is revealed only to have ever been a heuristic. Wells was self-consciously incorporating tropes in similar narratives about energy and evolution that had preceded his novel. The threat of a race of beings living underground was the basis for Edward Bulwer-Lytton's *The Coming Race* (1871), which was more explicitly concerned with questions of energy exhaustion and depletion. Like Wells, Bulwer-Lytton intertwines a thermodynamic plot and an evolutionary plot: the protagonist discovers a race of inner-earth beings whose bodies have adapted biologically to be able to control a form of quasi-electrical energy called "Vril." The ability to control this immensely destructive energy structures the political life of the civilization. The Vril live in perfect peace and equality since any individual could wipe out the entire society – an early vision of the nuclear age's "mutually assured destruction."

Similarly, the protagonist of Samuel Butler's *Erewhon* (1872) discovers a hidden society that has banned all technology more advanced than that of the Middle Ages, because their sages have predicted via evolutionary theory that machines will ultimately adapt to develop intelligence greater than that of humans and therefore pose an existential threat to human existence. For Butler, too, the speculative timescale of evolution undoes the difference between the natural and artificial; in this instance, artificial machinery obeys the principles of development by natural selection such that sentience is imagined to leap from the animal kingdom to machines. The timescales unfolded by the biological and physical sciences scrambled previous ideas about where one could draw the line between the social and the natural and hence the distinction between environment and society. An important effect of this new and fascinating confusion was the possibility that what in the present moment looked like progress, development, and providence might instead be symptoms of decline, degeneration, and dissipation.

Decadent Ennui As Environmental Affect

While speculative fiction took up scientific developments explicitly, it was not alone in contemplating a new sense of the environment as intertwined with society and extending deep into the past and future. Somewhat less obvious but arguably just as consequential was the ramification of this new *longue durée* sense of environment in decadent and aestheticist writing. As Denis Denisoff has observed, these movements have rarely been understood as salient to ecological thought because "decadence has been associated with the urban, the cultured, the artificial."[26] But the foundational metaphor of decadence was organic: that is, biological change has social causes and effects. Stephen Arata is one of many scholars who have noted the ideological traffic between biology and culture in discourses of decadence and degeneration: "From its modern beginnings ... the study of degeneration was at once a branch of biology and a form of cultural criticism."[27] Whether decadence was levied as an accusation or reclaimed as a rallying cry, it called upon not only the relation of the social and the natural, but also the very long timescale of their interrelation.

Joris-Karl Huysmans's *Á rebours* (*Against Nature*, 1884), the novel that Arthur Symons famously dubbed "the breviary of the decadence" and that Oscar Wilde's character Dorian Gray is fatefully "poisoned by," begins with a story about heredity, biology, and physiognomy.[28] Its protagonist is the last in the line of a family that "consisted in bygone days, of muscular warriors and grim-looking mercenaries" but has "grown progressively more effeminate" until its sole descendant, Duc Jean des Esseintes, is "a frail young man of thirty, nervous and anaemic."[29] The novel's plot centers on energy, but this is not the geophysical energy described by physicists, but rather an individual's vital energy that has been gradually depleted. Des Esseintes is "filled with an immense weariness"; his "passion [for women] was spent"; he "was oppressed by an overpowering sense of ennui"; and "having exhausted every possibility [of pleasure], as though worn out with the strain, his senses were overpowered by inertia, and impotence was close at hand."[30] The archetypal decadent figure is one for whom a degenerative hereditary teleology culminates in boredom, exhaustion, depletion, and inertia. The cultural logic of decadence depends on a story about biology and the dissipation of energy. It transposes science-fictional speculation about energy and entropy into a more refined aesthetic and formal register.

While concerns about the depletion of coal reserves and the heat death of the universe might seem far removed from the figure of the degenerated decadent, in fact a prevalent metaphor of energy joins these cultural phenomena. Decadent texts frequently make moves that echo narratives of energy exhaustion and depletion in the sciences. In his 1889 essay "A Note on Paul Bourget," Havelock Ellis extensively quotes Bourget's organic metaphor for decadence, which makes the connection between biology and energy explicit. On Bourget's account, the decadent individual no longer subordinates their energy to the social whole and creates anarchy as a result. The hyperindividuation we see in the character of des Esseintes, which causes him to withdraw from society into a world of interior sensations, exemplifies the social anarchy that Ellis fears, in which the efforts of the individual are directed inward rather than placed in the service of collective society. Decadent energy is self-consuming and entropic.

Decadent texts envision a complex relation between society and environment, which echoes the feedback loops of nature and society that late century science fiction was keen to explore. The workings of biology were not thought of as an external force acting on a humanity that was separate from the natural environment. Immediately after using the language of cells and energy to describe the relation of individual to society, Ellis moves on to Bourget's account of literary style:

> A similar law governs the development and decadence of that other organism which we call language. A style of decadence is one in which the unity of the book is decomposed to give place to the independence of the page, in which the page is decomposed to give place to the independence of the phrase, and the phrase to give place to the independence of the word.[31]

These metaphors assert what we might call the ideology of decadent environmentalism in its purest form: the individual *is* a cell; language *is* an organism. As such, not only do laws of nature apply across social/environmental or artificial/natural domains, but the cultural distinction between these domains is itself dissolved.

This cultural template exposes how some of the works of aestheticism and decadence that might seem to be most removed from a concern with nature, environment, and energy decline in fact derive from a cultural framework that conceives aesthetic sensitivity as a biophysiological phenomenon determined by the vast temporal scale of natural selection. The figure of the aesthete depleted of energy is among the most culturally memorable tropes of decadent writing, perhaps because it deftly crosses between biological and social domains. It finds early expression in Walter Pater's undergraduate essay "Diaphaneité" (1864), which meditates fondly on a "type of character" distinguished by a "colourless, unclassified purity of life" and by "a moral sexlessness, a kind of impotence, an ineffectual wholeness of nature."[32] Nobody would argue that Pater had in mind contemporaneous debates about declining coal reserves, thermodynamic entropy, or evolutionary progress. But the fascination with an "ineffectual" and unreproductively "sexless" and "impotent" figure lays the groundwork for later writers who would find aesthetic value in a mood of depletion and decay.

This notion of impotence and ineffectuality is one of the veins of Pater's thought that Wilde takes up in *The Picture of Dorian Gray*. As Jeff Nunokawa observes, there is a paradox at work in the novel, whose characters are strangely enthusiastic about being bored: "we may well wonder how anyone so absorbed by ennui has the energy to mention it with such élan."[33] In Wilde's novel, it is sometimes suggested that the cure for boredom with civilized society is to embrace an atavistic reversion to a more primitive biological type: "The worship of the senses has often, and with much justice, been decried, men feeling a natural instinct of terror about passions and sensations ... that they are conscious of sharing with the less highly organized forms of existence."[34] Wilde directly echoes Lankester's notion of the "less highly organized" degenerate forms, but inverts its moral valence. At the same time, the novel obliquely links modish ennui to planetary apocalypse as the characters banter: "'*Fin de siècle*,' murmured Lord Henry. '*Fin du globe*,' answered his hostess. 'I wish it were *fin du globe*,' said Dorian, with a sigh. 'Life is a great disappointment.'"[35] Wilde's novel understands the "environment" both as a cause for and as a site of decline but, unlike that in much science fiction, this decline is portrayed not as something to be feared but as something to be provocatively embraced.

While decadence may seem to operate in a social world far removed from material concerns with environmental change, in fact it illustrates how pervasive and mutable was the notion that society and nature intertwined with each other over long spans of time. Rather than distinguishing between literal and metaphorical senses of energy declining over time, the discourses of aestheticism and decadence depended upon a sleight of hand that substituted individual dissipation for biological decline and vice versa. Reading science fiction alongside decadent texts illustrates how culturally influential and widespread were biological and thermodynamic notions of long-scale environmental decline. But, more importantly, it shows how fictional and cultural texts actively theorized and undermined the distinction between individual and environment, between nature and society, between the given and the artificial. If speculative fiction most often echoed cultural concerns about degeneration and entropy, decadent texts are notable for their ability to play with the value systems that were mapped on to scientific concepts. They remind us that the relation between literature and environment is not passively mimetic but actively speculative, satirical, and subversive.

Notes

1. Jennifer Wenzel, *The Disposition of Nature: Environmental Crisis and World Literature* (New York: Fordham University Press, 2020), 16, 17.
2. Jason W. Moore, *Capitalism in the Web of Life: Ecology and the Accumulation of Capital* (New York: Verso, 2015), 16, 17.
3. Moore, *Capitalism*, 14.

4. E. A. Wrigley, *Energy and the English Industrial Revolution* (Cambridge: Cambridge University Press, 2010), 37.
5. Edward Hull, *The Coal-Fields of Great Britain: Their History, Structure, and Resources* (London: Edward Stanford, 1861), 188.
6. William Stanley Jevons, *The Coal Question: An Enquiry Concerning the Progress of the Nation, and the Probable Exhaustion of Our Coal-Mines* (London: Macmillan, 1865), xvi.
7. William Conybeare and William Phillips, *Outlines of the Geology of England and Wales* (London: William Phillips, 1822), 324.
8. Elizabeth Carolyn Miller, *Extraction Ecologies and the Literature of the Long Exhaustion* (Princeton: Princeton University Press, 2021), 12.
9. William Thomson, "On the Age of the Sun's Heat," *Macmillan's Magazine* 5 (March 1862), 388–93 at 388.
10. Choi Tina Young, "Forms of Closure: The First Law of Thermodynamics and Victorian Narrative," *ELH* 74.2 (2007), 304.
11. Charles Darwin, *On the Origin of Species* (Cambridge: Cambridge University Press, [1859] 2009), 360.
12. Herbert Spencer, *The Principles of Biology*, vol. 1 (London: Williams and Norgate, 1864), 445.
13. Edwin Ray Lankester, *Degeneration: A Chapter in Darwinism* (London: Macmillan, 1880), 30.
14. Max Nordau, *Degeneration*, 1st English trans. (New York: Appleton, [German 1892] 1895), 6.
15. Gillian Beer, *Darwin's Plots: Evolutionary Narrative in Darwin, George Eliot and Nineteenth-Century Fiction*, 3rd ed. (Cambridge: Cambridge University Press, [1983] 2009), 6; Buckland, *Novel Science*, 2.
16. H. G. Wells, *The Time Machine: An Invention*, ed. Nicholas Ruddick (Peterborough: Broadview, [1895] 2001), 91, 90.
17. Spencer, *Principles of Biology*, 445.
18. Wells, *The Time Machine*, 92.
19. Wells, *The Time Machine*, 111.
20. Wells, *The Time Machine*, 91, 90.
21. Wells, *The Time Machine*, 106.
22. Wells, *The Time Machine*, 144.
23. Wells, *The Time Machine*, 145.
24. Wells, *The Time Machine*, 147.
25. Wells, *The Time Machine*, 148.
26. Dennis Denisoff, *Decadent Ecology in British Literature and Art, 1860–1910: Decay, Desire, and the Pagan Revival* (Cambridge: Cambridge University Press, 2022), 4.
27. Stephen Arata, *Fictions of Loss in the Victorian Fin de Siècle* (Cambridge: Cambridge University Press, 1996), 2.
28. Arthur Symons, *The Symbolist Movement in Literature* (London: Constable, 1911), 139; Oscar Wilde, *The Picture of Dorian Gray*, ed. Joseph Bristow, Vol. 3, *The Complete Works of Oscar Wilde* (Oxford: Oxford University Press, [1891/1892] 2005), 290.
29. Joris-Karl Huysmans, *Against Nature*, trans. Margaret Mauldon (Oxford: Oxford University Press, [1884] 1998), 3.

30. Huysmans, *Against Nature*, 7, 8.
31. Havelock Ellis, "A Note on Paul Bourget," in *Views and Reviews: A Selection of Uncollected Articles, 1884–1932* (Freeport: Books for Libraries Press, 1970), 52.
32. Walter Pater, *Miscellaneous Studies: A Series of Essays* (London: Macmillan, 1895), 215, 216, 220.
33. Jeff Nunokawa, *Tame Passions of Wilde the Styles of Manageable Desire* (Princeton: Princeton University Press, 2003), 72.
34. Wilde, *The Picture of Dorian Gray*, 278.
35. Wilde, *The Picture of Dorian Gray*, 318.

4

CANNON SCHMITT

Blue Ecologies

On his visit to the distant future, the unnamed narrator of H. G. Wells's science fiction novella *The Time Machine* (1895) discovers a natural world transformed: "The air was free from gnats, the earth from weeds or fungi; everywhere were fruits and sweet and delightful flowers."[1] Already underway in the nineteenth century from which he set out, the wholesale remaking of the planet to suit human preferences, which the narrator elsewhere refers to as "the conquest of animated nature," has been completed.[2] Or nearly so. Later in his exploration of the year 802,701 CE, the sight of the Thames Estuary prompts a fleeting suspicion: "I thought then – though I never followed up the thought – of what might have happened, or might be happening, to the living things in the sea."[3] The portentous tone signals an unspoken hypothesis: that unlike life on land, marine life has continued evolving on its own, independent of human intervention and without regard to human desires.

Two scenes near the novella's end appear to confirm that hypothesis. First, on a beach an unspecified but immense number of years further into the future, a table-sized crab almost makes a meal of the Time Traveller. Finally, at the furthest extent of his temporal expedition, on the same beach but now 30 million years distant from Victorian Britain, the narrator witnesses what may be the last remaining animal life on the planet, a sea creature not so much predatory as disturbingly alien: "tentacles trailed down from it; it seemed black against the weltering blood-red water, and it was hopping fitfully about."[4] The main narrative of *The Time Machine* concerns the putative course of human evolution, which traces a parabola that reaches apogee centuries after the nineteenth. Following its subsequent descent, the novella dwells on the nightmarish time in which subterranean, simian Morlocks feed on childlike Eloi, the upper-world branch of the now speciated human family tree. But alongside that narrative Wells relates a shadow story of the sea that presumes not only its autonomy from, but also its long-continued threat to, the human.

Not all nineteenth-century sea stories are shadow stories. In poems such as Gerard Manley Hopkins's *The Wreck of the Deutschland* (written 1875–6) or Algernon Charles Swinburne's *Tristram of Lyonesse* (1882); in maritime fiction by Frederick Marryat, R. M. Ballantyne, Robert Louis Stevenson, and Joseph Conrad; in plays, from popular nautical melodramas to Charles Dickens's and Wilkie Collins's *The Frozen Deep* (1856), about the lost Franklin expedition that set out in 1845 to find the Northwest Passage – in these texts and many others, the ocean takes center stage. Their direct, sustained attention to salt water reveals much about contemporaneous blue ecologies, the varied ways the Victorians conceptualized the ocean environment and their relation to it. Far more numerous, however, are texts like *The Time Machine* in which the ocean makes an appearance but remains in the margins, an adjunct to the principal setting or action.

Nearly ubiquitous but frequently peripheral: the ocean in Victorian literature mirrors its place in the experience of the inhabitants of the island nation that was, from 1801 to 1922, the United Kingdom of Great Britain and Ireland. Consider: the furthest point from the coast in North America – what geographers call the continent's pole of inaccessibility – lies over 1,000 miles inland. But a scant 70 miles separate the shore from Britain's pole of inaccessibility, near Coton in the Elms in Derbyshire. Never far away, the ocean shapes the lives of Britons no less surely than it shapes the contours of the British Isles themselves. The obviousness of such an insight is belied by the fact that initially it could only be perceived by someone looking at Britain from elsewhere. Writing from Aotearoa/New Zealand in the 1990s and early 2000s, J. G. A. Pocock proposed a history that, "[f]ormed partly in an archipelago of the Southern Ocean, ... presents the islands including Britain as another archipelago."[5] A founding moment for the field of Archipelagic Studies, Pocock's innovation recognizes the resemblance between two widely separated constellations of islands. But it also asserts their connectedness to each other, to other archipelagoes (in the Mediterranean, the Indian Ocean, the Caribbean), to the water that surrounds them, and to continental land masses: "oceanic and planetary space must be part of a way of seeing the world."[6] We belong to one global ocean environment.

Historically, however, land and sea have been conceptualized as utterly distinct from, even hostile to one another. Christopher Connery argues that Western culture has been characterized from its inception by "antagonism toward the ocean" resulting in part from the ocean's resistance to attempts to know it. "[A]s close an approximation of the infinite as the visible, physical world can provide," in Connery's words, the ocean appears, in a telling metaphor, unfathomable.[7] The same illusion of infinitude has contributed to a longstanding conviction that the ocean is impervious to human activity. Its most lapidary articulation may be found in Lord Byron's *Childe Harold's Pilgrimage*, Canto the Fourth (1818): "Man marks the earth with ruin – his control / Stops with the shore." Like Wells, Byron figures the sea as beyond the reach of human designs. Also like Wells, he goes further. Apostrophizing the sea, the speaker of the poem continues: "upon the watery plain / The wrecks are all thy deed, nor doth remain / A shadow of man's ravage, save his own."[8] The ocean as land's opposite, unmarkable by humans and perilous to them when they venture not so much into as onto it: this constitutes the dominant blue ecology of the Victorian era.

Only recently has the first postulate of that ecology, the ocean's supposed inexhaustibility, been refuted. In *The Sea Around Us* (1951), even the great environmentalist and marine biologist Rachel Carson, as if channeling Byron, declares of the human: "He cannot control or change the ocean as, in his brief tenancy of earth, he has subdued and plundered the continents." Not until a decade later, in the preface to that book's second edition, does she acknowledge the ocean's vulnerability: "there has long been a certain comfort in the belief that the sea ... was inviolate, beyond man's ability to change and to despoil. But this belief, unfortunately, has proved to be naïve."[9] The ocean, we now know, is not unmarkable. But it still has the capacity to mark, to ravage us. In a concerning instance of how deeply literary and filmic depictions can determine ecological thinking, the twenty-first-century version of the danger the ocean poses centers on an apex predator. *Jaws* was published in 1974, and the film based on it was released the following year. Half a century later, we remain under the influence of the double synecdoche of Peter Benchley's title, which reduces the ocean to a Great White Shark and the shark to rows of serrated teeth. (Compare Wells on the giant crab of the far future, "its mouth all alive with appetite."[10]) But the Victorians, and with much more reason, most feared abiotic marine phenomena: wind, waves, storms, rocks, and reefs. Another synecdoche is at work here, one given utterance by Byron's speaker: "the wrecks are all thy deed." Arguably the most numerous representations of the ocean in Victorian literature involve shipwreck.

Take only a handful of the best known examples. In R. M. Ballantyne's Robinsonade, *The Coral Island* (1857), three boys survive the sinking of the *Arrow* only to encounter pirates and (by turns luridly or sentimentally portrayed) Indigenous Pacific Island peoples. Charlotte Brontë, at the end of *Villette* (1853), moots the likelihood of Monsieur Paul's death at sea to avoid specifying whether he returns from the West Indies to the novel's protagonist–narrator, Lucy Snowe. In *Dombey and Son* (1848), Dickens deploys shipwreck literally in the mistaken report of Walter Gay's drowning and figuratively in the account of Dombey's daughter Florence running away from home. Frequently occurring offstage, in narrative ellipses or at a distance from the main action, shipwreck in Victorian literature is functional: the source of plot devices or figurative conceits, a *deus ex oceano*. We can thus grasp the novels, poems, and plays in which wrecks feature as instances of what Nathan Hensley and Philip Steer refer to as "ecological form": the aesthetic shape of such texts registers "the nonhuman environment as central to the production of culture in modernity."[11] The same sea that destroys humans and thwarts their plans has, in connection with the stories it allows to be told, served as a kind of endlessly renewable natural resource.

On rare occasions, authors attempt to represent shipwrecks and the conditions that cause them directly – seemingly to demonstrate the impossibility of doing so successfully. In Joseph Conrad's *Typhoon* (1902), the description of the titular storm paradoxically confirms its ineffability: "Nobody – not even Captain MacWhirr, who alone on deck had caught sight of a white line of foam coming on at such a height that he couldn't believe his eyes – nobody was to know the steepness of that sea and the awful depth of the hollow the hurricane had scooped out behind the running wall of water."[12] At this moment of crisis, the ocean's incomprehensibility intensifies its perilousness. Its truth cannot be known, not even by the character who nearly dies witnessing it firsthand. We are in the realm of the sublime, but with a key difference. In Edmund Burke's 1757 account, sublimity results "when we have an idea of pain and danger, without being actually in such circumstances."[13] An affective phenomenon, the sublime draws on feelings of awe and fear – appropriate to the ocean, which Burke singles out as "an object of no small terror."[14] Conrad's "nobody was to know," however, moots an epistemological sublime: delight at the idea of unknowability.

Incomprehensible and implacable, the ocean in much of the Victorian imaginary took the form of a space apart that could be visited, but only at risk of death. Eschewing the complexities we now associate with ecological thinking, this blue ecology maps human relations with the ocean as an unadorned binary: us versus it. A more nuanced understanding of the ocean environment comes into focus in connection with a phenomenon that brought people into regular contact with the sea, a phenomenon sometimes destructive but more frequently limiting or shaping: the tide. "Time and tide will wait for no man," declares the narrator of Dickens's *Martin Chuzzlewit* (1844). "But all men have to wait for time and tide."[15] Dickens means this metaphorically, positing a numinous external force that humans must intuit and align themselves with – the "tide in the affairs of men" from Brutus's speech in Shakespeare's *Julius Caesar* (1599), which Dickens alludes to in his very next sentence. But behind the metaphorical lies the literal. Twice every twenty-four hours along the entire British coastline the level of the sea rises and falls. Waiting for the tide was a daily occurrence for many Britons in the nineteenth century.

Conrad built such waiting into the design of *Heart of Darkness* (1899). Marlow and his audience sit at anchor aboard the *Nellie* in the lower reaches of the Thames, unable to depart until the ebb tide allows them to make their way downriver and out into the North Sea. During that period of enforced inactivity, the tale of the journey up the Congo unfolds. A sailboat, the *Nellie* is at the mercy of tidal currents. Steam-powered vessels, the first of which date to the late eighteenth century, marked a shift, one noted by Conrad himself when, in *The Mirror of the Sea* (1906), he characterizes the essence of a steamer as its indifference to the ocean. But steam did not put an end to the influence of the tide. In Dickens's early short story "Out of Town" (1836), Wilkie Collins's sensation novel *The Moonstone* (1868), and other nineteenth-century fictions, mention may be found of a "tidal train": a railway service that connects to a steamer service, with train arrivals and departures timed to correspond with tide tables. Far from being rendered irrelevant by steam, the ocean's diurnal ebbs and flows sometimes determined the railway schedule.

Limiting and shaping for those onboard ships at sea or along the coast, the tide also impinged on life far inland. Britain's pole of inaccessibility is seventy miles from the shore, but the maximum distance to tidal waters is only half that. The tidal reaches of rivers affect vast regions of the country, and literary texts' frequent references to them index their importance. Take Dickens's *Great Expectations* (1861), in which the escaped convict Magwitch walks among large rocks placed along the shore of River Medway in Kent as stepping stones for use during high tide. Or consider the fictional river in the title of George Eliot's *The Mill on the Floss* (1860), the site of the "interrelations of hydrographic, social, and economic spheres" that Kyle McAuley refers to as "ecological entanglement."[16] A decisive factor in those interrelations, the tide on the Floss joins forces with the flood at novel's end to ensure Maggie Tulliver's death.

By far the most numerous nineteenth-century literary examples of the ecological entanglement of shore and sea via the tide occur in, on, and around the River Thames. The tidal reach of the Thames extends more than sixty-five miles inland, from the Nore at its mouth to Teddington Lock, built in 1810. Bisecting the whole of Greater London, the river is a constant presence in the daily lives of Londoners, actual as well as fictional, now as well as then. Like the ocean, the tidal Thames was understood as dangerous, the site of drownings both accidental and deliberate. In *Oliver Twist*, when Nancy refuses Rose Maylie's offer of rescue, Dickens has her gesture toward the river and ask: "How many times do you read of such as I who spring into the tide, and leave no living thing to care for or bewail them?"[17] But the Thames also gave life, or at least livelihood. Among the many odd job titles in Henry Mayhew's remarkable sociological survey, *London Labour and the London Poor* (1851), is that of "mud-larks," people who venture out onto the riverbed left exposed by the receding tide to collect metal, rope, pieces of coal, or anything else dropped by passing boats that might be sold. More macabre, "river finders" retrieve bodies from the water for the reward offered. Mayhew reveals some of the ways that, in life as well as in death, humans belong to the Thames's riverine and marine ecosystems.

No literary works attest to that belonging more frequently than Dickens's novels, including especially the last. *Our Mutual Friend* (1865) opens with a river finder, Gaffer Hexam, on the lookout for a submerged corpse: "The tide, which had turned an hour before, was running down, and his eyes watched every little race and eddy in its broad sweep."[18] A collection of handbills papering the walls of Hexam's house itemize his finds, which include apparent suicides such as "two young sisters what tied themselves together with a handkecher."[19] But drowning was not the only danger anticipated, as evidenced by a sentence in the earlier *Little Dorrit* (1857): "Through the heart of the town a deadly sewer ebbed and flowed, in the place of a fine fresh river."[20] Anything but Dickensian hyperbole, "deadly sewer" accurately portrays the Thames at mid century. Raw waste flowed into it unchecked, spreading cholera and culminating in the Great Stink of the summer of 1858, when, in the words of novelist and future prime minister Benjamin Disraeli, the "noble river" became "a Stygian pool, reeking with ineffable and intolerable horrors."[21] Dickens's and Disraeli's accounts both turn on a now familiar karmic irony: humans foul the Thames, the waters of which then threaten their own well-being.

Pollution in the ocean itself was more difficult to perceive, but the potential for extractive enterprises like whaling and fishing to affect entire marine ecosystems was beginning to be intuited. In the 1860s and again in the 1880s, a Royal Commission on the Sea Fisheries set out to investigate whether overfishing was possible – "and, if so, are the circumstances of the case such that [fisheries] can be efficiently protected?" The words are those of eminent scientist Thomas Henry Huxley, who reports the commission's finding that cod, herring, and mackerel were "inexhaustible."[22] This, "the most influential scientific pronouncement regarding North Atlantic fisheries during the middle of the nineteenth century," according to W. Jeffrey Bolster in *The Mortal Sea* (2012), set back nascent conservation efforts by decades.[23] But the very formation of the commission attests to a dawning awareness of the ocean's finitude, as does Huxley's concession that some fisheries, such as that for oysters, could be depleted.

The relatively few literary depictions of maritime extractive economies share the assumption of oceanic inexhaustibility. By far the most well known, Herman Melville's *Moby-Dick* (1851), minutely chronicles the harpooning and butchering of individual sperm whales but dismisses as implausible the prospect of the entire species being hunted to extinction. Jack London, another American author, devotes no small portion of *The Sea-Wolf* (1904) to the killing and skinning of fur seals. About a large herd of them the narrator observes:

> Coming from no man knew where in the illimitable Pacific, it was travelling north on its annual migration to the rookeries of Bering Sea. And north we travelled with it, ravaging and destroying, flinging the naked carcasses to the shark and salting down the skins so that they might later adorn the fair shoulders of the women of the cities.[24]

Although "illimitable" modifies only "Pacific," in an implied transferred epithet it characterizes that ocean's life forms as well. London's use of the verbs "destroying" and (especially) "ravaging" signals a protest against the seal hunt, but he can no more imagine damage done to a species or ecosystem than Melville can.

Cod rather than whales or seals are the focus of Rudyard Kipling's *Captains Courageous* (1897), set largely on a fishing boat on the Grand Banks off the coast of Newfoundland. In an unusually detailed depiction of work in a Victorian novel, Kipling relates the process of preparing fish for market: "The cod's liver dropped in the basket. Another wrench and scoop sent the head and offal flying, and the empty fish slid across to Uncle Salters, who snorted fiercely. There was another sound of tearing, the backbone flew over the bulwarks, and the fish, headless, gutted, and open, splashed in the tub."[25] The schooner aboard which this work is conducted is not a modern factory ship, but the assembly-line like process signals an industrial approach to exploiting the ocean's inhabitants. Looking back from the twenty-first century, when half of whale species face extinction and many fisheries have collapsed (including the cod fishery on the Grand Banks, where a moratorium was put in place in 1992), we can see the harm being done to a very exhaustible ocean. For the Victorians themselves, however, that harm was still largely invisible.

Largely but not entirely. In the 1850s, rail travel and the invention of the home aquarium combined with a fad for natural history to unleash hordes of vacationers on the tidepools along Britain's littoral. Among them were George Eliot and her partner George Henry Lewes. Eliot's journals from

May 1856 brim with enthusiasm for the strange organisms they collected from the waters of Ilfracombe on the North Devon Coast. In her journal entries, Anna Feuerstein has shown, Eliot developed a "secularized form of ecological thinking that emphasizes the interconnectedness of all life forms, and the alterity and agency of unfamiliar animal subjects."[26] Viewing the anemones, sea hares, pipefish, hermit crabs, brittle stars, aquatic annelids, and marine spiders she encountered as valuable in themselves, unconnected with what they might offer humans, and possessed of intricate relations with one another, Eliot begins to approach an understanding of marine ecology we recognize as our own.

And yet the close study that enabled such a perception threatened the very thing being studied. In *Father and Son* (1907), Edmund Gosse chronicles the destruction of the tidepools that had once formed a "ring of living beauty drawn about [Britain's] shores": "An army of 'collectors' has ... ravaged every corner of them. The fairy paradise has been violated, the exquisite product of centuries of natural selection has been crushed under the rough paw of well-meaning, idle-minded curiosity."[27] Gosse saddles his father, Philip Henry Gosse, the naturalist who invented the word *aquarium*, with "direct responsibility" for this "calamity."[28] Indeed, the older Gosse's guidebooks, including *A Naturalist's Rambles on the Devonshire Coast* (1853) and *Tenby: A Seaside-Holiday* (1856), did much to popularize seaside collecting. But so did Lewes's own *Sea-Side Studies* (1858), research for which took him and Eliot to Ilfracombe in the first place.

The mid century tidepool craze formed a small part of the increasing attention to the ocean and its creatures as inherently interesting and above all *knowable*. Demystifying the ocean's fancied infinity, Victorian science began to replace unfathomability with comprehension. Huxley indicates how far this went when he refers to the sea anemone as "a creature with which everybody ... must have become familiar, even to the limits of boredom."[29] His career well illustrates the path toward such familiarity. With strategic professional deliberation, he chose to devote his four years as surgeon's mate aboard HMS *Rattlesnake* to the study of rare and delicate marine organisms to which few others could have access. Later, he threw his support behind the 1872–6 *Challenger* expedition, a key milestone in the birth of oceanography. Sounding, dredging, and trawling its way across nearly 80,000 miles of ocean, the *Challenger* discovered over 4,000 new marine species – in the process, declared Huxley, "opening a new chapter in the history of the living world."[30]

As momentous as exploration of the deep sea was, it might be argued that the most important "new chapter in the history of the living world" opened by nineteenth-century science was the one having to do with ecology itself – which, Hensley and Steer point out, "[t]he Victorians invented."[31] Essential to that invention was Charles Darwin's theory of evolution. In *On the Origin of Species* (1859), Darwin insisted that grasping how evolution works requires keeping in mind the many and varied ways each organism relates to other organisms as well as to its physical surroundings. This is what we call "ecology," a term coined not by Darwin but by the German Darwinian Ernst Haeckel, for whom it meant "the whole science of the relations of the organism to the environment, including ... all the 'conditions of existence.' These are partly organic, partly inorganic in nature."[32] Even before he decided what to call it, Haeckel had practiced ecology in his 1862 study of Radiolaria, microscopic zooplankton found in all the world's oceans, and went on to develop it further in *Planktonic Studies* (1890). In the history of ideas, nineteenth-century blue ecology paves the way for ecology full stop.

Ecological thinking connects living organisms horizontally in space; evolutionary theory connects them vertically through time. Both together enabled Darwin to collapse the opposition between land and sea by locating human origins in the ocean. In *The Descent of Man* (1871), he points to the gill-like structure on the neck of human embryos and the likelihood that lungs developed from a swim-bladder as evidence that our distant forbears lived in the sea. Marine ancestors had already proven irresistible to poets and novelists. "There were shells, then fishes; then we came," declares Lady Constance in Disraeli's *Tancred* (1847).[33] In a feverish dream, the title character of Charles Kingsley's *Alton Locke* (1850) recapitulates the entirety of biological development, beginning with coral. Reconsidered in this context, the tentacled creature at the end of *The Time Machine* may signal that the novella's main narrative about human evolution and its peripheral narrative about the ocean are really one and the same: if human origins were aquatic, the human future might be as well. The dominant Victorian blue ecology viewed people and the sea not just as separate but opposed; an increasingly emergent one makes visible their thorough entanglement with one another.

Conversely, and finally, to write of "people" and "the sea" as if each were a single, monolithic entity ignores consequential distinctions. Pocock's exhortation to think in terms of "oceanic and planetary space" does not imply neglecting cultural, geographic, or ecological specificity. The Victorians recognized different oceans, each stratified into different zones. They also recognized, if only dimly, entirely other possibilities for conceptualizing those oceans and zones and humans' involvement in them. For instance, Charne Lavery identifies in Conrad's novels and short stories a "sense of disorientation produced in the face of [the] radical diversity" of the peoples and cultures of the Indian Ocean.[34] Oceania, too, unsettled certainties.

The encounter between European and Pacific Island peoples was, among other things, an encounter between two very different understandings of and relations with the ocean environment – a difference hinted at, among other places, in Robert Louis Stevenson's late fiction. At or just beyond the edges of nineteenth-century British literary and scientific ways of grasping the ocean environment, myriad alternative blue ecologies await.

Notes

1. H. G. Wells, *The Time Machine* (London: Penguin, 2005), 31–2.
2. Wells, *The Time Machine*, 66.
3. Wells, *The Time Machine*, 64.
4. Wells, *The Time Machine*, 85.
5. J. G. A. Pocock, *The Discovery of Islands: Essays in British History* (Cambridge: Cambridge University Press, 2005), 23.
6. Pocock, *The Discovery of Islands*, 15.
7. Christopher Connery, "*There Was No More Sea*: The Supersession of the Ocean, from the Bible to Cyberspace," *Journal of Historical Geography* 32 (2006), 494–511 at 495, 508.
8. *Lord Byron: The Complete Poetical Works*, ed. Jerome J. McGann, 7 vols. (Oxford: Oxford University Press, 1980), 2.184.
9. Rachel Carson, *The Sea Around Us* (New York: Oxford University Press, 1951), 15; Carson, *The Sea Around Us*, rev. ed. (New York: Oxford University Press, 1961), xi.
10. Wells, *The Time Machine*, 83.
11. Nathan K. Hensley and Philip Steer, "Ecological Formalism; or, Love Among the Ruins," in Nathan K. Hensley and Philip Steer, eds., *Ecological Form: System and Aesthetics in the Age of Empire* (New York: Fordham University Press, 2019), 5.
12. Joseph Conrad, *Typhoon, in Typhoon and Other Tales* (Oxford: Oxford University Press, 2002), 53.
13. Edmund Burke, "A Philosophical Enquiry into the Origin of Our Ideas of the Sublime and the Beautiful," in T. O. McLoughlin, James T. Boulton, and William B. Todd, eds., *The Writings and Speeches of Edmund Burke* (Oxford: Oxford University Press, 1997), 1.226.
14. Burke, "A Philosophical Enquiry," 1.230.
15. Charles Dickens, *Martin Chuzzlewit* (Oxford: Clarendon, 1982), 155.
16. Kyle McAuley, "George Eliot's Estuarial Form," *Victorian Literature and Culture* 48.1 (2020), 187–217 at 189.
17. Charles Dickens, *Oliver Twist* (Oxford: Oxford University Press, 1966), 316.
18. Charles Dickens, *Our Mutual Friend* (Oxford: Oxford University Press, 2008), 1.
19. Dickens, *Our Mutual Friend*, 22.
20. Charles Dickens, *Little Dorrit* (Oxford: Oxford University Press, 1979), 29.
21. Metropolis Local Management Act Amendment Bill – Leave, First Reading House of Commons Debates, *Hansard*, HC, vol. 151, cols. 1508, 15 July 1858.

22. Thomas Huxley, "*Inaugural Address. Fisheries Exhibition, London* (1883)," in Peter Hough, ed., *British Politics and the Environment in the Long Nineteenth Century* (London: Routledge, 2023), 1.124.

23. W. Jeffrey Bolster, *The Mortal Sea: Fishing the Atlantic in the Age of Sail* (Cambridge: Belknap, 2012), 141.

24. Jack London, *The Sea-Wolf* (Oxford: Oxford University Press, 2000), 140.

25. Rudyard Kipling, *Captains Courageous* (Oxford: Oxford University Press, 1995), 28.

26. Anna Feuerstein, "Falling in Love with Seaweeds: The Seaside Environments of George Eliot and G. H. Lewes," in Laurence W. Mazzeno and Ronald D. Morrison, eds., *Victorian Writers and the Environment* (London: Routledge, 2017), 189.

27. Edmund Gosse, *Father and Son: A Study of Two Temperaments* (Harmondsworth: Penguin, 1983), 125.

28. Gosse, *Father and Son*, 125.

29. T. H. Huxley, "On Coral and Coral Reefs," *Critiques and Essays* (New York: Appleton, 1887), 113.

30. T. H. Huxley, "The Problems of the Deep Sea," *Collected Essays*, 9 vols. (London: Macmillan, 1894–1901), 8.52.

31. Huxley, "The Problems of the Deep Sea," 8.9.

32. Quoted in Robert C. Stauffer, "Haeckel, Darwin, and Ecology," *Quarterly Review of Biology* 32.2 (1957), 138–44 at 140.

33. Benjamin Disraeli, *Tancred: Or, The New Crusade*, 3 vols. (London: Henry Colburn, 1847), 1.225.

34. Charne Lavery, *Writing Ocean Worlds: Indian Ocean Fiction in English* (London: Palgrave Macmillan, 2021), 25.

5

NATHAN K. HENSLEY

Aesthetic Form and Global Systems

Supply-Chain Sublime

The Victorian Empire was a world-spanning configuration whose networks of extraction, circulation, and exploitation remade the earth with profit in mind. The Empire's global system of domination and interchange is often thought of in terms of political economy. This makes sense: the interlinked formal and informal holdings of what was sometimes called "Greater Britain" were the result of planetary-scaled processes of social engineering that were also key steps in early phase capitalist globalization. "Not a bale of merchandise leaves our shores," said Radical MP Richard Cobden in 1836, a year before Queen Victoria began her reign,

> but it bears the seeds of intelligence and fruitful thought to the members of some less enlightened community; not a merchant visits our seats of manufacturing industry, but he returns to his own country the missionary of freedom, peace, and good government – while our steam boats, that now visit every port of Europe, and our miraculous railroads, that are the talk of all nations, are the advertisements and vouchers for the value of our enlightened institutions.[1]

Cobden's jingoistic paean to a beneficent British trade is often cited in political and economic histories of the Empire. Online searches yield references in the hundreds, some of which are citations to prior citations. The mirror-hall effect confirms that Cobden's statement has become a kind of synecdoche for British imperialism: a trope by which the whole can be expressed in part.

Today it reads as irony, given that the outcomes we have seen on the far end of Cobden's cultural export scheme so often look less like utopian Enlightenment and more like accelerating global inequality and (given his emphasis on early fossil infrastructure like "our steam boats" and "our miraculous railroads") climatological breakdown. Still, the passage is useful in capturing a certain rhapsodic faith in the uplifting capacities of global systems secured by British power. Linking economic development to cultural progress, Cobden's comment describes the marriage of ideas and money crucial to understanding empire as a total system. One complication is that Cobden actually opposed the formal annexation of territory and was, in the parlance of the time, "anti-imperialist." But his conception of words like "development" and "progress" enabled him to presume that an unfettered and fully globalized capitalism would lift up the world – and that Britain should lead the way in proving it. The result was what later historians have called "the imperialism of free trade."[2]

What does any of this have to do with *the environment*? This chapter presumes, first, that any consideration of Victorian environmental questions must address the earth-shaping project of Victorian imperial globalization; and second, that the political and economic questions animating Cobden's now infamous position on global trade are also at bottom ecological ones, and vice versa. Matters of political economy are also ecological. More specifically, the chapter suggests that Victorian literary works translated the systemic qualities of extraction-based globalization into aesthetic shape. Recent scholarship by Elaine Freedgood, Richard Menke, and Susan Zieger has described the supply-chain aesthetics of familiar Victorian literature, showing how works apparently unconcerned with "environment" or even "imperialism" at the level of explicit statement or overt theme might resolve into coded maps of resource capture, commodity circulation, and the exploitation of disposable populations across the imperium.

Zieger, for example, has shown how the famously hypermediated plot of Bram Stoker's *Dracula* (1897) – told through journal entries, telegrams, newspaper clippings, ship's logs, and phonograph recordings carved into wax cylinders, among other media forms – describes what globalization discourse today calls *logistics*. This term can be understood as "the art and science of efficiently managing the mobility of things and people," a techné of efficiency that is often associated with "global supply chains and their emblem, the shipping container."[3] What better shipping container than Dracula's coffin, Zieger notes, since this useful box brings the Count to England on circuits of seafaring trade, and enables the cargo itself – the vampire – to travel alongside the dirt from Transylvania without which he cannot, for lack of a better word, survive. One bioregion, packaged up, shipped off, and relocated to another.

It is no accident, perhaps, that the concept of the bioregion, or climatic zone amenable to certain forms of life but not others, is itself a Victorian invention. Formalized in the 1970s, the bioregion concept is traceable to the researches on plant life at various altitudes by Victorian botanist Joseph Dalton Hooker, whose career is itself a story of imperial travel and the linkage of disparate global environments under the banner of empire. In *Dracula*, Van Helsing refers to the Count's "earth-home, his coffin-home, his hell-home," which enables the undead traveler to circulate unharmed across disparate environments of the late Victorian globe. In this same way did Wardian cases – the sealed glass terraria popular after the 1840s – enable the movement of plants across the world, as work by Lynn Voskuil and Lindsay Wells among others has shown. These earth-homes helped connect disparate climatological zones or bioregions into new networks of exchange, commodification, and biological imperialism, and helped enable a new conception of "the world" as single system.

Seen this way, an invasive species narrative like *Dracula* discloses a kind of supply-chain sublime, with "sublime" here referring to the cognitive short-circuit that follows from confronting a total system whose vastness and complexity is structurally overwhelming to human consciousness. No single mind could properly account for the logistical networks, human relationships, and nonhuman elements (often redescribed as "raw materials") that united to form any one scene of Victorian domestic experience. Afternoon tea is one example, since this classic middle-class ritual was impossible without commodities that linked both ends of England's global imperial economy, the East Indies (tea) and the West (sugar). In this sense did the most quotidian experiences give physical shape to elaborate webs of human and nonhuman interaction, turning a newly globalized economy – and the forms of exploitation on which it depended – into the feeling of normal life.

In *Dracula*'s case, a highly mediated plot links different nodes in a global network and, in the process, gives literary shape to the almost unthinkably vast network of physical infrastructures and communicative relations enabling what Cobden described as the seed-spreading work of imperial globalization.[4] *Dracula* is perhaps special in obsessing so openly about the physical circuits and generic modes in which such linkages take form, since its narrative is told through any number of modern media channels, and tracks the material circulation of characters and information along railroad lines, shipping routes, and (in the case of the telegraphic messages recurring throughout the novel) copper wires strung across continents. But as Edward Said argues in his canonical *Culture and Imperialism*, such global networks are also present in the British novel generally, albeit most often in "allusions" that constitute "a structure and attitude of reference" rather than explicit mentions.[5]

In *Mansfield Park*, for instance, offhand references to the Antiguan planter economy buttress the moral logic of Jane Austen's domestic plot by sponsoring an ethical distinction between free choice and mastery. The leafy elsewhere of Antigua, in other words, enables the novel's England-based marriage plots by virtue of the wealth accumulated by an absentee planter class that is now available as inheritance or dowry. In a more mediated way, that slave colony also informs the moral distinction between "unfettered" choices and the other kind. It is worth recalling that slave-based monoculture plantations of the British sugar islands were early experiments in what is now termed "factory farming": predicated on the exhaustion of soil and the nonrenewable relationship to what business jargon now calls human capital. Yet, Said says, the scenes of colonial violence sustaining domestic comfort in the eighteenth century and afterwards are not treated directly in these novels, but instead with "aesthetic *silence* or *discretion*."[6] Such tropes suggest that British novels gave imaginative shape to networks of despoliation and accumulation they could not assimilate into direct expression.

Building on the insights of these and other interventions into the study of Victorian globalization, the rest of this chapter shows how two representative Victorian genres, the realist novel and the lyric poem, might be read in light of an early extraction economy whose aftermath we inhabit now. The hypercanonical test cases I examine here – George Eliot's *Middlemarch* (1871–2) and Matthew Arnold's "Dover Beach" (1867), along with an only slightly less famous text, Anthony Trollope's *The Eustace Diamonds* (1873) – have little to do with climate or environment in any obvious way: they are about love, or marriage, or ennui, or "industrialization," or whatever. But the question of what any text is *about* is in no way obvious, and my suggestion here is that the study of "Victorian Literature and Environment" can be opened beyond our most obvious understandings of aboutness to take account of texts and scenes unlikely to show up in a subject-heading search for "environment" or "environmental literature." A reading practice that construes ecological matters to inhere in sociopolitical ones, and that sees environmental issues as relating to key moral and philosophical concerns, might enable us to observe that relations of extraction and accumulation are part of the story of environment, too – and have been, ever since *the environment* was invented.

The Age of Improvement

To say that "the environment" was invented is to put provocatively a point that is actually obvious, which is that conceptual formations come into being in certain times and places in order to serve specific epistemological needs. The term "environment," for example, frequently coupled with "the," as the *Oxford English Dictionary* (*OED*) says, refers to the earth as a singular abstraction or ecological totality: "[t]he natural world or physical surroundings in general." This world-scaled abstraction was unavailable to the Victorians themselves, it turns out, who tended to describe environments, plural, from the middle French for the "action of surrounding something."[7] For example, Thomas Hardy's breakdown of his life's work into categories for the 1912 Wessex Edition included "Novels of Character and Environment."

Hardy's usage described not a holistic total system of living and nonliving beings, but the local zones in which characters in *Jude the Obscure* (1895) or *Tess of the D'Urbervilles* (1891), for instance, might flourish or not. (Mostly not.) The broader and singular version of environment in common usage today arrives into English only in the period following World War II, at the center of the period of vertiginous economic expansion and rapidly gathering ecological devastation that environmental historians call the Great Acceleration: in 1948, the year of my parents' birth, and just a few years before the field of Victorian studies was founded alongside the journal of that name.[8] In this sense are "Victorian literature" and "the environment" tangled together in complex relays of historical, ecological, and institutional relation.

Here we can emphasize that Victorian imperialism was a global system that reconfigured *the environment* in the strong, contemporary sense of that term. Between 1837 and 1901, the British Empire's effort to remake the globe had results not only for environments, plural – the bushlands of Australia, the boreal forests of Northern Canada, or the mangrove swamps of the Sundarbans in West Bengal, say, to pick just three bioregions reshaped significantly by imperial incursion. The Empire also reshaped "the environment," singular, since its coal-fired apparatuses for global connectivity and domination – the steam ships and railways of Cobden's fantasy – set path dependencies and infrastructural conditions for what is today a fully entrenched system of what Andreas Malm has called "fossil capitalism."[9] Under this rising system, nature would make way for progress or fuel it: forests would be cleared, hillsides stripped bare, mines sunk, canals dug, deserts irrigated into croplands, unproductive wastes transformed into spaces where extractive practices of accumulation, now understood as productivity, could transpire. It is worth observing that the term *productivity*, now an attribute of white-collar workers in a hyperspeed information capitalism, appeared first in the nineteenth century – and already in 1865, the OED tells us, could refer to "the limited productivity of soil," in other words: exhaustion.[10]

It would be possible to trace the dynamic relationship between ideologies of capture, extraction, and use, on the one hand, alongside their corollary term, exhaustion, on the other, as scholars like Elizabeth Carolyn Miller and Corbin Hiday have done, and to do so in any number of specific scenes across the imperium, only a few of which I can allude to in this short chapter. Menke, for instance, has shown how the print boom and much-vaunted rise of mass literacy in late Victorian cities relied upon a voracious new appetite for wood pulp in British Canada, where loggers were "denuding the primitive forests as fast as steam [would] permit."[11] This network-effect means that the ecological footprint of any number of seemingly domestic phenomena resolves into world-scaled grids of connectivity and degradation.

As the work of Miller, Hiday, and others suggests, any study of the relationship between progress and exhaustion would connect material scenes like the spruce forests of northern Ontario with philosophical ideas such as the ideologies of development being elaborated in places seemingly unrelated to sawmills and mineworks. These would include the pages of advanced literary and cultural journals like the *Westminster Review*, edited for a time by John Stuart Mill and, later, George Eliot. Inevitably this tracework would put us into contact with the ideology of improvement propounded by such theorists as Mill and fellow *Westminster*ite Herbert Spencer, whose "Progress; its Law and Cause" (1857) crisply articulated the concept of forward and upward historical motion that was a key driver of systemic connectivity across the British imperium. Here again, as always, material processes arise from ideological components and vice versa.

Long before Spencer and Mill, John Locke's *Second Treatise of Government* (1679) had influentially asserted that land was "improved" when wasted or nonprofitable spaces were transformed by labor into zones from which surplus could be extracted. As Locke explains in what would become a foundational text of liberal political theory, "the chief matter of property" is "not the fruits of the earth, and the beasts that subsist on it, but the earth itself."[12] Locke's influential account presumes that whatever areas of the earth are not yet mastered can be justifiably annexed for "improvement." Somewhat astonishingly, Locke explains that transforming wasted or unused lands into private property is the command of God, and that this process of successive enclosure is not a problem because there is plenty of land to go around: "there was still enough, and as good left."

In a world where the limits to growth have become obvious, this presumption of infinite expansion again reads as irony. In addition to punching holes in the now-naive-seeming idea that if one man drinks there will always be "a whole river of the same water left" – a theory now tested in drought-parched sectors of the American southwest, for instance – scholars have explained how Locke's ideology of wasted and unused land ignores Indigenous or non-agrarian land uses; construes uncolonized spaces as empty; and gives an alibi for expansion eminently useful to aspirational improvers since the early days of British capitalist expansion. For instance, in the planter Edward Long's *History of Jamaica* (1774), the authoritative source of knowledge about that place well into the Victorian era, he refers to the "judicious Locke" as his mentor.[13]

Long owned multiple plantations in Jamaica and helped transform vast swaths of forest into highly efficient engines for monoculture export trade – the envy of the planter class. As Catherine Hall has shown, Long conceptualized his extraction-based agriculture as improvement in strictly Lockean terms, and to the admiring wonder of his colleagues, designed these sites of exhaustion on principles of maximum efficiency. The benefits were obvious. "In our islands," he wrote, "the word *liberty* is in every one's mouth; the assemblies abound with the clamor of 'liberty and property'; and it is echoed back by all ranks and degrees, in full chorus."[14] We can presume that the hundreds of enslaved people who were worked to death in the boiling houses and canefields of Long's perversely named Lucky Valley estate were not part of the choir.

The obscenities of eighteenth- and early nineteenth-century slave-based monoculture might seem far removed from the topic of Victorian literature and environment, but it turns out that Victorian-era innovations in terraforming and global connection-making shared key features with these eighteenth-century forebears. Locke's principles of improvement would provide not only the explicit animating principles for Mill's 1859 *On Liberty*, which suggested that an upward developmental arc awaited those industrious enough to set it into motion, but also an entire tradition of political and social thought stemming from Mill's formulas. Mill's claim was that the world's nations could be divided into those that embraced "the spirit of improvement" and those better categorized as "the opponents of improvement."[15] This valorization of industrious forward development sponsored innovations ranging from early self-help books to continent-scaled transformations in earth systems. This general chorus was just one reason why Asa Briggs chose, for the title of his comprehensive study of the period from 1783 to 1867, *The Age of Improvement*.

Improvement across the Victorian imperium took different shapes in different places. Sometimes the transformation of uncapitalized nature into value was strikingly literal, as at the Kimberley diamond mine in South Africa (begun 1870), "the largest and most complete hole ever made by human agency," as Anthony Trollope said.[16] The Suez Canal (opened 1869) was another instance where improvement transformed the actual shape of the earth, since this new causeway enabled the traffic of goods and military force across the imperium and accelerated the steam-driven penetration of British trade into Africa, even as it demanded further garrisoning of troops and naval installations to "secure" this new passage. Eight years prior to the canal's opening, Trollope's "George Walker at Suez" (1861) could describe the area as "[o]f all the spots on the world's surface ... by far the vilest, the most unpleasant, and the least interesting" – even though it would be sustaining global trade in short order.[17] Forced labor was used to build the waterway itself, half a century after the much touted abolition of the British slave trade in 1807.

Written late in the century, Winston Churchill's celebratory account of counterinsurgency in the British Sudan, *The River War* (1897), reads as a love letter to improvement and the railroads and gunboats powered by improvement's main driver, steam. The future Prime Minister breathlessly reports that "[f]oundries, lathes, dynamos, steam-hammers, hydraulic presses, cupola furnaces, screw-cutting machines, and drills had been set up, and were in continual work" extending railways across the African continent.[18] Other times the earth-shaping aspirations of Victorian globalization were less material than ideological, as when the educator and politician Thomas Babington Macauley vowed to reshape the intellect of Indian students on the British mold in his famous "Minute on Indian Education" (1835); or when the mining magnate and colonial politician Cecil B. Rhodes, warm friend of Churchill's, said he would annex the planets if he could.

In the context of this interface between the ideological and material aspects of Victorian-era "improvement," it is worth observing that the diamonds removed from places like the Kimberley Mine were useful not only for their material value to metropolitan investors but also for their capacity to structure the imagination. In a chapter of *The Eustace Diamonds* called "The Diamonds are Seen in Public," for instance, Trollope's multiplot novel describes Lady Eustace entering a scene of immense social consequence to her, the drawing-room. Here, the subject of her marriage "had been so generally discussed, that the blaze of the stones immediately brought it to the minds of men and women. 'There she is, with poor Eustace's twenty thousand pounds round her neck,' said Laurence Fitzgibbon to his friend Barrington Erle. 'And there is Lord Fawn going to look after them,' replied the other."[19] Trollope describes the densely socialized site of interchange that is the British drawing room, on fire now with the "blaze of the stones." His syntax recodes the diamonds' use value or physical properties as something else, exchange value. Glittering chunks of concentrated carbon now signify as their worth in cash: Fitzgibbon notes that Lizzie is wearing not a necklace at all but "poor Eustace's twenty thousand pounds round her neck."

Kathy Psomiades has shown how Trollope's novel gives shape to the heteronormative traffic in women by which supposedly free actors enter marriage contracts under conditions of sexual domination.[20] In this way again do the domestic plot's most consequential social and political turns depend upon blazing bright things brought in from the darkest holes of the Victorian global system. Trollope himself seemed to suggest such a reading, given that in the 1884 *An Old Man's Love* he revisits the site of accumulation he'd seen firsthand nearly a decade before, and written into plot for *The Eustace Diamonds*. Of the Kimberley mine, he wrote that it was "foul with dust and flies; it reeks with bad brandy; it is fed upon potted meats; it has not a tree near it." Trollope goes on:

> It is inhabited in part by tribes of South African n – rs, who have lost all the picturesqueness of n – erdom in working for the white man's wages. The white man himself is insolent, ill-dressed, and ugly. The weather is very hot, and from morning till night there is no occupation other than that of looking for diamonds, and the works attending it. [D]iamond-searching is the occupation of the place; and if a man be sharp and clever, and able to guard what he gets, he will make a fortune there in two years more readily perhaps than elsewhere. John Gordon had gone out to Kimberley, and had returned the owner of many shares in many mines.[21]

Trollope's racist account of the southern African sacrifice zone describes the perfect inversion of what he understands to be the refinements of British society. But the passage also suggests the sinews of connection by which such scenes of anomie might link up to the drawing rooms in which the Lizzie Eustaces of the world wow and vex. The final turn of the passage describes the plot by which John Gordon "had gone out" to the frontier of accumulation but also, crucially, returned: improved from a flyblown imperial scammer into a respectable gentleman who owns stocks. It was in Griqualand West, incidentally, that the system of racial hierarchy known as apartheid was first conceived and deployed – administered by one William Owen Lanyon, who had begun his career in Jamaica.[22]

What Can That Have to Do with My Marriage?

Such movements only play out as literary device or biographical arc what Karl Marx argues in *Capital* – also a Victorian text, drafted in the British Library from 1863–5 – which is that the form of appearance for any commodity necessarily occludes the filth and violence in which value necessarily originates.[23] In George Eliot's *Middlemarch*, meanwhile, it is not diamonds but "purple amethysts" and "a pearl cross with five brilliants in it" that begin the plot of the book: "ornaments" that are, from Dorothea's perspective, "really of remarkable beauty."[24] The early episode enables Eliot to sketch Dorothea's self-denying personality against her sister Celia's more worldly embrace of the pleasurable. Dorothea's often cited desire to "live a grand life here – now – in England" advertises this multiplot novel's ambition to limn large-scale systems by way of the single storyline, and it is also this feature of the book, and not only its explicit mentions of political or social events, that makes it legible as a novel of ecological globalization.[25]

Already by 1962, critics had tired of pointing out *Middlemarch's* dominant metaphors of webs, tissues, and the interlaced scratches on the metal reflective surface known as a pier glass. The often remarked function of gossip in the novel is just one vocabulary by which Eliot emphasizes linkages and relation over the falsely isolated individual units that liberal theory of the period, led by Mill, understood as natural. Mill's 1859 *On Liberty* argued that "over himself, over his own body and mind, the individual is sovereign," while the first self-help book in history, Samuel Smiles' *Self-Help*, also of 1859, taught a generation of Victorians that they needed little other than their own hard work to improve themselves.[26] As scholars like John MacNeill Miller and Jayne Hildebrand have shown, against these individualizing fictions, Eliot positioned the interlaced and the collaborative – what Miller terms "the ecological plot."[27]

Some of the novel's most famous passages tell us that the squirrel's heartbeat and the growing grass cannot be perceived with normal orders of cognition: that the "roar which lies on the other side of silence" would deafen us if we could only learn to hear it.[28] This allusion to the imperceptible frequencies of the world beyond private human experience, like the evocation of imperial silences in books like *Mansfield Park* noted above, help us appreciate Eliot's effort to rewire the circuitry of our ethical sense. Along with the novel's key figures of webs, tissues, fibers, and "threads of connexion,"[29] such moments highlight the novel's interest in, first, the filigrees of relation connecting apparently disparate phenomena across an interspecies world system and, second, the threshold of perceptibility that renders some scenes invisible while making domestic dramas such as Dorothea's love plots leap into focus.

Eliot specifies that the context for such conventional plots is a vortex of changing social forms and shifting human relationships to the nonhuman world. *Middlemarch* depicts a moment of shifting land relations in the aftermath of eighteenth-century enclosure, as newly expanding fossil infrastructure (the railroads) and the alteration of medical knowledge, for instance, transform what had once been an agrarian and largely rural English society of peasants and aristocrats into one organized in ways we now understand to be modern. Taken as a whole, this multipronged investigation into sociopolitical modernization means that Eliot's novel, for all its emphasis on the unheard detail and the minor act, dramatizes processes that are fully global in scale. Its most brilliant work is to show how all these scales intersect.

Alluding to organized revolt against the rising industrial order, for instance, Mr. Vincy tells his daughter Rosamond of

> "this disappointment about [Rosamond's brother] Fred, and Parliament going to be dissolved, and machine-breaking everywhere, and an election coming on –"
>
> "Dear Papa! What can that have to do with my marriage?" [Rosamond asks.]
>
> "A pretty deal to do with it! We may all be ruined for what I know – the country's in that state! Some say it's the end of the world, and be hanged if I don't think it looks like it!"[30]

The exchange describes not just Vincy's anxiety but the aesthetic procedure of the novel itself. It asks what the background – framebreaking, "ruin," and "the end of the world" – might "have to do" with the marriage plot at the novel's foreground. Vincy's answer is also the novel's: "a pretty deal to do with it!"

Middlemarch's fundamental trick of scale, then, lets it see the major by way of the minor and vice versa. This means that when Eliot tells us that "every limit is a beginning as well as an ending,"[31] she construes systemic thinking as a narrative problem, and uses microscopes and pier glasses, for instance, as related tropes for describing the misleading, if inevitable, anthropocentrism of the novel as a form. Critic and novelist Amitav Ghosh has argued that the bourgeois novel is ill-equipped to narrate climatological change because it focuses on individual lives rather than relational ensembles. With Ghosh, Eliot acknowledges that the novel form she herself is working to perfect is nevertheless condemned to tell the story of isolated characters performing actions against a "backdrop."

This scenario can be considered a relic of the philosophical individualisms developed across the Victorian period, since it walls off characters into the false isolation of their own sensory worlds, when a more accurate description would see densely meshed networks of mutual action and collaborative interchange – as Charles Darwin, for instance, had proven in 1859's *On the Origin of Species*. *Middlemarch* investigates the occlusions by which regular human consciousness proceeds, and works to torque the procedures of the realist novel so as to expand our necessarily limited capacities for reading the world.

The Moon-Blanched Land

You are reading this chapter in a moment of climatological heating and collapsing infrastructure, at the far end of the modernizing processes Eliot documented in *Middlemarch*. At such a moment it is in no way certain why Victorian literature matters at all, nor yet what poetry, in its broadest sense, might do. (Poetry comes from the Greek *poiéō*, to make or do.) My answer has been to suggest that the formal features of certain nineteenth-century artifacts enable an expansion of our cognitive repertoire and are "environmental" insofar as they examine the intercalated histories of extraction, ecological transformation, and human experience at global scale.

One of the most beautiful poems of the nineteenth century, "Dover Beach" compresses all this work into a short lyric and ends this investigation of global systems and aesthetic form. In the poem, drafted first in

1851 and published only in *New Poems* (1867), Matthew Arnold's speaker is looking to the sea to index the fraught state of his own mind. Its famous first line, "The sea is calm tonight," mirrors formally the placidity it sees on the water: three beats of iambic verse – a trimeter – and the flattest verb in English, *to be*, create a perfect, powerful symmetry that is for the author of *Culture and Anarchy* the image of order itself, full, fair, and whole:

> The sea is calm tonight.
> The tide is full, the moon lies fair
> Upon the straits; on the French coast the light
> Gleams and is gone; the cliffs of England stand,
> Glimmering and vast, out in the tranquil bay.
> Come to the window, sweet is the night-air!
> Only, from the long line of spray
> Where the sea meets the moon-blanched land[.][32]

It's not static, exactly, but the permanence of this cyclical ebbing and flowing is again mirrored in Arnold's verse, in one of the Victorian era's greatest poetic effects: "Listen," the narrator continues, now addressing us and his lover directly, "you hear the grating roar / Of pebbles which the waves draw back, and fling, / At their return, up the high strand, / Begin, and cease, and then again begin."[33] *And then again begin*: the effect is musical: Sophocles heard this same cadence, Arnold says, because while the human world around us might crumble and go bad – while modernity might erode our most important institutions or even the capacity for relation itself – the sea is always the sea. Its sound, painful as it is, never goes away: it is an "eternal note."[34] In a gorgeous reading of this passage, Devin Griffiths describes its sedimented quality and being "swept" by it. The sound, he says,

> is an effect of overlapping forms, functions of meter, the stress pattern, the syntax, the caesuras and punctuation, assonance and dissonance, the withdrawing hiss of 'cease,' the plosive g's over which the line and its waves accelerate and break. It's the kind of seemingly irregular rhythm or tremulous cadence that … oceanographers struggled to explain before adopting wave function analysis.[35]

Griffiths finds in Arnold's famously melancholic verse a prototypical ecological form, where the wavelike motions of water itself are translated into literary effect by the lyric technologies of meter and sound.

Using the I-thou circuitry of lyric address, Arnold gives shape to the wave–function–effect by which his ocean is also that of Sophocles. In so doing he indulges in the fantasy of permanent stability in something called "nature" – a fantasy that, in our moment of rising seas and shifting baselines, has evaporated. Bill McKibben's *The End of Nature* – which argues that the permanent and unchanged nonhuman world had been definitively eradicated by means of human intervention – was published in 1989, when I was thirteen years old. In the long aftermath of that fantasy, it may be that Arnold's effort to find stability in chaos can help us appreciate how literary texts can compress affective moods, naturalistic analysis, and the ethical and political program of cognitive mapping – the attempt to measure the full scope of a world whose forms of appearance conceal as much as they disclose – into local details and small aesthetic effects: begin, and cease, and then again begin...

Like *The Eustace Diamonds* and *Middlemarch*, "Dover Beach" is famous not for its evocations of the flyblown and brutal ends of empire but for its depictions of inner life and something called "Victorian society." None of the works I've described here traces a single logistical supply chain to its bleak and disturbing terminus. None of them is "about" the environment as we know it today. But these familiar exhibits can be read for the global systems they nevertheless mediate into form, as their necessarily limited frames of analysis show as if through the scrim of their own occlusions the material facts of an extraction economy that was predicated on "improvement" but aimed, always, toward exhaustion. Attuning ourselves to the muted signals of this disaster, I contend, might enable us to hear the hiss and rush of a world, long in the making, where superstorms batter with increasing force what Arnold in "Dover Beach" calls "the naked shingles of the world."[36]

Notes

1. Cited in Anthony Wohl, "'Gold and Mud': Capitalism and Culture in Victorian England," *Albion: A Quarterly Journal Concerned with British Studies* 23.2 (Summer 1991), 275–82 at 275–6.
2. See John Gallagher and Ronald Robinson, "The Imperialism of Free Trade," *Economic History Review, (Second Series)* VI (1953), 1–15.
3. Susan Zieger, "Logistics," *Victorian Literature and Culture* 46.3–4 (2018), 749–52 at 749. doi.org/10.1017/S1060150318000736.
4. Susan Zieger, "Dracula's Cold-Chain," *Victorian Literature and Culture* 52.2 (2024), 355–74, doi:10.1017/S1060150323000955.
5. Edward Said, *Culture and Imperialism* (New York: Vintage, 1993), 62.
6. Said, *Culture and Imperialism*, 94, emphasis added.
7. *Oxford English Dictionary*, s.v. "environment, n." (Oxford University Press, September 2025), doi.org/10.1093/OED/4811513730.
8. Peter Engelke and J. R. McNeill, *The Great Acceleration: An Environmental History of the Anthropocene since 1945* (Cambridge: Belknap, 2016). The two previous paragraphs are adapted from Nathan K. Hensley, "Environment," *Victorian Literature and Culture* 46.3–4 (2018), 676–81.

9. Andreas Malm, *Fossil Capital: The Rise of Steam Power and the Roots of Global Warming* (London: Verso, 2016).

10. *Oxford English Dictionary*, s.v. "productivity (n.), sense 1," July 2023, doi .org/10.1093/OED/9290224495.

11. Richard Menke, "*New Grub Street*'s Ecologies of Paper," *Victorian Studies* 61.1 (Autumn 2018), 60–82 at 67–8.

12. John Locke, *Two Treatises of Civil Government*, ed. Thomas Hollis (London: A. Millar et al., 1764), https://shorturl.at/xFtHo.

13. Quoted in Catherine Hall, *Lucky Valley: Edward Long and the History of Racial Capitalism* (Cambridge: Cambridge University Press, 2024), 19.

14. Qtd. in Hall, *Lucky Valley*, 19, emphasis in original.

15. John Stuart Mill, *On Liberty* (London: John W. Parker and Son, 1859), www .gutenberg.org/files/34901/34901-h/34901-h.htm.

16. Anthony Trollope, *South Africa*, 2 vols. Collection of British Authors, Tauchnitz Edition. (Leipzig: Bernhardt Tauchnitz, 1878), 1.159. www.google.com/books/ edition/South_Africa/7dTQWwAhqyoC?hl=en&gbpv=1&bsq=hole.

17. Anthony Trollope, "George Walker at Suez," In *Tales of All Countries*, 2nd Series (London: Chapman and Hall, 1864), 261–78, Project Gutenberg, www .gutenberg.org/files/3718/3718-h.htm.

18. Winston Churchill, *The River War: An Historical Account of the Reconquest of the Soudan.* 2 vols. (London: Longman's, Green, & Co., 1900), 1.296.

19. Anthony Trollope, *The Eustace Diamonds* (*Fortnightly* Review, serial, 1871–3; London: Chapman & Hall, 1873), www.gutenberg.org/ebooks/7381.

20. Kathy Alexis Psomiades, *Primitive Marriage: Victorian Anthropology, the Novel, and Sexual Modernity* (Oxford: Oxford University Press, 2023).

21. Anthony Trollope, *An Old Man's Love* (Edinburgh: William Blackwood, 1884), www.gutenberg.org/cache/epub/25001/pg25001-images.html.

22. Alan Lester, Kate Boehme, and Peter Mitchell, *Ruling the World: Freedom, Civilization, and Liberalism in the Nineteenth-Century British Empire* (Cambridge: Cambridge University Press, 2021), 317–18.

23. Karl Marx, *Capital*, Vol. 1, trans. Ben Fowkes (London: Penguin, 1990), 925–6.

24. George Eliot, *Middlemarch* (1871–2), ed. David Carroll. (Oxford and New York: Oxford World's Classics, 1998), 12.

25. Eliot, *Middlemarch*, 27.

26. John Stuart Mill, *On Liberty and other Writings*, ed. Stefan Collini (Cambridge: Cambridge University Press, 2005), 13.

27. John MacNeill Miller, *The Ecological Plot: How Stories Gave Rise to a Science* (Charlottesville: University of Virginia Press, 2024); Jayne Hildebrand, *Novel Environments: Science, Description, and Victorian Fiction* (Oxford: Oxford University Press, 2023).

28. Eliot, *Middlemarch*, 182.

29. Eliot, *Middlemarch*, 88.

30. Eliot, *Middlemarch*, 332.

31. Eliot, *Middlemarch*, 779.

32. Matthew Arnold, "Dover Beach," in *New Poems* (London: Macmillan, 1877), 112–14 at 112. https://archive.org/details/newpoemsooarnogoog/page/n6/ mode/2up.

33. Arnold, "Dover Beach," 112.
34. Arnold, "Dover Beach," 112.
35. Devin Griffiths, "The Ecology of Form," *Critical Inquiry* 48.1 (Autumn 2023): 68–93 at 88.
36. Arnold, "Dover Beach," 113.

PART II

Imperialism and Colonialism

6

GRACE MOORE

Agricultural Ecologies

In 1838, the novelist William Howitt noted the "enviable" lives of English farmers, whom he described as "little kings" surrounded by "simple abundance."[1] As Howitt saw it, farmers spent their lives in a type of idyll, living well on a diet of "rich cream and milk, and unadulterated butter[,] ... their fruits ripe and fresh plucked from the sunny wall, or the garden bed, or the pleasant old orchard." Howitt's rosy vision of small-scale self-sufficiency suggests a golden age of agricultural prosperity, but in fact Queen Victoria's reign began and ended with periods of agrarian depression, which had global environmental consequences. This chapter commences with an exploration of how Victorian realist writers captured some of the major changes in British domestic agriculture, including alterations to the landscape, before shifting focus to Australia, which was increasingly perceived as an agricultural extension to Britain. Focusing on the work of the Australian-born writer Louisa Atkinson and the visiting English novelist Anthony Trollope, I examine agriculture's devastating effects on Australia's ecology.

Victorian Realism and Agricultural Innovation

In Britain, the development of large-scale farming that followed a sequence of Enclosure Acts during the nineteenth century saw the displacement of individual farmers from land that their families had worked for generations. The Corn Laws of 1815–46, which had been brought into effect to protect against the inundation of cheap grain from Europe at the end of the Napoleonic Wars, were frequently blamed for artificially inflating the cost of grain. However, prices were low in the century's first decades because more land had been turned over to farming when the trade restrictions had been introduced. The landed gentry who leased their land to farmers profited from the scenario, but the poorer classes struggled with high food prices. Indeed, the scarcity that underlies the plots of novels from the "hungry forties" like Elizabeth Gaskell's *Mary Barton* (1848), in which we see

77

families starving in cellars, may be traced back to the high cost of wheat and other grains.

Farming underwent significant changes over the century, many of which were tied to industrialism and the rise of what Greg Garrard terms "rural capitalism."[2] As the historian James Belich has expressed it, by the beginning of the nineteenth century, "Britain as a whole could no longer feed itself" and the consequences of this incapacity led to major ecological changes in Britain and across the globe, resulting in the emergence of what we today call "Big Agriculture."[3] Alfred W. Crosby expresses this idea in starker terms, commenting that "Accelerating urbanization, industrialization, and population growth obliged Great Britain to give up hope of autarchy," while he notes that, by the beginning of the twentieth century, British farmers were "producing only enough wheat to feed Britain for eight weeks annually."[4]

Mechanization was changing the pace of life on the farm, with threshing machines, drill seeds, and root slicers altering the speed with which crops could be processed and the rural vista. Thomas Hardy famously documented some of these changes in novels like *Tess of the d'Urbervilles*, published in 1891 but set in the 1870s. In an early chapter, Hardy details the work of a mechanical reaper intended to remove the standing corn, but which, the narrator reveals, also causes the deaths of small field-dwelling animals "unaware of the ephemeral nature of their refuge, and of the doom that awaited them."[5] As John Parham registers, the reaping machine causes "inevitable death in the middle of the field" through the displacement of field-dwelling creatures from their homes.[6] Later in the novel, Tess – abandoned by her husband, Angel Clare, who has travelled to Brazil to "experiment with that country's soil" as a farmer – goes to work on a "starve-acre" plot of a 100-acre holding.[7] We see her excavating swede roots (grown as part of the Norfolk four-course crop rotation, which, from the late seventeenth century onwards, altered Britain's biodiversity and made it possible to feed livestock in greater numbers), before she is later moved to a steam-threshing machine; a victim of a world changed by the agroindustry. As critics including Arnold Kettle and Raymond Williams have noted, Hardy shows us a world in transition.

The effects of industrial agriculture extended far beyond the countryside, as noted in "The Spirit of Modern Agriculture" (1876) by the novelist and journalist Richard Jefferies, best known for his 1885 postapocalyptic novel, *After London*, but also a keen observer of agricultural change. Writing of the many layers of industry supporting the agricultural boom, he comments, "there must also be considered the very extensive effect produced upon the iron trade, the consumption of coal, and in the multiplication of factories employing thousands of artisans."[8] While typically Victorian novelists – including Charles Dickens in *Bleak House* – envisioned the city expanding its limits and absorbing the countryside, Jefferies offered a different perspective through examining agriculture's wider reach. Though his concern is with the workforce, his commentary also captures some of the fossil fuel emissions that became a significant by-product of a system that was no longer localized: "The mere iron used in the construction of machines for tilling the land represents the labour and, consequently, the maintenance of thousands. Iron cannot be produced without coal ... and the use of steam for ploughing, threshing ... etc. also causes a direct consumption of coal in agriculture."[9] Jefferies continues to catalogue additional industries whose input was required to make large-scale farming effective. Notably, he lists "artificial manures" and guano, which, in addition to increasing soil nitrogen to unprecedented levels, also required "transhipment" from places like South America – a far cry from Howitt's earlier vision of an entirely self-sustaining farmstead, in which everything (including manure) was produced on site.

Anthony Trollope parodies the "search after unadulterated guano" in his novel *Orley Farm* (1861), in which the gentlemanly Lucius Mason – mistakenly believed to be the heir to the farm – seeks to implement intensive agricultural methods.[10] Mason rushes to Liverpool to acquire the purest dung and renders himself absurd in his bid to bring science into agriculture. As Allen MacDuffie has argued, these new fertilizers pushed the land "beyond its 'natural' carrying capacity," contaminating lakes and rivers through run-off, and fueling an unsustainable population growth.[11] Jefferies also comments on the movement of machinery, materials, and crops over large distances which, to a modern reader, is indicative of an accelerated depletion of resources, and agriculture's growing carbon footprint.

While the period from 1850 to 1870 was regarded as one of prosperity in Britain, by the early 1870s agriculture had experienced a downturn that, a decade later, was recognized as a major crisis. In "The State of Farming" (1881), Jefferies describes the agricultural industry as "shaken to pieces": "There are some signs that the bottom of agricultural depression has been reached. Wheat, stock, produce of all kinds, are down to an unremunerative price. Disease appears at intervals ... From all sides accounts come in of farms vacant, lands to let at any rent, almost, land to sell, and no one to buy it."[12] So pronounced was the state of reversal that it is reflected in the Sherlock Holmes story "The Adventure of the Speckled Band" (1892), where the catalyst for the villainous Grimesby Roylott's crimes is a decline in the value of his deceased wife's estate, caused by a fall in agricultural prices.[13]

The Great Agricultural Depression lasted from 1873 until 1896, and Britain increasingly looked to its empire for a solution. Nicholas Daly notes that "Britain had ceased to be primarily an agricultural nation, and had become a net importer of food. Grain came from the mid-western states of the U.S.; by the end of the century refrigeration meant that meat could be imported from as far away as Australia, New Zealand, and South America."[14] In this time of agricultural decline, Britain looked to what Crosby has termed "Neo-Europes" or colonies of settlement, which led to "ecological imperialism."[15] Its distant colony, Australia, enjoyed a period of prosperity from the 1850s until the late 1880s, becoming a major supplier of both meat and grain. As the climate historian Julia Miller observes, settler farmers made the most of these conditions, unaware that the "sustained high rainfall" that made this possible was a result of the combined effects of La Niña and Interdecadal Pacific Oscillation.[16]

At the beginning of his influential treatise *Elements of Practical Agriculture* (1834), the Scots agriculturalist David Low warned that "the practice of the farmer must be varied to suit the differences of climate."[17] Migrant farmers were often ill-prepared for the tribulations of farming in intense heat and therefore caused untold damage by "seeking to remake the continent's interior as a paddock for England."[18] The Australian environmental historians Tom Griffiths and Libby Robin describe settler forays into Australian agriculture as "like giant experiments in ecological crisis and management, sometimes a horrifying concentration of environmental damage and cultural loss."[19] They emphasize that "improvement" was a key term for early settlers in Australia, and that "Improvement was nostalgic; it was dismissive of indigenous environmental knowledge systems; it was aggressive as well as progressive." This approach to the land sought to "tame" its wild otherness through pastoralization, "clearing" it of native vegetation to make way for the planting of European crops, or the farming of imported livestock.[20] As Miller points out, clearance also "assumed the inferiority of indigenous plants," with settlers believing that the removal of vegetation would "dry and sweeten the soil."[21]

Ecocide and the Settler Novel

The Australian novelist, botanist, and nature writer Louisa Atkinson (1834–72) documented many of the environmental difficulties faced by settler farmers. Her novels, which are largely forgotten today, combine sensation fiction and romance plots with depictions of Australian rural life. In her fiction, Atkinson represents the Australian bush as a challenge to be endured and overcome by would-be agriculturalists, although her work also captures the damage that settler society inflicted upon the land.

In her first novel, *Gertrude the Emigrant* (1857), Atkinson highlights the difficulties faced by migrant farmers. The novel's refined young heroine, Gertrude, is adjusting to life as a servant on a cattle station in rural New South Wales after the deaths of her parents. While the novel is primarily a romance, the narrative also reveals the impact of farming on the landscape as Gertrude responds to the strangeness of her new surroundings. Atkinson shows stockmen riding for days on end in search of new acreages, and highlights the "hundreds of miles" that they needed to travel in order to oversee their herds and flocks.[22] Many Australian farms were of an enormous scale and, as Coral Lansbury has observed, "Properties, to be financially rewarding, ran into thousands of acres, extending from breeding country, through fattening country, to holding paddocks close to market."[23] In *Gertrude*, Atkinson depicts the acquisition of new territory as a transaction, with the novel's romantic hero Ned Tudor interacting respectfully with Indigenous Australians, who show him their ancestral lands in exchange for a fee. In reality, land was all too frequently acquired by force, with the clearance of scrub often masking the removal of people. The politician Edward Gibbon Wakefield may have written in his *Letter from Sydney* (1829) of "millions upon millions of acres … to be had for nothing," bemoaning, "what is more, there are not people to take them," but the assertion that Australia was *terra nullius* was an expedient myth which obscured large-scale theft and widespread colonial violence.[24]

Atkinson was acutely aware of the brutality that underpinned Australian agriculture. In both her fiction and newspaper columns, she wrote of various forms of clearance, including the ringbarking of trees (a technique involving the removal of a circle of bark from the circumference of the trunk to cut off the flow of sap and cause the tree to die). *Gertrude* contains several representations of cleared landscapes, including a scene where the narrator describes a view of fallen trees as "bleached white, or charred by some bush fire."[25] For Gertrude, the scene is "not unlike a graveyard,"[26] a parallel pointing to the sustained ecocide that settler society was enacting in the interests of pastoralizing Australia, as well as the clearance of First Peoples from the land.

Atkinson's final novel, *Tressa's Resolve* (published posthumously in 1872), stages some of the immense difficulties faced by migrant farmers. The eponymous heroine's suitor, Tyrell Love, learns that he must make his own way in the world and turns to farming, believing that it will offer him a swift and reliable income that will allow him to marry. Searching for an appropriate plot on which to establish himself, Tyrell moves through country that the narrator describes as "forlorn."[27] As a metropolitan dweller, he is alarmed by the scale and inhospitable nature of the outback, with the narrator observing, "Hitherto Tyrell Love's acquaintance with the bush had been the barren scrub around Sydney; here was a new style of country. Trees 200 feet in height and of huge girth; the rich vegetable mould carpeted by ferns of the most exquisite forms and lively greens."[28] Initially, Tyrell is charmed and pays a deposit on forty acres of land. Yet before long he realizes the formidable task he has taken on. Atkinson's narrator comments that he "was too inexperienced to calculate the amount of toil which would be needed to convert that dense primeval forest into a farm."[29] The novel continues to recount the exhausting work involved in Europeanizing the Bush: "One by one must the huge trees fall, and when fallen they must be burnt and the brush cleared away; then there would be numerous stumps and the wide roots beneath the soil."[30] Tyrell, who is not robust, soon realizes that he will never be able to clear the land alone, so he must abandon his dream to "convert his forest possessions into fields of golden grain."[31]

Importantly, the hero does not triumph over the landscape. Similarly, in a subplot, another would-be farmer, "a Queensland squatter" living in a "torrid climate," is forced from his sheep station, partly through a prolonged drought, which sees his sheep dying from thirst, and partly because he does not understand Australian weather conditions and their effect on farming.[32] Atkinson's fiction was serialized in newspapers and she frequently used it to teach readers about the land. It is therefore not unreasonable to conclude that she designed these plots to demonstrate the difference between European and Australian farming, just as she had used an early story, "The Burning Forest" (1853), to highlight the dangers of fire in the parched Antipodean woods.[33]

Atkinson's nature writing is subtle in its representation and understanding of how European farming techniques were altering the local climate. She was unusual in that she had spent considerable time in the company of Indigenous Australians, and much of her knowledge of Australian plant life was gleaned from their teachings. In an article for the *Sydney Mail* published in 1871, Atkinson demonstrates her understanding that "a far more careful style of cultivation" was needed in a climate notable for its extremes.[34] She reports a conversation with an old man, who remarks that "the land's no good now, for I have known it grow wheat eighteen years running." She then continues to argue against an instinctive knowledge of farming, asserting that: "Some people argue that the earth was made for man and must support him, and that his instinct will teach him how to cultivate it. Many a ruined farmer has tried the truth of this hypothesis."[35] Embedded in Atkinson's assessment, and in her depictions of failed farmers in *Tressa's Resolve*, is a critique of the arrogance with which settler society approached the Australian environment and a prescient understanding of the damage that farming was causing.

Anthony Trollope and the Visitor's Perspective

Anthony Trollope was an astute observer of environmental change across the globe. So seriously did the Victorians consider the interplay between travel writing and understandings of the environment that his travelogue

South Africa (1878) was reviewed in the scientific journal *Nature*. The reviewer "W. J. L." noted the author's interest in irrigation and the problems the arid landscape posed for imported European plant life, suggesting that in his lifetime Trollope was a respected environmental commentator.[36] Nowhere, however, was he more attentive to the environment than on his two visits to Australia in the early 1870s.

In 1869, Trollope's son Frederic had set up as a squatter – that is, someone usually from a wealthy background who takes up residence on Crown land and begins to develop it. Through his father's generosity, Fred was able to purchase a sheep station in New South Wales, where he kept 10,000 sheep on 27,500 acres. His career as a pastoralist was short-lived and by 1875, Fred was preparing to sell up, while his father made a second visit to Australia to help him discharge his debts.

Anthony Trollope knew from childhood that agriculture was a precarious business. His father had attempted, without success, the life of a gentleman farmer during the period of economic recession following the Napoleonic Wars. It was his mother, the entrepreneurial Frances Trollope, who eventually reversed the family fortunes through her writing. As Trollope noted in his autobiography, his own son was similarly unsuccessful in his Australian ventures. However, he was clear that Fred was not to blame for his farm's failure, remarking "I rejoice to say that this has been in no way due to any fault of his. I never knew a man work with more persistent honesty at his trade than he has done."[37] Nigel Starck observes that "Frederic Trollope's station ... was simply not big enough," while P. D. Edwards (quoted in Starck) suggests that climatic factors also played a significant part in Fred's failure, since he lacked the cash reserves to see him through the prolonged drought that followed a period of "good rains" in 1872.[38]

While Fred's foray into farming was brief (*c.* 1869–75), it shaped Trollope senior's focus as he traveled around the Australian colonies. The travelogue he wrote to fund his first trip (1871–2), *Australia and New Zealand*, incorporates remarkable amounts of information about farming, some of which the novelist gleaned through interviews with agriculturalists and laborers and some from copious research into costs, land use, revenue from sales of crops and animals, and export figures. During his time in New South Wales, Trollope learned a great deal about how the unpredictable weather affected settler farmers. In *Australia and New Zealand*, he remarks that the climate "is the most severe enemy which the free-selecter [*sic*] has to encounter in New South Wales. Land capable of producing cereals he can obtain, but through the uncertainty of the climate he cannot be secure of his crop. Once in three years his crop is good, – but twice in three years it will hardly pay the price of production."[39]

In a later trip to South Australia, Trollope was struck once again by the precarity of the farmer's existence, this time in relation to the cultivation of wheat. He was shocked to learn that, "In one year the red rust will almost destroy the crop, in another year, – as happened during the harvest-time of 1872 ... a cloud of locusts will come and eat up wheat and grass throughout the country."[40] Impressed as he was by the enormity of the agricultural business, he also recognized that it was an industry fraught with risk.

His commitment to recording everything he saw meant that Trollope often inadvertently captured the adverse effects of transposing European farming methods to the southern hemisphere. He saw the wholesale importation of domestic animals like cows and sheep to be of great benefit to the colony. However, the millions of sheep who inhabited Australia around the time of Trollope's visit (over 40 million in 1870) had already caused lasting damage; in addition to the felling of tens of thousands of trees to make way for grazing, the animals' hooves compacted the earth, making it less permeable to rain, when it came.[41]

Trollope's novella *Harry Heathcote of Gangoil* (1874) explores some of the dangers associated with farming in the Bush, while also detailing how agriculture was changing Australia's ecology. In an early chapter, the young squatter Harry asks one of his workers, "what does a man live for except to alter things?"[42] We see Harry, as a sheep farmer, clearing land and fencing the boundaries of his property. He is almost obsessively afraid of arsonists, and the novella includes a number of scenes in which Harry expresses his terror of a fire "which should get ahead before it was seen, and scour across the ground, consuming the grass down to the very roots over thousands of acres."[43] Harry's fear of losing his livelihood to fire reflects a concern that haunted many migrant farmers. Yet the depth of his anxiety can also be read as a displacement of his knowledge that he is farming on land stolen from its traditional custodians. Indeed, in the opening chapters, he voices concerns that he will be moved from the land as a mere "tenant of the crown," and the narrator's emphasis on Harry's tentative sense of entitlement gestures to his subconscious knowledge that he is an impostor.[44] The bushfire becomes a signifier of Australia's otherness and of the threat in the inherent and sustained un-tameability of the land, its climate, and its first people. Trollope's figuring of the fire renders action against indigenous ecology an act of preemptive self-defense.

Trollope's decision to set his novella in Queensland might have been driven by a need to differentiate his son from the hot-headed Harry, yet he may also have been guided by a widely held belief in the territory's superior farming conditions. Jude Piesse notes that: "Trollope's decision to write about Queensland, a colony he had very little direct experience of, triggered a great deal of criticism concerning the dubiousness of his geographical

84

knowledge, accompanied by general annoyance at his less than documentary accounts of 'Bush Life.'"[45] Certainly the climate and vegetation were very different from those of New South Wales, but the location also enabled the novelist to examine a number of additional agricultural issues.

A key element of the plot of *Harry Heathcote* involves a falling-out between Harry and his neighbor Giles Medlicot over access to water. Medlicot is the owner of a sugar plantation and, as a free selector, he has a greater legal entitlement to the land. He takes possession of some river frontage, to allow the transportation of sugar hogsheads to the sea, which threatens to restrict Harry's flock's access to the water. The mill is run by Polynesian laborers "who crept silently among the vats and machinery, shifting the sugar as it was made."[46] While the reader learns little of their story, the presence of these Pacific Island characters highlights the entanglement between exploited landscapes and peoples. The transportation of convicts from England to Australia was abolished in the 1860s and led to a shortage of unpaid labor. To offset this change, between 1862 and 1904 more than 62,000 Pacific Islanders were kidnapped or coerced into traveling to Australia, where they were enslaved as plantation workers. Medlicot's workers are likely to have arrived in Queensland via this route; yet in the novella they are barely visible. Trollope shows them to have less agency than any of the other characters, less even than the resistant landscape to which they have been brought. The novelist's engagement with these workers is so slight that they are little more than part of the scenery, yet their presence highlights another shameful human element of the settler agricultural venture.

Trollope met and befriended a number of Australian sugar-growers and devoted an entire chapter of his travelogue to sugar and South Sea Island labor. He became interested in how refinery owners could set up on a small scale, compared to the huge plantations he had seen in the West Indies. He was also reluctant to engage with what he termed the "hardship of labour," clearly having been influenced by his plantation-owning friends.[47] Yet in *The Tireless Traveller* (1875), he returned to the subject, standing by his belief that "sugar cannot be grown by white labour. It is too costly, and the European cannot stand the heat," and emphasizing the value of the Pacific worker.[48] Trollope acknowledges the practice of kidnapping and equivocates about whether Queenslanders have been involved in it. Importantly, he declares "Let us have no slavery in God's name," but, unable to resolve the issue, he moves on.[49]

Having written extensively on sugar during his time in the West Indies (1858–9), it is unsurprising that Trollope was drawn to the subject during his Australian travels. At the time of his visit, sugar looked set to overtake wool as Queensland's primary source of revenue. As the historian Peter Griggs points out, Queensland's tropical and subtropical ecology was unsuitable for the cultivation of cereal crops, thus remaining mostly undisturbed until the 1860s, when planters began to clear forests to experiment with tobacco, bananas, and sugar.[50] The latter had been grown on a small scale since the early 1830s, and it was the cost of importing sugar from overseas that led to government inducements for local growers. The Sugar and Coffee Act of 1864 allowed those with an interest in cultivating sugar cane favorable terms when leasing land from the government. The industry was devastating to the environment of the northeast of Australia and, as Griggs observes, the effects were not limited to the initial clearance of forests to make way for plantations. Deforestation was an ongoing process, owing to the need to supply building materials and firewood for sugar mills, while the sugar's transportation for sale required further clearances for the building of railway tracks.[51]

For Trollope, farming was key to settler society's claim on the land. On his first visit, he was struck by how "advancing science has carried out and acclimatized, not only men and women, but beasts, birds, and fishes, fruit and vegetables, rich grasses, and European trees, with a rapidity and profusion of which our grandfathers never dreamed, and which even our fathers never ventured to anticipate."[52] He also drew parallels between what he saw as the languor of the native wildlife and a lack of vigor on the part of the first peoples. For Trollope, both the ecology and its first custodians would inevitably and naturally yield to the more robust species and methods brought from England. On his return to Australia, however, Trollope admits that "in occupying these lands we commit a terrible injustice," but he attempts to legitimize the colonial venture by interpreting agricultural success as a sign of divine approval; as he chillingly expresses it, "The land becomes ours with its fatness – and the people disappear."[53] In adopting this position, Trollope aligned himself with those who asserted that Indigenous Australians had no sovereignty over the land of their ancestors because they had not cultivated it. Yet, as the historian Bill Gammage has argued, sophisticated farming systems based on understanding the seasons, the rhythms of the land, and what animals wanted – rather than only what they *needed* – operated in Australia long before 1788.[54]

Having created a dependency on colonial farming through unsustainable extractivist practices, the British deployed those same techniques overseas. Rather than drawing upon the sophisticated climatic and environmental knowledge of those who had lived on the land for tens of thousands of years, settler farmers imposed a failed pastoral model from the northern hemisphere upon a drought-stricken land, as they do today.[55] The result has been a continuum of colonial ecocide that was obscured through the rhetoric of entitlement and ownership that was, in turn, tied to the greatest possible exploitation of the land and its resources.

Notes

1. William Howitt, *The Rural Life of England*, Vol. 1 (London: Longman, 1838), 124.
2. Greg Garrard, *Ecocriticism* (London: Routledge, 2004), 110.
3. James Belich, *Replenishing the Earth: The Settler Revolution and the Rise of the Anglo-World, 1783–1939* (Oxford: Oxford University Press 2009), 441.
4. Alfred W. Crosby, *Ecological Imperialism: The Biological Expansion of Europe, 900–1900*, 2nd ed. (Cambridge: Cambridge University Press, 2004), 306.
5. Thomas Hardy, *Tess of the d'Urbervilles*, ed. Simon Gatrell (Oxford: Oxford University Press, 1988), 93.
6. John Parham, "Was There a Victorian Ecology?," in John Parham, ed., *The Environmental Tradition in English Literature* (Farnham: Ashgate, 2002), 156–71 at 170. On Hardy and the effects of industrialism on agriculture, see also Arnold Kettle, *An Introduction to the English Novel*, Vol. 2 (London: Routledge, 2016); and Raymond Williams, *The Country and the City* (London: Verso, 1993).
7. Hardy, *Tess of the d'Urbervilles*, 260.
8. Richard Jefferies, *Agriculture and the Land: Richard Jefferies' Essays and Letters*, ed. Rebecca Welshman (Edinburgh: Edinburgh University Press, 2019), 64.
9. Jefferies, *Agriculture and the Land*, 64.
10. Anthony Trollope, *Orley Farm* (London: The Trollope Society, 1993), 21.
11. Allen MacDuffie, *Victorian Literature, Energy, and the Ecological Imagination* (Cambridge: Cambridge University Press, 2014), 57.
12. Jefferies, *Agriculture and the Land*, 111.
13. Arthur Conan Doyle, "The Adventure of the Speckled Band," in *The Penguin Complete Sherlock Holmes* (London: Penguin, 1981), 244–73 at 265.
14. Nicholas Daly, "Britain," in Michael Saler, ed., *The Fin-de-Siècle World* (London: Routledge, 2014), 117–30 at 126.
15. Crosby, *Ecological Imperialism*, 297.
16. Julia Miller, *La Niña and the Making of Climate Optimism: Remembering Rain* (Chamonix: Palgrave, 2019), 7.
17. David Low, *Elements of Practical Agriculture* (London: Longman, 1847), v.
18. Cameron Muir, *The Broken Promise of Agricultural Progress: An Environmental History* (London: Routledge, 2014), 2.
19. Libby Robin and Tom Griffiths, "Environmental History in Australasia," *Environment and History* 10.4 (2004), 439–74 at 443.
20. Robin and Griffiths, "Environmental History," 444.
21. Miller, *La Niña*, 33.
22. Louisa Atkinson, *Gertrude, the Emigrant: A Tale of Colonial Life* (Sydney: University of Sydney Library, 2002), https://digital.library.sydney.edu.au/nodes/view/11774, 77.
23. Coral Lansbury, *Arcady in Australia: The Evocation of Australia in Nineteenth-Century English Literature* (Melbourne: Melbourne University Press, 1970), 160.
24. Edward Gibbon Wakefield, *A Letter from Sydney, and Other Writings* (London: J. M. Dent & Sons, 1929), 7. The Australian historian Lyndall Ryan worked extensively on colonial violence, mapping massacre sites and counting victims from 1788 onwards, https://c21ch.newcastle.edu.au/colonialmassacres/map.php.
25. Atkinson, *Gertrude*, 151.

26. Atkinson, *Gertrude*, 151.

27. Louisa Atkinson, *Tressa's Resolve* (Canberra: Mulini, 2004), 46.

28. Atkinson, *Gertrude*, 46.

29. Atkinson, *Gertrude*, 47.

30. Atkinson, *Gertrude*, 48.

31. Atkinson, *Gertrude*, 50.

32. Atkinson, *Gertrude*, 35.

33. Grace Moore, "'Raising High Its Thousand Forked Tongues': Campfires, Bushfires and Portable Domesticity in Nineteenth-Century Australia," *19: Interdisciplinary Studies in the Long Nineteenth Century* 26 (2018). https://19 .bbk.ac.uk/article/id/1506/.

34. Louisa Atkinson, "Hanging Rock on the Southern Road," in *Excursions from Berrima and a Trip to Manaro and Molonglo in the 1870s* (Canberra: Mulini, 1996), 22.

35. Atkinson, *Gertrude*, 22.

36. W. J. L. "Trollope's 'South Africa'," *Nature* (April 11, 1878), 463–4.

37. Anthony Trollope, *An Autobiography* (London: Trollope Society, 1999), 215.

38. Nigel Starck, *The First Celebrity: Anthony Trollope's Australian Odyssey* (Bath: Lansdowne Media, 2014), 46.

39. Anthony Trollope, *Australia and New Zealand*, Vol. 1 (London: Trollope Society, 2002), 269.

40. Trollope, *Australia and New Zealand*, 188.

41. Wray Vamplew, ed., *Australians. Historical Statistics* (Fairfax, Syme & Weldon, 1987), 128.

42. Anthony Trollope, *Harry Heathcote of Gangoil*, 1874 (London: Trollope Society, 1998), 37.

43. Trollope, *Australia and New Zealand*, 27.

44. Trollope, *Australia and New Zealand*, 9.

45. Jude Piesse, *British Settler Emigration in Print, 1832–1877* (Oxford: Oxford University Press, 2016), 71.

46. Trollope, *Australia and New Zealand*, 28.

47. Trollope, *Australia and New Zealand*, 136.

48. Anthony Trollope, *The Tireless Traveler: Twenty Letters to the Liverpool Mercury* (Berkeley: University of California Press, [1875] 1978), 179.

49. Trollope, *The Tireless Traveler*, 179.

50. Peter D. Griggs, "Deforestation and Sugar Cane Growing in Eastern Australia, 1860–1995," *Environment and History* 13.3 (August 2007), 255–83.

51. Griggs, "Deforestation," 257.

52. Trollope, *The Tireless Traveler*, 3.

53. Trollope, *The Tireless Traveler*, 124.

54. Bill Gammage, *The Biggest Estate on Earth: How Aborigines Made Australia* (Sydney: Allen & Unwin, 2011), 211–17.

55. On Indigenous Australian farming and land management, see Bruce Pascoe's *Dark Emu: Aboriginal Australia and the Birth of Agriculture* (Brunswick: Scribe, 2018).

7

LINDSAY WELLS

Empire, Environment, and Botanical Art in British India

Bright red flowers float at the center of the two images, their colors thrown into relief by plain white backgrounds. Delicate shading lends volume to the glowing blooms, while line conveys the strength of the foliage and stems. As our eye lingers over these pictures, additional details begin to reveal themselves – the lattice of veins adorning every leaf, the pinpricks of ink embellishing the petals, the patches of shadow suggestive of depth. A flourish of cursive script appears at the bottom of each page and identifies both plants as species of rhododendrons. The first is a hand-colored engraving (Figure 7.1) of the Himalayan tree rhododendron – *Rhododendron arboreum* – from the third and final volume of *Exotic Flora* (1823–7), a book series compiled by English botanist William Jackson Hooker. The second is an opaque watercolor drawing (Figure 7.2) from *Specimens of Flowering Plants* (c. 1830s–40s), an album commissioned by a British military captain from five Indian artists in the state of Madras (Tamil Nadu). When compared with one another, these two compositions not only disclose the importance of images to colonial plant science, but also raise questions about the power of botanical illustration to visualize environments with nuance and complexity. One picture distills the rhododendron down to its simplest structural components, while the other alludes to the flower's relationship with other living beings. One embraces the political function of art as an emblem of authority while the other pushes against the colonial milieu in which it was designed. One speaks to a desire to control the vegetal world while the other courts scrutiny on the ethics of doing so. This chapter shows how botanical illustrations can join works of literature in illuminating the ties between ecological thought, cultural production, and British imperialism in the nineteenth century.

By arranging cut specimens on an empty page, both *Exotic Flora* and *Specimens of Flowering Plants* dislodge the rhododendrons they depict from their natural habitats – a representational strategy that, in the words of Beth Fowkes Tobin, "was employed ... to assert European systems of

Figure 7.1 Robert Kaye Greville (artist) and Joseph Swan (engraver), *Plate 168: Rhododendron Arboreum*, hand-colored engraving, 23.5 × 30 cm.
Source: Printed in William Jackson Hooker, *Exotic Flora*, Vol. 3 (Edinburgh: William Blackwood, 1827). From the Collection of The Lloyd Library and Museum.

Figure 7.2 Artists' names now unknown, *Rhododendron: Rhododendron Rustica*, watercolor and bodycolor, 60.5 × 48 cm (manuscript).
Source: Figured in *Specimens of Flowering Plants, Collected by Captain Frederick Parr* (*c.* 1830s–40s). Oak Spring Garden Foundation, Upperville, VA.

control over the natural resources of the world."[1] As Lorraine Daston and Peter Galison add, the purpose of scientific illustration at this time was "to standardize the ... observed objects of the discipline by eliminating idiosyncrasies" that might hinder the identification of plants by naturalists.[2] Drawn according to the conventions of Western botanical art, our two rhododendrons fit comfortably within this framework and reflect the role that standardized imagery played in advancing scientific research across the former British Empire. It is just as crucial, however, to analyze the differences between these pictures as their many similarities for, as I will argue in this chapter, their distinct treatment of line, texture, and other formal elements animate contrasting insights into vegetal life. Whereas the illustration in *Exotic Flora* primarily concentrates on summarizing botanical morphology, the one in *Specimens of Flowering Plants* explores a moment of touch and connection across biological kingdoms.

Covered in a fine mesh of spidery lichen, the stem of the rhododendron in *Specimens of Flowering Plants* supports a miniature ecology of diverse lifeforms: along with the blossom itself, we have the fungi and algae from which most lichens are jointly comprised. Through its tactile manipulation of line, the watercolor foregrounds the interdependence of these organisms in a manner that foils colonial attempts to excise plants from the environments they occupy. Both the contents and composition of this drawing gesture toward the ecosystem that nurtured the rhododendron's growth and, in consequence, convey how vegetation supplies the necessary conditions for other entities to thrive. Whether performing photosynthesis or nourishing animals and humans, plant life interacts with the world in ways that sustain and generate a multispecies vitality – "lighting up the space around it," explains Michael Marder, "with lived meaning-making activity."[3] Though decontextualized in negative space, the illustration in *Specimens of Flowering Plants* mobilizes the expressive potential of lichen to communicate both the symbiotic properties and environmental immersion of the rhododendron that Hooker's *Exotic Flora* entirely sidesteps. It thus subverts the mandate that conformity should take precedence over all other concerns in the production of botanical art and exposes how Britain's colonial scientific regime failed to erase Indigenous perspectives on native plants. Placing *Exotic Flora* and *Specimens of Flowering Plants* into dialogue with one another allows us to reevaluate the environmental affordances of botanical illustration as an artistic genre, while also demonstrating how emerging theories from critical plant studies can enrich our understanding of Anglo-Indian scientific exchanges in the nineteenth century.

Beginning in the early modern period, British botanists stationed in India turned to native artists to document the plants they encountered while working there – a practice that grew in step with the East India Company's political presence on the subcontinent after 1608. Combining European and Indian compositional techniques, these illustrations braided together a variety of aesthetic traditions to convey information about plant structure, distribution, and growth habits to colonial scientists.[4] British patrons commissioned thousands of such drawings from Indian draftsmen in the nineteenth century, yet most of these images remain at the margins of research on the ideological function of botanical art during the age of empire. If we accept, as many scholars have, that Indian illustrations formed a cornerstone of colonial plant science throughout this period, we must also consider how they complicate the familiar claim that botanical drawings uniformly effaced the ecological context of living flora. As the lichens in *Specimens of Flowering Plants* remind us, the environmental stakes embedded in nineteenth-century Indian botanical studies warrant deeper consideration.

After reviewing past scholarship on colonial botany and botanical art, I will return to the two rhododendrons illustrated in *Exotic Flora* and *Specimens of Flowering Plants*. In some respects, both of these works corroborate the argument that scientific diagrams impede environmental inquiry as opposed to foster it. At the same time, they tell a parallel story about art's capacity to undermine empire even while serving its interests and proponents. Because the lichen in *Specimens of Flowering Plants* does not directly assist with our classification of the pictured rhododendron, it unsettles the expectation that botanical art should remove all traces of a plant's environment for the sake of visual consistency. The illustration, therefore, resists sublimation into the entwined orders of colonial science and colonial power that dictated botany across the British Empire. As I will demonstrate, the ecology envisioned in this watercolor facilitates a capacious outlook on vegetal vitality that is fundamentally antithetical to the pursuit of colonial hegemony.

Colonial Functions of Botanical Art

Often defined by its ostensible lack of context, botanical illustration may, at first glance, seem ill-suited for exploring how visual culture can provide insights into multispecies entanglement. Isolation and idealization are arguably two of the most distinctive characteristics of the genre, epitomized by the method of arranging solitary specimens on an empty page. The frequent addition of magnified or dissected details further emphasizes this sense of fragmentation, as does the lack of overt references to a plant's habitat. Other hallmarks of Western botanical illustration include unnatural lighting and limited shadow, as well as the use of composite images that show plants in flower and fruit simultaneously.[5] If asked to select a standard nineteenth-century example of this formula, the engraving of *Rhododendron arboreum* from William Jackson Hooker's *Exotic Flora* would fit the bill. Neatly arranged upon cream-colored paper, this image features a horizontal spray of cut blossoms, with enlarged views of the plant's corolla, stamens, and pistil positioned beneath. Crisp leaves protrude at various angles below the central globe of flowers, each of which are individually depicted as full-blown blooms. By allowing floral structure and morphology to dictate its composition, this diagram underscores the centrality of taxonomic classification to European botany. Its subject of a Himalayan flower, meanwhile, invites us to consider how histories of colonial plant collecting intersected with those of art and science in the nineteenth century.

Simple in both its design and layout, the rhododendron engraving from *Exotic Flora* typifies the representational paradigm of Western botany, which Jim Endersby describes as capturing "not what the plant looked like, but what it *ought* to look like" (emphasis in the original).[6] Evidence of insect damage, seasonal decay, or even oxidized discoloration at the cut stem are excluded from view, leaving in their stead a polished display of floral perfection. Although British botanists wrote at length about the environments in which they collected foreign plants in the nineteenth century, this information seldom made its way into the pictures for their books. European botanical artists of the period were taught to prioritize the general over the particular and the fixed over the variable in order to substantiate what Daston and Galison term "a science about the rules rather than the exceptions of nature."[7] Instead of recording facts about a specific flower or tree, drawings were intended to provide naturalists a generic snapshot of botanical taxa; this, in turn, assisted with the study of economically useful vegetation in the service of empire.

As director of the Royal Botanic Gardens at Kew from 1841 to 1865, William Jackson Hooker oversaw the introduction of countless foreign plants into British soil, including numerous rhododendrons that were native to Asia. In 1847, his son Joseph Dalton Hooker launched a multiyear botanical collecting expedition that brought additional rhododendrons to the attention of Victorian gardeners, who embraced the plants as fashionable exotics. From the grounds of Audley Court to the landscapes of Wessex, rhododendrons also found their way into works of fiction, where, as Elizabeth Hope Change notes, they registered the "global network" of environments that underpinned British horticulture.[8] Mary Elizabeth Braddon was particularly fond of incorporating these flowers into the settings of her novels, one of which – *Hostages to Fortune* (1875) – speaks at length about a rhododendron arbor near an English castle. Here we read that the novel's protagonists "enter a paradise of purple and green – a verdant alley between high walls of rhododendrons, which have grown to absolute trees. Birds are singing, bees humming; for the rest there is silence as in a world newly made, solitude as on the shores of the Amazon."[9] On the one hand, this passage evokes a multisensory ecosystem of plants, animals, and insects that attends to the vibrancy of more-than-human nature. On the other hand, it employs the common imperialist trope of reimaging foreign environments (such as the Amazon) as wholly unpopulated, thereby sanctioning Britain's claims to the vegetation that grew there. Crystal Palace architect Joseph Paxton, for example, declared in 1849 that many of the regions visited by travelling botanists had "perhaps never before, since their creation, [been] impressed with a human foot" – an erasure of Indigenous people that dovetailed with the reductive aesthetics of scientific plant drawings.[10] Botanical illustrations played an integral part in advancing colonial collecting efforts throughout the nineteenth century for, like the plants themselves, they were inherently portable.

While living plants often perished in transit, images of them could freely circulate between Britain and its colonies, thereby rendering draftsmanship a valuable instrument of overseas empire-building. As scholarship on colonial botany has routinely pointed out, scientific drawings aided the appropriation of plants by visually transforming them into discrete commodities. Any element deemed inessential to a specimen's identification (and, by extension, possible commercialization) was omitted from view, obscuring in the process both its ecological relationship to the wider world and its cultural significance to Indigenous communities.[11] Sliced into pieces and mounted onto paper, the plants in such illustrations painted a piecemeal picture of the sites in which colonial scientists conducted their research. Like maps or geographical surveys, these botanical drawings evaded by design any direct confrontation with the social and environmental impact of colonial expansion. Nicholas Thomas refers to these pictorial practices as "discursive deprivation," while Daniela Bleichmar points out how they sanctioned the "extractive vision of nature" upon which European empires depended.[12] Marshaled toward not just scientific goals, but also ideological ends, the creation and dispersal of botanical illustrations carried real-world consequences throughout the nineteenth century.

By the time William Jackson Hooker began printing *Exotic Flora* in the 1820s, the colonial cities of Madras (Chennai) and Calcutta (Kolkata) had emerged as important scientific hubs of the East India Company, an organization deeply invested in economic botany, or the study of useful plants. The Company's collecting activities, in turn, sparked a demand for images that could keep administrators in Britain apprised of this scientific research. From the late eighteenth century onward, British naturalists regularly contracted native artists in India to prepare illustrations for their publications. Thousands of plant drawings, for example, were produced by Indian draftsmen for William Roxburgh during his tenure as superintendent of the Royal Botanic Garden in Calcutta, which was founded by the East India Company around 1787. Roxburgh's successor at the Garden, Nathaniel Wallich, continued to work with Indian artists well into the 1830s, as did his fellow botanists Francis Buchanan-Hamilton, Hugh Francis Clarke Cleghorn, and John Forbes Royle. Another prominent patron at this time was the surgeon-botanist Robert Wight, who commissioned plant drawings from the renowned Telugu botanical artists Rungiah and Govindoo. While the names of most Indian illustrators went unnoted by their British employers, several have survived to the present day, including Vishnupersaud and Gorachaud, who worked with Wallich, Royle, and Buchanan-Hamilton. Drawings by these and many more artists subsequently appeared in Roxburgh's *Plants from the Coast of Coromandel* (1795–1819) and Wallich's *Plantae Asiaticae Rariores* (1829–32) – texts that laid the foundation for colonial plant science in nineteenth-century India. Examined at length by Mildred Archer in the 1960s, Indian botanical art has received sustained attention from scholars for several decades, with the work of Martyn Rix, Theresa Kelley, Savithri Preetha Nair, Henry J. Noltie, and Ray Desmond paving the way for its critical reappraisal.[13]

Following the distribution of their drawings abroad, Indian botanical illustrators gained swift recognition among the scientific communities of nineteenth-century Britain. One of Hooker's earliest encounters with their pictures came when he oversaw the publication of a treatise by Wight in his magazine *Botanical Miscellany* (1830–3), featuring numerous colored plates after sketches by Rungiah. Hooker later observed in a review of Wight's text that a collection of nearly 2,000 drawings had been formed in Calcutta "with the aid of native artists, whose talents for flower-painting are truly astonishing."[14] Hooker's familiarity with the work of Indian illustrators helps us better understand his personal interest in colonial botanical art while also demonstrating how British and Indian scientific drawings developed coevally in the nineteenth century. Images of plants were just as mobile as plants themselves, and they constantly pulled artists and botanists together into each other's orbit. Hooker's inclusion of Indian illustrations in some of his own publications shows how British and Indian botanical studies grew in tandem like twining vines, twisting and reshaping one another as people, plants, and pictures traversed the empire. Nevertheless, it is important to acknowledge just how deeply texts like *Exotic Flora* were also aligned with colonial practices of data collection and valuation.

Because botanical illustrations by British artists often reduced entire ecosystems down to disembodied motifs, they contributed to the conceptual process of naturalizing colonial power hierarchies in the name of science. According to Endersby, the "nineteenth-century rhetoric of scientific illustration" hinged upon the avoidance of "quirks or idiosyncrasies," which could jeopardize a drawing's utility in classifying plant life.[15] An unusual display of growth or overabundance of flowers ran the risk of misleading botanists about the identity of a specimen, hence the absence of such anomalies from many illustrations. No petal is left out of place in the tree rhododendron from *Exotic Flora*, which even clips some of the plant's leaves to fit them on the page. In the preface to *The Art of Botanical Drawing* (1873), Victorian plant hunter Frederick William Burbidge warned draftsmen against the deceptive dangers of superfluous detail, bemoaning how: "The sensitive feelings of many a true naturalist have again and again been subjected to severe shocks by would be artists, who in painting their subjects have introduced some one or more natural objects as accessories, which latter are but too frequently wretched burlesques on what they are intended to represent."[16] The removal of what is peculiar or unique to a single plant as opposed to its entire species had crystallized into an attribute of Western botanical art by the early Victorian period, as had the visual excision of plants from their immediate environments. This renders the inclusion of lichen in our second rhododendron illustration from *Specimens of Flowering Plants* all the more remarkable.

Ecological Insights of Colonial Botanical Art

The rhododendron watercolor in *Specimens of Flowering Plants* adheres to the parameters of European botanical art while also challenging them head-on through its excess of organic detail. In comparing this image to the engraving from *Exotic Flora*, my aim is not to impose a strict division between British and Indian botanical illustrations from the period, and nor is it to reinforce such well-worn binaries as center/periphery that oversimplify how intellectual exchange operated within this context. As both David Lowther and Kapil Raj contend, the study of natural history in nineteenth-century India was uneven in terms of colonial power dynamics yet co-constitutive in its production of scientific knowledge.[17] Diverse in regional origin, the botanical drawings of Indian illustrators amalgamated a wide array of genres and techniques, with stylistic influences ranging from Mughal and Rajput decorative art to textile designs and miniature painting. These elements were then combined with European rules of perspective to craft intricately detailed images of plants, which Roxburgh began sending back to Britain as early as the 1790s.[18] At once driven by the scientific agendas of imperialism and operating independently from them, the networks of artistic patronage that once funded botanical art in India elude uniform definition just a readily as the drawings themselves. Tobin, for instance, has suggested that some of the images commissioned by the Calcutta Botanic Garden "convey an energy that cannot be contained" by the strictures of Western botany, disturbing in the process the colonial tendency to decontextualize plants in order to exploit them.[19] Writing more recently on the Calcutta Botanic Garden, Khyati Nagar argues that Indian botanical art "marks a moment in the story of colonial science where the production of knowledge was not entirely dependent on metropolitan science."[20] Sita Reddy likewise refers to this body of pictorial work as "a multi-genre and *dispersed* archive," in that it connected individuals across vast geographies (emphasis in the original).[21] We might further think of Indian botanical drawings as a rich repository of ecological insights, maintained through inconspicuous – yet by no means inconsequential – details like lichen on a flower stem.

India stood as a major center of scientific image-making throughout the nineteenth century, with native artists supplying illustrations to not only large botanical surveys, but also informal albums meant for private consumption. *Specimens of Flowering Plants* falls into this latter category and, while little is known about the five draftsmen from Tiruchirappalli who created it, their watercolors demonstrate how Indian illustrators altered the blueprint of European botanical art and, more broadly, circumvented the limits of colonial perspectives on Asian flora. The inclusion of lichen in *Specimens of Flowering Plants* encourages viewers to contemplate the habitat of the pictured rhododendron and imagine how long it might have been growing there (long enough, we are to assume, for lichen to appear in the first place). In one of her essays on Victorian art and climate change, Kate Flint has singled out lichens as prime examples of the "commonplace natural phenomena" that help us to investigate "timescales of earthly continuance that differ from human ones."[22] *Specimens of Flowering Plants* destabilizes the conventional formula of Western botanical art through its abundance of cascading lichens; accordingly, it retains space for ecological intricacy in ways that upset the extractive use of scientific images by nineteenth-century Britons. Here botanical drawing leaves behind the colonial desire to generalize, perfect, and consume nature in order to alternatively explore a set of environmental relationships with no immediately apparent economic use value.

In contrast to the carefully labeled engraving in *Exotic Flora*, the watercolor in *Specimens of Flowering Plants* bears the solitary title of "Rhododendron," with an additional line in pencil specifying "Rhododendron Rustica." *Rhododendron rustica* corresponds to no known species of rhododendron, which suggests that the scribe may have been using the qualifier "rustica" in the Latin sense to simply mean "rural." *Rhododendron arboreum* – which we saw in *Exotic Flora* – is one of the most common rhododendrons that grows in South Asia, being especially concentrated in the Himalayan foothills. The plant has evergreen foliage and ruby-red blossoms, and its branches often play host to a mantle of lichens, which Joseph Dalton Hooker took note of in his botanical treatise *The Rhododendrons of Sikkim-Himalaya* (1849–51). "I beheld the Rhododendrons in all their magnificence," he writes in this text, adding how "the *Rhododendron arboreum* is first met with, its branches often loaded with pendulous mosses and lichens, especially *Usnea*."[23] *Usnea* belongs to the *Parmeliaceae* family of lichen-generating fungi and typically takes the form of fruticose lichen, a defining characteristic of which is three-dimensional growth. The lichen in our watercolor bears a resemblance to many species of *Usnea*, and if viewed from a distance, it seemingly transforms the underlying rhododendron into a web of writhing lines. Pushing against the more static hallmarks of Western botanical art, this image visualizes how plants can produce ecologies through acts of touch and growth.

In both form and facture, the rhododendron watercolor in *Specimens of Flowering Plants* draws attention to the physical materiality of vegetal life. Through the medium of lichen, viewers become aware of how plants like the rhododendron forge tactile relationships within an ecosystem – a process at odds with the colonial impulse to fix and dismantle nature for scientific study. In the watercolor, the lichen introduces a lively burst of lines to the drawing, heightening in the process the texture of the rhododendron and, by extension, its three-dimensional presence upon the page. Extending downward, this haphazard growth beckons viewers to imagine the spongey surface of the stem if grasped by their hands, its numberless filaments bending to the touch. The finest of these extremities are reminiscent of roots or capillaries, their trailing curves both anchoring the flower to the picture plane and projecting it outward. Vivified by line and texture, the lichen undercuts the perception of the rhododendron as a lifeless object such that it also obstructs the objectifying gaze of the colonial botanist. *Specimens of Flowering Plants* weaves the haptic energy of plant life directly into the design of its rhododendron watercolor, whereas *Exotic Flora* suppresses this same energy in favor of building a floral archetype. Although both works were commissioned by British patrons for the benefit of colonial science, they contribute unequally to the botanical project of empire. By refusing to eliminate ecological context wholesale, the watercolor in *Specimens of Flowering Plants* betrays the illusion that British political and intellectual authority in nineteenth-century India was absolute. As enduring as the template of Western botanical art was, we must continue to probe the boundaries of its influence by analyzing drawings that defied its principles of abstraction and detachment. This approach will center the accomplishments of Indian artists more prominently in our understanding of botanical illustration in the nineteenth century while also expanding arguments about the genre's ecological insights as a mode of representation.

Through its dynamic handling of lichens and rhododendrons, *Specimens of Flowering Plants* visualizes the cooperative nature of vegetal touch. As organisms that generate their own food, plants maintain an interactive relationship with the world while seeking out the water, light, and nutrients they need to perform photosynthesis. This process embodies what Emanuele Coccia calls "a cosmogony in action," in that it yields the proper circumstances for non-plants to flourish.[24] Through photosynthesis, for example, plants release oxygen into the atmosphere and turn water and carbon into energy, their touch transforming inorganic matter into the very substance of being. The rootedness of the vegetal world stands at odds with the economic and political objectives of colonial science, which seeks to remove plants from the environment (both figuratively and literally) in order to control them. Vegetal biorhythms hold the potential to build worlds, and in recent years scholars from a variety of fields have stressed the importance of recognizing how plants, to quote biologist Beronda Montgomery, "possess powerful abilities to modify their environment to support their own growth as well as that of others."[25] The illustrations that I have focused on in this chapter point toward new ways of examining the joint histories of art, plants, and empire in the nineteenth century – ways of reading botanical illustrations against the grain of their own imperialist production while also scrutinizing the arguments that surrounded them in their own day. These works demonstrate what art history and visual analysis can bring to current conversations about Victorian culture and the environment as well as why plants deserve a more prominent place in our future scholarship.

Notes

1. Beth Fowkes Tobin, *Picturing Imperial Power: Colonial Subjects in Eighteenth-Century British Painting* (Durham: Duke University Press, 1999), 201.
2. Lorraine Daston and Peter Galison, *Objectivity* (Princeton: Princeton University Press, 2007), 63.
3. Michael Marder, "The Place of Plants: Spatiality, Movement, Growth," *Performance Philosophy* 1.1 (2015), 185–94 at 190.
4. Henry J. Noltie, "Indian Export Art? The Botanical Drawings," in William Dalrymple, ed., *Forgotten Masters: Indian Painting for the East India Company* (London: Philip Wilson, 2019), 78–103.

5. Gill Saunders, *Picturing Plants: An Analytical History of Botanical Illustration* (Berkeley: University of California Press, 1995), 85–100.
6. Jim Endersby, *Imperial Nature: Joseph Hooker and the Practices of Victorian Science* (Chicago: University of Chicago Press, 2008), 125.
7. Daston and Galison, *Objectivity*, 68.
8. Elizabeth Hope Chang, *Novel Cultivations: Plants in British Literature of the Global Nineteenth Century* (Charlottesville: University of Virginia Press, 2019), 14.
9. Mary Elizabeth Braddon, *Hostages to Fortune*, 3 vols. (London: John Maxwell, 1875), 1.263.
10. Joseph Paxton, "Introductory Address," *Paxton's Magazine of Botany, and Register of Flowering Plants* 16 (1849): 1–3 at 1.
11. Beth Fowkes Tobin, *Colonizing Nature: The Tropics in British Arts and Letters, 1760–1820* (Philadelphia: University of Pennsylvania Press, 2005), 168–97.
12. Nicholas Thomas, "Licensed Curiosity: Cook's Pacific Voyages," in John Elsner and Roger Cardinal, eds., *The Cultures of Collecting* (Cambridge: Harvard University Press, 1994), 116–36 at 119; Daniela Bleichmar, *Visible Empire: Botanical Expeditions & Visual Culture in the Hispanic Enlightenment* (Chicago: University of Chicago Press, 2012), 152.
13. Mildred Archer, *Natural History Drawings in the India Office Library* (London: Her Majesty's Stationery Office, 1962); Martyn Rix, ed., *Indian Botanical Art: An Illustrated History* (New Delhi: Lustre Press/Roli Books, 2021); Theresa M. Kelley, *Clandestine Marriage: Botany and Romantic Culture* (Baltimore: Johns Hopkins University Press, 2012), 162–209; Savithri Preetha Nair, "Native Collecting and Natural Knowledge (1798–1832): Raja Serfoji II of Tanjore as a 'Centre of Calculation'," *Journal of the Royal Asiatic Society* 15.3 (2005), 279–302; Henry J. Noltie, *Indian Botanical Drawings 1793–1868: From the Royal Botanic Garden Edinburgh* (Edinburgh: Royal Botanic Garden Edinburgh, 1999); Ray Desmond, *The European Discovery of the Indian Flora* (Oxford: Oxford University Press, 1992).
14. William Jackson Hooker, "Illustrations of Indian Botany, Principally of the Southern Parts of the Peninsula. By Richard Wight, M.D., &c. &c.," *Botanical Miscellany* 2 (1831), 90–97 at 90.
15. Endersby, *Imperial Nature*, 112.
16. Frederick William Burbidge, *The Art of Botanical Drawing* (London: Winsor & Newton, 1873), 10–11.
17. David A. Lowther, "The First Painting of the Red Panda (*Ailurus fulgens*) in Europe? Natural History and Artistic Patronage in Early Nineteenth-Century India," *Archives of Natural History* 48.2 (2021), 368–76; Kapil Raj, "Colonial Encounters and the Forging of New Knowledge and National Identities: Great Britain and India, 1760–1850," *Osiris* 15, *Nature and Empire: Science and the Colonial Enterprise* (2000), 119–34.
18. Noltie, "Indian Export Art?"
19. Tobin, *Picturing Imperial Power*, 201.
20. Khyati Nagar, "Between Calcutta and Kew: The Divergent Circulation and Production of *Hortus Bengalensis* and *Flora Indica*," in Bernard Lightman, Gordon McOuat, and Larry Stewart, eds., *The Circulation of Knowledge*

between Britain, India and China: The Early-Modern World to the Twentieth Century (Leiden and Boston: Brill, 2013), 153–78 at 176.

21. Sita Reddy, "Foreword," in Martyn Rix ed., *Indian Botanical Art: An Illustrated History* (New Delhi: Lustre Press/Roli Books, 2021), 6–9 at 7.

22. Kate Flint, "Ruskin and Lichen," in Kelly Freeman and Thomas Hughes, eds., *Ruskin's Ecologies: Figures of Relation from Modern Painters to the Storm-Cloud* (London: Courtauld Books Online, 2021), unpaginated, https://shorturl.at/7Vo4y.

23. Joseph Dalton Hooker, *The Rhododendrons of Sikkim-Himalaya* (London: Reeve, Benham, and Reeve, 1849–51), 12.

24. Emanuele Coccia, *The Life of Plants: A Metaphysics of Mixture*, trans. Dylan J. Montanari (Cambridge: Polity Press, 2019), 10.

25. Beronda L. Montgomery, *Lessons from Plants* (Cambridge: Harvard University Press, 2021), 136.

8

SUKANYA BANERJEE

The Agricultural Roots of Realism
Lal Behari Day's *Govinda Samanta*

"To one who has never been out of town, the prospect of the open country must be striking and pleasant."[1] These lines from Romesh Chunder Dutt's *The Peasantry of Bengal* (1874) serve at once to justify and complicate the author's intentions in writing *Peasantry*, a socioeconomic treatise on nineteenth-century rural Bengal. On the one hand, Dutt entices readers with the pastoral pleasures offered by the countryside. Yet, as if to deliver on the expectation of a countervailing revelation invited by the clause "the open country *must* be striking and pleasant" (italics mine), Dutt fittingly concludes the paragraph with the contrasting observation: "A spot so secluded seems devoted to peace and rural happiness; – alas! it is the home of poverty, suffering, and ignorance."[2]

Economist, historian, novelist, Dutt was one of the first and very few Indians appointed to the elite ranks of the Indian Civil Service in the nineteenth century. Amongst the early Indians to mount a systematic critique of the economic policies of British rule, he authored the two-volume *Economic History of India* (1902, 1904). Significantly, even as such an effort yielded a methodical accounting of the agricultural output of the country, it also generated interest in rural, agricultural life. More specifically, it drew attention to the figure of the *raiyat* – the agricultural laborer – and his life and surroundings. Dutt's objective in *Peasantry* in fact lay in drawing attention to the condition of the *raiyats*, "the cultivating classes" in Bengal, who failed to secure legislative redress on account of the fact that the realities of their situation were either unknown or misrepresented to the colonial state.[3] Dutt's focus on the *raiyat* indicates the extent to which such a figure came to occupy a central place in nationalist economic and political discussions over the latter half of the century. On the one hand, the intervention by Dutt and his contemporaries Dadabhai Naoroji and M. G. Ranade is clearly occasioned by their awareness of the extent to which colonial power is tied with agricultural interest, an awareness that reminds us of the etymology of "colony": from the Latin *colonus*, meaning "farmer." On the other hand, in its particular depiction of rural life, Dutt's economic treatise also recalls the literary genre of the georgic. Although such an association is not surprising, given the georgic's imbrication with agriculture as well as empire, the georgic has, to my knowledge, not been invoked in literary analyses of "rural writing" in nineteenth-century India – leave alone Bengal – even as the authors in question readily engage with it.[4] A critical hesitation to engage the georgic may bespeak its own uncertain position in nineteenth-century English literary discourse. But such reticence may also, understandably, underline a postcolonial reluctance to frame Indian writing in English in derivative terms.[5]

However, given the inescapable prominence of the georgic *qua* georgic in the texts under study in this chapter, it becomes necessary to consider the georgic in its transimperial mode.[6] Such a reading does not assume a radial importation of the georgic from the metropole to the colony; rather, it considers its emergence in the late nineteenth century both as a mode of colonial critique and as a crucial marker in the evolving history of nineteenth-century realism. In other words, to recall the georgic in discussions of Indian rural writing not only accounts for the place of the georgic in colonial critique but also points to how the georgic's imbrication with the vicissitudes of agricultural life offered a self-conscious template for a literary rendition of the everyday along an aesthetic of "plainness" that scaffolded the beginnings of the realist novel in nineteenth-century India. Such a rendition ensured that the beginnings of realism were forged through an irreducible connection with rural, agricultural life around the same time that the fortunes of domestic realism were on the wane in late Victorian Britain. To read the transimperial georgic, then, is to extend the story of realism, tracking it elsewhere and otherwise. It is also to disaggregate the handy notion of everyday realism into its constitutive multispeciated components that otherwise get obscured by the social, anthropocentric remit of realism.

The georgic, with its preoccupation with agricultural labor and the land, bears a long literary history dating back to Hesiod's *Works and Days* and, more prominently, Virgil's *Georgics*. Its fortunes received a fillip from the seventeenth century onward, as a result of both a Baconian move towards inquiry of "ordinary and common matters" and changing views of the land as precipitated by unfolding capitalist relations.[7] Though initially the English georgic demarcated the distinction between the town and country, sharply differentiating between trade and agriculture, John Dryden's 1697 translation of Virgil's *Georgics* inaugurated a tradition of emphasizing the interplay between agriculture and commerce, indeed between England and its forays into empire-building.[8] However, the growing awareness of the inequities of colonialism and the dependence of colonial agricultural production on enslaved labor rendered the aesthetic melding of agriculture and empire problematic. By the end of the eighteenth century, the georgic almost retreated into the pastoral.[9] In the second half of the nineteenth century, Paddy Bullard notes, "the line of the georgic literature grows more faint."[10] In picking up the colonial variant of the georgic within the context of the late nineteenth-century empire then, one is compelled to ask what it means for the georgic to become instrumental in a critique of colonial rule voiced by colonial subjects, given that the georgic conventionally afforded a perspective that was male and free.[11] What are the implications of the georgic recalling colonialism to its agricultural roots? How does this formulation bear upon our literary mappings?

In order to address these questions, I turn to a novel, also published in 1874 – Lal Behari Day's *Govinda Samanta, or Bengal Peasant Life*. *Govinda Samanta*, I suggest, not only explicitly invokes the georgic tradition but can be read as a georgic itself. Even as Dutt's treatise in *Peasantry of Bengal* gestures to the literary in its invocation of the rural, it does not purport to exceed the scope of its socioeconomic analysis. Day, on the other hand, self-consciously writes a novel on rural life in ways that demonstrate how the georgic, though originally poetic in form, extends across other literary forms as well.[12] A compatriot of Dutt's in nineteenth-century Bengal, Day came from a far more modest background. Born into a Bengali Hindu family, he grew up amidst straitened circumstances and was educated in a Christian missionary school. Day converted to Christianity and spent part of his life as a missionary (he was known as the Rev. Lal Behari Day). He also taught in different colleges in and around Calcutta. Unlike Dutt, Day spent much of his life in rural and semirural areas, thereby gaining firsthand knowledge of rural life. In 1872, he participated in a competition organized by the wealthy zamindar – landowner – Joy Krishna Mukherjee, who announced a fifty-pound reward for "the best novel, to be written either in Bengali or in English, illustrating the 'Social and Domestic Life of the Rural Population and Working Classes of Bengal.'"[13]

That Mukherjee saw it worthy enough to establish rural life as a novelistic theme evidences the extent to which the novel, still finding its footing in India, was called, in its mimetic capabilities, to highlight the "agricultural question," so to speak. That the guidelines for the competition allowed for the novel to be written in English or Bengali also indicates a desire to expand the novel's reach beyond a middle-class, Western-educated (and therefore bilingual) Bengali audience. Indeed, it indicates a desire to reach audiences in Britain as well. *Govinda Samanta* was adjudged the best entry in the competition. The first edition was published in London by Macmillan in 1874, and a new edition in 1879. The novel was well received both in India and Britain, even catching the eye of Charles Darwin, who in 1881 wrote to its publishers: "I see that the Rev. Lal Behari Day is editor of the *Bengal Magazine*, and I shall be glad if you would tell him, with my compliments, how much pleasure and instruction I derived from reading, a few years ago, his novel, *Govinda Samanta*."[14]

Given that the georgic is didactic in nature, it is not surprising that Darwin derived "instruction" from *Govinda Samanta*, a novel revolving around the life of the eponymous *raiyat*, Govinda Samanta. But one may very well query Darwin's limning of "pleasure," not least because Day concertedly abjures any interest in providing the readerly pleasure afforded by conventional tropes. As Day states in the opening chapter, readers should forsake any expectation of "Romantic adventures, intricate evolutions of the plot, striking occurrences."[15] Instead, he cautions, "The reader is to expect here a plain and unvarnished tale of a plain peasant, living in this plain country of Bengal – I beg the pardon of the sublime poet who sang of the hills of Hooghly and the mountains of the Twenty four Parganas – told in a plain manner."[16]

To Day's dubious credit, he reorients literary expectations in order to deliver on the promise of "plainness." If plainness is posited in contrast to "romantic adventures, intricate evolutions of the plot, and striking occurrences," then the novel achieves plainness through the fact that it aspires to little more than depicting the humdrum monotony of peasant life. However, such depiction is not by way of a purportedly mimetic, documentary realism. Although scholars such as Rochelle Pinto have rightly noted the ethnographic elements of the novel, the novel's ethnographic quality does not detract from Day's highly self-conscious narratorial style.[17] As becomes clear from the onset of the novel, we have a reflective narrator who lays bare his narrative choices, letting us know what he will focus on and what, consequently, he will skim over. In clearly directing what exactly we should look at and for how long, the narrator actually renders transparent his own "varnishing" of village life. But, paradoxically, such varnishing – a key if counterintuitive element of any realist depiction – helps realize the novel's desired objective of plainness. In fact, the narrator cites Darwin himself to double down on his point about the novel's plainness. Even "love scenes" exceed the remit of plainness. As he points out, "I would fain introduce love scenes ... Unlike the butterfly whose courtship Darwin assures us is a very long affair, the Bengali does not court at all. Marriage is an affair managed entirely by the parents and guardians of bachelors and spinsters."[18] Although such a sociological observation marks a discontinuity between the natural world and its social counterpart by way of defending the absence of a courtship plot in the novel, it is through the imbrication of the natural and social world – an imbrication that continually questions the division between the two – that the novel achieves its plainness. In so doing, the novel proffers an aesthetic of the everyday that becomes the hallmark of Day's transimperial rendition of the georgic, which at once forwards a line of colonial critique while also adding another chapter to the story of literary realism.

The novel is set in fictional Kanchanpur, a hamlet that the narrator locates with geographical precision, "six miles to the northeast of the town of Vardhamana or Burdwan."[19] Noting that though drawn from various castes, the villagers belong mainly to the "agricultural class,"[20] the narrator introduces us to the members of the Samanta family, *raiyats*, who farm the plot that the family rents from the village landowner. The novel begins with the birth in the Samanta household of a male child, the eponymous protagonist Govinda. To say that the novel traces the life of Govinda is only partly true. To be sure, the novel follows the fortunes of Govinda as he matures into a young man and, upon the death of the older male members, takes on the family mantle to manage its farming obligations. But despite endowing him with an eponymous status, the novel is not too interested in Govinda's life. We hardly get to know him and the novel does not seem too invested in developing his character. Even Govinda's schooling is given short shrift. His father, Manik Samanta, keen that Govinda receive the benefits of formal education, enrolls him in the village school. But as Manik's mother, Alanga – the family matriarch – disapprovingly reminds Manik, "We have been born tillers of the ground, and we must remain tillers of the ground all our life. Besides, did your fathers ever learn to write and to read?"[21] As it happens, Govinda soon has to leave school because of an unfortunate turn of events and joins his family in the fields. The impossibility of Govinda moving away from the life that he was born into may well be part of the point that Day, the educationist, is trying to make about the difficulties of rural life. But if that is the case, then the point is only lightly made, for there is no desire expressed by any of the characters for an alternative to farming. The spatiotemporal horizons of Kanchanpur seem sufficient, and any express disquiet is on account of the difficulties of agricultural life. The portrayal of such difficulties, however, is meant to sharpen the focus on such an existence rather than supersede it. In fact, it is the shared agricultural labor – in which human, animal, and the vegetal are coparticipants – that takes precedence in the novel. No wonder, then, that the character of Govinda recedes into unimportance and serves more as a relay for marking the cycle of agricultural events in the novel. In a chapter titled "The Navanna" (The New Rice), for instance, the narrator describes the festival in which the first fruit of the paddy fields is offered to the gods before they are consumed by humans, a festival not to be confused, he intones, with "the general harvest, which occurs about a month after."[22] The significance of the festival is underlined by the observation that "Govinda is not to go out today with the cows; neither his father nor his uncle is to work."[23] Even as the mention of Govinda is instrumental in bringing the festival to life, as it were, the festival itself is evidently alive with a range of entities, ranging from the nonhuman to the extra-human: paddy, cows, the gods.[24] And that Govinda is only a bit player in this ensemble is evident in the preceding chapter that is devoted entirely to paddy.

In "All about Paddy," the narrator launches a lengthy description of paddy cultivation, enumerating the various kinds of paddy – the chief source of dietary sustenance in Bengal, its requisitions, and the proper means to cultivate it. In all of this, it is paddy that emerges as the key player:

> There is nothing peculiar in the process of cultivating paddy. The ground is ploughed and harrowed, and then the seed is sown by the hand. In the course of a few days, the seed germinates and sprouts. Before the setting in of the rains, about the middle of June, great attention is paid to irrigation, the cares of which cease only when beneficent heaven sends down rain in copious show-ers. But the Bengal husbandman is not without anxiety. If there be a drought, the paddy is parched up; if there be too much rain, the plant is drowned and rots. ... In the swampy districts of Bakharganja and Jasahar (Jessore) the paddy stalk rises sometimes to the height of ten or twelve feet; though in the high land of Vardhamana and Birbhum it seldom attains a greater height than six or eight feet.[25]

Significantly, paddy is cast in an agentive role – "the seed germinates and sprouts," "the paddy stalk rises sometimes to the height of ten or twelve feet" – whereas the husbandman stands by to minister to it, a role ren-dered and obscured through the use of the passive voice: "great attention is paid to irrigation." Indeed, the attention that paddy demands and the extent to which it dictates peasants' lives cede the ground, as it were, to paddy, thereby detracting from an anthropocentric hierarchy. While such de-anthropocentrism is now commonly identified with ecologically attuned writing, I am interested in considering how it is precisely through this entan-gled multispeciated context that plainness is imagined. But before doing so, I want to consider more fully how the georgic or, rather, *Govinda Samanta* as georgic, in addition to producing plainness on a literary register, also proffers a critique of colonial practices on a political one.

Govinda Samanta's lengthy exegesis on paddy cultivation might seem anomalous only if we were to expect the novel to have a more characterolog-ical investment in Govinda's life. The exegesis is entirely in keeping, however, with the didactic inclinations of the georgic. The novel self-consciously invokes the georgic. The "rural scene" in the title of an earlier chapter, "Describes a

Rural Scene, and Ushers Our Hero into the World," not only provides the setting but is also of interest in and of itself because much of the chapter is devoted to describing the fields Govinda's family works, the cattle they own, and, yes, the paddy they grow: the rural scene, in other words, indexes an inalienable relationality between the human and nonhuman, against and through which individual identities begin to morph. The rural component of the milieu is emphasized to the extent that the chapter spends considerable time describing a key agricultural tool, the plough. Dwelling on the plough is not an uncharacteristic feature of the georgic, and the chapter, which quotes lines from Dryden's translation of the *Georgics* in its epigraph, takes explicit warrant from the progenitors of the georgic: "As some of our readers may not have seen a Bengal plough, it is as well to describe it here; and we do not think the object is too low to be described, especially when we remember that it exercised in antiquity the genius of two such poets as Hesiod and Virgil."[26]

The attentiveness with which the narrator describes the plough also extends, as we have seen, to the process of cultivating paddy. If all of this falls within the remit of the georgic, then it also enables the georgic to double up as a critique of colonial policies of land cultivation and management. Later chapters of the novel take up the question of indigo cultivation. Even as indigo is not cultivated in Kanchanpur, the marriage of Govinda's sister to a *raiyat* forced to grow indigo allows for the novel to engage with the travails of those working at the mercy of the English indigo planters, whose ruthless means rendered indigo cultivation a scandal and topic for agitation and protest in mid nineteenth century Bengal. Dinabandhu Mitra's play *Neel Darpan* (The Indigo-Planting Mirror), which highlighted the plight of a native family ravaged by the brutalities of indigo cultivation, was published to popular acclaim in 1860. In response to official inquiries that were prompted in no small measure by native outcry, the colonial state largely did away with the system of indigo plantation in Bengal by the end of the decade. Yet *Neel Darpan* acquired a totemic status over the course of the 1870s as growing nationalist consciousness hailed the play as firing an early salvo at the inequities of colonialism. *Neel Darpan* may well have acquired a nationalist afterlife after the horrors of indigo cultivation had already ceased, but for Day to make note of indigo cultivation in the 1870s seems a curious choice. While it may be in keeping with the prior historical setting of the novel, Day was by all accounts a votary of the colonial state. Or at least he apparently saw no reason to explicitly position himself against it (he had been raised in missionary schools). In his reading of the novel, Satya P. Mohanty suggests that Day's "descriptive realism" is ideologically motivated, a sign of a strategic "neutrality."[27] Yet because of his firsthand experience in the rural districts, Day was also all too acquainted with the ills of colonial agricultural practice. The insistence and force of his descriptive thrust seems to push beyond a strategic neutrality. For him to write a novel whose generic form warrants extensive description of the methods of cultivation in fact draws attention to colonial lapses as a function of genre rather than premeditated critique. In other words, it is the descriptive mode that the georgic extensively deploys that doubles up as critique, leaving in abeyance the specificities of Day's position vis-à-vis the colonial state, a position that was ambivalent but by no means singular.[28]

In *Neel Darpan*, Mitra draws attention to the ills of indigo cultivation to be sure, but very little is mentioned in the play about indigo or the specific nature of its cultivation.[29] Instead, we witness the miseries inflicted upon the peasants and small-scale cultivators by reading of the difficulties they experience in their personal and social lives. In *Govinda Samanta*, on the other hand, Govinda's brother-in-law, Madhava, who is forced to grow indigo in his field, suffers enormous hardship on account of the unscrupulous practices followed by the profit-hungry planters and their overseers. However, the hardships endured by the *raiyats* is explained by and through a detailed description of the various stages involved in indigo cultivation, prompting the narrator to comment on the human as well as ecological damage inflicted by the indigo crop, which "exhausts the power of the soil, and is in every respect unremunerative to the raiyat."[30] None of these details is present in Mitra's play. Of course, the difference in form – novel vs. drama – might explain *Govinda Samanta*'s ability to accommodate such extended description. But it is as much a matter of form as of genre that distinguishes the two texts in terms of their depiction of indigo cultivation. *Neel Darpan*, despite the title's explicit mention of indigo, centers on social relations, whereas *Govinda Samanta* (despite its anthropocentric title) remains entrenched in the relation between the *raiyats*, their land, and their crops. Small wonder, then, that towards the end of the novel, Day summarily dispenses with Govinda and his family, ending the novel, in the final three chapters that Day tacked on after he submitted his entry to the competition, with the description of a famine that devastates the Bengal countryside, a description that implicitly questions colonial policies even though the narrator ostensibly lauds the government for limiting the damage inflicted by famine.[31]

Despite (or because of) the fact that there is no significant character development in the novel, the turns in the plot are circumstantially induced and take the form of injustices meted out to the peasants, be it by English planters or native landowners. While his brother-in-law suffers at the hands of the indigo planter, Govinda and his immediate family face enormous privation on account of the rapacious practices of the local landowner, Jaychand Raya Chaudhuri, whose henchmen destroy Govinda's home and crops because he had not paid arrears. By the end of the novel, Govinda loses his land and is forced to eke out a living as a day laborer in a nearby town, where he dies an ignominious and early death. Depictions of figures such as Raya Chaudhuri illuminate Dutt's point in *Bengal Peasantry* regarding the need to highlight the plight of the *raiyat*, who also suffers at the hands of native landowners and their intermediaries. As Priyamvada Gopal notes, in this section of the novel, Day offers a "surprisingly fierce critique" of the system whereby the British, post-Permanent Settlement, entrusted the supervision of the rural peasantry to the local aristocracy.[32]

In *Govinda Samanta*, Govinda and his family's interactions with the native landowners and the indigo planters are set off against the familiar cadences of their agricultural life. In contrast to the steadying pattern of the *raiyats'* daily routine, the incidents involving the native landowners and the indigo planters are both exorbitant and disruptive. They offer moments of suspense and intrigue – we wonder if the landowner will make good on his threats to destroy Govinda or are shocked that he does indeed burn down part of Govinda's dwelling. But as the introductory chapter implies, the point of the novel is not to revel in such heightened moments. The novel's didacticism perhaps lies most in its directing of readerly pleasure away from the exorbitant and toward the more flattened affective graph of the everyday. Day's stated preference for "plainness" is realized in the novel through the rhythm and practices of an agricultural life. The georgic framing of the novel ensures that we are always aware of the vicissitudes of such a life: the ceaseless labor, the possibility of crop failure, and the certainty of recalcitrant animals. Of course, in a novel that ends with a devastating famine, the agricultural life hardly offers a pastoral retreat. Moreover, agriculture is in contention with what might be considered "natural," and nature itself is not predictable.

Nonetheless, the attention to agricultural details in the novel not only functions as colonial critique but also accounts for the introduction of a literary aesthetic of plainness arrived at through an attentiveness to the familiar, ordinary aspects of life brought home by an emphasis on a multispeciated everyday. The normal course of the *raiyat's* lives is far from comfortable; however, the formalization of their labor into and through the predictable pattern of the everyday is comforting. This predictability is conveyed through an attentiveness to the natural (nonhuman) environment, manifesting itself in mundane forms that reassuringly structure the *raiyat's* lives in ways that can be foretold down to minute details:

> As Badan [Govinda's uncle] had about thirty-six *bighas*, or nearly twelve acres, of land, he had only one plough and therefore two bullocks. ... As they were, in a manner, the support of the family, particular care was bestowed upon

them. Gayaram every morning and evening filled their tubs with chopped straw, well soaked in a solution of water and oil-cake. ... The oldest cow, named Bhagavati, gave only three quarters of a *seer* of milk in the morning and half a *seer* in the evening ... and the last, though not the least in value called Kamdhenu (the cow of desire) gave every morning three *seers* of milk as thick as the juice of the fruit of the *Ficus Indica*, and two *seers* in the evening.[33]

The assurance rising from such specific details renders the novel's all-too-human plot turns – such as the indigo planter's incursions and Raya Chaudhuri's rapacity – as unwelcome and intrusive, proximate as they are to the "striking occurrences, hair-breadth escapes, and scenes of horror" that Day otherwise deplores while limning his literary aesthetic.[34]

The multispeciated agricultural focus, then, is not extraneous to the novel-as-georgic, nor does it or merely provide the setting. Rather, such a focus constitutes the bulk of the novel while also accounting for its vaunted plainness. On the one hand, the rhetorical tools yielding this plainness, such as the extended descriptions of indigo planting, also serve as colonial critique. On the other hand, in their constitutive iterability, the plainness and structural predictability proffer an aesthetic of the everyday that carries another kind of pleasure, another (novel) source of wonder. In what is now hailed as an early and "radical" credo of realist fiction in India,[35] Day states in the preface to his readers:

You are not to expect anything marvelous or wonderful in this little book. My great Indian predecessors ... Valmiki, Vyas, and the compilers of the Puranas, have treated kings with ten heads and twenty arms ... And some of my European predecessors like Swift and Rabelais, have spoken of men whose pockets were capacious enough to hold a whole nation of diminutive human beings, and of giants ... Such marvels, my reader, you are not to expect in this unpretending volume. The age of marvels has gone by; giants do not pay now-a-days.[36]

Govinda Samanta offers pleasure that is decidedly of the non-marvelous kind. It is worth noting the salience of quotidian, everyday pleasure in the latter decades of the century, for it was at the same time that domestic realism was on the wane in Britain as metropolitan readerly attention shifted to adventure, fantasy, and the thrills of *fin de siècle* gothic. Moreover, if, as has been argued, the everyday became a commonplace of twentieth-century modernism,[37] then a novel such as *Govinda Samanta* might well be worth thinking more about as a nineteenth-century colonial precursor. The everyday that the novel constitutes through its embrace of a multispeciated rural environment not only comments on the varying fortunes of realism in Britain and India but also creates space for questioning colonial policy at its very roots.

Notes

1. Romesh Chunder Dutt, *The Peasantry of Bengal* (Calcutta: Thacker, Spink and Company, 1874), 60.
2. Dutt, *The Peasantry of Bengal*, 61.
3. Dutt, *The Peasantry of Bengal*, vi.
4. For an extensive study of Indian writing about nineteenth-century rural life in Bengal, see Bipasha Raha, *The Plough and the Pen: Peasantry, Agriculture and the Literati in Colonial Bengal* (New Delhi: Manohar, 2012).
5. For a consideration of the implications of reading nineteenth-century Indian literature through a derivative framework, see Meenakshi Mukherjee, *Perishable Empire: Essays on Indian Writing in English* (Delhi: Oxford University Press, 2000), 1–30.
6. I understand the transimperial as a heuristic that keeps alive the "asymmetries, tensions, and collaborations" between and across different constituencies of empire. Sukanya Banerjee, "Transimperial," *Victorian Literature and Culture* 46.3/4 (2018), 925–28 at 927.
7. Francis Bacon, *The Advancement of Learning* (1605), qtd. in Paddy Bullard Paddy Bullard, "A Survey of English Georgic Writing, 1521–2021," in Paddy Bullard, ed., *A History of English Georgic Writing* (Cambridge: Cambridge University Press, 2023), 1–36 at 7.
8. Karen O'Brien, "Imperial Georgic, 1660–1789," in Gerald MacLean, Donna Landry, and Joseph P. Ward, eds., *The Country and the City Revisited: England and the Politics of Culture, 1550–1850* (Cambridge: Cambridge University Press, 1999), 160–70 at 163.
9. O'Brien, "Imperial Georgic," 174.
10. Bullard, "A Survey," 17.
11. Charlie Kerrigan, "Environment and Empire: Georgic through Time," in Bullard, ed., *A History of English Georgic Writing*, 334–61 at 345.
12. Bullard, "A Survey," 1.
13. Lal Behari Day, "Preface," in *Bengal Peasant Life* (London: Macmillan, 1879), vii.
14. Qtd. in G. MacPherson, *Life of Lal Behari Day: Convert, Pastor, Professor and Author* (Edinburgh: T. and T. Clark, 1900), 134.
15. Lal Behari Day, *Govinda Samanta or The History of a Bengal Raiyat* (London: Macmillan, 1874), 3.
16. Day, *Govinda Samanta*, 4.
17. Rochelle Pinto, "*Govinda Samanta*, or, Eluding Ethnography in the Colonial Novel," in Baidik Bhattacharya and Sambudha Sen, eds., *Novel Formations: The Indian Beginnings of a European Genre,* (Ranikhet: Permanent Black, 2019), 98–134.
18. Day, *Govinda Samanta*, 3.
19. Day, *Govinda Samanta*, 5.
20. Day, *Govinda Samanta*, 10.
21. Day, *Govinda Samanta*, 60.
22. Day, *Govinda Samanta*, 204.
23. Day, *Govinda Samanta*, 204.
24. As Meghna Sapui notes, though, it is worth keeping in mind that even as the "new rice" ceremony indexes the "harmonious ecology of relationships" in the

novel, *Govinda Samanta* also reveals caste distinctions as they operate through gustatory practices. Meghna Sapui, "Edible Empire: Foodways and Literature in British India," unpublished book manuscript (in progress, shared with me by the author), 107–8. For a reading of gods as extra-human, see Parama Roy, "The Strange Ecologies of Empire," *Victorian Literature and Culture* 49.1 (Spring 2021), 73–106; Mayanthi Fernando, "Uncanny Ecologies: More-Than-Natural, More-Than-Human, More-Than-Secular," *Comparative Studies of South Asia, Africa, and the Middle East* 42.3 (December 2022), 568–83.

25. Day, *Govinda Samanta*, 202.
26. Day, *Govinda Samanta*, 17.
27. Satya Mohanty, "The Epistemic Work of Literary Realism: Two Novels from Colonial India," in Ulka Anjaria, ed., *A History of the Indian Novel in English* (Cambridge: Cambridge University Press, 2015), 45–58 at 52.
28. Raha, *The Plough*, 102.
29. Sukanya Banerjee, "Drama, Ecology, and the Ground of Empire: The Play of Indigo," in *Ecological Form: System and Aesthetics in the Age of Empire* (New York: Fordham University Press, 2018), 21–41.
30. Day, *Govinda Samanta*, 319.
31. Day, *Govinda Samanta*, 375.
32. Priyamvada Gopal, *The Indian English Novel: Nation, History, and Narration* (Oxford: Oxford University Press, 2009), 27. For an analysis of the Permanent Settlement, see Ranajit Guha, *A Rule of Property for Bengal: An Essay on the Idea of Permanent Settlement*, 1962 (Durham: Duke University Press, 1996).
33. Day, *Govinda Samanta*, 34.
34. Day, *Govinda Samanta*, 3.
35. H. S. Mohapatra and J. K. Nayak, "Writing Peasant Life in Colonial India: A Comparative Analysis of Lal Behari Day's 'Bengal Peasant Life' and Fakir Mohan Senapati's 'Chha Ana Atha Guntha,'" *Toronto Review of Contemporary Writing Abroad* 14.3 (Spring 1996), 29–40 at 30.
36. Day, *Govinda Samanta*, 2–3.
37. Bryony Randall, "A Day's Time: The One-Day Novel and the Temporality of the Everyday," *New Literary History* 47.4 (Autumn 2016), 591–610.

9

PHILIP STEER

British Values, Indigenous Knowledge, and Settler Colonial Environments

In their call to approach the Victorian era as a "wide" rather than "long" nineteenth century, Sukanya Banerjee, Ryan D. Fong, and Helena Michie ask: "How might ecology look from other parts of the empire?"[1] In the parts of the British Empire at the center of this chapter – the settler colonies of Canada, Australia, and New Zealand – their ecologies began to look very different once the Victorians arrived. As Anthony Trollope reflected after visiting Australia and New Zealand, settlement was premised on thoroughgoing environmental transformation: "[A]dvancing science has carried out and acclimatized, not only men and women, but beasts, birds, and fishes, fruit and vegetables, rich grasses and European trees, with a rapidity and profusion of which our grandfathers never dreamed, and which even our fathers hardly ventured to anticipate."[2] The natural environment was a prominent theme of the writing produced in all the colonies, but only relatively recently has settler literature begun to receive sustained consideration from the perspective of Victorian studies. At the same time, calls for the decolonization of Victorian studies are also prompting a search for means of taking into account Indigenous knowledge and perspectives in imperial contexts. This expanding remit is enabling a long-overdue reckoning with a key arena of British culture's global impact in the nineteenth century. Taking a wider look at the nineteenth century has the potential to encompass not only the forms of environmental understanding produced by British writers in those new locations but also the Indigenous knowledges that circulated within settler print culture.

The sheer volume and vibrancy of settler writing about the natural environment is being brought to ever greater visibility by the ongoing digitization of colonial newspapers and periodicals. This expanding archive highlights the importance of poetry in providing localized responses to environmental conditions and changes, affirming Jason R. Rudy's observation that the genre was "signally important to the ways British emigrants thought of themselves and the work of British colonialism."[3] Notably, these local bodies of literature did not stand alone but intersected with other prominent spheres of cultural production. At the broadest level, settler writers drew on and reworked British and North American models of form and aesthetics. Their work also existed in a dynamic relationship with other domains of colonial knowledge, including legal regimes, economic developments, scientific inquiry, and political debates. At the same time, settler writing was superimposed upon the ways that environments were comprehended, shaped, and valued by Indigenous populations. It is not possible in this chapter to offer a comprehensive overview of the variety of ecosystems that were encountered (and often destroyed) through Victorian settler colonialism, or the print cultures that developed in their midst. Yet underlying this complexity was a common story: the Victorian literature produced in the settler colonies was at the forefront of mediating diverse conceptions of the environment within a system that otherwise ruthlessly prioritized its economic exploitation. In what follows, I offer three brief case studies that highlight different dimensions of this mediating role. First, through considering representations of forests in New Zealand, I outline literature's capacity to articulate and assess diverse conceptions of environmental value. Second, I discuss the use of writing to comprehend unfamiliar and unpredictable environments with reference to accounts of aridity and drought in Australia. Finally, I reflect on how non-Indigenous critics might approach nineteenth-century Indigenous writing about the environment by focusing on the poetry of Mohawk and Canadian author E. Pauline Johnson.

Evaluating the Environment

The settler encounter with the colonial environment was profoundly shaped by a variety of Victorian conceptions of value and raised questions about how differences between them might be evaluated. While settler literature's ability to articulate a positive response to the precolonial environment derived in large part from Romanticism's privileging of wilderness, this paled into insignificance alongside the normative value ascribed to agriculture across economic, ecological, and aesthetic domains. Conversely, colonization was premised on the devaluation not only of Indigenous environmental relations and perspectives, but also of the idea that nonhuman nature might have inherent worth. These Indigenous perspectives had a limited visibility within settler print culture and were carefully framed to minimize their claims upon modernity. In this section, I demonstrate the role of literature in mediating these overlapping conceptions of environmental value by focusing on one specific context for settlement – the forests of New Zealand.

Faced with the dense forests that covered much of the New Zealand landscape, Victorian settlers saw the abstraction of developmental time made real. Keith Thomas summarizes the conventional wisdom: "The progress of mankind was from forest to the field ... Untamed woodlands were thus seen as obstacles to human progress."[4] This temporal perspective could be expressed in almost reverential portrayals of the forest as a space outside of history, which often overlooked any prior human presence, or through drawing on the Gothic's historicist sensibilities to portray an inhospitable ecosystem whose intransigence was at least implicitly associated with Indigenous sovereignty. William Satchell's novel *The Toll of the Bush* (1902) presents the "primeval solitudes" of the forest as actively antagonistic towards the settler population, and its settler characters draw on a Māori vocabulary to express that enmity: "What wonder if it be true, as the bushmen believe, that the forest demands its toll of the destroyers. It needs no stretching of the imagination to believe that in this great silent outburst of life there is a soul that can offer resistance. ... Uto is the word ... payment in expiation."[5] Similarly, ethnographic accounts of Māori environmental knowledge that circulated within and beyond settler society relegated those insights to a premodern past by framing them as being of poetic or romantic interest. As E. B. Tylor wrote in *Primitive Culture* (1871), "the Maori poet's shaping of nature into nature-myths" produced "masterpieces of an art belonging rather to the past than to the present."[6] This poetic framing is evident in historian and ethnographer James Cowan's wide-ranging summary of Māori forest knowledge, "Te Wao-Nui-a-Tane" (1902), the title referring to Tāne, the god of the forest, and the trees that trace their descent from him. Published in a literary magazine, the piece begins with the proposition that any settler with "imagination or poetry in his nature" must inevitably enter "in some degree into the feeling of reverence with which the ancients regarded the forest primeval."[7] Keeping this knowledge at a historical distance by deeming it "enchanted" and "curious" is of a part with dismissing an informant as "a sturdy relic of paganism stranded on the shores of modern progress."[8] While such comments are partial and highly tendentious, they nevertheless stand in contrast with the majority of settler writing about the environment that simply ignores the longstanding Māori relation with the forest.

The idea of the forest's premodernity was generally mobilized to validate its destruction in the name of development, but it also chimed with Romantic ideas of sublimity in ways that could lead to positive, noneconomic assertions of value. Not all of New Zealand's forest environments were viewed in sublime terms, however, for only certain tree species possessed the necessary properties of awe-inspiring size and age – most notably the kauri, known to grow over 160 feet tall and to live for thousands of years. Thus, the painter and poet Alfred Sharpe could rhapsodize about one such forest:

> Like the grand aisles of some Titanic temple
> The mighty trunks rose dim;
> I felt, within that hushed and holy stillness,
> As standing on the rim
> Of things unseen, known only to the seraphs,
> And to the cherubim.[9]

Romantic sentiments like these are also notable for the environmental insights they do not admit. On the one hand, the object of admiration is singled out and isolated, offering little opportunity to imagine either the kauri as participant in a wider ecology or a sustained human presence alongside its "hushed and holy stillness." On the other hand, the evocation of spiritual qualities displaces existing Indigenous metaphysical understandings. In the case of the kauri, for instance, Mānuka Hēnare points out that Māori view it as "imbued at its birth with its own tapu, meaning its potentiality to be a remarkable tree," as well as possessing its own hau, a life-force that "gives sustenance and life to associated flora and fauna."[10] Settler celebrations of noneconomic environmental value therefore need to be read from two perspectives at once, attending to absence as well as effusiveness.

Literature also provided settlers with a means of comparing forms of environmental value, and especially of reflecting on the contest between economic and aesthetic priorities. That comparative work could take satiric form, as in a poem by George Phipps Williams that describes a man "solemnly gazing" at a "kingly" tree:

> You may safely conclude that the subject is *this*,
> Of the deep meditation in which he is sunk,
> *Not* the glorious beauty he's inwardly drunk,
> But the number of feet he can cut from its trunk.[11]

More commonly, such acts of evaluation were cast in elegiac tones that combine feelings of loss with a sense of historical inevitability. Those concerns were expressed most influentially by the politician and historian William Pember Reeves's "The Passing of the Forest," which presents deforestation as a significant aesthetic loss to the colony: "Is this the price we pay, / The price for progress – Beauty swept away?"[12] The poem conveys a sense of inevitability as "progress" takes its seemingly destined course, but it also demonstrates, through its appeal to a collective "we," how the perception of loss is limited to the settler population as bearer of aesthetic perception.

Comprehending the Environment

Colonial environments and the changes wrought by settlement presented all manner of challenges to comprehension, ranging from the introduction of species that prove to be invasive to the unexpected impacts of defor- estation on hydrological cycles. Deviations of climate from British norms proved especially troubling in Australia, not only because of the agricultural basis of settler economies but also because the ideological basis of the set- tler project depended on the thoroughgoing replication of Britishness in the colonies. As an anonymous poet reflected in the early 1880s, a full century after colonization began, a recent drought had "baffled" settler expecta- tions and ambitions.[13] Whereas early settlers believed Australia's weather would be "ordered," in line with the regularity of British seasonal progres- sion, Indigenous conceptions of seasonality hinge on the idea that seasonal change does "not happen at particular times, but in specific sequences."[14] Such climatic challenges to British expectations were at their most intense in Australia's inland semi-arid and arid bioregions, known colloquially as the outback. In this section I survey the social function performed by settler literature in contexts of environmental uncertainty by highlighting a range of Australian responses to aridity and drought.

The conceptual difficulty posed to British settlers by arid environments is evident in the emotional responses that they generate, which cover a spec- trum from bemusement and disdain to fear and anger. Writings about the outback by the prominent late century author Henry Lawson express deep frustration at the intransigent climate yet also employ irony to manage that uncertainty. That frustration is on display in an essay on local liter- ature, "Some Popular Australian Mistakes," which posits a fundamental mismatch between literary language and arid environments: "A plain is not necessarily a wide, open space covered with waving grass or green sward, like a prairie ...; it is either a desert or a stretch of level country covered with wretched scrub .... An Australian lake is not a lake; it is either a sheet of brackish water or a patch of dry sand."[15] Several of Lawson's ballads describe the experience of traversing this landscape, and they channel feel- ings of disdain at its deviations from inherited climate expectations into expressions of ironic surprise. In "The Paroo 'River,'" the speaker enter- tains idyllic visions of their riverine destination – "I longed to hear a stream go by / And see the circles quiver" – until his more experienced companion comes across "a strip of ground" that is "just a little hollowed," and announces that they have arrived:[16]

> I stood awhile, as in a dream,
>   "Great Scott!" I cried, "is that it?
> Why, that is some old bridle-track!"
>   He chuckled, "Well, I never!
> It's nearly time you came out-back –
>   This is the Paroo River!"[17]

Lawson's irony also performs an educative function. In describing the environment's recalcitrance, irony's doubleness provided a mechanism by which settlers could begin to comprehend that difference and inhabit it imaginatively.

The unpredictability of drought presented a profound challenge to settler cultural and economic certainties, and in the absence of accurate weather prediction or climatological models, literary responses participated in and reflected on attempts to fit it into other explanatory frameworks. For example, as Joseph Hardwick observes, "providential explanations flourished in early colonial Australia because they provided settlers with a sense of order and regularity in what appeared to be a variable and chaotic climate."[18] One prominent expression of this providential mindset was the observance of so-called humiliation days, state-sanctioned exercises in prayer and fasting intended to break a drought, and poetry provided a vehicle for affirming that providential ethos:

> The day was kept throughout the land,
> The rain came down in showers;
> And thus, in mercy to us all,
> God on us blessings pours.[19]

A more light-hearted view is offered in W. H. Dean's "The Parsonage Debt," where the need for rain clashes with a vicar's plan to hold a fundraising event: "I know, Lord, we needed a downpour of rain, / We have prayed for it all through the land, / But spare it, I pray, till some other day."[20] With the drought breaking despite this plea, the poem mocks religious small-mindedness but nevertheless reaffirms a providential view of the climate through answered prayer. At the same time, other writers employed poetry to convey deep skepticism toward the idea that the climate observed a divine logic. V. North's "A Western Story" describes a lack of rain so crippling that "in bitterness men muttered, 'God has cursed the / land throughout,'" and the observance of a humiliation day is dismissed as superficial by those suffering most directly: "And we read how in the townships they were offering prayers for rain: / There the drought affected pockets – here it taught starvation's pain."[21] Such examples point to the complex social function performed by settler literature amidst an environmental uncertainty experienced unevenly across different parts of the population.

Approaching Indigenous Writing

Engaging with nineteenth-century Indigenous writing on environmental matters in contexts of settler colonialism is a necessary yet fraught undertaking – and especially so for non-Indigenous critics. Ryan D. Fong writes of the need for engaging "Indigenous forms of expression more responsibly within our work in Victorian literary studies" as a central response to the field's "role in perpetuating the ideologies of settler colonialism and our responsibility to undertake the work of dismantling them."[22] Writing about the environment is central to this critical mission.

Although Indigenous peoples' ecological knowledges are highly localized and specific, Kyle Whyte (Potawatomi) argues that they share the commonality of deriving "economic vitality, cultural flourishing, and political self-determination from the relationships they have established with the plants, animals, physical entities, and ecosystems."[23] Nevertheless, while Indigenous writing in English was widespread – especially for purposes of advocacy and protest – there are relatively few instances of the use of Western poetic and fictional genres. Penny van Toorn points out that, in the Australian context, "there are no known pre-20th century Indigenous authored novels, plays or poems," whereas "humble" genres such as letters and petitions preferred by early Aboriginal authors nevertheless demonstrate "complex forms of language, narrative, political argument and self-construction."[24] On the one hand, Victorian studies is thus confronted with Indigenous writing's refusal to conform to its genre preferences. On the other, Victorianists lacking Indigenous insight also risk reinscribing a colonial dynamic if they assume Indigenous texts and references are fully legible to their usual interpretive approaches. At the least, Indigenous literature demands to be located as carefully and precisely as possible in cultural and historical terms through the foregrounding of Indigenous scholarship. In this section I focus on the prominent Mohawk writer Emily Pauline Johnson to offer a provisional demonstration of the need for literary interpretation to be informed by Indigenous environmental knowledge.

Johnson was one of the most prominent Indigenous writers to engage with British literary forms during the nineteenth century. Born to a settler mother and a Mohawk father, she was a member of the Haudenosaunee (Iroquois) confederacy and grew up on the Six Nations reserve at Grand River, Ontario. Author of *The White Wampum* (1895) and two subsequent collections of poetry, as well as numerous essays, Johnson chose during the 1890s to write and perform under her grandfather's name of Tekahionwake, and to "emphasize the Indigenous content of her poems" by assembling an "Indian costume" that could "play to settler audiences' expectations of stage Indians."[25] Rick Monture (Mohawk) argues that Johnson's legacy is "both useful and damaging to Indigenous peoples in Canada" due to the tension in her work "between her Iroquois identity and the desire to make herself, and all Iroquois, more acculturated Canadians."[26] That tension is often seen to play out in a distinction in Johnson's writings between those texts that foreground Indigenous perspectives and those that represent the natural environment in less culturally marked ways. Thus, her biographers point out that "only eight of the thirty-six poems in *The White Wampum* present explicitly Native subject matter," and contrast these with her "canoeing and nature poems, which strongly resemble similar verse by non-Native Canadian poets of the 1890s but, in the perception of contemporary and later readers, acquire an Indian inflection due to the public identity of their author."[27] However, Beth Brant (Mohawk) counters that Johnson's writings about the natural world express a Mohawk nationalism, and distinguishes her "great love for ... the Canada of oceans, mountains, pine trees, lakes, animals and birds" from the settler regime of "politicians and racism that attempted to regulate her people's lives."[28] In other words, even if Johnson's nature poetry might on the surface appear comparable to that of her settler contemporaries, it is nevertheless important to be open to the potential that it is informed by Haudenosaunee environmental understanding.

The risk that a non-Indigenous interpreter of Indigenous writing will reproduce a colonial dynamic is especially heightened in a field such as Victorian Studies that is so invested in the culture of the colonizer. A less domineering approach seems to require, at a minimum, an attempt to foreground an Indigenous worldview in the interpretation through the work of Indigenous writers and scholars. Prefacing a discussion of Johnson's nature poetry with a sketch of contrasting settler and Haudenosaunee perspectives therefore lays the groundwork for interpretations that might move beyond colonizing perspectives. On the settler side of the equation, portrayals of the natural environment offered by Canadian poets in the 1880s and 1890s were "largely guided by American nature writers," as D. M. R. Bentley points out, and especially by the work of John Burroughs.[29] Burroughs's influential essay "Nature and the Poets" (1881) firmly asserted a materialist view of the natural world. "It is the soul the poet interprets, not nature," Burroughs argues: "Nature is a dead clod until you have breathed upon it with your genius ... A tree, a cloud, a bird, a sunset, have no hidden meaning that the art of the poet is to unlock for us."[30] From a Haudenosaunee perspective, by contrast, James Costello and Brenda E. LaFrance (Mohawk) describe a relational cosmology that regards people – having been made last by the Creator – as "younger brothers and sisters to all of Creation."[31] The Haudenosaunee peoples are therefore oriented toward environmental gratitude and obligation, as exemplified in the institution of the Thanksgiving Address: "Our first instruction from the Creator is to recite the Thanksgiving Address, thereby acknowledging each particular natural or supernatural component of the environment with gratitude. Each component complements the natural, observable order and represents the parts of Creation: the things upon the ground with thanksgiving upward to the things in the sky world above."[32] The Thanksgiving Address is also a political statement, for its recitation reaffirms the unity of mind that enabled the establishment of the Haudenosaunee Confederacy.[33] Highlighting these contrasting dispositions towards the natural world aligns with Banerjee et al.'s call to "lateralize the British point of view or experience" in the nineteenth century by placing it "alongside and adjacent to other cultural moments and experiences with which it is nonetheless intimately connected."[34] At the same time, it is important to emphasize the brevity and shallowness of the account I have offered and thus to regard it as indicative rather than authoritative.

The interpretive significance of these divergent contexts can nevertheless be glimpsed by comparing one of Johnson's nature poems, "At Husking Time" (1891), with a Canadian settler poet's work on a similar seasonal theme, Archibald Lampman's "An Autumn Stream" (1895). Lampman describes a bleak and chilly scene where "patches of white corn / in the wind complain," and the landscape crystallizes the speaker's sense of melancholy:

> All things that be
> Seem plunged into silence, distraught,
> By some stern, some necessitous thought:
> It wraps and enthralls
> Marsh, meadow, and forest; and falls
> Also on me.[35]

Here, the environment becomes an index to the settler "soul," as in Burroughs's materialist account of nature poetry. To a reader attuned to read autumnal imagery in such "stern" terms, the opening lines of Johnson's poem may initially suggest a similar sense of decline: "At husking time the tassel fades / To brown above the yellow blades."[36] Yet in contrast to Lampman's "distraught" and depopulated landscape, the initial hint of energy conveyed by Johnson's iambic pentameter presages not only the sight of "merry lads and maids" involved in bringing in the corn harvest, but also the actions of multitudinous other living beings, including the "thieving raids" of crows, the "sly racoon with craft inborn," and the "saucy chipmunk."[37] Arguably, however, the most significant contrast with Lampman's version of the environment is hiding in plain sight: ó:nenhste, the corn itself. Whereas his "white corn" simply catches the settler's eye as another symbol of despondency, Johnson knew corn to be one of the Three Sisters, along with beans and squash, who grew from the body of the first woman, Earth Mother, and who remain "a foundational component" of the "cultural practices that shape Haudenosaunee relationship to the universe."[38] The story of the first harvest of the Three Sisters further explains that corn "leaves last after she has fully matured and is able to sustain the people throughout the winter months," and thus she also sustains relations of mutual responsibility and continuity: "the sisters need the people just as the people need them, in order to care for them in a way that ensures they can keep returning to the fields every year."[39] Approaching Johnson's "stalks and stubble, sacked and torn / At husking time" from the perspective of Haudenosaunee environmental knowledge,[40] shifts the poem away from the tropes of settler nature poetry and toward being read as an expression of thanksgiving for corn and its sustaining powers – and thus as an affirmation of Haudenosaunee self-determination.

Conclusion

This chapter suggests how the call for Victorianists to consider a "wide" nineteenth century might enable new approaches to the literature produced amidst the environments of the settler colonies. Those diverse settings were united in being the setting for what environmental historian Geoff Park describes as "the furious, meticulous work of Britain's mission": the voracious extraction of wealth from natural resources; a thoroughgoing determination to establish agricultural ecosystems; the belated realization of unanticipated environmental harms; and a willful disregard of Indigenous environmental relations and knowledge.[41] Writers in the colonies also drew on a common formal inheritance – the historicizing structures of romance and Gothic, the aesthetic principles of the picturesque and the sublime, and modes of irony and satire – which provided lenses through which settlers could view individual species and entire landscapes. At the same time, however, inherited forms could bend or break when faced with unfamiliar conditions. As New Zealand author Mary Colborne Veel observed:

> A Browning or Keats I would pity
> If writing his rhymes in this city:
> Or say that we fly from the town
> And seek Nature! – All barren and brown,
> Stretch out a monotonous plain,
> Too crude for a fanciful strain,
> Too vast for a poet to sing.[42]

Nevertheless, in constituting one of the most prominent noneconomic means by which the natural world was assessed and evaluated, literature functioned for settlers as a powerful and pervasive form of environmental knowledge. The intensely local referentiality of much settler writing means that its cultural and political stakes are often most evident when approached as a response to a particular place at a particular time. A local approach draws attention to the importance of the periodical press, and the newspaper in particular, as the seedbed of settler literary culture. At the same time, poetry is brought into focus as a key genre of ecological insight alongside travel literature, landscape painting, and photography. Moreover, engaging the local also brings to the fore the need to attend to the silences and omissions that profoundly structure settler literature, most notably those surrounding Indigenous peoples and their relations with nonhuman nature.

Notes

1. Sukanya Banerjee, Ryan D. Fong, and Helena Michie, "Introduction: Widening the Nineteenth Century," *Victorian Literature and Culture* 49.1 (2021), 1–26 at 11.
2. Anthony Trollope, *Australia and New Zealand* (Cambridge: Cambridge University Press, 2013), 1.3.
3. Jason R. Rudy, *Imagined Homelands: British Poetry in the Colonies* (Baltimore: Johns Hopkins University Press, 2017), 14.
4. Keith Thomas, *Man and the Natural World: Changing Attitudes in England 1500–1800* (London: Allen Lane, 1983), 195.
5. William Satchell, *The Toll of the Bush* (Auckland: Auckland University Press, 1985), 96, 224.
6. Edward Burnett Tylor, *Primitive Culture: Researches into the Development of Mythology, Philosophy, Religion, Art, and Custom* (Cambridge: Cambridge University Press, 2010), 1.286, 1.293.
7. James Cowan, "Te Wao-Nui-a-Tane," *New Zealand Illustrated Magazine* (1902), 200–9 at 200.
8. Cowan, "Te Wao-Nui-a-Tane," 203, 208, 207.
9. Alfred Sharpe, "A Reminiscence," *New Zealand Herald* (December 18, 1880), 3.
10. Mānuka Hēnare, "In Search of Harmony: Indigenous Traditions of the Pacific and Ecology," in Willis J. Jenkins, Mary Evelyn Tucker, and John Grim, eds., *Routledge Handbook of Religion and Ecology* (London: Routledge, 2016), 129–37 at 133.
11. George Phipps Williams, "A Globe-Trotter's Views on New Zealand," *Colonial Couplets: Being Poems in Partnership* (Christchurch: Simpson & Williams, 1889), 19–23 at 21, 22, original emphasis.
12. William Pember Reeves, "The Passing of the Forest," *New Zealand Herald* (24 December 1892), 8.
13. "Sigma," "The Late Drought," *Toowoomba Chronicle and Darling Downs General Advertiser* (February 23, 1884), 1.

14. Chris O'Brien, "Imported Understandings: Calendars, Weather, and Climate in Tropical Australia, 1870s–1940s," in James Beattie, Matthew Henry, and Emily O'Gorman, eds., *Climate, Science, and Colonization: Histories from Australia and New Zealand* (New York: Palgrave Macmillan, 2014), 195–211 at 198, 205.

15. Henry Lawson, "The Bush and the Ideal," *The Bulletin* 17.889 (1897), 2.

16. Henry Lawson, "The Paroo 'River,'" *The Bulletin* 14.743 (1894), 2.

17. Lawson, "The Paroo 'River,'" 2.

18. Joseph Hardwick, *Prayer, Providence and Empire: Special Worship in the British World, 1783–1919* (Manchester: Manchester University Press, 2021), 169.

19. R. E. Kemp, "After the Drought," *Kiama Independent, and Shoalhaven Advertiser* (8 February 1866), 4.

20. W. H. Dean, "The Parsonage Debt," *Molong Argus* (August 5, 1898), 1.

21. V. North, "A Western Story," *The Queenslander* (February 9, 1889), 257.

22. Ryan D. Fong, "The Stories Outside the African Farm: Indigeneity, Orality, and Unsettling the Victorian," *Victorian Studies* 62.3 (2020), 421–32 at 422.

23. Kyle Whyte, "Settler Colonialism, Ecology, and Environmental Injustice," *Environment and Society* 9.1 (2018), 125–44 at 126.

24. Penny van Toorn, *Writing Never Arrives Naked: Early Aboriginal Cultures of Writing in Australia* (Canberra: Aboriginal Studies, 2006), 3.

25. Carole Gerson and Veronica Strong-Boag, *Paddling Her Own Canoe: The Times and Texts of E. Pauline Johnson (Tekahionwake)* (Toronto: University of Toronto Press, 2000), 109, 110–11, 116.

26. Rick Monture, *We Share Our Matters | Teionkwakhashion Tsi Niionkwariho:ten: Two Centuries of Writing and Resistance at Six Nations of the Grand River* (Winnipeg: University of Manitoba Press, 2014), 64, 65.

27. Gerson and Strong-Boag, *Paddling Her Own Canoe*, 115.

28. Beth Brant, "The Good Red Road: Journeys of Homecoming in Native Women's Writing," *American Indian Culture and Research Journal* 21.1 (1997), 193–206 at 195.

29. D. M. R. Bentley, *The Confederation Group of Canadian Poets, 1880–1897* (Toronto: University of Toronto Press, 2004), 147.

30. John Burroughs, "Nature and the Poet," *Pepacton* (Boston: Houghton, Mifflin, 1901), 9–114 at 111–12.

31. James E. Costello and Brenda E. LaFrance, "The Haudenosaunee Environmental Protection Process (HEPP): Reinforcing the Three Principles of Goodmindedness, Peacefulness, and Strength to Protect the Natural World," in Chrstine Sternberg Patrick, ed., *Preserving Tradition and Understanding the Past: Papers from the Conference on Iroquois Research, 2001–2005* (New York: New York State Education Department, 2010), 61–8 at 63.

32. Costello and LaFrance, "Haudenosaunee Environmental," 62.

33. Jennifer Wemigwans and Lanna MacKay, "The Haudenosaunee Ohén:ton Karihwatéhkwen Thanksgiving Address: Moving beyond the Havoc of Land Acknowledgements," *Engaged Scholar Journal* 9.2 (2023), 1–21 at 9.

34. Banerjee et al., "Introduction," 5.

35. Archibald Lampman, "By an Autumn Stream," *Lyrics of Earth* (Boston: Copeland and Day, 1895), 42–4 at 43, 43–4.

36. E. Pauline Johnson, "At Husking Time," in Carole Gerson and Veronica Strong-Boag, eds., *E. Pauline Johnson, Tekahionwake: Collected Poems and Selected Prose* (Toronto: University of Toronto Press, 2002), 78.

37. Johnson, "At Husking Time," 78.

38. Lois Stevens and Joseph Brewer, "Ka'tshatstásla: 'Strength of Belief and Vision as a People' – Oneida Resilience and Corn," *Journal of Agriculture, Food Systems, and Community Development* 9.B (2019), 225–38 at 229.

39. Stevens and Brewer, "Ka'tshatstásla," 229.

40. Johnson, "At Husking Time," 47.

41. Geoff Park, *Ngā Uruora | The Groves of Life: Ecology & History in a New Zealand Landscape* (Wellington: Victoria University Press, 2018), 27.

42. Mary Colborne Veel, "The Poet's Lament," in Douglas B. W. Sladen, ed., *A Century of Australian Song* (London: Walter Scott, 1888), 501–503 at 501.

PART III

Vegetal and Animal Correlations

10

CATHERINE MAXWELL

Floral Poetics

Writing is rooted in the vegetable world. A book's pages are its "leaves" – the Latin word "folio," meaning "sheaf or leaf of paper," is still used to designate manuscript pages or more commonly a book printed on paper sheets of a large size. In most instances the pages themselves are of vegetable composition, originally deriving from the leaves of plants. The word "paper" derives from "papyrus," the pith of an aquatic sedge, laminated and pressed as sheets and widely used as a writing surface throughout the ancient Mediterranean world until the second century CE. In other cultures, various tree barks (mulberry, fig, and breadfruit, for example) were pounded down to make a thin writing surface, while there was a long practice of writing on palm leaves in India and Sri Lanka. Strips of bamboo shoot bound together served a similar purpose in China before the invention of paper around the second century CE. Although processing techniques and end-products varied, paper from recycled plant cellulose maintained its sway for almost two millennia. Obtained from a variety of sources including pulped linen and cotton rags, discarded hemp rope, canvas, and sometimes bark, cellulose was broken down, mixed with water, strained, and dried on screens to make paper sheets. The manufacture of wood-pulp paper is a relatively modern process which became widespread only in the 1840s. Vegetable elements have also played their part in other writing materials. Ink, made from a variety of natural substances, might contain soot or charcoal from carbonized wood, or tannic acid derived from oak-tree galls, while traditional writing implements have included reed or bamboo pens.[1]

When it comes to literary writing, the connection between plants and poetry has a long history, starting with the ancient Greek idea of poems as flowers (*anthoi*), with the anthology (*anthologia*), the garland (*stephanos*), and, later the *florilegium*, being a gathering or collection of poets' or writers' finest flowers. In English, the word "posy," meaning a small bunch of flowers held in the hand, is a variant of "poesy," an old word for "poetry," suggesting an intimate association between the two, with "posy" also occasionally used as a name for a collection of poems, as in *A Sweet Nosegay or Pleasant Posye* (1573) by Isabella Whitney, reputedly England's first woman poet and professional writer. Botanical nomenclature has been widely used in English titles since at least the sixteenth century, usually to denote a collection of poems either as a floral gathering such as a sheaf, wreath, bouquet, or nosegay, or, alternatively, as a space such as a wood, grove, or a contemplative or idyllic garden retreat where a choice selection of flowers bloom. Nineteenth-century examples of such titles include Walt Whitman's *Leaves of Grass* (1855), A. Mary F. Robinson's *A Handful of Honeysuckle* (1878) and *An Italian Garden* (1886), R. L. Stevenson's *A Child's Garden of Verses* (1885), and Eugene and Annie Lee-Hamiltons' *Forest Notes* (1899). Elkin Mathews's ten-volume "Shilling Garland" series (1895–8), later collected in two volumes as *Elkin Mathews' Garland of New Poetry* (1898–9), featured new verse by up-and-coming poets of the day such as Laurence Binyon, Mary E. Coleridge, and Robert Bridges, while *The Garland of New Poetry by Various Writers* (1898) included new and unpublished verse by contributors to the earlier series.

Alongside such collections which might or might not contain poems featuring plants and flowers are more particularized floral titles like Mark André Raffalovich's *Tuberose and Meadowsweet* (1885) or William Allingham's *Flower Pieces* (1888), volumes in which most or large swathes of the poems are dedicated to specific flowers. Other particularized titles such as May Probyn's *Pansies: A Book of Poems* (1895) or Theodore Wratislaw's *Orchids* (1896) feature only one or two flower poems, using the floral theme in a more allusive way – in the latter case to indicate the decadent exoticism of the book's contents.

Commenting on the use of named floral gatherings for collections, Dahlia Porter notes how, in particular, "the field of nineteenth-century annuals was lush with these figures."[2] These start with the famous *Forget-Me-Not* launched in 1823 and include titles such as *The Amaranth*, *The Bouquet, Chaplet, The Coronal, The Garland*, and *The Winter's Wreath*.[3] Claiming that "This efflorescence of the botanical metaphor was spurred by a vigorous debate about the purpose, audience, and content of poetic collections around 1800," Porter suggests that "Romantic era collections of poetry were not just metaphorically but also materially conditioned by the projects of botanical collecting, preservation, classification, description, and illustration of the previous century."[4] Botanical collecting and classification is an undoubted influence, although the links between poetry and plants are greatly enhanced throughout the nineteenth century by what might be called "the Victorian culture of flowers," a vastly increased interest not only in wild and garden plants and flowers, their acquisition, and cultivation, but also in pictorial, decorative, and ornamental schemes and images as well as in floral symbolisms. Pondering the many examples of flowers and leaves found pressed in nineteenth-century poetry texts as "souvenirs of Romantic reading," Andrew M. Stauffer declares that botanical material "was persuasively and complexly involved with poetry as it was written, published, and read in this era." With poets aware "that floral botanical practices were part of the field of reception: publishers and illustrators designed books that called them forth and echoed them; and readers engaged in this layered scene of instruction as they inserted blossoms and buds between the leaves."[5]

Yet in addition to more modern "floral botanical practices," English poetry arguably has its own longstanding green tradition sprung from "seminal" biblical and classical mythological sources. This revives memories not only of the gardens and groves of Eden, the Song of Solomon, the Elysian Fields, and Arcadia – along with the rural idylls of ancient eclogues, pastoral, and bucolic verse – but also mythical stories of transformation in which certain plants have their origins in human bodies and identities, and in which human identities merge into those of plants. This will be an important theme in what follows but we might start by observing that even nineteenth-century poets often retain a special association with flowers and plants that become signs of their identities. Some of those interleaved blossoms and buds mentioned by Stauffer, as well as possibly referencing particular poems, might be mementoes of the poets themselves. In "Lines on the Death of Sir Walter Scott," Joanna Baillie observes of her subject's grave at Dryborough: "Flower, herb, or leaf by children yet unborn / Will often from thy verdant turf be torn, / And kept in dear memorial of the place."[6] Samantha Matthews remarks that "the violets removed from Keats's grave in Rome and preserved in books were legion," and elsewhere I have shown how Keats and Shelley are associated with the violet and its scent, a flower that variously signifies music, mourning, remembrance, and regeneration.[7] The Victorian artist Charles Ricketts designed a border of violet flowers and leaves for the opening pages of his 1898 Vale Press edition of Keats's poems and a border of pansies (also from the *Violaceae* family) for his 1901 Vale Press edition of Shelley's poems, presumably recalling the poet's short lyric "Remembrance" – "Pansies let *my* flowers be: / On the living grave I bear" – and the figure of the mourning "Frail Form" in "Adonais" (1821), usually identified with Shelley himself, whose "head was bound with pansies overblown, / And faded violets, white, and pied, and blue."[8] Other poets have come to be associated with specific flowers they hymned such as Chaucer with the daisy, called in *The Legend of Good Women* "the emperice, and floure of floures alle," Blake with the sunflower, and Wordsworth with the daffodil.[9] William Allingham in the sequence "Flowers and Poets" in his *Flower Pieces* ignores such conventional associations to assign his own symbolic flower to each of his chosen subjects, musing subjectively on the links between Chaucer and the wallflower, Milton and the agave, Keats and the hyacinth, Shelley and the Egyptian lotos, and Tennyson and jasmine.[10]

The garland or wreath that may denote a poetry collection can also signify a poet's crown or chaplet bestowed as an award for verse-making. Traditionally this would be bay laurel (*Laurus nobilis*), sacred to Apollo, the god of music and lyrical poetry, being the transformed body of Daphne, his unwilling inamorata, whom he nonetheless pledges to honor by making her leaves evergreen, wearing them wreathed in his hair and on his bow and lyre, and by decreeing that they are carried in triumphal military processions.[11] Yet in classical times a poet's crown could be made of other leaves such as myrtle, olive, ivy, and vine. The second canto of Elizabeth Barrett Browning's narrative poem *Aurora Leigh* (1856) opens with Aurora, an aspiring woman poet, surprised by her cousin Romney as she is playfully yet symbolically crowning herself with a wreath of ivy on the morning of her twentieth birthday. She subsequently parries his patronizing remarks about women's poetry, refusing his marriage proposal to defend her chosen career and the importance of poetry as a spiritually renovative force. As Ellen Moers has shown, Aurora's crowning scene alludes to Germaine de Staël's celebrated novel *Corinne, ou L'Italie* (1807), whose heroine, a renowned late eighteenth-century female poet, is honored, like the celebrated poets Petrarch and Tasso, by being crowned with laurels at the Capitoline Hill in Rome.[12] This famous episode had also inspired another source for Barrett Browning, "Corinne at the Capitol" (originally "Corinna at the Capitol," 1826), a well-known poem depicting this coronation by the popular British poet Felicia Hemans, which celebrates its female subject with the lines: "Radiant daughter of the sun! / Now thy living wreath is won."[13] Images of wreaths and garlands are thus commonplace on the covers and frontispieces of Victorian poetry books while the German publisher Ernest Nister produced a "Laurel Wreath" series of decorative color-illustrated editions of famous texts including poetry titles such as Barrett Browning's *Sonnets from the Portuguese* (1891), Tennyson's *A Dream of Fair Women* (1892), and Edward FitzGerald's translation of *The Rubáiyát of Omar Khayyám* (1904).

By the Victorian period, flowers are an essential part of the poetic fabric, with poetry writing and poethood commonly seen as intertwined with images of flowers. While flower-wreathed annuals and poetry books are conceived and marketed as attractive gifts, the lyric poem itself is frequently seen as a flower and often a floral offering, one that has the power to endure while actual flowers fade and die. It is commonplace for a prefatory or a dedicatory poem to include images of the poet's poems as flowers or leaves thus reprising the "folio-page" connection (though "leaf," as in "rose-leaf," can also mean "petal"). In "Dedication 1865," written for Edward Burne-Jones, which closes *Poems and Ballads* (1866), Algernon Swinburne is simultaneously self-deprecating and self-assured, referring to his verse as "the firstfruits of me" (and thus implying that it may be negligible or immature), while also alluding to the poet's crown and reprising Shelley's image in "Ode to the West Wind" of his poems as "dead thoughts" blown "Like withered leaves to quicken a new birth!":[14]

> Let the wind take the green and the grey leaf,
>   Cast forth without fruit upon air;
> Take rose-leaf and vine-leaf and bay-leaf
>   Blown loose from the hair.[15]

Addressing her grandparents in the dedicatory sonnet that prefaces *Songs and Sonnets of Springtime* (1881), Constance Naden asks them to "Accept this wreath, entwined in April hours: / Yours was the garden where the seed was set, / To you I dedicate the opening flowers."[16] In the prefatory sonnet to *A Handful of Honeysuckle*, Mary Robinson imagines the poems of her first published collection as the flowers of her title – "I gather from the hedgerows where they spring, / These sunshine-yellow flowers, grown sweet i' the air," offering their apparent simplicity to her readers in an elegant gesture of self-deprecation.[17] Olive Custance in the initial poem of *Opals* (1897), "Love's Firstfruits," recycles her title image from Swinburne's "Dedication," offering her lover in her poems "the fruitage of first love," grown from a "flower but faintly touched with passion's pink" into a mature fruit "framed in girlhood's life of leaves."[18]

In lieu of a prefatory floral lyric, Mark André Raffalovich includes two lines from Swinburne's flower poem "Relics" (1873) on the title page of *Tuberose and Meadowsweet* – "Such words of message have dead flowers to say … / Before I throw them and these words away" – indicating that his own flower-themed poems carry an important communication.[19] Immediately beneath this quotation is the frontispiece image of a rose with the Latin motto "Sub hoc signa vinces," a near quotation of the motto that accompanied the Emperor Constantine's vision of the cross "In hoc signa vinces" ("In this sign you shall conquer"), betokening his success in battle after his conversion to Christianity. However, Raffalovich's emendation "sub," meaning "under," signifies "under the rose," a phrase that alludes to the rose as a sign for secrecy and confidentiality, and thus hints at the efficacy of discretion and the "coded" nature of his own floral poetic collection which celebrates love between men. Poetry as plant allows a different kind of expressive outlet for the disabled poet Eugene Lee-Hamilton, prostrated by a long-term illness. In his poetic "Introduction" to *The New Medusa, and Other Poems* (1882) he refers to Xavier Boniface Santine's popular novel *Picciola* (1836), which features a political prisoner who endures his long confinement by cultivating into a strong plant a small seedling grown through the cracks of his exercise yard. The plant which becomes his friend and companion he calls by the Italian feminine diminutive "Picciola" meaning "dear little one." Exclaiming "Oh such another Picciola hast thou, / My prison-nurtured Poetry, long been," Lee-Hamilton declares:

> This book is all a plant of prison-growth,
> Watered with prison water, not sweet rain;
> The writer's limbs and mind are laden both
> By heavy chains.[20]

English elegy, shaped by classical models, also calls on plants and flowers as an essential part of its formal content. Following the famous example of Milton's "Lycidas" (1636), the elegiac poet's offering of flowers as part of his funerary celebration is a tradition that continues into nineteenth-century elegies in which poets commemorate their fellow poets with floral tributes, as in Shelley's *Adonais*, Letitia Landon's "Stanzas on the Death of Mrs Hemans" (1835), and Swinburne's "Ave atque Vale" (1868), with the "flowers" often signaled as interchangeable with verse itself. In the first stanza of Swinburne's elegy the speaker asks his dead "brother" poet, Charles Baudelaire, subsequently acknowledged as "the gardener of strange flowers,"[21] what he would prefer as a farewell offering – the more conventional "rose or rue or laurel," "quiet" or "simple" wildflowers, or exotic "fiery blossoms,"[22] more typical of his notorious *Les Fleurs du mal* (1857). Yet, as I have shown elsewhere, Swinburne himself tends to prefer those quiet or simple wildflowers, so his elegy with its rather overblown descriptions of Baudelairean flowers – "Green buds of sorrow and sin, and remnants grey, / Sweet-smelling, pale with poison"[23] – also suggests that he is putting some distance between himself and his illustrious precursor.[24] Later in the poem the speaker also represents himself as offering to "the gods of gloom" more palatable fare – "And what of honey and spice my seedlands bear, / And what I may of fruits in this chilled air."[25] Tennyson in stanza 8 of "In Memoriam A. H. H." (1850) imagines planting "this poor flower of poesy" on Arthur Hallam's tomb "That if it can it there may bloom, / Or dying, there at least may die."[26] Paying tribute to Charlotte Brontë in "Haworth Churchyard" (1855), Matthew Arnold declares "Strew with laurel the grave of the early-dying!" noting that her premature death "leaves / Half her laurels unwon … yet green / Laurels she had."[27] Commemorating his friend Arthur Hugh Clough in "Thyrsis" (1865), Arnold's verse revives "The coronals of that forgotten time,"[28] the now many vanished flowers of the Oxfordshire countryside they once explored together. Laurence Binyon opens his *Lyric Poems* (1894) with "In Carissimam Memoriam A. S. P.," an elegiac dedication to his beloved aunt Agatha Sophia Phillips (not a poet but the muse who encouraged him to write), offering to lay "these few leaves" on her grave:

> Now my flowers' poor grace
> I bring to bloom or fade; I little care.
> Ah let them fade and die in that dear place!
> It is enough, if they have faded *there*.[29]

In *Underneath the Bough* (1893), Katharine Bradley, writing for the poetic duo that is Michael Field, compares other poets (implicitly herself and Edith Cooper) to defoliating branches – "Slowly we disarray / Our leaves grow few" – in contrast to the recently departed Robert Browning who is evergreen and "fills fresh as Apollo's bay, / The Hand of God."[30]

More commonly in elegiac verse the deceased, rather than being evergreen, is a flower, something beautiful but fragile, evoking the shortness of life, as in the words of the biblical book of Job (14 v.1) used in the Christian funeral service: "Man that is born of a woman is of few days, and full of trouble. He cometh forth like a flower, and is cut down." That flower is often cut down prematurely or doomed like Keats in "Adonais": "The bloom, whose petals nipp'd before they blew / Died on the promise of the fruit, is waste; / The broken lily lies."[31] The phrase "the flower of" most often denotes peak perfection, as when Tennyson's speaker in "In Memoriam" mourns the day "I lost the flower of men,"[32] with the Greek elegiac poets frequently associating the phrase "the flower of youth" with brevity and death.[33] The elegiac poem as flower thus specifically preserves the fading dead flower of the deceased. A type of self-elegy, Shelley's influential poem "The Sensitive-Plant" (1820) evokes the *Mimosa pudica* which shies away from touch or contact and has often been read as an allegory of the poet; it tells a kind of cautionary tale using the image of the vulnerable plant and its need for nurture and a sympathetic environment to signify the optimal conditions for creative flourishing. Shelley returned to the image of the vulnerable poet as plant in his later unfinished poem "The Zucca" (dated January 1822), in which a dying plant, seen as a fellow spirit, is rescued, and nursed back to life by the sympathizing hypersensitive speaker.

Like "Adonais" and "The Sensitive-Plant," much other English poetry has its roots vitalized by vegetal classical myth via Ovid's *Metamorphoses*, a highly influential Latin poetical text which includes tales of botanical transformation, the coming-into-being of new plants and flowers from human bodies. These foundational stories commemorate figures including Adonis (anemone), Clytie (heliotrope), Daphne (laurel), Hyacinthus (hyacinth), Mintha (mint), Myrrha (myrrh tree), Narcissus (narcissus), and Syrinx (reed). Some of these plants and flowers become mnemonic texts, being marked or stained – usually with blood – thereafter telling the story of the one whose trace or wound they commemorate. In *Metamorphoses* Book 10, Aphrodite changes the blood of her slain lover Adonis into the blood-red anemone, while Apollo inscribes "Ai, Ai," words of lamentation, on the petals of the flower that he creates from the shed blood of his dead lover, the beautiful Hyacinthus.

Various of these plant myths germinate individual Victorian poems – Michael Field's "Apollo's Triumph" (featuring Daphne) and "Mintha"; John Addington Symonds's "The Daffodil I: Narcissus Flower"; and Elizabeth Barrett Browning's "A Musical Instrument" (1860) featuring Pan violently creating a flute from the reed.[34] In Ovid's tale the reed is Syrinx, the nymph Pan had frantically pursued who escaped him by her metamorphosis. Pan then found that his frustrated sighs over the hollow reed drew forth her musical voice and, charmed by this, transformed her into his own personal set of pipes. Barrett Browning's poem enlarges on that second metamorphosis, with the god ruthlessly "Making a poet out of a man." Pan's aggressive fashioning of the reed into a musical instrument strongly suggests the suffering involved in gaining poethood, and specifically perhaps – despite the generic "man" – female poethood. Noticeably Barrett Browning does not name or gender her reed – perhaps to universalize her message, perhaps to minimize the disturbing sexual implications of Pan's brutalizing treatment. Less than a month after her death, Francis Turner Palgrave's *Golden Treasury of English Songs and Lyrics*, one of the most famous Victorian anthologies of poetry, appeared in July 1861. It may have lacked a floral title, but its frontispiece vignette by Thomas Woolner, engraved by Charles Henry Jeens, pictured Pan blowing on a flute, an evident allusion to the Pan-Syrinx story which links poets and poetry to plants. Alfred Tennyson, Palgrave's friend, would later remark of Swinburne: "He is a reed through which all things blow into music."[35]

Contrasting with more overtly Ovidian stories, Thomas Hardy's more speculative "Transformations," from *Moments of Vision* (1917), apparently set in a churchyard, muses how recent human remains, absorbed into nature's cycle of decay and regeneration, might inform or enter into the vegetal life he sees around him. Yet the imagined sentience of the meta-morphosed dead nudges the poem back to its pagan classical roots, disso-ciating it from the purely natural rhythms of material decomposition and conversion:

> Portion of this yew
> Is a man my grandsire knew,
> Bosomed here at its foot:
> This branch may be his wife,
> A ruddy human life
> Now turned to a green shoot.
>
> These grasses must be made
> Of her who often prayed,
> Last century, for repose;
> And the fair girl long ago
> Whom I often tried to know
> May be entering this rose.
>
> So, they are not underground,
> But as nerves and veins abound
> In the growths of upper air,
> And they feel the sun and rain,
> And the energy again
> That made them what they were![36]

The same Ovidian spirit enters "Rain on a Grave," where thinking about his first wife's death, Hardy imagines that:

> Soon will be growing
>   Green blades from her mound,
> And daisies be showing
>   Like stars on the ground,
> Till she form part of them –
> Ay – the sweet heart of them,
> Loved beyond measure
> With a child's pleasure
>   All her life's round.[37]

Again, this is a transformation that does not erase the identity of the deceased as Hardy hopefully and tenderly imagines his wife's body and spirit entering into the fragrant centers of the daisies on her grave – fittingly flowers with which she had a special lifelong affinity and which in both their appearance and fragrance seem emblematic of her innocent nature.

Thus, while many elegiac poems preserve and commemorate the dead flower of the deceased, other poetic flowers spring directly from more literal botanical embodiments of dead or transformed bodies, taking nourishment from them and channeling their energies.

But if the poem is a flower, poets may also represent themselves as gardeners or sowers and their creative consciousness as a bower or garden plot. As previously seen in "Ave atque Vale," Swinburne refers to his "seedlands" and Baudelaire as "the gardener of strange flowers," while an early Tennyson poem, "The Poet's Mind" (1830), imagines that secluded mental space as a "garden" hedged round by flowering "laurel-shrubs,"[38] which help keep out sneering detractors. In a later sardonic lyric, "The Flower" (1864), Tennyson portrays himself as a poetic innovator whose original, distinctively different bloom meets with critical disapproval:

> Once in a golden hour
>   I cast to earth a seed.
> Up there came a flower,
>   The people said, a weed.
> To and fro they went
>   Thro' my garden-bower,
> And muttering discontent
>   Cursed me and my flower.

However, when his poetry finally flourishes, imitators "steal" his style and the verse they produce becomes widely acknowledged and approved. Moreover,

> Most can raise the flowers now,
>   For all have got the seed.
> And some are pretty enough,
>   And some are poor indeed;
> And now again the people
>   Call it but a weed.[39]

Tennyson is contemptuous about his poetic successors, but A. E. Housman in "LXIII: I Hoed and Trenched and Weeded," the last poem in *A Shropshire Lad* (1896), is more generous about his legacy. As in Tennyson's poem, the speaker finds the flowers he labored to produce are unappreciated – "The hue was not the wear." However, he persists:

> So up and down I sow them
>   For lads like me to find,
> When I shall lie below them,
>   A dead man out of mind.

Drawing on the New Testament parable of the sower from Matthew 14. 3-8, which depicts the way a message may be either ignored or heeded and further disseminated, his hope is that:

138

> But here and there will flower,
>   The solitary stars,
>
> And fields will yearly bear them
>   As light-leaved spring comes on,
> And luckless lads will wear them
>   When I am dead and gone.[40]

In the light of Housman's own homosexuality, a theme that underpins *A Shropshire Lad*, the poem suggests his wish that his gay successors will "wear," that is own and acknowledge, his poems (and presumably their own indebted poems) after he himself has died. The "poems as flowers" here function as a badge of gay identity – a more bucolic, less flamboyant version of Oscar Wilde's "green carnation." Indeed, it transpires that Housman sent a copy of *A Shropshire Lad* to Wilde after he left Reading Gaol, although before that Robert Ross had learnt some of the poems and recited them when visiting him in prison. Later, during his exile in France, Wilde wrote to Laurence Housman praising "your brother's lovely lyrical poems."[41]

These and other floral associations are arguably integral to much Victorian poetry where of course "actual" flowers with their own particular significations are frequently the focus of verse. For if the poem is a flower, the flower is also often a poem being an archetypal subject for poetry. A survey of such flower portraits and their purposes must await another more studied examination, but I conclude by noting how such poems can also revive the ideas already explored in this chapter when floral depictions reassert their essential bond with poetry. Thus Michael Field delight in hymning the natural qualities of lilies – "Brown and gold and tiger-brown, / Wreathing many a spotted crown," "Burnished, tumultuous, immense" – in a celebratory lyric that addresses Christ while remembering his own words about the resplendent "lilies of the field" that "toil not, neither do they spin" because they are clothed and cared for by God (Matthew 6.28).[42] Yet Field's signature lilies are also an aestheticist or "art for art's sake" motif – "They do not spin / And yet such fabulous beauty win" – while the lyric's title "Poets" (1908) and its opening line "Consider them thy poets, how they grow, / Thy lilies of the field"[43] identifies the flowers with lyric artists who produce pure beauty without fretting about its utility. Thus, a poem or poet may be a flower, but flowers may also be poems or poets.

Notes

1. Mark Kurlansky, *Paper: Paging through History* (New York: W. W. Norton, 2016).
2. Dahlia Porter, "Specimen Poetics, Botany, Reanimation and the Romantic Collection," *Representations* 139 (2017), 60–94 at 61.

3. See Frederick Winthrop Faxon, *Literary Annuals and Gift-Books: A Bibliography with a Descriptive Introduction* (Boston: The Boston Book Company, 1912).

4. Porter, "Specimen Poetics," 61, 62.

5. Andrew M. Stauffer, *Book Traces: Nineteenth-Century Readers and the Future of the Library* (Philadelphia: University of Pennsylvania Press, 2021), 21.

6. Joanna Baillie, "Lines of the Death of Sir Walter Scott," *The Dramatic and Poetical Works of Joanna Baillie* (London: Longman, Brown, Green, and Longmans, 1851), 794.

7. Samantha Matthews, *Poetical Remains: Poets' Graves, Bodies and Books in the Nineteenth Century* (Oxford: Oxford University Press, 2004), 12; Catherine Maxwell, *Scents and Sensibility: Perfume in Victorian Literary Culture* (Oxford: Oxford University Press, 2017), 77–80.

8. Percy Bysshe Shelley, "Remembrance" and "Adonais," *Shelley: Poetical Works*, ed. Thomas Hutchinson, rev. G. M. Matthews (Oxford: Oxford University Press, 1970), 643, 439.

9. Geoffrey Chaucer, "The Legend of Good Women," in F. N. Robinson, ed., *The Works of Geoffrey Chaucer*, 2nd ed. (Boston: Houghton Mifflin Co., 1957), 486.

10. William Allingham, "Flowers and Poets," *Flower Pieces* (London: Reeves and Turner, 1888), 15–25.

11. See Ovid, *Metamorphoses*, Book 1, 553–67.

12. Ellen Moers, *Literary Women* (New York: Doubleday & Co., 1976), 182.

13. Felicia Hemans, "Corinne at the Capitol," in *The Poetical Works of Felicia Hemans* (London: Ward, Lock & Co., 1882), 324.

14. Shelley, *Shelley: Poetical Works*, 579.

15. Algernon Charles Swinburne, "Dedication 1865," in Kenneth Haynes, ed., *Poems and Ballads* (London: Penguin, 2000), 234.

16. Constance C. W. Naden, "Dedication," *Songs and Sonnets of Springtime* (London: C. Kegan Paul, 1881), v.

17. A. Mary F. Robinson, "Honeysuckle," *A Handful of Honeysuckle* (London: C. Kegan Paul, 1878), iv.

18. Olive Custance, "Love's Firstfruits," in *Opals* (London: John Lane, 1897), 1–2.

19. Mark André Raffalovich, *Tuberose and Meadowsweet* (London: David Bogue, 1885), iii; Swinburne, "Relics," originally published as "North and South" (1873), then in *Poems and Ballads*, 2 (1878). See Algernon Swinburne, *The Collected Poetical Works of Algernon Charles Swinburne*, 6 vols. (London: Chatto & Windus, 1904), 3.28.

20. Eugene Lee-Hamilton, "Introduction," in *The New Medusa and Other Poems* (London: Elliot Stock, 1882), 7–11 at 8.

21. Swinburne, "Ave atque Vale," *The Collected Poetical Works*, 3.52.

22. Swinburne, "Ave atque Vale," *The Collected Poetical Works*, 3.50.

23. Swinburne, "Ave atque Vale," *The Collected Poetical Works*, 3.57.

24. See Maxwell, *Scents and Sensibility*, 101.

25. Swinburne, "Ave atque Vale," *The Collected Poetical Works*, 3.54.

26. Tennyson, "In Memoriam A. H. H.," in Christopher Ricks, ed., *The Poems of Tennyson in Three Volumes*, 2nd ed., 3 vols. (Harlow: Longman, 1987), 2.327.

27. Matthew Arnold, "Haworth Churchyard" *Arnold: The Complete Poems*, ed. Kenneth and Miriam Allott, 2nd ed. (Harlow: Longman, 1979), 427.

28. Arnold, "Thyrsis," *Arnold: The Complete Poems*, 544.

29. Laurence Binyon, *Lyric Poems* (London: Elkin Mathews, 1894), 9, 11.

30. Michael Field, *Underneath the Bough* (London: George Bell & Sons, 1893), 31.

31. Shelley, "Adonais," *Shelley: Poetical Works*, 433.

32. Tennyson, "In Memoriam," stanza 99, *The Poems of Tennyson*, 2.419.

33. See William Brockliss, *Homeric Imagery and the Natural Environment*, Hellenic Studies Series 82 (Washington, DC: Center for Hellenic Studies, 2019), 312–13.

34. Michael Field, "Apollo's Triumph," *Underneath the Bough* (1898), 79; "Mintha," *Wild Honey from Various Thyme* (London: T. Fisher Unwin, 1908), 11; John Addington Symonds, "The Daffodil I: Narcissus Flower," *The Century Guild Hobby Horse* 2.8 (October 1887), 121; Elizabeth Barrett Browning, "A Musical Instrument," (1860), collected in *Last Poems* (1862), *The Poetical Works of Elizabeth Barrett Browning* (London: Smith, Elder & Co., 1904), 538.

35. Hallam Tennyson, *Alfred Lord Tennyson: A Memoir*, 2 vols. (London: Macmillan, 1897), 2.85.

36. Thomas Hardy, "Transformations," in James Gibson, ed., *The Complete Poems of Thomas Hardy* (London: Macmillan, 1976), 476.

37. Hardy, "Rain on a Grave,"in Gibson, ed., *The Complete Poems of Thomas Hardy*, 341–2

38. Tennyson, "The Poet's Mind," *The Poems of Tennyson*, 1.245.

39. Tennyson, "The Flower," *The Poems of Tennyson*, 2.684.

40. A. E. Housman, "LXIII: I hoed and trenched and weeded," in *A Shropshire Lad* (London: The Richards Press, 1896), 95–6.

41. See Housman to Seymour Adelman, 21 June 1928 in *The Letters of A. E. Housman*, ed. Henry Maas (London: Rupert Hart-Davis, 1971), 267; *The Complete Letters of Oscar Wilde*, ed. Merlin Holland and Rupert Hart-Davis (New York: Henry Holt and Company, 2000), 923.

42. Michael Field, "Poets," in Marion Thain and Ana Parejo Vadillo, eds., *Michael Field: The Poet: Published and Manuscript Materials*(Peterborough: Broadview Press, 2009), 221.

43. Field, "Poets," 221.

11

MICHAEL MARDER

Vegetal Ontology in Emily Dickinson's Poetic Herbarium

It is hard to tell where, in Emily Dickinson's corpus, plants end and words begin. An avid gardener and herbarium-maker, she had the habit of sending pressed plants together with her letters and poems to family and friends. Thus "her poetry, for the most part privately 'published,' was often enclosed in letters pinned together by flowers, or in bouquets that made the poem concealed at the flowers' center and the flowers themselves one message."[1] The practice and theme of "a flower in a letter" was not idiosyncratic to Emily Dickinson but, like the tendencies of the plants themselves, seeded itself among various writers from across national frontiers. And it was poetry that proved especially conducive to the practice. Indeed, Elizabeth Barrett Browning dedicated to the genre an entire twenty-stanza poem.[2] Poems spoke silently from, with, and through flower arrangements – and often enough they did so *about* flowers. Not only the form and content of the messages were vegetal; so was the act of sending, disseminating the herbarium as so many seeds, spores, or grains of pollen, preceded by lovingly tending to plants in a garden or hothouse conservatory, walking in forests and meadows, gathering and preserving flowers. For Dickinson, an herbarium was a poetry collection, while a poetry collection was an herbarium, expressing fragility and tenacious preservation, humid vitality and dryness, mortality and the afterlife of mortal remains, vegetal and human.

Dickinson and the Victorian Tradition

Dickinson's poetic herbarium speaks to a tradition that flourished in various countries during the nineteenth century and reaches back to earlier epochs. One might place Dickinson within a tradition that was popular among Victorians, with her as an American reminding us that the notion of "Victorian" has porous boundaries as far as both literature and politics are concerned. Analogous practices and preferences, like genres and authors, developed across nationalities, geographies, and time periods. In

The Wayward Nun of Amherst, Angela Conrad lists St. Hildegard of Bingen and her creative principal of *viriditas* among Dickinson's mystical precursors.[3] This broad network of dissemination can be sensed in an early poem of Dickinson's from 1859 that encrypts vegetal sending in the sending that is the poem itself:

> Angels, in the early morning
> May be seen the Dews among,
> Stooping – plucking – smiling – flying –
> Do the Buds to them belong?
> Angels, when the sun is hottest
> May be seen the sands among
> Stooping – plucking – sighing – flying –
> Parched the flowers they bear along.[4]

An angel (*angelos*) is a messenger, an envoy. The message these angels carry is composed of buds and flowers as much as written or spoken words, the budding promise of a future, which they encounter and pluck with a smile in the morning dew, and the parched, invariably betrayed realizations of that promise in a future of no-future. The angels of plants deliver the messages of life and death, of a flourishing future and a futureless future, of the forest and the desert, the moist budding of vitality and mortiferous desiccation. They deliver both with the same patient gestures, along the same trajectories of stooping, plucking, flying … with but one difference: a smile here, a sigh there.

The entire drama of Hildegard's visions is condensed in these poetic lines. In particular, Dickinson seems to be restaging the elemental and cosmic clash of *viriditas* – "greenness," or the self-refreshing power of finite existence that reaches its apotheosis in plants – and *ariditas* – "dryness," or the scorching heat of sin understood in the extra-moral sense of everything that contravenes life and its renewal. Is the actual drying of plants in preparation for their admission to an herbarium complicit in the dynamics of *ariditas*? Do postal-vegetal angels transmit, with an invariable sigh, a message of death, regardless of the kind of future they carry along? Even the desert sands, embodying mortiferous *ariditas*, are incapable of driving flowers away, parched as they may be, nor of dealing a lethal blow to the tenacious capacities of *viriditas*. As another nineteenth-century poet of plant life, Christina Rossetti, has inquired, in "Yea I have a Goodly Heritage":

> But if my lot be sand where nothing grows? –
> Nay who hath said it? Tune a thankful psalm:
> For, though thy desert bloom not as a rose,
> It yet can rear thy palm.[5]

Fifteen-year-old Emily, penning a letter to her close friend Abiah Root on September 25, 1845, asks:

> Have you any flowers now? I have had a beautiful flower-garden this summer; but they are nearly gone now. It is very cold to-night, and I mean to pick the prettiest ones before I go to bed, and cheat Jack Frost of so many of *the treasures* he calculates to rob to-night. Won't it be a capital idea to put him at defiance, for once at least, if no more? I would love to send you a bouquet if I had an opportunity, and you could press it and write under it, The last flowers of summer. Wouldn't it be poetical, and you know that is what young ladies aim to be now-a-days.[6]

This line of reasoning holds an important insight regarding Dickinson's adaptation of the creative principal of *viriditas*. As summer fades into fall, flowers wilt until they are finally "robbed" by the premonition of winter. In keeping with ancient and medieval metaphorology, the seasons represent times of life: the promise of youth in the spring, the adult vigor of the summer, the maturity and decline of the fall, and wintery death, replete with the hopeful anticipation of rebirth the following spring. Dickinson's approach, however, is at the same time allegorical and literal: delivering their angelic missives, delivering *themselves* as angelic missives, plants provide her with a way of dealing with the inexorability of death and of its extreme cold, matched only by the equally unbearable lethal heat of desert noon. Refracted through the time of plants, the seasons are not only the actual seasons, but also stand-ins for the stages of life, interwoven with death.[7]

A similar mix of literalness and allegoricity is applicable to an herbarium. "Cheating" Jack Frost is robbing him of what he was going to rob, namely the vegetal "treasures" that convey life itself. But to cheat death, "to put him at defiance, for once at least," the maker of an herbarium has to incorporate its strategy into her actions, to pluck the prettiest flowers a little before their seasonally appointed time, to make a bouquet out of them, which would be preserved by her addressee. The herbarium provides Dickinson with an apparatus for mobilizing death against death, playing along and disrupting its routines.

Epistolary herbaria are collaborative affairs, commenced in the company of plants and entrusted to other human beings for further elaboration. As such, they remain radically incomplete, breathing with life. In a previous letter to Abiah Root, dated May 7, 1845, Dickinson will have written:

> My plants look finely now. I am going to send you a little geranium leaf in this letter, which you must press for me. Have you made you an herbarium yet? I hope you will if you have not, it would be such a treasure to you; 'most all the girls are making one. If you do, perhaps I can make some additions to it from flowers growing around here.[8]

Again, the herbarium is deemed a "treasure," conveying a living vegetal form stolen from the clutches of death, albeit at the price of this form's humid vivacity. But if the apparatus of the herbarium is one that mobilizes death against death, then it does so also by de-privatizing death, by smudging the lines not only between vitality and mortality, but also between dispersal and gathering, not least thanks to the postal service.[9] And this smudging approximates the features of vegetal ontology itself, where the one and the many, articulation and disarticulation, gains and losses, and, finally, life and death aren't the polar opposites they are habitually taken to be.

The dispersal of a plant herbarium and poems (or, according to a prevalent mid Victorian pun, "'posies' and 'poesie'"[10]) is informed by the techniques of neutralizing death. The addressee is thoroughly implicated in the structure and process of the angelic address, not just as its recipient but as an active participant. On the face of it, the gendered references in the letters (cheating *him*, Jack Frost, who "calculates to rob" many treasures tonight, before "I go to bed"; "what young ladies aim to be now-a-days"; "'most all the girls are making one," an herbarium) indicate that teenage Emily's endeavor is unfolding in the context of Victorian repression and a displacement of human sexuality onto plant sexuality. The apparently disincarnate figure of the angel may be also pinned onto this historico-cultural constellation. Objectively correct, such a reading runs the risk of overlooking that there is much more to her words and deeds than this: the lighter side of irony, "Wouldn't it be poetical, and you know that is what young ladies aim to be now-a-days,"[11] or, in a poem, "Tis sweet to know that stocks will stand / When we with Daisies lie – / That Commerce will continue – / And Trades as briskly fly,"[12] and the seriousness of joining the stirrings of vegetal ontology, of vegetalizing *oneself*.

Dickinson was fascinated with and well versed in botany. Judith Farr observes that influences would have likely included major contemporary botanists from both the US and Britain such as Asa Gray and Erasmus Darwin.[13] She did not, however, aim to convert herbaria into scientific tools, which would undersign and intensify death's final verdict. In a poem, she brands as monstrous the scientific procedure dealing with plant:

> I pull a flower from the woods –
> A monster with a glass
> Computes the stamens in a breath –
> And has her in a "class"![14]

Or, in another piece:

> If the foolish, call them *'flowers'* –
> Need the wiser, *tell*?

> If the Savants 'Classify' them
> It is just as well![15]

Her negative reaction to the scientific method brought to bear on plant specimens was, no doubt, a rejection of attempts to class and classify *her*. Now, this tacit substitution of the plants for herself or of herself for the plants does not take place on an equal footing (or rooting); instead, the young poet views flowers as superior:

> Flowers – Well – if anybody
> Can the ecstasy define –
> Half a transport – half a trouble –
> With which flowers humble men:
> [...] Have a system of aesthetics –
> Far superior to mine.[16]

Emily Dickinson's influential predecessor, Elizabeth Barrett Browning, likewise doubts even the possibility of naming, let alone classifying, a living rose; when such practices succeed, the rose is as good as dead: "O Rose! who dares to name thee? / No longer roseate now, nor soft, nor sweet; / But pale, and hard, and dry, as stubble-wheat ..."[17] In an inversion of Shakespeare's "A rose by any other name ...," this is a name without the rose, the name as a shipwreck of a sailing past. Beneath all the systems of classification imposed on them, flowers are as definable as ecstasy – which is to say: undefinable and indefinite in their finitude. They "humble men" by suspending determinate judgments halfway, by troubling static hierarchies, by transporting themselves (or parts of themselves: pollen, seeds ...) elsewhere. Nor are herbaria aesthetic tools. The plants' peculiar "system of aesthetics" (a system of ecstasy, of transport, of indeterminacy externalized, available to the senses, human and not only) is declared "[f]ar superior to mine," which, anything but a narcissistic wound, is a reason for admiration, joyous wonder, and respect. A similar sense of wonder shines through George Eliot's lines "When flowers with upturned faces gazing drew / My wonder downward, seeming all to speak / With eyes of souls that dumbly heard and knew."[18]

The Poetics of a Biocentric Face

Many among Dickinson's early poems speak from the standpoint of the plants themselves (notably, of flowers) about the redemptive reversal or suspension of time, immanent and imminent in its fine-grained materiality. To be sure, the poet does not usurp the position of plants; rather, she painstakingly vegetalizes herself, in gardening as much as in poetizing, in the making of herbaria as much as in her epistolary practice. If "she expresses her feelings in terms of flowers and gardening," it is because her feelings have *become* vegetal.[19] That is also why, from an anthropocentric perspective, her thinking appears incoherent. As a critic notes: "In other Dickinson poems we find that thought has lost not only existential mastery of sequence but also cognitive dominion over sense perception. Perceptions simply crowd in too thick and fast to be arrangeable in a single chromatic sequence."[20]

Consider, for example, a poem in which Dickinson assumed the non-identity of an anemone flower:

Summer for thee, grant I may be
When Summer days are flown!
Thy music still, when Whippoorwill
And Oriole – Are done! –
For thee to bloom, I'll skip the tomb
And row my blossoms o'er!
Pray gather me –
Anemone –
Thy flower – forevermore![21]

This short poem may be read as a kind of manifesto for the practice of creating herbaria, the "herbarium manifesto," voiced by a plant that is about to be admitted into the collection. From the edge of death, the time of vigorous life is recovered. Anemone-Emily – the name of the flower set apart from the rest of the text between dashes and on a poetic line dedicated just to it – implores to be "Summer for thee" after "Summer days are flown"; gathered into an herbarium, she will embody time after time, the future of time past. In an herbarium, Anemone-Emily defies death ("I'll skip the tomb"), fluttering between a delicate infinitely finite life, brittle in its dryness, on the one hand, and eternity ("forevermore"), on the other. Gathering her ("Pray gather me") is gathering oneself and, in the same stroke, gathering time from its dispersion into the modalities of past, present, and future – a gathering that will, in its turn, be dispersed, shared with the addressees of flower poems and epistolary fragments of herbaria. Such a gathering does not foreclose death ("'Departed' – both – they say! / i.e., gathered away"), but apportions death otherwise, ridding it of its sting in the process.[22] Rossetti, for her part, treats (in a poetic dialogue paradoxically lacking closure) vegetal death as a symbol of *any* death whatsoever: it stands for the absolute discontinuity, rupture, and non-recoverability: "Nay, a bud once plucked there is no reviving, / Nor is it worth your rearing now, nor worth indeed my own; / The dead to the dead, and the living to the living. / It's time I go within, for its time now you were gone."[23]

A plant prepared for inclusion in an herbarium is a stop frame of existence. Here, the ecstasy that is the undefinable essence of flowers is at once glimpsed and slips away from the gaze and the grasp. At best, it is a glimpse of elusiveness itself, glimpsing the limits of the glimpse, an intimation of what George Eliot christens "the soul of visible things [that] shows silent happiness." Immediately following these lines from Eliot's *The Spanish Gypsy*, we read about "The wingéd life that pausing seems a gem / Cunningly carven on the dark green leaf."[24] The continuation of an afterlife, for Dickinson, is possible only thanks to a series of discontinuities, the intermittencies of being, punctuated by pauses and lapses, some of them indefinitely long. Hence,

> When Roses cease to bloom, Sir,
> And Violets are done –
> When Bumblebees in solemn flight
> Have passed beyond the Sun –
> The hand that paused to gather
> Upon this Summer's day
> Will idle lie – in Auburn –
> Then take my flowers – pray![25]

Mirroring the momentary pause of an active hand gathering summer flowers is the totally "idle" hand of the deceased lying in Mount Auburn cemetery, which Dickinson visited at the age of sixteen.[26] The wilting of roses, the passage of bumblebees "beyond the Sun," and the end of the violets complete the catalogue of disruptions that are, in one way or another, associated with mortality, violets being a staple Victorian symbol of death. Nonetheless, something is passed along despite the passing of flowers, of their pollinators, and of the hand that touched them – something recommences (fitfully, spasmodically, sporadically) as the giving of existence beyond its spatiotemporal edges. "Then take my flowers – pray!" is an offer from a hand that is no longer vitally active, that cannot give anything in the physiological, biological, or behavioral senses of the term. Only this gift of a hand that does not grasp and that does not intend, only this offering of a flower that is on the verge of becoming no-longer-flower and that is forevermore a flower in an herbarium, matters. So much so that it will be the storehouse of the treasure that is vegetal vitality in the mode of an afterlife.

The gift, then, is given out of the absolute impotence of giving. But it presupposes a prior act of taking. In those moments when her self-vegetalization falters, Dickinson is riddled with guilt, doubt, and regret. "Nobody knows this little Rose – ," she proclaims in a poem, "It might a pilgrim be / Did I not take it from the ways / And lift it up to thee." Musing about the bees, butterflies, bird, and breeze who will miss the flower, she sighs: "Ah Little

Rose – how easy / For such as thee to die!"[27] The judgment she passes on herself is even harsher in another poem, which begins with the lines,

> I robbed the Woods –
> The trusting Woods.
> The unsuspecting Trees
> Brought out their Burs and mosses
> My fantasy to please.[28]

The one previously accused of robbery was Jack Frost and the icy breath of death he embodied. The rhyme "breath : death" peppering many of Dickinson's poems carries a number of crucial thematic and semantic associations in Victorian poetry, also around the figure of flowers. Rossetti, for example, ends "Emblem Flowers" with "violets of fragrant breath, / For death,"[29] Whether creating an herbarium of plants and words is putting an end to their immediate life and inexhaustible possibilities or whether it is saving the fading being of flowers is no longer an either/or scenario: the maker of an herbarium robs the robber and rescues vegetal and verbal forms from oblivion by repeating this basic thievish gesture, albeit repeating it otherwise.

More interesting, perhaps, is Dickinson's take (an interpretation is also a "take," a taking, a grasping, and so an extraction of one string of sense from a throng of countless others) on the ease of death for the creature "such as" a rose. My hypothesis is that her poetic, epistolary, and herbarizing practices are the intersecting and mutually reinforcing experiments in her self-vegetalization. Thus Richard B. Sewall is right to note, "Take Emily's herbarium far enough, and you have *her*."[30] Dickinson's practices are motivated neither by the mimesis of plants nor by an identification with them: in each of these instances, the herbarium would have functioned as a mirror, a speculative instrument for better recognizing oneself, where – transformed as it may be – the human self (if not the self *as such*) is retained. Simultaneously allegorical and literal, self-vegetalization is awash in paradox, which is a tributary to the paradoxes of vegetal ontology.

Two words – "such as" – ooze with the ambiguities of the poet's take on plants and herbaria, the take that lets go what it plucks, presses, and preserves (and also lets go itself) in the very act of plucking, pressing, and preserving. The rose referred to with the words "such as thee" is no longer *this* singular and unique, perhaps unnamable flower, whom "nobody knows." She becomes, by the poem's closing line, an exemplary case of ease in death. The rose is idealized in the precise philosophical sense of getting unglued from her *thisness*, growing vaguely universal; the transition from "such as" to "as such" is seamless. Despite her generic rendering, however, the rose is still an addressee, a *thee*, which indicates another kind of distance than the idealizing "such as" or "as such." And this is not even to mention that "such as thee" includes the author of these lines, becoming a rose in an herbarium of words and flowers – that is, in the discontinuous continuity of her pilgrimage.

The rose's ease of dying is similarly paradoxical. *This* rose dies easily, when its blooming time is over, but the rosebush lives on. The practice of "dead-heading," removing the faded or dead flowers from a plant, stimulates further blossoming. Besides *this* rose, the one "such as thee" dies with comparable ease, but the iterations and the iterability of "such as," let alone "as such," resist death. In a scientific herbarium, the death of a singular plant is overcome in the generality of the species it represents as a preserved specimen, such as a rose, which stands for the rose as such. The ease of dying betokens the ease of vanquishing death. Dickinson's poetic herbaria also bet on this loophole, but they do so by means other than the subsumption of the singular in the general.

What is needed for one to die? In "I haven't told my garden yet …," it turns out that in lieu of biological vitality and its cessation, the prerequisite for dying is a face, or, more precisely, having a face:

> I haven't told my garden yet –
> Lest that should conquer me.
> I haven't quite the strength now
> To break it to the Bee –
> I will not name it in the street
> For shops would stare at me –
> That one so shy – so ignorant
> Should have the face to die.[31]

In a proto-Heideggerian mood, I could say that to have a face is to be able to face death as one's own possibility. Do plants have a face – indeed, face*s*? It would not be easy (in fact, it would be next to impossible) for them to die were they to be bereft of this feature. To overcome death, it would be enough to dispense with the face of the dying one. And yet, the ease of plant death is contingent upon a loose relation of a plant to its faces: a flower, for instance, does not have faces; it does not lay claim to its own finite being as its indisputable first (and last) possession. A flower does not *have* faces; it *is* its faces, the sentient surfaces of petals, leaves, stocks with which it faces the sun and the no less sentient faces of the roots, in touch with the earth. Plants are all faces *and* they do not have a face. Hence, it is both all too easy and exceptionally difficult for them to die.

Conventionally, an herbarium embodies an effort to preserve the faces of plants, to tear them away from death, to put an end to the movements of growth and decay alike. What is then preserved amounts not to the faces but to the death masks of plants. Dickinson's herbaria do something else altogether. On the one hand, the appearance of jasmine on the first page of the herbarium she made at Amherst Academy may be read in light of the language of flowers that was current in the nineteenth century, where this plant connoted the affairs of the heart, whether passion or separation.[32] On the other hand, according to her poetry, jasmine "is" ecstasy itself – the uncontainable – unleashed, just after the threshold of death has been passed:

> Kill your Balm – and its Odors bless you –
> Bare your Jessamine – to the storm –
> And she will fling her maddest perfume –
> Haply – your Summer night to Charm.[33]

It is after jasmine is exposed "to the storm" or even killed that "she will fling her maddest perfume" in olfactory ecstasy, a trace of jasmine's nonidentity, of her being outside or beside herself. To commence an herbarium this way is to make a silent (vegetal) statement about the *a priori* failure of conventional herbaria and to face the faces of plants gathered there at the threshold of life and death, which is a mutable edge of vegetal being.

The olfactory ecstasy of jasmine exposed to mortal danger is received as a blessing there where play is deadly serious:

> She died at play,
> Gambolled away
> Her lease of spotted hours,
> Then sank as gaily as a Turk
> Upon a Couch of flowers.[34]

These other flowers, too, die playfully, throwing themselves to chance ("haply"), with the scents they release in their final hour irreducible to the biochemical signaling of danger. Herbaria are the visual-tactile expressions of vegetal ecstasy. Hence, in Barrett Browning's *A Drama of Exile* (1845), flower spirits likewise proclaim:

> We are spirit-aromas
> Of blossom and bloom.
> We call your thoughts home, – as
> Ye breathe our perfume, –[35]

But, according to Dickinson, jasmine spearheads the ecstatic being of plants at the olfactory level, which, in Victorian poetry, is closely linked to thinking.

The Vegetal Cycles of Life–Death

Utterly ecstatic, Dickinson's poetic herbaria strive to live up to life – to vegetal life, in the first instance. Her rejection of the botanical segregation of species is the underside of her unconditional acceptance of this life's diversity. So, the Amherst herbarium "included meadow blooms and sophisticated garden varieties, sometimes existing side by side on the same page."[36] Dickinson proclaims herself "grateful for the Roses / In life's diverse bouquet,"[37] where the plucked flowers of the bouquet are not inconsistent with life and where "diversity" is not an indifferent term for a multiplicity of differences, but a precondition for singularization, for discernment and affective attachment.

To live up to life is, probably, the most human of goals; all other living beings live their lives without trying to live up to anything, to the extent that they are lived by the life (or by the lives) coursing through them. How could something so seemingly trivial as an herbarium be of any use in this endeavor? Dickinson's herbaria of plants and words are literal and allegorical laboratories where living up to life involves an intimate engagement with death, supplemented with the symbioses of various forms of vitality and modes of expression. Thus:

> By a flower – By a letter –
> By a nimble love –
> If I weld the Rivet faster –
> Final fast – above –
> Never mind my breathless Anvil!
> Never mind Repose!
> Never mind the sooty faces
> Tugging at the Forge![38]

Flowers and letters, the nimbleness of love and the heaviness of "my breathless Anvil" weld, articulate, fasten, bring together disparate elements in divergent fashions, both forging and letting-show or letting-grow. This is the poetic herbarium in a nutshell, in the process of its gathering. And death is never far beyond the horizon: "the sooty faces / Tugging at the Forge" are, as faces, those who are prone to die. That they replace the hands, whose job it usually is to tug at the forge, is indicative of their work as faces, which is to elaborate on death within the framework of living up to life.

No sooner does such an elaboration commence than death sheds its purely negative associations and becomes "Night's possibility." Speaking in a mix of the singular and the plural from the standpoint of plants, the poet contends:

> We are the Flower – Thou the Sun!
> Forgive us, if as days decline –
> We nearer steal to Thee!
> Enamored of the parting West –
> The peace – the flight – the Amethyst –
> Night's possibility![39]

In the finite stretch of time that is a life, the sun is "the parting West," approached as "days decline." Growing toward and blossoming unto this nocturnal sun is what decades later Heidegger will call "being-toward-death." In an herbarium, as an herbarium, the trajectories of the astronomical sun and the nocturnal sun intersect. At this point of intersection, they belong to the past, however: the solar energy that convoked a flower into being, in doing so, turned it into a heliotrope of death. Henceforth, an herbarium commemorates and eclipses the two suns. In another, albeit related, key, George Eliot emphasizes the synesthetic commemoration of the sun by plants in their very corporeity: "Surely, these flowers keep happy watch, – their breath / Is their fond memory of the loving light."[40]

Dickinson's nocturnal theme returns in a poem pairing flowers and children:

> As Children bid the Guest:
>
> 'Good Night'
> And then reluctant turn –
> My flowers raise their pretty lips
> They put their nightgowns on
> As children caper when they wake
> Merry that it is Morn –
> My flowers from a hundred cribs
> Will peep, and prance again.[41]

Children's reluctant turning in at night bespeaks human irreconcilability with death, the irreconcilability that, although the poem operates with a simile between children and "my flowers," is not at all characteristic of plants, who without protest "put their nightgowns on." Dying (and being reborn) is a daily ritual, seeing that the night itself dies the next morning. From this ritual, the time sequence of lives and deaths is strung together, with all the punctuations, intervals, and silences separating them, as well as with everything that is left unsaid about what happens between the first and the second "As ..." of the poem. So then is an herbarium one of the creatures of the night or does it reinterpret the merry reawakening of the morning?

Recalling jasmine's "maddest perfume," released in the moment of its death, it would be fair to say that awakening is part of night's ecstasy, while turning in for the night is part of the day's prancing vitality. This uniquely vegetal mix of light and darkness, of a luminous closure and an obscure openness, is also featured in Barrett Browning's *A Drama of Exile*, where a spirit announces: "Filtered through roses did the light enclose me."[42] In Dickinson's view, in turn, an herbarium is life–death and day–night, spanning the ostensible extremes in the manner of vegetal ontology. Along these lines, the young poet writes that her "Tambourin" would only "break in wilder song / When Winter shook the boughs," audibly reverberating with jasmine's olfactory ecstasy at the hour of its death.[43]

In a letter to Abiah Root, dated May 16, 1848, Dickinson complains that there "are not many wild flowers near, for the girls have driven them to a distance, and we are obliged to walk quite a distance to find them, but they repay us by their sweet smiles and fragrance." She then adds:

> The older I grow, the more do I love spring and spring flowers. Is it so with you? While at home there were several pleasure parties of which I was a member, and in our rambles we found many and beautiful children of spring, which I will mention and see if you have found them, – the trailing arbutus, adder's tongue, yellow violets, liver-leaf, blood-root, and many other smaller flowers.[44]

Nearness to flowers in space and in time is the grid of Dickinson's poetic herbarium. It is a nearness that is craved, desired to the point of becoming-plant, but without erasing the distance to the "many and beautiful children of spring." Finding them, despite all the challenges, is finding oneself – othered, vegetalized, moving against the strongest current of life in a life ("The older I grow, the more do I love spring and spring flowers"). The gathering and dispersal of an herbarium, collectively made with others be they human or vegetal, are tokens of this distant nearness. The one and the many, life and death, day and night, plants, words, silences, seasons, faces, surfaces, senses commune, threading into and out of one another on its pages. Far from a simple rebirth named "spring," the chance an herbarium grants to whomever gains entry into it is that of a continuation of what is done and over with, a continuation without continuity, despite itself. Like "[t]he stem of a departed Flower," which "[h]as still a rank / The Bearer from an Emerald Court / Of a Dispatch of Pink."[45]

Notes

1. Judith Farr, *The Gardens of Emily Dickinson* (Cambridge: Harvard University Press, 2004), 3.
2. Elizabeth Barrett Browning, *The Poems of Elizabeth Barrett Browning* (London: Frederick Warne & Co, 1850), 356–7.
3. Angela Conrad, *The Wayward Nun of Amherst: Emily Dickinson and Medieval Mystical Women* (New York: Garland Publishing, 2000).
4. Emily Dickinson, *The Complete Poems of Emily Dickinson*, ed. Thomas H. Johnson (Boston: Little, Brown & Company, 1960), 47.
5. Christina Rossetti, *Poems of Christina Rossetti*, ed. William M. Rossetti (London: Macmillan 1904), 129.

6. Emily Dickinson, *The Letters of Emily Dickinson*, vol. 1, ed. Thomas H. Johnson (Cambridge: The Belknap Press of Harvard University Press, 1958), 21.
7. Dickinson, *Letters*, 13.
8. Dickinson, *Letters*, 13.
9. Farr, *The Gardens of Emily Dickinson*, 4.
10. Farr, *The Gardens of Emily Dickinson*, 4.
11. Dickinson, *Letters*, 21.
12. Dickinson, *Complete Poems*, 36.
13. Farr, *The Gardens of Emily Dickinson*, 9, 282.
14. Dickinson, *Complete Poems*, 36.
15. Dickinson, *Complete Poems*, 79.
16. Dickinson, *Complete Poems*, 64.
17. Dickinson, *Poems*, 371.
18. George Eliot, *Poems of George Eliot* (New York: Thomas Y. Crowell & Co, n.d.), 393.
19. Farr, *The Gardens of Emily Dickinson*, 38.
20. Helen Vendler, *Poets Thinking: Pope, Whitman, Dickinson, Yeats* (Cambridge: Harvard University Press, 2004), 68.
21. Dickinson, *Complete Poems*, 20.
22. Dickinson, *Complete Poems*, 32.
23. Dickinson, *Poems*, 208.
24. Rossetti, *Poems*, 58.
25. Dickinson, *Complete Poems*, 21.
26. Dickinson, *Letters*, 36.
27. Dickinson, *Complete Poems*, 22.
28. Dickinson, *Complete Poems*, 24.
29. Rossetti, *Poems*, 293.
30. Richard B. Sewall, "Science and the Poet: Emily Dickinson's Herbarium and 'The Clue Divine,'" *Harvard Library Bulletin* 3.1 (Spring 1992), 11–26 at 11.
31. Dickinson, *Complete Poems*, 27.
32. Farr, *The Gardens of Emily Dickinson*, 42, 99.
33. Dickinson, *Complete Poems*, 109.
34. Dickinson, *Complete Poems*, 39.
35. Elizabeth Barrett Browning, *Poetical Works in Six Volumes*, Vol. 1 (London: Smith, Elder & Co., 1890), 18–19.
36. Farr, *The Gardens of Emily Dickinson*, 21.
37. Dickinson, *Complete Poems*, 46.
38. Dickinson, *Complete Poems*, 52–3.
39. Dickinson, *Complete Poems*, 52.
40. Dickinson, *Poems*, 116.
41. Dickinson, *Complete Poems*, 62–3.
42. Browning, *Poetical Works*, 51.
43. Dickinson, *Complete Poems*, 85.
44. Dickinson, *Letters*, 66.
45. Dickinson, *Complete Poems*, 637.

12

DENNIS DENISOFF

Queer Ecology and the Animal in Walter Pater and William Sharp

There is a story about Walter Pater's cat getting hold of one of his volumes of Paul Bourget's *Essais de psychologie contemporaine* (1889) and then proceeding to tear up the section containing the essay about Charles Baudelaire. "[A]s Baudelaire was such a lover of cats," Pater is said to have mused, "I thought she might have spared him."[1] The anecdote is gently comic, the sweet scene capturing Pater, the renowned leader of British aestheticist philosophy, engaging in that bemused forgiveness so many of us have extended to our domestic pets when they've chewed a book, knocked over a glass, or crashed on our keyboard. Pater's openness to acknowledging his affection for the feline is refreshing, capturing his pleasure in the sharedness of their daily lives, the two of them consuming Bourget's work together. It also captures a deep mental intimacy, the man so quick to toy with the idea that cats do read if not our writing, then at least we humans ourselves, albeit in a way that we only ever partially understand. What most interests me in this anecdote is not the idea that Pater pretended to believe the cat could understand the written word, but that he so easily entertained considering the world through the lens of the nonhuman. The difference between, on one paw, wondering whether a cat can think like a human and, on the other, imagining what it might be like to think like a cat captures the inter–subjectivity of queer ecology on which this chapter focuses.

To date, scholarship in the field of queer ecology has predominantly addressed the ways in which the natural environment creates a space for people's transgressions of normative erotic and sexual practices. It is presented as an accommodating or even encouraging context for human–human explorations of unconventional desires. What Pater's cat emphasizes, however, is that this world is not a passive context for human explorations, but a set of forces, human and otherwise, maneuvering amongst each other on an ongoing basis. In literature, these cross-species engagements are usually ignored or perceived as symbolic of human characters thoughts or actions. When they are acknowledged in their own right, these connections are represented as rare, unconventional, or even excessive to the edge of deviance. They are, however, utterly common. And yet they are still nevertheless queer because the experiences, sensations, and thoughts of other animals demand the decentering of our human perspectives and affective reactions.

In *What Animals Teach Us about Politics* (2014), Brian Massumi engages with the political benefits of trying, even though we will fail, to understand the sense we have of ourselves "as humanly standing apart from other animals; our inveterate vanity regarding our assumed species identity, based on the specious grounds of our sole proprietorship of language, thought, and creativity."[2] Massumi is not speaking of developing sympathy or empathy, or of giving nonhumans the status of personhood (conceptually or legally) – common strategies of Victorian animal rights activism. Rather, he asks one to imagine replacing one's privileged notion of selfhood with an appreciation of the equally valid, incomprehensible subjectivity conceived of by a nonhuman creature. Victorian authors such as Pater and William Sharp were keenly invested in nature and its relation to pleasure and the aesthetic imagination; both have also explored nonhuman animals as offering alternative subject positions uninvested in accommodating the human. In this chapter, I consider these two writers' explorations of nonhuman animals' experiences and thoughts as underappreciated, everyday intimacies. In doing so, my analysis looks at Victorian literature that does not necessarily engage with nonnormative human sexuality but does acknowledge an eco-centric imaginary that is queer in its destabilizing of systems of erasure and oppression before the classificatory efforts of modern scientific and legal discourses had come to dominate the sexual and gendered landscapes.

Queer Ecology in the Victorian Context

It was in the Victorian period that, as Michel Foucault put it, the "temporary aberration" of the sodomite shifted to the "species" of the homosexual.[3] The term "species" generally refers to a group of like organisms that can both procreate and produce fertile offspring. That said, there are exceptions such as organisms that rely on asexual reproduction. The term "typological species" refers more broadly to a category of organisms that simply conform to certain fixed properties.[4] Foucault similarly presents "species" as a culturally reified identity category. For Foucault, the concept of the modern homosexual as identity arose through a discourse of typological species. At the same time, the categorization of homosexuals as species would have implied a dehumanization of gay pleasures and kinships as nonnormative threats to human (read: white, male, middle-class, heterosexual) authority.

The field of queer ecology studies addresses the desires and attractions that characterize relations among humans and other elements of their environment, as well as the eco-politics regarding reliances and mutual influences among these diverse species. To date, its emphasis has been on the ways in which nature has served as a sort of privacy screen behind which humans could explore their unconventional attractions to other humans. "Queer" in this formulation is taken from the rich field of studies – rooted in the trans, feminist, gay, and AIDS-related activism of the latter half of the twentieth century – regarding human–human relations that disrupt assumptions regarding acts and interests considered appropriate and wholesome (predominantly those privileging heterosexuality and procreation). Pioneered in large part by Catriona Mortimer-Sandilands, the analysis of humans' queer experiences within their organic ecology has addressed the ways in which an escape to less populated locales such as the hinterlands, the backwoods, or thinly populated farmlands, have allowed people to realize and engage their same-sex desires, often without having to adopt some permanent queer self-identification.[5] The model extends a tradition that goes back at least to the classical formulation of the homoerotic pastoral, while also recognizing its presence in more contemporary renderings of men's experiences living as adventurers and frontiersmen. The hospitable, pastoral vision is apparent in works such as Mary Elizabeth Braddon's *Lady Audley's Secret* (1862) and E. M. Forster's *Maurice* (written 1913–14, published 1971), where nature is portrayed as a benign environment that nurtures civilized, European male–male intimacy. Meanwhile, in escapist adventure literature such as Rider Haggard's *She* (1886) and Joseph Conrad's *Heart of Darkness* (1899), the untamed and uncertain quality of both the landscape and daily existence roughs up the edges of the lifestyle norms that characterize settled or urban society. Within this space of indeterminacy, male–male admiration and hero worship are enhanced by situations demanding occasions of codependence and intimacy as individuals struggle to survive. At the same time, the authors of the latter works often melded the Indigenous peoples with the inhospitable organic ecology, rather than with intruding human foreigners. This representation essentializes the white, European male as the primary signifier of the human but it also demonstrates the imaginative ease by which the system was prepared to acknowledge the overlap of some types of humans with other animals, in accord with Foucault's own slippery notion of the homosexual species.

Cameron Clark and E. L. McCallum describe these sexualized ecologies as portraying "white male same-sex eroticism in positive spaces of refuge, relaxation, and sensual discovery."[6] Of course neither the pastoral idyll nor the escapism of the wilds has ever been realistically sustainable – despite the inspiring conclusion near the end of Forster's novel, with Maurice's lover Alec famously declaring they "shan't be parted no more, and that's finished."[7] It's never finished, even if common male privilege did allow for a considerable margin of secrecy and self-determination for many men (as, in another sense, so has the invisibility extended to those deemed to be of an inferior or inconsequential gender, class, race, or species). With the spectrum of sexual and emotional ambiguities that characterize the Victorian Age, some people did create lifestyles whose unacknowledged status assisted in their long-term sustainability, but many disenfranchised people could not. As Clark and McCallum posit, "for queer and trans writers, especially writers of color, ... ecology does not appear as a neutral ontology of inter-relations but one that originates through the violent theft or loss of home, kinship, belonging, and official records of personhood."[8]

Their observation likewise points, if not intentionally, to an oversight within queer ecology studies itself – the disregard for the contributions and interests of the nonhuman species that populate any ecology and that regularly experience the theft and loss of home, kinship, and personhood. To focus queer ecological inquiry on its benefits and detriments to exclusively humans regarding either their fulfillment of desires and self-identity or their responsibilities and stewardship regarding environmental abuse is to engage in conversation with only part of the collective in which the field claims to be invested. Less often explored but equally important are the nonnormative engagements that humans have within their organic ecologies, and particularly with other animal species. Examples can be found in a range of fictions, including Louisa May Alcott's "Lost in a Pyramid, or a Mummy's Curse" (1869), Ouida's *Puck* (1870), Anna Sewell's *Black Beauty* (1877), Thomas Hardy's *Far from the Madding Crowd* (1874), and Algernon Blackwood's "The Willows" (1907). These shared subject positions are queer not because of engagements seen as unconventional, but because the authors use them to disrupt the very conventions by which kinship and intimacy are recognized and articulated. The Victorians practiced various models of friendship, kinship, intimacy, and co-reliance that had not yet been categorized as either essentially normal or deviantly heterodox. Therefore, one finds the ecologically queer not simply in escapist visions of rare human-human sexual fulfillment, but also in everyday cross-species experiences. Authors such as Pater and Sharp worked with such ambiguities around desire and kinship to capture animal intimacies that can, today, be difficult to recognize through the history and terminology of our present moment. Rather than attempt to translate such intimacies for the sake of others' understandings, both authors in distinctly different ways considered whether the verbal arts could be used to settle in with another's signaled pleasure from a moment's engagement. This was not an effort on the authors' part to recognize the communicative methods of nonhumans, but to gesture toward an appreciation of less recognized, less empowered cross-species affections, acceptances, and identifications.

Pater and the Wolf: The Passion of the Beast

Pater's story about the cat shredding Bourget's monograph was recorded in an essay by Arthur Symons, poet and preeminent theorist of Symbolism and Decadence. He begins the essay by quoting Pater's claim that, in addition to Michelangelo and Leonardi da Vinci, there are other lesser artists who evoke a "'peculiar quality of pleasure'" unique to them, and who have "'their place in general culture, and must be interpreted to it by those who have felt their charm strongly, and are often the objects of a special diligence and a consideration wholly affectionate, just because there is not about them the stress of a great name and authority.'"[9] Pater's description of a peculiar pleasure felt from those who lack cultural status recalls the ease he displayed in his affection for his cat. He enjoyed the society of other people well enough but was never entirely comfortable unless "among very intimate friends," among whom it would be no exaggeration to include his cats over the years. A. E. Benson offers a particularly astute description of such human-feline connections, noting Pater's "unceasing delight in watching the ways and habits of pet animals. His own domestic cats, indeed, were kept and lovingly tended, observed and interpreted, with a subtle and discriminating sympathy."[10] He goes on to note Pater's appreciation of "the extraordinary relation that may exist, such perfect confidence, such unrestrained affection, while yet there is no communication of thought, and so little comprehension on either side of what is really passing in the mind." Meanwhile, as Catherine Maxwell argues, Pater's "feline affinities" also acted "as a means of affiliation between those [people] with similar literary, intellectual, and artistic leanings," cats, in their seeming inconsequentiality, proving easy mediators for human-human connections among Pater and others of his aesthetic circle.[11]

Symons describes one evening at dinner the "quaint, solemn, and perfectly natural way in which [Pater] took up the great black Persian, kissed it, and set it down carefully again on his way upstairs."[12] It is the lack of self-consciousness on Pater's part in this public display of affection that stands out for Symons, as it had for Benson. Later in the essay, Symons relays a discussion with Pater about their mutual admiration of fairs, in which the latter recalled "the minute, coloured impression of the booths, the little white horses of the 'roundabouts,' and the little wild beast shows."[13]

What struck Pater most forcefully was one occasion on which he saw a French peasant being drawn not to the exoticism and vibrancy of the caged tiger but instead to "the wolf, a creature he might have seen in his own woods." The strongest attraction for the man in the anecdote is with what Pater recognized as the kinship with others from one's locale, as well as a sense of one's own position in the ecological scheme of things.

In the preface to *The Renaissance: Studies in Art and Poetry* (first published as *Studies in the History of the Renaissance* in 1873), Pater asks regarding any object of influence, "Does it give me pleasure? and if so, what sort or degree of pleasure? How is my nature modified by its presence, and under its influence?"[14] Such sensitivity to pleasure but especially to the changing self in relation to one's natural ecological context suggests the author's keen awareness of biological intimacy, the physical proximity, and interactions among different species groups, or taxa, during their life cycles. Within the field of evolutionary biology, it is argued that such intimacy results in developments of species specialization that are influential and supportive among the various taxa of the local ecology.[15] The concept recalls Ernst Haeckel's *History of Creation* (1880), in which he marks the expansive potential of the term "ecology," characterized by "the mutual dependence of all living creatures on one another, and in general the universal connection between cause and effect."[16] In a bionetwork formulation, no pure nature can exist *out there* for humans or any other organisms because one is always a constituent element of an ecological web. Nature, then, is never just a backdrop for human action. Meanwhile, Haeckel's reference to "all" living creatures and a "universal connection" foreshadows the general shift in environmentalist thought over the past two centuries from an attention to local issues to a greater awareness of the broader, even global impact of local actions.

Pater himself questioned the separability of the local and the global. It is the immediate and experiential, he proposes, that gives the sharpest access to a sincere emotional engagement with a more vast and indeterminable force, but just as often the aesthetics of nature are not configured by a specific item of beauty. Of Michelangelo with his preference for depicting "blank ranges of rock, and dim vegetable forms" rather than a particular stone or plant, Pater writes: "he penetrates us with a sense of that power which we associate with all the warmth and fulness of the world, and the sense of which brings into one's thoughts a swarm of birds and flowers and insects. The brooding spirit of life itself is there; and the summer may burst out in a moment."[17] Pater's queer ecological vision appreciates the immediacy or familiarity with the object of pleasure, but extensively because it evokes a sense of a broader, universal ethics.

Pater was nowhere as explicit about animal rights as his contemporaries such as Francis Power Cobbe, Ouida, and Henry Salt. But his keen sense of the place of the animal in aesthetic pleasure makes a distinctly original contribution to Victorian animal rights politics and in particular to its ethics of kinship and intimacy. Consider his "Study of Dionysus: The Spiritual Form of Fire and Dew," which appeared in the *Fortnightly Review* in 1876 and then, posthumously, in *Greek Studies* (1894). The essay addresses the Greek god – characterized by wildness, chaos, and human sacrifice – as a precursor of Christ in his role as a benefactor of humanity, but as one who more fully embodies the energy of the beastly than did the gentle figures that came with later schools of spiritual belief. We find the god passing into an identity that, Pater imagines, affords the perspective of another species. This is not a benign conflation of the human with the more-than-human, but the experience of a state of being that can be understood even as "an enemy of human kind," the "were-wolf."[18] Dionysus, he writes, "is connected with the fears, the dangers and hardships of the hunter himself, lost or slain sometimes, far from home, in the dense woods of the mountains, as he seeks his meat so ardently; becoming, in his chase, almost akin to the wild beasts – to the wolf."[19] Here we understand why, at the fair, the French peasant's keen interest in the wolf likely reflected empathy and respect, as opposed to the objectification that comes with a curiosity in more exotic creatures such as the tiger.

In the case of Dionysus as portrayed by Pater, the idea of cross-species empathy as a type of queer intimacy is brought home by a "fierce hunger and thirst" that in conventional society constitutes an immoral passion that is to be constrained,[20] represented as a form of dangerous animality in works such as Robert Louis Stevenson's *Strange Case of Dr. Jekyll and Mr. Hyde* (1886) and Bram Stoker's *Dracula* (1897). In one sense, animality constitutes a threat to modern humanist civility while, in another, it is embodied not by a rejection of the beast but by a dangerous intimacy, a familiarity with it as part of the human. The animality presented in Pater's essay is not any sort of actual transformation from one species or another, nor is it a symbolic suggestion of an animalistic or primitive state of human development. Rather, Dionysus experiences the world through the passion of the animal, having taken on a visceral perspective that is part of the bionetwork. Such queerness resides not in identity but in the relationality that slakes, temporarily, an impassioned hunger.

William Sharp's Eco-poetics of Embodiment

Pater's friend William Sharp was particularly intense in his aestheticizing approach to channeling the passion of the other, captured in both his eco-pagan poetry and his Celtic novels. Scholars have written on Sharp's gender queerness – his declaration that "in some things I am more a woman than a man," what Flavia Alaya calls a "sexual tension within himself," or what Terry Meyers refers to as his "self-division" and "trans-gendering."[21] During the second half of his career, he wrote and published both as himself and as Fiona Macleod, the latter pseudonymous works proving more popular. It is, however, not the queerness of a writer or artist that is the singular trait by which a queer ecology need be registered. As I have been arguing, the field is as invested in cross-species – and so, nonnormative – emotional and sensual relations, as well as in the standpoint of the nonhuman in such relations. Sharp's oeuvre reflects such a sustained effort to imagine the sensual reality of nonhumans.

In his memoirs, edited by his wife Elizabeth Sharp, Sharp mentions reading *Primitive Folk*, by the French ethnographer Élie Reclus. This study of the Inuit, the Kolarians of Bengal, and other Indigenous ethnic groups made Sharp recognize, he writes in his diary, "a definite law in the evolution of sexual *morale*, I am sure if one could only get at it. The matter is worth going into, both for Fundamental and contemporary and Problematical Ethics."[22] Meyers considers this a reference to Reclus's discussion of Inuit homosexuality, and the incorporation of male-to-female transvestism into its culture, a section of Reclus's work that Havelock Ellis also addresses.[23] However, the introduction to Reclus's study also offers a reconsideration of Western anthropocentrism:

> We have manuals of natural history which, dividing animal and vegetable species into two categories, the useful and the noxious, affirm that neither reason nor conscience exists except amongst men; books which reproach the ass for his stupidity, the shark for his greed, and the tiger for his fierceness. But who are we that we should take up such a lofty position with regard to the intellectual and moral weaknesses of those who have preceded us?[24]

It is unclear whether Reclus is distinguishing all humans across time as intellectually and morally equal, or affirming that nonhuman animals may likewise have intellectual and ethical capabilities that humans have not adequately considered.

Reclus develops his suggestion for greater respect for other species later in his study, when he offers a problematic summary of the similarities he finds between the Inuit and seals:

> The Esquimaux connects the seal closely with man. He has the habits, character, appearance, even the physiognomy of this animal, which like himself is amphibious. ... Both he and it are thick-set, all trunk, voracious, both are gay and domestic, both have great, soft, intelligent eyes. At first sight one has no

great opinion of either of these awkward lumps of flesh, but it is astonishing
to find how much judgment and good nature is revealed by a close observation
of them. It is noteworthy that the beast is more jealous in love than his human
compatriot.[25]

The species may differ, Reclus suggests, but the similarities arising from their
shared ecology prove more relevant to their sense of selfhood. When Reclus
mentions the formulation elsewhere in his study, it is usually through consid-
erations of earth-centered spiritualities and mysticism, which speak directly to
the neopaganism of much of Sharp's own writing. In a paraphrased conversation in Reclus's work between an Innuk and a missionary, when asked about
nonhuman animals in heaven, "the missionary declared 'we have the Lamb,
we have a lion, an eagle, a calf ... but not your sea-calf; we have – ' The Innuk
interrupted, 'That's enough; your heaven has no seals, and a heaven without
seals cannot suit us!'"[26] Reclus's comingling of the Innuk with another species feeds into the colonialist tendency to associate non-Western people and
cultures with nonhuman animals as a denigration that implicitly sanctions
their oppression and exploitation. In this instance, what it also does is present Reclus's reader's with a pseudo-scientific attempt to recognize a human
self-identifying based on cross-species intimacy.

Much of Sharp's poetry can be read as attempts not simply to represent
but to enter into the sensual correspondences among the animal, vegetal,
and elemental. Such poetic efforts lack the explicit intellectual articulations found in Pater's essays. Instead, deeply invested in meter, alliteration,
euphony, and often tortured grammar, the poems struggle to transpose the
sensual experience of another species onto the readers, offering a rare,
avant-garde effort to use poetics to explore eco-sensuality. Sharp's most
innovative works in this regard appear in his collection of poems, *Sospiri
di Roma* (1891), which he wrote while in Rome, reading and writing about
Reclus's study. One of his most frequently anthologized pieces, "The
White Peacock," is unique among the collection's works for its particularly intense turn to impressionism and formal innovation to impact the
reader's own breathing and mental engagement with the poem's subject.
The gossamer imagery of "The White Peacock" is excessive, smothering,
fostering a sense of immersion into a nonhuman realm. No people appear
in the poem. Instead, the entire piece focuses on the blue, gold, and white
lushness of a surreal landscape, punctuated by an occasional peacock. In
his diary, Sharp refers to the piece as "a study in Whites for Théodore
Roussel."[27] A friend of James McNeill Whistler, Roussel was a self-taught
artist who often created dreamy, aqua landscapes of the Thames. Sharp's
"a study in Whites" echoes Whistler's own painting titles – *Symphony in*

White, No. 1 (1862); *Symphony in White, No. 2* (1864); and so on – while the poem evokes, as much as anything, a piece of the blue and white china admired by aesthetes such as Oscar Wilde and, indeed by this time, the general public who had developed a penchant for an aestheticist style of house beautification. Meanwhile, the rich imagery of Sharp's piece recalls the immersiveness of Whistler's *Peacock Room* (1876–7), a space buried in ornate blue and gold detail, with even the entire ceiling painted with peacock feathers that, on closer observation, also appear to be hundreds of unblinking eyes.

The saturated quality in Sharp's poem is particularly dehumanizing. As if ignoring regular breathing practices, the poem doesn't offer a main verb until its twenty-eighth line, exactly halfway through the work. While the sentences are very long, the lines are short – mostly five or six syllables each – with no consistent rhythm, resulting in an awkward staccato effect:

> Here where the sunlight
> Floodeth the garden,
> Where the pomegranate
> Reareth its glory
> Of gorgeous blossom;
> Where the oleanders
> Dream through the noontides;
> And, like surf o' the sea
> Round cliffs of basalt,
> The thick magnolias
> In billowy masses
> Front the sombre green of the ilexes:
> Here where the heat lies
> Pale blue in the hollows,
> Where blue are the shadows
> On the fronds of the cactus,
> Where pale blue the gleaming
> Of fir and cypress,
> With the cones upon them
> Amber or glowing
> With virgin gold:
> Here where the honey-flower
> Makes the heat fragrant,
> As though from the gardens
> Of Gulistan,
> Where the bulbul singeth
> Through a mist of roses,
> A breath were borne:[28]

"Gulistan" is Persian for "The Flower Garden," referring to perhaps the most famous collection of prose and poetry written by Persian author Saadi in 1258 CE. The plural verb "were" does not fit grammatically with the single subject "breath," suggesting the breath is borne of multiple subjects, the cohesion of exhalation arising vaguely from the ecological context at large. The sentence is in the passive voice, the subject or subjects remain indeterminate, in accord with the languidness of the entire piece and the lack of an individualized agent. While the rhythm is choppy, the grammatical repetition of "here" and "where" causes pulsations that are shared by the elements described in the poem and the reader's own act of reading. In this way, the poem encourages an intense sense of collective embodiment, with descriptions that anthropomorphize aspects of the natural ecology: pomegranates "rear[]" their heads, the hot African wind "foldeth his soft wings in the sunlight / And lieth sleeping," the collective breath moves "dreamlike," until finally, on the forty-fifth line, we get the second main verb of the sentence: "Cream-white and soft as the breasts of a girl, / Moves the White Peacock."[29] And then soon, again, "Here, as the breath, as the soul of this beauty, / White as a cloud through the heats of the noontide / Moves the White Peacock."[30] In a letter written in 1880, Sharp translated the Italian word "sospiri" as "spiritual breath," describing it as a force that passes through all things "like a vague wind blowing through intricate forests."[31] Appropriately, then, the titular animal of Sharp's poem is not a singular entity but "the soul of this beauty," more accurately understood as the embodiment of a vast eco-spirituality. The poem's difficult form and proliferation of sensual imagery buries narrative action, as the excess of detail and breathlessness of line structure move the work from a description to an embodied experience.

"The White Peacock" is an attempt on Sharp's part not to describe or theorize cross-species intimacy or sensual pleasure, but to have the reader experience the sensuality of the other not as peacock but as a bionetwork of mutual influences. By the time Sharp was writing, his mentor Pater had effectively and famously theorized animal familiarity as an imaginative engagement fundamental to aesthetics. Sections of *The Renaissance*, *Greek Studies*, and other of his works make use of a sensual prose style to draw a reader into a stronger affective sense of the eco-aesthetics he attempts to articulate. Meanwhile, Sharp's investment in species intimacies is apparent in the formal qualities of poems like "The White Peacock," which are often keen to explore losing the self within the subjectivity of nonhumans. Queer in its emphasis on humans' relations with other species, this aesthetic field is also queer in its disruption of anthropocentrism's privileging of the human and the heteronormative. Encouraging imaginative engagements with others who are a part of one's ecology, Pater's and Sharp's works pivot away from the assumption that only (a select group of) humans understand the environment and know what is best for it, and encourage us to envision becoming more open, affectively and politically, to the concerns, histories, and futures of other members of our eco-communities.

Notes

1. Arthur Symons, "Walter Pater," *Figures of Several Centuries* (London: Constable, [1906] 1916), 316–35 at 330.
2. Brian Massumi, *What Animals Teach Us about Politics* (Durham: Duke University Press, 2014), 3.
3. Michel Foucault, *The History of Sexuality*, trans. Robert Hurley, Vol. 1 (New York: Pantheon, 1978), 43.
4. John Maynard Smith, *Evolutionary Genetics* (Oxford: Oxford University Press, 1989), 273–4.
5. Catriona Sandilands, "Queer Ecology," in Joni Adamson, William A. Gleason, and David N. Pellow, eds., *Keywords for Environmental Studies* (New York: New York University Press, 2016), 169–71.
6. Cameron Clark and E. L. McCallum, "Nature Bites Back: The Anti-pastoral Thesis in Queer and Trans Studies," *Regeneration: Environment, Art, Culture* 1.1 (2024), 1–20 at 2.
7. E. M. Forster, *Maurice* (London: Penguin, [1971] 1987), 210.
8. Clark and McCallum, "Nature Bites Back," 11.
9. Symons, "Walter Pater," 316.
10. A. C. Benson, *Walter Pater* (London: Macmillan, 1906), 190.
11. Catherine Maxwell, "Atossa to Pansie: Walter Pater, Edmund Gosse, and their Cats," *Studies in Walter Pater and Aestheticism*, 7 (Autumn 2022), 1–27 at 2.
12. Symons, "Walter Pater," 329–30.
13. Symons, "Walter Pater," 330.
14. Walter Pater, *The Renaissance: Studies in Art and Poetry* (London: MacMillan, [1873] 1888), x.
15. J. Ollerton, "Biological Barter: Patterns of Specialization Compared across Different Mutualisms," in N. M. Waser and J. Ollerton, eds., *Plant-Pollinator Interactions: From Specialization to Generalization* (Chicago: University of Chicago Press, 2006), 411–35.
16. Ernst Haeckel, *The History of Creation* (New York: Appleton, [1868] 1880), 94–95.
17. Pater, *The Renaissance*, 77, 79–80.
18. Walter Pater, *Greek Studies* (New York: Macmillan, 1895), 42.
19. Pater, *Greek Studies*, 42.
20. Pater, *Greek Studies*, 77, 79–80.
21. Flavia Alaya, *William Sharp –"Fiona Macleod"* (Oxford: Oxford University Press, 2016), 27, 127; Terry Meyers, *The Sexual Tensions of William Sharp* (New York: Peter Lang, 1996), 6, 4.
22. William Sharp, *A Memoir*, ed. Elizabeth A. Sharp (New York: Duffield, 1910), 177.

23. Meyers, *Sexual Tensions*, 21.
24. Élie Reclus, *Primitive Folk: Studies in Comparative Ethnology* (London: Walter Scott, 1891), viii.
25. Reclus, *Primitive Folk*, 16.
26. Reclus, *Primitive Folk*, 104.
27. Sharp, *A Memoir*, 179.
28. William Sharp, *Sospiri di Roma* (Rome: La Societá Laziale, 1891), 45–6.
29. Sharp, *Sospiri di Roma*, 45.
30. Sharp, *Sospiri di Roma*, 47.
31. Sharp, *A Memoir*, 31.

13

ELIZABETH CHANG

Plant Agency

To imagine the possibilities of plant agency in Victorian literature is also to imagine the limits of that agency. As much as plant life during the Victorian era could be scientifically or fantastically theorized to have far-reaching intentions and actions made evident in ways newly comprehensible to human eyes, it could also be rendered comprehensible through the suppression of these intentions and actions. For every vegetable mass that spread invasive tendrils towards a British colony or a British adventurer in fiction, another plant, potted and pruned, peacefully obeyed instructions from a domestic gardening manual in a British greenhouse. Both of these scenarios illuminate the century's understanding of what kinds of things plants might do and, by inference, how plants might think or feel (or, by contrast, *not* think or feel) about those actions. In asking and answering questions regarding what plant agency means for Victorian writers, we must return to these questions of presence and absence. What plants take action? What plants are acted upon? Literature's foundational parameters – of expression, representation, and embodiment – seem to demand that writing about plants be done with exploratory and revelatory purpose. When reading literature of the nineteenth century, whether scientific, aesthetic, philosophical, or narrative, in search of agential plants, we seek evidence of plant intention. Equally, though, plants in Victorian literature offer something else: action without apparent direction, existence without understandable intent. How might we also there find plant agency, in either individual or general terms?

Agency, plant or otherwise, has often been described through relationality: the habitual, accidental, or intended consequences of one agent's actions on another. Plants are easy to describe as the recipients of action, but harder to place as active agents themselves, especially when working through forms of literature, like the Victorian novel, that were neither initially explicitly concerned with these questions nor valued by later scholars for such data. As a result, much work involving nineteenth-century literature in the related and growing fields of critical plant studies, vegetal and more-than-human geographies, and environmental humanities more generally has involved efforts to identify and nuance the premises of this relational understanding while simultaneously attending to the complexities and differences of plant biological form.[1] To search a nineteenth-century novel for such evidences is hard for reasons both botanical and narratological, though these vibrant and expanding fields do offer welcome interdisciplinary possibilities.

One immediately apparent challenge is the profound discrepancy between plant and human delineations of scale, shape, and individual boundary in literary representation, especially when using a broadly popular historical definition of plants that might include such non-plant things as fungi and bacteria. Additionally, key derived indicators of agency including mobility, activity, and attention, while famously studied in Charles Darwin's works on botany such as *On the Movement and Habits of Climbing Plants* (1875) and *On the Power of Movement in Plants* (1880), are harder to track as independent plant phenomena through other genres of Victorian writing.[2] This is because the narrative conditions by which the agential action of plants might be registered in fiction and nonfiction of the time generally have demanded a human referent to reflect their presence – going against more recent efforts to diminish or remove human-centric framings in theorizations of plant agency. In both Victorian fiction and nonfiction, it is nearly impossible to see plants without finding people. This is as true for investigations of subjectivity and characterization as for problems of chronology, logical progression, and narrative structure. Plants, whether growing rank in the garden of an unused brewery in Charles Dickens's *Great Expectations* (1861), uprooted by floods in George Eliot's *The Mill on the Floss* (1860), or shading a wedding celebration in Thomas Hardy's *Under the Greenwood Tree* (1872), gain meaning through human reference even as human understanding acknowledges the mismatch of the forms.[3]

How then to describe a plant in independent literary and narrative terms? Modern definitions of the distinctive qualities of plants – what has been called their "plantiness" – have refenced the capacity for photosynthesis, specific modes of reproduction, movement, communication, and multicellular cellulose-based form. Though none of these characteristics can singularly apply to every plant, any specific plant can be described in scientific terms by some combination of these capacities. These qualities, however, are not often the ones highlighted when plants appear in Victorian poetry and fiction, since those genres tend to prefer qualities of aesthetic and sensory pleasure, nutritive value, or medical function. Recognizing this, Bertholde Schoene has asked if "authentic plantness [must] always remain at odds with and somehow protrude from human narration," a perhaps unanswerable question.[4] This chapter instead aims to follow Lesley Head's reminder that "each species, even each plant, has its own dynamic manifestations of form and relations – with humans and otherwise," in order to recognize not just the authenticity but also the abundance of plants claiming agency and presence both in popular narrative and in the living world.[5]

I offer two case studies drawn from Victorian literature that interact with these manifestations and protrusions to complicate the anthropomorphic ground of agentic activity, albeit without abandoning it entirely. The first study addresses Victorian practices and critiques of plant miniaturization, exploring through negative example the question of a plant's units of ethical standing as an inevitable consequence of its form and scale. The second addresses the peripatetic journeys of invasive plants through nineteenth-century texts, considering the relationship between plant taxonomy and narrative form. In the poetry and novels mentioned, plants make brief but densely significant appearances that refer to a much wider discourse – significantly, one deeply intermixed with the global realignments of the British Empire. Natani Meeker and Antónia Szabari propose that contemporary scholars "prioritize[e] not the steady accumulation of knowledge about plants but the speculative drive to bring plant life into relation with human experience."[6] This drive, I suggest, can work backwards as well as forwards as we look to the literature of the past to speculate on the glancing views it allows us of its plants' agentic life.

Miniature Plants

Altering a tree into a tiny version of itself was an Asian horticultural process long known to and often written about by Britons. Clarke Abel, a naturalist appointed to Lord Amherst's 1816 Embassy to the Qing emperor's court, notes in his memoir of the voyage that, in China, "[a]lmost all the dwarf plants seen in the gardens were elms, twisted into grotesque shapes." He describes the practices as that of "taking up a young plant and putting it in a pot too small to allow the spreading of its roots[,] ... wounding the bark in different places, so as to cover it with scars which might seem to be the consequence of decay; ... tying the branches to each other, and giving them all kinds of curves."[7] John Livingstone, a British surgeon resident in Macao, makes a point in his 1820 report of meticulously describing the Chinese practice of "dwarfing trees and shrubs" because, "[h]owever much a correct taste may depreciate the art," the subject is worth attention as "it may, in several respects, extend our information regarding the laws of organic life."[8]

Efforts at describing this Chinese practice, whether in Livingstone's inductive biology lesson or in the more sensational British travel reports from China that reprinted his remarks, presume two notable characteristics of these plant specimens: first, that they possess a specific, organic, vegetable form that human hands may attempt to obscure but can never eliminate, and second, that those specific forms suffer when forced to change. As Livingstone goes on to explain, "some Chinese feel gratified in expending considerable sums of money in giving those poor tortured trees freedom; a sufficient proof that they possess the kindlier affections, and that they believe that vegetables are endowed with sensation, as well as animals."[9]

Livingstone's comment signals the discussion of plant miniaturization as an early attempt to theorize vegetal pain and suffering within figurative capacities of anthropomorphic form and language. But it also stages, in quite dramatic terms, the "dynamic manifestation of form and relations" between plants and humans that Lesley Head described. Agricultural botany had long been concerned with methods of sizing plants for purposes of nutritional and economic productivity, but what some British visitors called the Chinese "koo-shoo" (古樹, literally "ancient tree," though such arrangements were properly termed 盆景 or 盆栽) offered an opportunity to explore humans' intentional manipulation of plants as an ornamental and therefore useless practice, one that depends for its emotional resonance on a recognition of the pain and desires of the plant itself. Victorian literature has been shown to find many routes to empathetic connection; here it finds more hospitable pathways through vegetable sensation than human affection.

By the Victorian era, the opening of Japan to British trade broadened the European understanding of East Asian horticultural practices, and the expansion of the British Empire introduced many more horticultural varieties to popular British knowledge. Attention to what William Wordsworth once called "freaks / Of human care industriously perverse" continued throughout this time, with the influential landscape designer William Robinson deeming Japanese gardeners "past masters of the art of torturing plants."[10] Laurence Oliphant, private secretary to Lord Elgin, remarked on Japanese "forest-trees ... seen in flower-pots ... their unnatural branches spread out laterally like the fingers of a deformed hand," and the adventure novelist H. Rider Haggard, by the end of the century, called these miniature specimens "abortions and a mockery to their kind."[11]

The heavy figurative effects at work here represent a pathway through Victorian literature to some of the theoretical questions arising from the initial acknowledgment of independent plant agency as understood through human-inflicted plant suffering. Chief among these is the leveraging of notions of human disability. In these anecdotes, the revisionist timescale and constrictive growing conditions create the living plants' antitheses, the manipulated plants existing as, in Haggard's word, "abortions." Many biologically defined monstrosities traveled through Victorian literature in the *fin de siècle* and "Oriental" tortures played a frequent role in their making. But beyond these yellow peril fictions, as they were known, the trope of the perverse plant signaled other revisions of form and scale.

Michael Marder has summarized that a "plant in its singularity is a collective being, a loose and disorganized assemblage, and, hence, a community of plants that do not comprise a unified whole, do not constitute either an individual or an organism."[12] More succinctly, "[p]lants are easy to take for granted," and their free-growing collective communities are easily set aside as discrete units of ethical regard or responsibility precisely because their expansive ways of being are so antithetical to Victorian rules of order.[13] By contrast, miniaturized plants, isolated in individual containers, turn the spotlight on intimate gestures of affect and care as singular modes of relation both in horticultural practice and in forms of fiction. The miniaturized tree is especially useful for engaging with these boundaries because trees have long been seen as most easily made to echo human forms and intentions, while also often being seen as particularly suggestive of national and racial affiliations. A topiary small enough to fit in a container superimposes the mobility and intimacy of a domestic houseplant onto the singularity and historicity of a centenarian heritage tree. Hence the dismay of English landscape lovers from Wordsworth to Haggard at the miniaturization of the English oak in particular.

Yet it is important to note that, beyond miniaturization's particular tortures, most of the Victorian era's horticultural developments – including practices of grafting, forcing, and training, as well as the manipulation of growing conditions in greenhouses and conservatories – arose as part of the great project of acclimatizing global plant life to domestic cultivation in Britain, and thus also in service of yoking individual affection to broader affiliative claims. As the British reach spread across climate zones, the return of exotic specimens to the British Isles as both proof of and reward for that reach required new procedures to support these non-native introductions. The understanding of plant agency was thus facilitated by conceptions of selfhood that were developing through the expansions of the British Empire.

Victorian authors used the recognition of plant pain to explore questions of individual agency through empathetic means, in both their nonfiction prose and their novels.[14] That is, plant agency was interpellated through affective recognition; plants did not need to match human lifespans or standards of size and shape, so long as their singular emotional response to pain and pleasure rang true. The lurid details of "Oriental" dwarfing gave vivid negative testimony to plant pain, while at the same time, other writings admired the satisfaction of a geranium on a sunny windowsill or similar registers of plant pleasure. In either case, the allure of vegetal charisma came in direct relation to the compliance of its subjects, an appeal routed back through fictional human characters in turn.

Throughout the nineteenth century, Asian and other exotic plant life interested literature chiefly for possessive reasons: to describe specimens in writing made part of wider ongoing efforts to observe, collect, and circulate botanical specimens relevant to the interests of the British Empire's plantations, kitchens, laboratories, and pleasure gardens, among other spaces. When these efforts took unexpected turns, the understanding of plant agency was also rewritten. What once had been called "acclimatization" was now termed "invasion."

Invasive Plants

In describing plant miniaturization in the previous section, I focused closely on horticultural techniques as they took rhetorical and narrative shape in literature. In this section I shift attention to the plants themselves and the forms of freedom in which they might engage. The significant evolutions of gardening practice during the Victorian era can be understood in part as an acknowledgement of independent plant agency. Controlled formalities of geometrical beds and symmetrical rows made up of greenhouse flowers popular earlier in the century gave way to the "wild gardening" favored by landscape designers like William Robinson, a naturalistic style favoring densely planted drifts of mixed perennials. As Robinson observed, "[t]o most people a pretty plant in the wild state is more attractive than any garden denizen ... It is free, and taking care of itself."[15] The larger context of his popular gardening advice books and periodicals, however, makes it clear that such attractive wildness can be achieved to human aesthetic satisfaction only as a simulation requiring intense human labor and cultivation. Truly wild plants had no place in the plotted garden.

Victorian writers by and large saw this division as a good thing; the kind of wild plants that actually did take care of themselves in the nineteenth-century novel usually ended up exercising forms of agency uncongenial to human interests.[16] While the pathos of the captive miniature tree depends on a reader's emotional investment in the tree's thwarted liberty, the depredations of the invasive plant rest on the reader's interest in seeing such liberties removed or reversed. This interest only increases the more the plant diverges from a potted plant's singularity and towards a heterogeneity of form that evades anthropomorphic parallelism – a growing occurrence amid the British Empire's efforts of bio-diversification, transplantation, and botanical assimilation. With the nineteenth century's many varieties of plant species finding so many new forms and new homes, indeed, mutually intelligible terms of identification struggled to keep up with these species' free growth and movement. They could not all be dismissed as simply "a pretty plant in the wild state."

Fiction and poetry, with their vast spread of vernacular botanical descriptors, begin to mark out the intricacies of this struggle from the moment they invoke the natural world. Narrative form admits the possibility of wildly variable frames, scales, and identifications to broker human–plant relations: characters admire a willow, some firs, or a forest and grow fearful of a thorn, an upas tree, or a wilderness. In Eliot's *Middlemarch* (1871) alone, readers must distinguish between Dorothea Brooke's figurative "Chinyrose" bloom, Mary Garth's garden of drying rose petals, the jasmine and hollyhock that adorn Mr. Dagley's decrepit tenancy, and the garden "Yewwalk" where Casaubon takes his refuge, among many other horticultural references deeply significant to character and yet quite uneven in specificity and scale of reference.[17] While these acts of recognition alone already suggest faint human perception of plant intention by their very appearance, it is especially interesting to consider the ways that varieties of naming embed a history of botanical exchange elucidating the operations of plant agency on a global scale.

Human circulations of and with plants, whether through agricultural importation and exportation, scientific exchange, souvenir and personal trade, or inadvertent transmission, are part of the history of imperial expansion, and have drawn attention to the effects of plant circulation on the environments, economies, and societies involved in these exchanges. Following the work of scholars like Anna Tsing, such circulations have recently been examined from a vegetal perspective; "plants act on us as much as we act on them," conclude David Nally and Gerry Kearns in their study of the history of the potato.[18] Indeed, it is within the history of plant exchange and importation that some of the clearest intentional language denoting plant agency and plant mobility comes to be employed. In addition to Linnaean binomial nomenclature, names specific to the scientific or vernacular terminologies of different languages, and translated and mistranslated versions of those names, we also find categories that insist on distant origins like "exotics," "non-natives," and "aliens," and others that attest to destructive intention like "introductions," "colonizers," and "invaders," as well as the simple and absolute interpellation of alterity that is the category of "weed."[19] When nineteenth-century novels choose some, or all, or none of these terms, we see the relayed effects of plant intentions yet again in operation.

Lynn Voskuil has explained that the invasive "red weed" in H. G. Wells's *The War of the Worlds* can be interpreted in other ways beyond

its customary designation as cautionary tale of non-native botanical introduction, but only if readers recognize, as Wells did, "the vital, dynamic,
cosmopolitan qualities of biophysical matter, most notably its capacity to
elude human cultural control."[20] As Voskuil and other environmental historians and ecologists point out, for Victorians "invasiveness" as a descriptive
botanical quality was not a particularly concerning term. While non-native
introductions were certainly noted, it was often with the intent of praising the flexibility and utility of a globally adaptative species. When reading
Victorian fiction, where Linnean namings are less frequently found, the vernacular identification of invasive species often carries its own associations.

This was the case with the genus *acacia* which was both widely planted in
the nineteenth century and often present in fiction of the time.[21] Christian
Kull and Haripriya Rangan have definitively studied the complexities of
the "acacia exchanges" that circulated these plants globally, encouraging
us to understand "wandering plants as active agents in region-forming
processes" and to recognize that "plant introductions both shape and are
shaped by distinct regional convergences of ecology, livelihoods, politics,
and ideology."[22] Within the genus, the *acaia mearnsii*, commonly known
as black wattle, which was exported from its native Australia to be grown
as a source for tannin, especially in Southern Africa and the *acaia dealbata*,
known as silver wattle or, to Victorians, mimosa-tree and also native to
Australia and equally widely exported for use as fuel, both appear by their
common names in nineteenth-century British novels and travel narratives
written from the Cape Colonies (now South Africa).

Though current scholarship argues that today these trees are "among
the most conspicuous [and] damaging ... invasive species," neither kind
is depicted as a particular threat to their new ecological settings in these
writings.[23] Thus, when we read of the plantations of black wattle or of
the freely growing mimosa-tree in H. Rider Haggard's two Cape Colony
novels of 1885, *Jess* and *The Witch's Head*, we have multiple compounding
conditions by which to consider the agency of these plants, both as individual specimens and as an actively-dispersing species. The black wattle,
like other invasive species naturalized in Haggard's novels, is most usefully
understood as the latter, since its fictional presence is usually kept under
conditions of strict cultivation.

The mimosa-tree, by contrast, makes a more notable entrance into *The
Witch's Head*'s adventurous pages. On a ride through the forest, a character notices an unusual botanical action by "one of the flat-crowned
mimosa-trees" which suddenly rises and flips in the air to show its roots
instead of its crown. Though this "'Alice in Wonderland' sort of performance on the part of the tree" is quickly explained as the work of an

elephant "pulling up mimosa-trees as easily as though they were radishes" and the narrative just as quickly distracted by an elephant hunt, the knot of allusions is worth some pause.[24] In these few sentences, the tree first has its seemingly independent actions gain explanation through allusion to a British children's classic, then is likened to a staple of the English vegetable garden itself originally imported from Asia, all the while existing itself as a transplant with a name allusive to the titular (though unrelated) *mimosa pudica* of a famous Romantic poem, Percy Shelley's "The Sensitive Plant" (1820). Amid all this, of course, the performative tree is only "one of" the stand of invasives growing across the novel's landscape, each awaiting their own "sort of performance."

Kull and Rangan have described "bundled movement" as a heuristic for the combined circulation of botanical, horticultural, and social knowledge that can be understood to travel with the species of plant exchanges. Their emphasis on the burgeoning human activity embedded in plant life gains fuller meaning when paired with Voiskul's description of culture's planty overflow as "unpredictable natural excess not subsumed by the human – and capable of escaping our notice, our intervention, and our management."[25] This imagined yet particular mimosa tree – quixotic, mobile, performative – demonstrates both sides of these excess conditions within the pages of the novel. Though the frame of reference and the literary form are human, the distribution and presence of these trees are of their own making, multiplying at the edge of human notice.

Narratological form, and in particular the gestures towards nonhuman narratologies that the mimosa and elephant offer to us here, can thus be understood to accommodate the intentions and actions of plants, even if only by not absolutely disallowing their existence.

Each act of plant recognition – in scientific nomenclature, in what Dickon in Frances Hodgson Burnett's *The Secret Garden* (1911) would call its "country name," in analogy, or in literary allusion – itself grants a plant agency from the very occasion of its invasion into the lines of the written text. But agentic plants do not always require the supports of narrative movement. Shelley's *mimosa* poem, favored by Victorians for its apparently innocuous themes, lyrically invokes a full garden in growth and death, one by one: the Sensitive plant of the title, but also snowdrop, violet, tulip, "Naiad-like lily of the vale," moss, grass, pines and later "ugly weeds," "thistles, nettles, and darnels rank," and "plants, at whose names the verse feel loath," among so many more.[26] Though the decay of the garden and the death of the Lady who tends it seem distressing, Shelley's conclusion forestalls such empathies. "Whether the Sensitive Plant ... / Now felt this change, I cannot say" the poet insists, explaining that "That garden sweet, that lady fair / ... In truth have never passed away:/ 'Tis we, 'tis ours, are changed; not they" (l.288-91, l.304-7). Shelley's verse, often understood to embed the resilience of human revolution beneath its "sweet shapes and odours," can also in its lyrical catalogue be understood to describe the persistence of plant intention and agentic purpose (l.305).[27]

These accommodations of scientific, narrative, or lyric literary form to the plant as referent suggests that plants, when given names, even changeable or non-referential ones, are also given narrative possibility and so, by extension, a kind of agency – an agency that then extends through the readers to the plants of the living world. To recognize these plant names and the impressions they leave – whether of delight, fear, scholarly interest, or aesthetic pleasure – is also to register the effects of an agency relayed through its rippling effects.

At the beginning of this chapter, I suggested that plant agency could be recognized in Victorian literature often only through its absence or suppression. In cataloging some specific descriptions of individual species, I have also proposed that plant agency can be brought into focus through particular acts of close reading and observation that we see best in edge cases – a miniature plant scarred in root and limb or an invasive tree turned upside down in its colonial landscape. These moments of sidelong attention do not, of course, return to us the plant itself as it once lived and grew. But perhaps by following the trailing path of Victorian literary plants rather than always their human observers, contemporary readers themselves can become more plant-aligned. Doing this, I think, will aid in recognizing the flexible and nonhierarchical effects of the surrounding vegetable world in contemporary literary and physical environments as well. Plant agency, of course, by no means depends on human recognition. However, both plant and human existences can gain heightened, collaborative, mutually supportive embodiment and expression when such recognition, even glancingly, is granted.

Notes

1. On plant agency, see Owain Jones and Paul Cloke, "Non-human Agencies: Trees in Place and Time," in Carl Knappett and Lambros Malafouris, eds., *Material Agency* (Boston: Springer US, 2008), 79–96; Anna M. Lawrence, "Listening to Plants: Conversations between Critical Plant Studies and Vegetal Geography," *Progress in Human Geography* 46.2 (April 2022), 629–51.
2. See Mary Bowden, "Vegetal Being in Samuel Butler's *Erewhon*: The Narrative Challenge of Nineteenth-Century Plant Science," *ISLE: Interdisciplinary Studies in Literature and Environment* 28.3 (Autumn 2021), 966–85.
3. On Hardy, see Elizabeth Carolyn Miller, "Dendrography and Ecological Realism," *Victorian Studies* 58.4 (2016), 696–718.

4. Berthold Schoene, "Arborealism, or Do Novels Do Trees?" *Textual Practice* 36.9 (September 2, 2022), 1435–58 at 1440.

5. Lesley Head, Jennifer Atchison, and Catherine Phillips, "The Distinctive Capacities of Plants: Re-thinking Difference via Invasive Species," *Transactions of the Institute of British Geographers* 40.3 (July 2015), 399–413 at 404. See also Hannah Pitt, "On Showing and Being Shown Plants – A Guide to Methods for More-Than-Human Geography," *Area* 47.1 (March 2015), 48–55.

6. Natania Meeker and Antónia Szabari, *Radical Botany: Plants and Speculative Fiction* (New York: Fordham University Press, 2019), 24.

7. Clarke Abel, *Narrative of a Journey in the Interior of China* (London: Longmans, 1818), 221.

8. John Livingstone, "Account of the Method of Dwarfing Trees and Shrubs, As Practised by the Chinese, Including Their Plan of Propagation from Branches," *Transactions of the Horticultural Society of London* 4 (1822), 224.

9. Livingstone, "Account of the Method," 228.

10. William Wordsworth, *The Thirteen-Book Prelude*, ed. Mark L. Reed, 2 vols. (Ithaca: Cornell University Press, 1991), 2.84; William Robinson, *The English Flower Garden: Design, Arrangement and Plans*, 4th ed. (London: John Murray, 1895), 321.

11. Laurence Oliphant, *Narrative of the Earl of Elgin's Mission to China and Japan in the Years 1857, '58, '59* (London: W. Blackwood, 1859), 173; H. Ryder Haggard, *A Gardener's Year* (London: Longmans, 1905), 183–4.

12. Michael Marder, "Resist Like a Plant! On the Vegetal Life of Political Movements," *Peace Studies Journal* 5.1 (2012), 24–32 at 29.

13. Lesley Head and Jennifer Atchison, "Cultural Ecology: Emerging Human–Plant Geographies," *Progress in Human Geography* 33.2 (April 2009), 236–45 at 236–7.

14. On houseplants, see Lindsay Wells, "Vegetal Bedfellows: Houseplant Superstitions and Environmental Thought in Nineteenth-Century Periodicals," *Victorian Periodicals Review*, 54.1 (2021), 1–23. On "hierarchy of ethical regard," see Hannah Pitt, "Questioning Care Cultivated through Connecting with More-Than-Human Communities," *Social & Cultural Geography* 19.2 (February 17, 2018), 253–74.

15. William Robinson, *The Wild Garden, or, Our Groves & Shrubberies Made Beautiful by the Naturalization of Hardy Exotic Plants* (London: John Murray, 1870), 11.

16. See Elizabeth Chang, "Killer Plants of the Late Nineteenth Century," in Lara Karpenko and Shalyn Claggett, eds., *Strange Science: Investigating the Limits of Knowledge in the Victorian Age* (Ann Arbor: University of Michigan Press, 2017), 81–101.

17. George Eliot, *Middlemarch* (New York: Penguin, 2015), 452, 484, 370, 452.

18. David Nally and Gerry Kearns, "Vegetative States: Potatoes, Affordances, and Survival Ecologies," *Antipode* 52.5 (September 2020), 1373–92.

19. See Jodi Frawley and Iain McCalman, eds., *Rethinking Invasion Ecologies from the Environmental Humanities* (New York: Routledge, 2014).

20. Lynn Voskuil, "Victorian Plants: Cosmopolitan and Invasive," *Victorian Literature and Culture* 49.1 (April 2021), 27–53 at 43.

21. On Victorian taxonomy of the acacias mentioned, see G. Bentham, "Revision of the Suborder *Mimoseæ*," *Transactions of the Linnean Society of London* 30 (London, 1875), 335–664.

22. Christian A. Kull and Haripriya Rangan, "Acacia Exchanges: Wattles, Thorn Trees, and the Study of Plant Movements," *Geoforum* 39.3 (May 2008), 1258–72 at 1261.

23. David M. Richardson and Marcel Rejmánek, "Trees and Shrubs As Invasive Alien Species – A Global Review," *Diversity and Distributions* 17.5 (2011), 788–809 at 789.

24. H. Ryder Haggard, *The Witch's Head*, 3 vols. (London: Hurst and Blackett, 1885), 3.5.

25. Kull and Rangan, "Acacia Exchanges," 1261; Voiskul, "Victorian Plants," 42.

26. Percy Shelley, "The Sensitive Plant," in Donald Reiman and Sharon Powers, eds., *Shelley's Poetry and Prose* (New York: W. W. Norton, 1977), 210–19, lines 21, 213, 228, 232.

27. On Shelley's revolutionary interests while writing this poem, see Elisa Cozzi, "P. B. Shelley, George William Tighe, and the Irish Roots of 'The Sensitive-Plant,'" *Romanticism* 30.1 (2024), 42–55.

PART IV

Environmental Uses and Abuses

14

ELIZABETH CAROLYN MILLER

"A Little in the Mining Way"

Victorian Literatures of Extraction

In the preface to his 1825 publication *A General Guide to the Companies Formed for Working Foreign Mines*, Henry English hazarded that "this Pamphlet cannot be otherwise than acceptable" given its publication "at a period when Joint Stock Companies, particularly those formed for Mining Operations, engage so large a share of the public attention."[1] At the dawn of the Victorian era, mining operations in Britain and overseas were indeed becoming a source of wide public attention, even fascination, as the economy and culture shifted toward those of an extraction-based society, one grounded in the extraction of finite underground materials. Despite the volatility and uncertainty of individual mining operations at the time, wild fortunes were to be made, it was thought, through mining investment, especially overseas. The association of mining with sudden wealth can be gleaned from the number of Victorian literary plots that turn on the sudden acquisition of mineral riches from overseas, whether in Mary Elizabeth Braddon's *Lady Audley's Secret* (1862), Wilkie Collins's *The Moonstone* (1868), or Anthony Trollope's *John Caldigate* (1879). Some novels obscure the nature of this wealth, but its minerality clings about it nonetheless: in Charles Dickens's *Great Expectations* (1861), for example, Pip is made a gentleman on the strength of an Australian fortune that crashes down on him unexpectedly, but while the novel was published in the midst of the mid-century Australian gold rushes, it is set in the early decades of the nineteenth century, so the novel grounds Magwitch's Australian fortune in shepherding rather than gold. Even in this early century setting, however, Pip's friend Herbert Pocket already presumes that a young man with limited prospects must look to mining to make his way: "I shall not rest satisfied with merely employing my capital in insuring ships. ... I shall also do a little in the mining way."[2]

Herbert Pocket's phrasing, "a little in the mining way," suggests his own unfamiliarity with mining in the industrial era, for it was not something to be done in half measures. The era had seen a massive acceleration of mining in terms of the depths plumbed and the volumes extracted, and this was largely an effect of the new role of fossil fuels in nineteenth-century industry. Kenneth Pomeranz has explained the impact of early nineteenth-century British coal in fomenting the era's world-historical economic shifts: "no matter how far back we may push for the origins of capitalism, *industrial* capitalism, in which the large-scale use of inanimate energy sources allowed an escape from the common constraints of the preindustrial world, emerges only in the 1800s."[3] This "escape" occasioned an acceleration in industries of all kinds, including mining, and more and more coal was increasingly demanded as the motive power of daily industry. Britain's early development of industrial coalmining, and its coal-rich subsurface, had put it in a dominant position to cater to that demand, and as Edward Hull marveled at the time, "it appears that almost every country in the world is dependent, to a greater or less degree, on Great Britain for its coal supply."[4]

By the time William Jevons published *The Coal Question: An Inquiry Concerning the Progress of the Nation, and the Probable Exhaustion of Our Coal-Mines* in 1865, the possibility that Britain would run out of coal, thus completely derailing the basis for daily life, had already begun to worry many social thinkers. Jevons's book takes for granted that Victorians had already become accustomed to a motive power utterly untethered from the vagaries of the season or weather:

> The first great requisite of motive power is, that *it shall be wholly at our command, to be exerted when, and where, and in what degree we desire.* The wind, for instance, as a direct motive power, is wholly inapplicable to a system of machine labour, for during a calm season the whole business of the country would be thrown out of gear.[5]

Jevons's volume suggests that by 1865 coal had come to seem indispensable in Britain, and that this created, counterintuitively, a sense of vulnerability: "our anxiety must be indefinitely increased in reflecting that *while other countries mostly subsist upon the annual and ceaseless income of the harvest, we are drawing more and more upon a capital which yields no annual interest, but once turned to light and heat and force, is gone for ever into space.*"[6] The problem with coal, in Jevons's view, is that it does not regenerate – at least not on human timescales. Unaware that coal combustion released particulates into the atmosphere that contribute to the greenhouse gas effect, Jevons thought coal just disappeared "into space." Jevons's musings suggest how coal combustion ushered in an extraction-based economy that was premised, unprecedentedly, on a nonrenewable, finite underground resource, and they convey how this fact in itself required significant cultural adjustment. They also anticipate how coal brought with it a way of life that Naomi Klein would later describe as "extractivism": a "nonreciprocal, dominance-based relationship with the earth, one purely of taking … the opposite of stewardship, which involves taking but also taking care that regeneration and future life continue."[7]

The term "extraction," on which "extractivism" is based, often refers to the mining of underground mineral resources, but is also used more generally to describe, as Sandro Mezzadra and Brett Neilson put it, "the forced removal of raw materials and life forms from the earth's surface, depths, and biosphere."[8] The term is helpful because it points to a disjuncture between extracted resources and the environments and lifeworlds in which they were embedded, and the ways that these environments and lifeworlds are often disturbed to the point of being sacrificed in the wake of extractive industry. Under extractivism, the bits of earth that are removed and sold have value, not the extractive zone from which they are taken. To pay attention to extractivism is to be cognizant of the centrality of natural resources to colonialism and capitalism and of the resource imbalance between wealthy colonial powers and the places that have been exploited by them. Looking back to the Victorian period, a focus on extraction helps us see how British literature responded to the epochal emergence of a society reliant on finite underground resources – including but not limited to coal – and to the material relations at the heart of imperialism.

This chapter explores how various Victorian writers conceived of the rise of an extraction-based society and looks to the literary archive for early impressions of extraction's wider social significance. My 2021 book *Extraction Ecologies and the Literature of the Long Exhaustion* offers a longer discussion of this subject, focused on different literary texts than the ones I discuss here, but the topic is pervasive in literature of the era and one of the points I want to emphasize in this chapter is the extent to which extractivism informs Victorian literature even when it is not obviously *about* mining and extraction. Thus this chapter will engage both texts that are directly about mining and texts that are not.

In our current era of climate change, I am far from alone in looking back to nineteenth-century literature to ask how we became so enmired in fossil fuels and how our culture transformed in line with such developments.[9] Heidi C. M. Scott sums up the magnitude of the changes effectively: "By unleashing the astonishing power of fossil fuels using the steam engine, coal introduced more changes to life, environment, and society than the world had seen in the previous twelve thousand years of the agricultural era[.] … This was the single largest leap in energy consumption in history, made visible in the coal-gray skies hulking above nineteenth-century cities."[10] The wide social significance of such changes was not lost on the major thinkers of the day. Jevons, an economist, believed that "England's manufacturing and commercial greatness" depended on the coal supply, and he worried about exhaustion's cultural as well as its economic implications: "material decay may ... involve us in moral and intellectual retrogression"[11] In the second edition of *The Coal Question*, revised and published a year after the first one, he went so far as to outline a series of social reforms that should be taken during coal's heyday to guard against such retrogression in the leaner times of the future. He argued, for example, for "a far more general restriction on the employment of children in manufacture," so that children could be educated into citizenry, thus preventing a future fall into barbarism, and he argued for universal education: "anything which we may lose or spend now in education and loss of labour will be repaid many times over by the increased efficiency of labour in the next generation."[12]

Children often loomed large in discussions of coal and coal exhaustion, for the future was the battleground of these discussions. Not only did children represent Britain's future population, threatened by a potential depletion of coal, but child labor was also one of the first areas where Britain was willing to put a check of any sort on rampant coal extraction. The Mines and Collieries Act of 1842 prohibited children under ten from working in the mines and thus began to correct a situation where shockingly young children had often been employed as trappers or putters. Trappers were typically the youngest workers in the coal mines, and they played a crucial role in workplace safety, as Peter Kirby describes:

> Underground ventilation currents were maintained by the installation of trapdoors that were frequently attended by young children. "Trappers" were required to open such ventilation doors momentarily to allow the passage of coal tubs and then to ensure that they closed again to maintain the correct circulation of air currents. This was a simple procedure but was crucial to the safety of the entire workforce. Young trapdoor keepers would sometimes fall asleep in the warm, dark, atmosphere of the mine ... resulting in an interruption of ventilation.[13]

The role of the putter was another job often given to young children, and Louis Simonin's *Mines and Miners; Or, Underground Life* (1868) describes it thusly: "boys, called *putters*, perform a task ... drawing four-wheeled trams along the low and narrow levels, which are sometimes not more than a yard high. With belts round their waists they couple themselves by a chain to the tram, and draw it along, occasionally on their hands and feet, over the uneven and often muddy roads."[14]

Depictions of child trappers and putters animated some of the earliest anti-extractivist literature in Britain, including Elizabeth Barrett Browning's 1843 protest poem "The Cry of the Children," which gave voice to the children working in mines and factories of the age. Originally published in *Blackwood's Edinburgh Magazine* in August 1843, "The Cry of the Children" had an important role in the early 1840s public outcry against children's work in the mines, and it has been credited with having a direct political impact on child labor legislation in Britain and elsewhere.[15] The structure of the poem is a dialogue between the speaker, who is distraught by the condition of the child workers and frantically trying to call attention to it, and the children themselves, who are numbed and deadened to sentiment and sensation altogether. In one passage, the speaker exhorts them, "Go out, children, from the mine and from the city – / Sing out, children, as the little thrushes do – / Pluck you handfuls of the meadow-cowslips pretty / Laugh aloud, to feel your fingers let them through!" But the children respond, "Are your cowslips of the meadows / Like our weeds anear the mine? / Leave us quiet in the dark of the coal-shadows, / From your pleasures fair and fine!"[16] An oft-circulated illustration of child putters hard at work had appeared in *The Condition and Treatment of the Children Employed in the Mines and Collieries of the United Kingdom* (1842), which was published just before the poem, and Barrett Browning gave the putters a line in "The Cry of the Children": "For, all day, we drag our burden tiring, / Through the coal-dark, underground."[17] Toward the end of the poem, the insensate children finally wake up and Barrett Browning concludes with their passionate question to readers: "'How long, O cruel nation, / Will you stand, to move the world, on a child's heart[?].'"[18]

Less well known, but no less an illuminating literary response to child labor in the mine is Joseph Skipsey's poem "Mother Wept" from his 1878 volume *Miscellaneous Lyrics*. If the child miners were crying in Barrett Browning's poem, here it is the mother crying as her son prepares to begin working in the pit. The poem opens, "Mother wept, and father sighed; / With delight a-glow / Cried the lad, 'to-morrow,' cried, / 'To the pit I go.'"[19] Only four quatrains, the poem is much shorter than "The Cry of the Children," but like Barrett Browning, Skipney draws his poem's pathos from the child's insensibility to the tragedy of their position. Skipsey's lad is actually excited to enter the mine – to achieve a rite of passage that is social in nature, as is evident from the description of his town's response in the final quatrain: "'May he,' many a gossip cried,' / 'Be from peril kept;' / Father hid his face and sighed, / Mother turned and wept."[20] Skipsey had himself begun working as a trapper boy in the mine at age seven, and his father, a pit overman, had died when Skipsey was only four months old, having been "shot dead by a special constable while trying to defuse an altercation between pitmen and police during a bitter miner's strike."[21] "Mother Wept" complicates the victimhood of child workers in the mine by depicting its lad as something like a willing victim, one who has evidently been socially conditioned to envision his future in the mines despite the risks and dangers of the work, of which his parents are all too aware. Martha Vicinus calls "Mother Wept" "the culmination of half a century of educating the miners and the public by trade unions and their literary spokesmen," and she connects the poem to the "continuous literary tradition" of England's coal miners.[22]

If this tradition was continuous, mining itself proceeded in a less steady manner in the nineteenth century, characterized rather by rapid jumps forward and surges of acceleration and change. The stark, sudden changes that industrialization wrought on the life and landscape of nineteenth-century Britain are perhaps one reason why the novel of the recent past was such a common literary form during this period. Kathleen Tillotson has observed that beginning in the 1840s, many novelists "were coming to prefer a setting which was neither historical nor contemporary, but which lay in a period from twenty to sixty years earlier," and she describes "the wish to record change, in its process or by implied contrast" as one of the reasons for this shift.[23] Helen Kingstone has similarly argued that novels set within the time of "living memory" were significant in the nineteenth century to a greater degree than before or since, and she mentions Dickens's *Great Expectations* as one such novel that "would have been received by [its] first readers as taking more or less specific, and often very pointed, retrospects" and as "making implicit commentaries on the trajectory of the period between setting and writing."[24] Although neither Tillotson nor Kingstone raises the prospect that rapid industrial change was the prompt for the rise of the novel of the recent past, I would suggest that the changes wrought by coal-fired industry were dramatic enough to make living memory and its gap from the present a subject of new interest for novelists. Thinking about this drive to trace industrialism's transformations as part of the motivation for the novel of the recent past in this era helps us see the connection between literary works that are directly focused on extraction, such as "The Cry of the Children" and "Mother Wept," and those that are much less obviously about extraction, like Dickens's *Great Expectations*.

Great Expectations was published in 1861, but it takes place in the first decades of the century, prior to the rise of the railways and before the 1830s when steam power achieved definitive sway within British industrial production. The novel is a *bildungsroman*, and as Pip grows, the century and its industrial economy grow with him. Indeed, as with many nineteenth-century novels of the recent past, we could think of *Great Expectations* as a *bildungsroman* for industrialism: as Pip recalls early in the novel, "steam, was yet in its infancy."[25] If steam power is in its infancy at the time of the novel's opening, it seems to possess what we might call great expectations. What is perhaps most interesting about the gap between the novel's publication and its setting is that Dickens does not choose to depict a pre-steam or pre-industrial era but rather a period of transition when new and old forms of energy intermingled. Joe, for example, is the novel's figure of constancy – "there was no change whatever in Joe," Pip reflects at one point – and his forge, powered by fire, represents a more traditional form of production dependent on hard physical labor rather than steam-powered machinery.[26] Joe "stick[s] to the old work," as he says.[27] The sheer muscular strength demanded by the forge is evident in the fight between Joe and Orlick, two blacksmiths going "at one another, like two giants. But, if any man in that neighbourhood could stand up long against Joe, I never saw the man."[28] Joe's gift, however, is his ability to regulate this iron-wielding power in a way that no inhuman engine could ever do: Pip thinks of him as like a "steam-hammer," but one that can "crush a man or pat an eggshell, in his combination of strength with gentleness."[29] As a child, Pip had been tricked by Orlick into believing "that the Devil lived in a black corner of the forge, and … that it was necessary to make up the fire, once in seven years, with a live boy, and that I might consider myself fuel."[30] Though a childish belief, it reflects the forge's association with the premodern and its dependence on human energy rather than engines. But Pip's path will not be Joe's, and in the world of manufacture, steam power is quickly coming to replace the human muscular power of traditional forms of production. If Pip had once believed in that ancient technology of "the forge as the glowing road to manhood and independence," "once was not now."[31]

The setting and details of Dickens's novel often serve to reflect on industrialization and industrial heritage and on the rapid changes in life and land that had been occasioned by steam power in the early nineteenth century. Take, for example, Pip's description of the River Thames toward the end of the book, which focuses on sites that may have been remembered by his earliest readers though they could no longer be seen:

> Old London Bridge was soon passed, and old Billingsgate Market with its oyster-boats and Dutchmen, and the White Tower and Traitor's Gate, and we were in among the tiers of shipping. Here were the Leith, Aberdeen, and Glasgow steamers, loading and unloading goods, and looking immensely high out of the water as we passed alongside; here, were colliers by the score and score, with the coal-whippers plunging off stages on deck, as counterweights to measures of coal swinging up, which were then rattled over the side into barges; here, at her moorings was to-morrow's steamer for Rotterdam, of which we took good notice; and here to-morrow's for Hamburg, under whose bowsprit we crossed.[32]

Old London Bridge was demolished in 1832, and Billingsgate Market, where one could purchase oysters, eels, and fish, was transformed in 1850 when a market building was erected to replace the sheds of the past. If Dickens offers readers a trip through a riverside London that no longer exists, it is also evident that coal is the reason it no longer exists. The passage calls our attention to colliers and coal-whippers, and thus to the growing importance of coal to the era's maritime culture, but the bulk of the passage focuses on the steamships that had begun to travel to relatively nearby destinations – Leith, Aberdeen, Glasgow, Rotterdam, and Hamburg – at this point in the century. Pip as narrator emphasizes how preliminary all this was to what was to come: "At that time, the steam-traffic on the Thames was far below its present extent ... of steam-ships, great and small, not a tithe or a twentieth part so many."[33] By the time Dickens's novel was published, readers would have been able to catch steamships bound for almost anywhere, but the first transatlantic steamships between Britain and the United States did not sail until 1838 and the Peninsula and Oriental Steam Navigation Company (P&O) did not launch its first steamship route to India until 1842; thus Pip's options for steamship travel were much more limited.

Even while depicting such an early stage of steamship travel, *Great Expectations* emphasizes "the steamship's status as a wonder of the modern age," as Jonathan Stafford puts it, one whose "means of propulsion was particularly seen as a radical departure from sail ... constituting the industrialisation of travel at sea."[34] When Pip and Magwitch attempt to catch a steamship further down the Thames, the sublime scale and inexorability of the new industrial technology are brought home to Pip: "She was nearing us very fast, and the beating of her paddles grew louder and louder. I felt as if her shadow were absolutely upon us ... I heard them calling to us, and heard the order given to stop the paddles, and heard them stop, but felt her driving down upon us irresistibly."[35] By the time *Great Expectations* was published, the screw propeller had mostly replaced the paddlewheels of earlier steamships, so the passage again serves to locate the novel in the recent industrial past, but what is most notable about the passage is how relentlessly inhuman the coal-fired steamship already is. An accident ensues where Magwitch is brought "under the keel of the steamer ... struck on the head in rising," and he will eventually die of the injury.[36] This recalls another Victorian novel of the recent past, George Eliot's *The Mill on the Floss*, published in 1860 – just a year prior to *Great Expectations* – and set in the 1820s and 1830s. The heroine of Eliot's novel, Maggie Tulliver, is famously killed at the end of the novel when the river on which she lives floods and the boat carrying Maggie and her brother collides with some fragments of broken machinery caught up in the river's current. Maggie and Tom Tulliver see "death rushing on them" and "the next instant the boat was no longer seen upon the water."[37]

Like *Great Expectations, The Mill on the Floss* is a novel of the recent past that is published in the context of England's industrial heyday but looks back to the earlier advent of the coal economy. In the case of Eliot's novel, a mill's transition from water power to steam power marks the change, but both Eliot's and Dickens's novels endeavor to record and historicize the rapid technological and energy changes of the century and both participate in a broader literary engagement in this period with extractivism and the emergence of an extraction-based society. Such engagement is visible in the literary resonance of other kinds of mineral extraction beyond coal, too. As noted earlier, one of the strange effects of *Great Expectations*'s setting in the recent past is the ghostly presence of the Australian gold rushes in the novel. These were well underway when it was published in 1861, but had not yet happened in the time the novel is set. Late in the novel we find out that Magwitch had hoped to leave to Pip "certain lands of considerable value" in New South Wales, the state where the Australian gold rush would begin in 1851.[38] Writing in the midst of those gold rushes, Dickens might have wanted readers to imagine those agricultural lands bearing much richer fruit in the gold rushes to come, after the time the novel is set. The novel's emphasis on Miss Havisham's jewels and Estella's inheritance of them is yet another means by which Dickens positions extracted commodities at the heart of the novel's strange forms of intergenerational transfer. Just as Magwitch makes Pip a gentleman through his Australian lands, Miss Havisham makes Estella a lady through her jewels, and after she goes to live in London, Estella tells Pip that she is to "write to [Miss Havisham] constantly" and "report how I go on – I and the jewels."[39] Both Miss Havisham and Magwitch live vicariously by means of the extracted wealth – portable property – that they bestow on their young protégés.

Diamonds and gold are called on as symbols more commonly than coal in Victorian literature, but coal was at the root of Britain's great industrial wealth. Few writers and artists of the nineteenth century depicted underground mines directly, and as Louis Simonin wrote in 1868, "the colliery population ... is a world in itself, which has been little studied till now ... the philosopher, the savant, the artist, the romance writer, have not sufficiently examined him."[40] This lack of attention was no doubt due in part to the class bias of literature and the arts, and the paucity – at least until the early twentieth century – of working-class writers and artists with knowledge of mining. Even without such direct accounts, however, reflections on extraction-based life and what it meant for British society, British Empire, and British futures are everywhere apparent in the literature of the era. From shifts in genre and setting, such as the preeminence of the novel of the recent past which catalogued industrialism's rapid transformations, to direct appeals for checks to extractivism's worst forms of exploitation, such as we find in Barrett Browning's and Skipsey's poems, extraction was a shaping force and central concern of nineteenth-century literature. The influence went the other way, too, of course: narratives and discourses of extraction also transformed the way industry and the environment were imagined and thought of in this period. Taken together, extractivism was a framework of understanding through which nineteenth-century literature passed, and which passed through nineteenth-century literature, at a historical moment when the grounding of life was shifting under writers' feet.

Notes

1. Henry English, *A General Guide to the Companies Formed for Working Foreign Mines* (London: Boosey & Sons, 1825), preface, n.p.
2. Charles Dickens, *Great Expectations* (Peterborough: Broadview, 1998), 214.
3. Kenneth Pomeranz, *The Great Divergence: China, Europe, and the Making of the Modern World Economy* (Princeton: Princeton University Press, 2000), 16.
4. Edward Hull, *The Coal Fields of Great Britain: Their History, Structure, and Resources.* 5th ed., rev. (London: Rees, 1905), 398.
5. W. Stanley Jevons, *The Coal Question: An Inquiry Concerning the Progress of the Nation, and the Probable Exhaustion of Our Coal-Mines* (London: Macmillan, 1865), 122, original emphasis.
6. Jevons, *The Coal Question*, 307, original emphasis.
7. Naomi Klein, *This Changes Everything: Capitalism vs. The Climate* (New York: Simon & Schuster, 2014), 169.
8. Sandro Mezzadra and Brett Neilson, "Operations of Capital," *South Atlantic Quarterly* 114.1 (January 2015), 2.
9. See, for example, Allen MacDuffie, *Victorian Literature, Energy, and the Ecological Imagination* (Cambridge: Cambridge University Press, 2014); and *Climate of Denial: Darwin, Climate Change, and the Literature of the Long Nineteenth Century* (Stanford: Stanford University Press, 2024); or Jesse Oak Taylor's *The Sky of Our Manufacture: The London Fog in British Fiction from Dickens to Woolf* (Charlottesville: University of Virginia Press, 2016).
10. Heidi C. M. Scott, *Fuel: An Ecocritical History* (London: Bloomsbury, 2018), 4.
11. Jevons, *The Coal Question*, ix.
12. W. Stanley Jevons, *The Coal Question: An Inquiry Concerning the Progress of the Nation, and the Probable Exhaustion of Our Coal-Mines*, 2nd ed., rev. (London: Macmillan, 1866), xxiv–xxv.
13. Peter Kirby, *Child Workers and Industrial Health in Britain, 1780–1850* (Woodbridge: Boydell & Brewer, 2013), 142.
14. Louis Simonin, *Mines and Miners; Or, Underground Life*, trans. and ed. H. W. Bristow (London: Mackenzie, 1868), 118.
15. Marjorie Stone, "Witness Narratives and Working-Class Suffering: 'The Cry of the Children,' Corn Law Rhymes, and Elizabeth Barrett Browning's Unpublished Hunger Ballad," *Victorian Studies* 62.4 (Summer 2020), 616–43.
16. Elizabeth Barrett Browning, "The Cry of the Children," *The Norton Anthology to English Literature*, Vol. E (New York: Norton, 2005), 1174–78, ll. 57–64.

17. Browning, "The Cry of the Children," 73–4.
18. Browning, "The Cry of the Children," 153–4.
19. Joseph Skipsey, "Mother Wept," *A Book of Miscellaneous Lyrics* (Bedlington: printed for the author by George Richardson, 1878), 119, ll. 1–4.
20. Skipsey, "Mother Wept," 13–16.
21. Bridget Keegan and John Goodridge, "Modes and Methods in Three Nineteenth-Century Mineworker Poets," *Philological Quarterly* 92.2 (Spring 2013), 238.
22. Martha Vicinus, *The Industrial Muse: A Study of Nineteenth Century British Working-Class Literature* (London: Croom Helm, 1974), 60, 61.
23. Kathleen Tillotson, *Novels of the Eighteen-Forties* (Oxford: Clarendon, 1954), 92.
24. Helen Kingstone, *Victorian Narratives of the Recent Past: Memory, History, Fiction* (London: Palgrave Macmillan, 2017), 3–4, 141.
25. Dickens, *Great Expectations*, 82.
26. Dickens, *Great Expectations*, 487.
27. Dickens, *Great Expectations*, 254.
28. Dickens, *Great Expectations*, 148.
29. Dickens, *Great Expectations*, 173.
30. Dickens, *Great Expectations*, 146.
31. Dickens, *Great Expectations*, 140.
32. Dickens, *Great Expectations*, 456.
33. Dickens, *Great Expectations*, 456.
34. Jonathan Stafford, *Imperial Steam: Modernity on the Sea Route to India, 1837–1874* (Manchester: Manchester University Press, 2023), 36.
35. Dickens, *Great Expectations*, 456.
36. Dickens, *Great Expectations*, 466.
37. George Eliot, *The Mill on the Floss* (Peterborough: Broadview, 2007), 516–17.
38. Dickens, *Great Expectations*, 469.
39. Dickens, *Great Expectations*, 298.
40. Simonin, *Mines and Miners*, 250–1.

15

ELLA MERSHON

The Victorian Capitalocene
Olive Schreiner on the Frontier

The Anthropocene marks humanity's emergence as a planetary force capable of altering the geophysical earth such that future generations will see humanity's presence in the geological record for ages to come. But recently the quest to declare the Anthropocene an official geological epoch hit a major roadblock. In March 2024, the Subcommission on Quaternary Stratigraphy voted down a proposal to declare 1952 the year in which the Anthropocene began. In a statement about this decision, the International Union of Geological Sciences underscores several critiques of the Anthropocene, two of which speak directly to the Victorian Capitalocene. First, they note that anthropogenic environmental destruction "long predates the mid 20th century" and that the Anthropocene can be traced back to the Industrial Revolution and the Victorian era. Second, they stress that human environmental impacts are "time-transgressive" and "spatially and temporally variable."[1] That is, human planetary impact is uneven and asymmetrical; there is no globally synchronous marker for the Anthropocene.

This stratigraphic issue poses more than a methodological problem for geologists; it resonates with far-reaching critiques of the Anthropocene. Critics have been uncomfortable, for example, with the Anthropocene's assumption of a homogenous humanity, in which all humans are equally responsible for environmental damage. Rob Nixon argues that a homogenizing view of the human species "risks concealing – historically and in the present – unequal human impacts, unequal human agency, and unequal human vulnerabilities."[2] Hence, critics have argued that the present environmental crisis must be addressed with more sociopolitical nuance and, in response, an ecocritical cottage industry has churned out a bevy of "cenes" now vying with each other: Capitalocene, Plantationocene, Chthulucene, Technocene, and so on.

This chapter takes up the idea of the Capitalocene for several reasons. First, the Victorian period witnessed rapid industrialization that led to fossil-fueled modernity – an acceleration of production and consumption sped along by globalized transportation (railways and steamships) and global telecommunications (transnational telegraphy). Second, this global economy relied upon the Victorian colonial frontier to provide cheap inputs – often at grievous cost to local inhabitants. Third, the nineteenth century was awash in critiques of capitalism, from Thomas Carlyle's diatribes against *laissez-faire* economics to John Ruskin's invectives against capitalism's "illth" (as opposed to "health") to Karl Marx's socialist critique of the intertwined fates of exploited workers and environments. I employ "Victorian Capitalocene" to suggest the term's origins in nineteenth-century economic and intellectual developments.

Numerous popular texts reflect the Victorians' awareness of the role of global systems of extraction and exploitation in maintaining their lifestyles. These include Charles Dickens's *Great Expectations* (1861), Wilkie Collins's *The Moonstone* (1868), Robert Louis Stevenson's *Treasure Island* (1883), Rider Haggard's *She* (1886), and Joseph Conrad's *Heart of Darkness* (1899). Colonial perspectives on frontier capitalism include: from Canada, Susanna Moodie's *Roughing It in the Bush* (1852); from South Africa, Thomas Pringle's *Poetical Works* (1837) and Sol Plaatje's *Native Life in South Africa* (1916); from Australia, Marcus Clarke's *For the Term of His Natural Life* (1874) and Thomas Browne's *Robbery Under Arms* (1888); from New Zealand, Frederick Maning's *Old New Zealand* (1863) and William Satchell's *The Land of the Lost* (1902). To show how the Capitalocene can be brought to bear on literature, this chapter turns to Olive Schreiner, a South African writer whose experimental texts have been labeled proto-modernist, proto-feminist, and, more recently, proto-environmentalist.

Central to my analysis is Schreiner's *Trooper Peter Halket of Mashonaland* (1897), a fictional critique of British imperialism that takes aim at Cecil Rhodes and his British South African Company, exposing his incursions into Rhodesia (modern Zimbabwe). Tapping into the cultural fantasy of Great Zimbabwe as the biblical land of Ophir (an ancient site of gold), Rhodes's company violently annexed Mashonaland and Matabeleland in their pursuit of gold mines. Rhodes's company was met with intense African resistance (the *Chimurengas* of 1893–4 and 1896–7), and Schreiner's text traces, through the main character Peter's colonial gaze, tales of Black female resistance. The first edition of *Trooper Peter*, featuring a photographic frontispiece of three executed Black men hanged as "rebels," sent shockwaves across London, the British Empire, and beyond.[3] Published while the British parliamentary subcommittee was investigating Rhodes's role in the 1895–6 Jameson Raid on the mineral-rich Transvaal, *Trooper Peter* was Schreiner's calculated attempt to mobilize protest against Rhodes, hoping that public outcry would prompt the government to strip Rhodes's company of its Royal Charter. Ultimately, Rhodes was not indicted for the Mashonaland and Matabeleland invasions but was forced to resign as Prime Minister of the Cape. This chapter reads *Trooper Peter* alongside Schreiner's better known texts, *The Story of An African Farm* (1883) and *From Man to Man* (1926), to illuminate her critique of colonial capitalism and Rhodes's brutal expansionism. Schreiner rebukes capitalism's frontier process and challenges hierarchical constructions of nature and humanity. More specifically, Schreiner's novel exposes capitalism's normalization of racial and sexual exploitation, while also imagining alternative modes of more-than-human solidarity.

Victorian Capitalocene

What is the Capitalocene? Andrea Malm, David Ruccio, Donna Haraway, Tony Weis, and Jason Moore all start using the term in the 2010s. For Moore, the term addresses what he sees as the fundamental pitfall of the Anthropocene, namely that it reinforces the artificial separation of nature and humanity, thus perpetuating the human exceptionalism that eco-critics have been striving to dismantle. Various strands of eco-critical thought have sought to make the human just one lifeform among a mass of non-human plants, animals, and technologies. But against the decentering logic of cyborgs, assemblages, and hybrids, the Anthropocene returns us to the seemingly dated notion of Humanity's separation from Nature, with these two terms capitalized to signal that they are always and inevitably constructions limited by the culture in which their meanings have formed. Moore contends that this division conceals "a dirty secret of modern world history," namely that "capitalism was built on excluding most humans from Humanity – Indigenous peoples, enslaved Africans, nearly all women." From the imperial capitalist perspective, "these humans were not Human at all. They were regarded as part of Nature, along with trees and soils and rivers – and treated accordingly."[4] The Capitalocene contends that there has never been a homogenous humanity acting on nature: capitalism brutally dehumanizes certain populations and deems them part of nature, which is itself assumed to be separable from and inferior to the human.

Differentiation lies at the root of capitalism, which, as Marx established, functions via the alienation of labor from the means of production. The real division of labor mirrors the ontological separation of nature and humanity. This ontological paradigm has force in the material world; that is, revolutions in theories of nature shape revolutions in material production. Capitalism works with the forces of empire and science to render nature a foreign, controllable entity that humans are then justified in subordinating and using, legitimating capitalism's violent appropriation of "Cheap Nature."[5] By this logic, the nature/humanity dualism becomes "complicit in the violence of modernity at its core": it is no less than the source of all oppressive hierarchical dualisms, including race, gender, sex, and Eurocentrism.[6]

Against this false dualism, the Capitalocene posits that the economy and the environment are not separate systems. Just as capitalism seizes and wields nature, nature shapes and determines the course of capitalism's development. Even as colonial, scientific, and capitalist systems taxonomize and rationalize nature, nature is "busy shuffling about the biological and geological conditions of capitalism." Hence, humanity and capitalism are united in one all-encompassing "web of life," which refers to nature as a whole: "nature as us, as inside us, as around us … as a flow of flows."[7] Despite his call to oneness, Moore emphasizes capitalism's countervailing push toward division, since "human organizations are premised on internal variation," such as the workings of race, class, and gender. This variation unfolds as "bundles of human and extra-human natures, interweaving biophysical and symbolic natures at every scale."[8] Hence, Moore's Capitalocene strives to grasp the multiscalarity of human and nonhuman power systems as they unfold through material processes and symbolic registers.

Despite the Capitalocene's recent coinage, its intellectual origins can be found in the nineteenth century. The notion of the Capitalocene builds on the work of Marx and speaks to various strands of socialism, working-class radicalism, and communitarianism that developed in the Victorian period. Its great synthetic projects – Alexander von Humboldt's *Kosmos* (1845–62), Robert Chamber's *Vestiges of the Natural History of Creation* (1844), Herbert Spencer's *First Principles* (1862), Charles Darwin's *On the Origin of Species* (1859) – express similar attempts to grasp the multiscalarity of human–earth histories. Indeed, Darwin's "entangled bank" encapsulates multispecies interdependence.[9] With its "web of complex relations," the entangled bank not only embodies a "war" among species, but also the "dependence of one being on another" and the "mutual relation of all organic beings."[10] The notion of a "web of life" picks up on Darwin's "web of complex relations" and resonates with web imagery laced throughout the works of Charles Dickens, George Eliot, Thomas Hardy, Walter Pater, and others.

Schreiner similarly insisted on what, in *African Farm*, she refers to as the "deep union" of all life and nonlife.[11] Her work explores what Gerald Monsman calls "the unity underlying all nature" and "unity in multeity."[12] Schreiner's belief in unity counters patriarchal hierarchies and envisions equitable forms of relationality premised on "hopes of recharged love and generosity."[13] Hence, Ivan Kreilkamp argues that Schreiner foregrounds the vulnerability shared by humans and nonhumans to create a "wider sense of fellowship and empathy."[14] In this way, Schreiner resists the separation of humanity and nature, advocating for humanity's enmeshment in the universe's "deep union." However, Schreiner never loses sight of capitalism's divisiveness. In *African Farm*, for example, she uses the manipulative, sadistic grifter, Bonaparte Blenkins, to represent the exploitative impulses of colonial capitalism. His devious machinations all have one goal: to gain possession of the farm. In his quest for colonial land, Blenkins performs in miniature what Moore calls capitalism's "frontier process" where "endless accumulation and endless geographical appropriation are joined at the hip."[15] Meanwhile, in *Trooper Peter*, Schreiner offers a large-scale depiction of capitalism's frontier process in its portrayal of the British South African Company under Cecil Rhodes – a man iconized by Edward Linley Sambourne in his 1892 cartoon in *Punch* magazine as straddling the African continent in a scalar distortion as the Rhodes Colossus.

Rhodesian Capitalism in the Web of Life

Trooper Peter tells the story of Peter Halket, a working-class English youth turned South African immigrant who has abandoned prospecting to enlist as a trooper, a soldier in the paramilitary force of the British South Africa Company. In Part I of the novel, Peter gets separated from his crew and waits up through the night on a hillock. Fatigued, hungry, and a little unhinged, his mind drifts between memories of childhood, fantasies of vast fortunes, and recollections of imperial violence. Peter's musings reveal how much he has accepted the racist and sexist ideology of imperial expansion and capitalist exploitation of South Africa.[16] Moreover, his musings reveal how imperial ideology imagines South Africa as existing solely as a frontier for white capitalist exploitation.

Peter's capitalist fantasy takes Rhodes as his model: "all men made money when they came to South Africa, – Barney Barnato, Rhodes ... why should not he!"[17] Peter's fever dream revolves around setting up his own company, where "men with big names" take shares and float the company, but without anyone "having to pay anything" and everyone selling out at the right time.[18] Peter's naive understanding of corporate finance trenchantly satirizes the speculative finance driving South African imperialism at the end of the century. Mining investments were focused on the stock market rather than on colonial development – on, as Ian Phimister puts it, "speculation rather than production."[19] The primary object was not actual gold production but the off-loading of shares onto the public. Hence, Peter's fantasy captures the (un)reality of late Victorian imperial speculation, where "appearance was everything."[20]

But Schreiner shows that white men's dreams have real costs for Black Africans. The first intimation of imperial violence comes as an eerie absence. Lost on the open plains, Peter encounters "no signs of human habitation, but the remains of a burnt kraal, and a down-trampled and now uncultivated mealie field."[21] The company's forces have destroyed habitations for thirty miles around and the Mashona have fled. Undoing the logic of settler colonialism, the company does not cultivate the land: its scorched-earth policy leads to the destruction of kraals, the abandonment of farmland, and the internal exile of the Mashona. As Kreilkamp notes, the word "kraal" could refer to either pens for keeping animals or Black African encampments, and as such it "spatializes a designation of creaturely nonhumanness that is ambiguously a matter of race and species."[22] Schreiner thus shows how colonial deterritorialization operates through a racialized humanity/nature dualism, where Black Africans are animalized and subsumed into the natural habitat, which the colonizers deem expendable.

Peter's role in the violent dehumanization of Black Africans haunts his waking dreams. As he drifts into a fragmented nightmare, Schreiner's psychological realism reveals the intertwining of symbolic and biophysical natures:

> As he looked into the crackling blaze, it seemed to be one of the fires they had made to burn the natives' grain by, and they were throwing in all they could not carry away: then, he seemed to see his mother's fat ducks waddling down the little path with the green grass on each side. Then, he seemed to see his huts where he lived with the prospectors, and the native women who used to live with him; and he wondered where the women were. Then – he saw the skull of an old Mashona blown off at the top, the hands still moving. He heard the loud cry of the native women and children as they turned the maxims on to the kraal; and then he heard the dynamite explode that blew up a cave. Then again he was working a maxim gun, but it seemed to him it was more like the reaping machine he used to work in England, and that what was going down before it was not yellow corn, but black men's heads; and he thought when he looked back they lay behind him in rows, like the corn in sheaves.[23]

Characteristic of her proto-modernism, Schreiner portrays Peter's kaleidoscopic consciousness as he free-associates between memories of imperial violence and English pastoralism. As he recalls burning the Mashona's food supplies, starving them out of their homelands, Peter remembers his mother's fat ducks – a juxtaposition of feast and famine that is only sharpened when we later learn that Peter's mother "never would kill our ducks."[24] Her care and kinship with the ducks, only taking their feathers and eggs and letting them die of old age, becomes the ecofeminist counterpoint to the imperial sexual violence of Peter, who "used to live with" two Black African women – a euphemistic representation of domestic cohabitation that conceals the women's enslavement and sexual exploitation.[25] These fraught juxtapositions culminate in the disturbing overlay of maxim gun and reaping machine. Not only is the dehumanizing convenience of the automatic weapon conjoined to mass agriculture's callous threat to humans and other species, so poignantly critiqued in Thomas Hardy's *Tess of the d'Urbervilles* (1891), but the Black Africans are conflated in Peter's mind with the vegetal landscape as not just dispensable but utterly unworthy of consideration.

The gun-as-reaper destabilizes the boundary between colony and metropole and reverses the dynamics of domestic agriculture "from producing food for others to producing others as food."[26] Inverting the expectations of colonial pastoralism and the logic of ghost acres – the outsourcing of food production to the colonies to sustain domestic industrialization – Schreiner shows that these acres are not ghosted: they are inhabited and cultivated by the Mashona.[27] They are the grounds of "the lives of the ghostly dispossessed – the bodies displaced, starved, colonized ... killed, exterminated."[28] Wielding gun-as-reaper, Peter embodies a techno-imperial Grim Reaper: the traditional scythe is replaced by the first fully automatic machine gun invented in 1884 and widely used in the Scramble for Africa with devasting consequences. Haunted by his role in the Mashona's dispossession, Peter's mind shows how rationalized conceptions of agricultural land – controlled by the industrial reaper – dovetails with racialized conceptions of colonial territory – subjugated by industrial gun. The common denominator is the organic ecology made governable and exploitable, allowing for the horrific conversion of "black men's heads" into "corn in sheaves."

Into this disturbing scene comes a mysterious figure whom the reader is encouraged to view as Christ. Excited to have company, Peter regales the Stranger with the story he always trots out to amuse male audiences about his betrayal by two Black women he used to own. One day he catches them talking with a Mashona man. Thinking nothing of it, he goes on his way, returning to find them departed, leaving behind their Western clothing but taking any weaponry they could find and even "the lid off the tea-box to melt into bullets."[29] Peter concludes that the women have gone off with the Mashona man, likely one of the women's husbands and the recipient of the cartridges she had previously begged off him:

> If I'd had any idea that day who that bloody n[----] was ... I'd have given him one cartridge in the back of his head more than ever he reckoned for! ... I shouldn't have minded so much ... though no man likes to have his woman taken away from him; but she was going to have a kid in a month or two ...

I expect they did away with it before it came; they've no hearts, these n[----];
they'd think nothing of doing that with a white man's child. They've no hearts;
they'd rather go back to a black man, however well you've treated them ...
though I never gave her a blow all the time she was with me.[30]

Clearly, Peter has been fully indoctrinated into the racial and sexist ideology
of colonial expansionism. Unable to acknowledge the political agency of the
Black women, Peter directs his misogynist ire at the man as assumed authority. Lost on Peter is the irony that he blames the Mashona man for "taking"
his woman when he has done exactly this to the Mashona man by taking
his wife. The Stranger's only reaction upon hearing the story is "infinite sad-
ness," encouraging the reader to recognize Peter's unchristian treatment of
the Black women.[31] Furthermore, since his tale normally garners "applause
and sympathy" from white male settlers, it forces readers to grapple with
the normalization of Black women's racial, sexual, and labor exploitation
within the operations of colonial expansionism.[32]

In this novel, Schreiner demonstrates that Rhodes's violent expansionism
perpetuated what Katherine McKittrick calls the "ongoing spatial project"
of "racial-sexual domination."[33] Schreiner's representation of race remains
a deeply thorny issue, but broadly speaking, "her anti-racist views developed over the second half of her life."[34] Elsewhere in her oeuvre Schreiner
depicts Black women as submissive victims and one-dimensional racist car-
icatures, as in her portrayal of the "kaffir" women in *African Farm*. But
here the Mashona women are shown to have political agency and cunning,
using Peter's ammunition to arm the African resistance. Nevertheless, the
reader has access to Black female resistance only through the distorting
lens of Peter's racist ideology. Hence, we might agree with Sylvia Wynter,
who contends that white feminism cannot imagine the figure of the Black
woman: "she is outside the bounds of reason."[35] Schreiner's narrative could
be read as suggesting that Black women are dangerous Others who must be
contained by white sexual oppression. However, I read it as performing the
bigoted limitations of white patriarchal consciousness – a limitation later
exposed by the Stranger in his attempts to convert Peter.

As they talk through the night, the Stranger encourages Peter to acknowledge his complicity in colonial capitalism's violence. Through stories and
allegories, the Stranger presses Peter to rethink the branding of Black
Africans as rebels, asking him to put himself in the Mashona's position.
One of these stories focuses on two Mashona women who fled from Peter
during the company's raid on their village:

When you took away all the grain, and burnt what you could not carry,
there was one basketful that you knew nothing of. The women stayed
[hidden in a cave], for one was eighty, and one near the time of her giving

birth ... Every day the old woman doled grain from the basket ... every day the old woman gave the young one two handfuls and kept one for herself, saying, "Because of the child within you." And when the child was born and the young woman strong, the old woman took a cloth and filled it with all the grain that was in the basket; and she put the grain on the young woman's head and tied the child on her back, and said, "Go, keeping always along the bank of the river, till you come north to the land where our people are gone."[36]

The Stranger's tale of Black female solidarity offers a poignant counterpoint to Peter's callous tale of racialized sexual domination. In Peter's tale, the Black women are sexual chattel – things bought, sold, and fought over by men. In the Stranger's tale, they are fellow survivors, bound together through suffering, kinship, and intergenerational care. They exemplify Christ's suffering and fortitude, while the older woman embodies his self-sacrifice. The Black women are not represented as dangerous or alien. Instead, they are folded into a wide-reaching conception of fellow-feeling and empathy, suggesting that a white feminist such as Schreiner could try to imagine Black female experience (even if such imagining was necessarily imperfect) and could appreciate her doubly vulnerable place in the Victorian Capitalocene – subject to racial *and* sexual commodification.

But to call the Stranger's perspective Christian fails to capture his worldview. He is "not more with one people than with another."[37] His "Company" – a foil for Rhodes's company – includes people from "every race," "every land," and "every religion."[38] While Laura Chrisman reads him as representing "transcendental humanism," the Stranger's faith is explicitly more-than-human.[39] Its origins lie in deep time: "no man living can conceive of its age." It springs from the soil itself: "on this earth it begun."[40] And its geological roots contain the wellspring of compassionate care: "when the dicynodont bent yearningly over her young, and the river-horse ... called with love to his mate; and the birds ... flew in the sunshine calling joyfully to one another ... the fore-dawn of this kingdom had broken on the earth."[41] In this way, the Stranger's faith reflects Schreiner's belief in the deep unity of human and nonhuman life.

Indeed, the Stranger's tale of Black female solidarity directly mirrors Schreiner's depiction of meerkats in *From Man to Man*. Meerkats exemplify "passionate love for one another" and "endless self-sacrifice" in their willingness to hazard their lives to save each other. Schreiner notes how "older males and females grow gaunt and thin in the breeding-time, because almost all food they find is brought to lay at the feet of the young."[42] The older meerkat and the older Black woman perform nearly identical acts of self-sacrifice. Just as the older meerkat lays food before the young, the older Black woman gives the young pregnant woman "two handfuls and kept one for herself," ultimately sending the young woman off with "all the grain," leaving herself to starve in the cave. Hence, stories of protective care reveal the "binding moving creative force [that] moves at the very heart of things":[43] "From the mysterious drawing together of amoeba to amoeba … on through all the forms of sentient life … always this stretching out, uniting, creative force … drawing together creatures of like and unlike kinds, bringing into all the forms of friendship and union and love, it lies at the root of existence." The Stranger's tale of Black female self-sacrifice draws Peter into an understanding of the binding force that joins all animals into "friendship," "union" and "love." While the animalization of Black bodies has long been in the service of white supremacy and racial subjugation, Schreiner's creaturely commonality strives to undo racialized and sexualized hierarchies through deep interconnection.[44] Like Moore, Schreiner understands that capitalism is a way of organizing nature into exploitable resources shaped by oppressive racial and sexual ideologies. But she holds out hope that nature's "close internetted lines of interaction" offer lessons not only in competition, but also in cooperation.[45] Even more radically, she sees in nature the promise of compassionate care, fellowship, and love.

Peter at the Hanging Tree

The Stranger successfully converts Peter. In Part II of the novel, Peter is sent forth to profess his new conviction that colonial capitalism is unjust. Reunited with the company, he protests his captain's treatment of a captive Mashona man. The captain declares the man a spy who must be "hanged tomorrow."[46] In a spirited speech, Peter challenges the captain, defending the Mashona's right to "fight for their country" and to "fight for freedom," encouraging him to recognize that "all men were brothers."[47] It is implied that the Mashona man is the husband of Peter's enslaved mistress – the man he threatened to kill. In a complete reversal, he asks permission to take the man back to his people and tell them that "it's not their land and their women that we want."[48] As punishment, the captain forces Peter to be his executioner. But, in the dead of night, Peter frees the man, whose escape wakes the camp. Chaos ensues and, when things settle, Peter is dead. It is strongly implied that the captain shot him.

Peter is buried where he was shot, under the same tree that the Mashona man was bound to: "a short stunted tree; its thick white stem gnarled and knotted; while two stunted misshapen branches, like arms, stretched out on either side."[49] With its central trunk and two arms, the tree is shaped like the Cross, symbolically aligning the Mashona man and Peter with Christ's crucifixion. But this cross-like tree is twisted and deformed, suggesting a perversion of both Christianity and Schreiner's vision of unity. In *African Farm*, the tree is the ultimate symbol of "deep unity." Noting how the "bifurcating and rebifurcating" branches of blood vessels and the branching "metallic tracery" of rocks are the "same exact shape" as the tree, Schreiner asks: "how are these things related that such deep union should exist between them all? Is it chance? Or, are they not all the fine branches of one trunk, whose sap flows through us all?"[50] Reimaging Darwin's "Tree of Life," which covers the earth with "its ever branching and beautiful ramifications,"[51] Schreiner suggests that the tree's branching form reveals the world's morphological and spiritual unity.

But, under Rhodes's genocidal capitalism, the Tree of Life becomes the Hanging Tree. The Mashona man's captivity and Peter's subsequent burial under the cruciform tree returns the reader to the book's frontispiece – the image of three executed Black men hanged as rebels. Peter tells the Stranger about the hangings in gruesome detail, including how the colonists made the assumed spies jump down from the tree and hang themselves.[52] In this way, the captain's plan to execute the Mashona man as a spy is not a freak instance of tyranny within Rhodes's company, nor are the earlier hangings a cruel anomaly in an otherwise just system. Rather, through repeated figuration of the hanging tree, Schreiner insists that racial exploitation and racial injustice are built into the fabric of the Victorian Capitalocene.

The novel's ending, nevertheless, works to affirm the tree's promise of unity. When Peter frees the captive man, Schreiner describes his closeness to the tree: "the black man hung against the white stem, so closely bound to it that they seemed one."[53] The arboreal intertwining of Black and white intimates humanity's racial unity, which is then physically materialized in Peter's burial: "he was lying under the little tree, with the red sand trodden down over him, in which a black man and white man's blood were mingled."[54] Rewriting fears of miscegenation, their comingled blood encodes an image of shared vulnerability that – while not erasing the differential experience of living under white supremacy and anti-Black violence – unites the working-class Englishman and Black African as they are both "trodden down" by the forces of the Victorian Capitalocene. In this way, the novel's ending expands the tale of Black female solidarity, with Peter's death opening a pathway to cross-racial solidarity. Even if the affectionate ties of deep affinity are perverted by the terrors of racial capitalism, Peter's sacrificial death aligns him with the motherly dicynodont, the passionate river-horse, and the selfless Black woman – all bound together in the web of life.

Notes

1. International Union of Geological Sciences, March 20, 2024, www.iugs.org/_files/ugd/f1fc07_40d1a7ed58de458c9f8f24de5e739663.pdf?index=true.
2. Rob Nixon, "The Anthropocene: The Promise and Pitfalls of an Epochal Idea," in Gregg Mitman, Marco Armiero, and Robert S. Emmett, eds., *Future Remains: A Cabinet of Curiosities for the Anthropocene* (Chicago: University of Chicago Press, 2017), 25.
3. Janet Remmington, "Olive Schreiner, Race and Black South Africa," in *Olive Schreiner: Writing Networks and Global Contexts* (Edinburgh: Edinburgh University Press, 2023), 118.
4. Jason Moore, *Anthropocene or Capitalocene?: Nature, History, and the Crisis of Capitalism*, (Binghamton, NY: Kairos, 2016), 78–9.
5. Jason Moore, *Capitalism in the Web of Life: Ecology and the Accumulation of Capital* (London: Verso, 2015), 2, 18.
6. Moore, *Capitalism*, 4.
7. Moore, *Capitalism*, 2, 3.
8. Moore, *Capitalism*, 9.
9. Charles Darwin, *On the Origin of Species*, 1859 (Oxford: Oxford University Press, 2008), 59.
10. Darwin, *Origin of Species*, 58, 59, 51, 52.
11. Olive Schreiner, *The Story of An African Farm* (Oxford: Oxford University Press, [1883] 2008), 118.
12. Gerald Monsman, *Olive Schreiner's Fiction: Landscape and Power* (New Brunswick: Rutgers University Press, 1991), 105, 91.
13. Dan Wylie, "Olive Schreiner and Virginia Woolf: Proto-Ecofeminists?," in Jade Munslow Ong and Andrew Van der Vlies, eds., *Olive Schreiner: Writing Networks and Global Contexts* (Edinburgh: Edinburgh University Press, 2023), 61–82 at 68.
14. Ivan Kreilkamp, *Minor Creatures: Persons, Animals, and the Victorian Novel* (Chicago: University of Chicago Press, 2018), 152.
15. Moore, *Capitalism*, 107.
16. Andrew Van der Vlies, "Coetzee's Schreiner, Schreiner's Coetzee: Provincialising Allegory" in *Olive Schreiner: Writing Networks and Global Contexts* (Edinburgh: Edinburgh University Press, 2023), 302. See also J. M. Coetzee, "Farm Novel and 'Plaasroman' in South Africa," *English in Africa*, 13.2 (1986), 1–19.
17. Olive Schreiner, *Trooper Peter Halket of Mashonaland* (London: Unwin, 1905), 28.
18. Schreiner, *Trooper Peter Halket*, 30–2.
19. Ian Phimister, "Late nineteenth-century globalization: London and Lomagundi perspectives on mining speculation in southern Africa, 1894–1904," 28.
20. Phimister, "Late nineteenth-century globalization," 28.
21. Schreiner, *Trooper Peter Halket*, 14.
22. Kreilkamp, *Minor Creatures*, 157.
23. Schreiner, *Trooper Peter Halket*, 38–40.
24. Schreiner, *Trooper Peter Halket*, 79.
25. Schreiner, *Trooper Peter Halket*, 79.
26. Laura Chrisman, *Rereading the Imperial Romance: British Imperialism and South African Resistance in Haggard, Schreiner, and Plaatje* (Oxford: Oxford University Press, 2000), 136.

27. For the role of "ghost acres" in Britain's industrialization, see Kenneth Pomeranz, *The Great Divergence: China, Europe, and the Making of the Modern World Economy* (Princeton: Princeton University Press, 2001).

28. Banu Subramaniam, *Ghost Stories for Darwin: The Science of Variation and the Politics of Diversity* (Bloomington: University of Illinois Press, 2014), 122.

29. Schreiner, *Trooper Peter Halket*, 65–6.

30. Schreiner, *Trooper Peter Halket*, 68–70.

31. Schreiner, *Trooper Peter Halket*, 71.

32. Schreiner, *Trooper Peter Halket*, 68.

33. Katherine McKittrick, *Demonic Grounds: Black Women and the Cartographies of Struggle* (Minneapolis: University of Minnesota Press, 2006), 121.

34. Remmington, "Olive Schreiner," 115.

35. Quoted in McKittrick, *Demonic Grounds*, xxv.

36. Schreiner, *Trooper Peter Halket*, 105–7.

37. Schreiner, *Trooper Peter Halket*, 101.

38. Schreiner, *Trooper Peter Halket*, 103.

39. Chrisman, *Rereading*, 143.

40. Schreiner, *Trooper Peter Halket*, 145.

41. Schreiner, *Trooper Peter Halket*, 148.

42. Olive Schreiner, *From Man to Man; or Perhaps Only* (London: Virago, 1982), 211.

43. Schreiner, *From Man to Man*, 175.

44. For a searching account of race and animalization in Schreiner, see Kreilkamp, *Minor Creatures*, 148–80.

45. Schreiner, *From Man to Man*, 144.

46. Schreiner, *Trooper Peter Halket*, 219.

47. Schreiner, *Trooper Peter Halket*, 223–4.

48. Schreiner, *Trooper Peter Halket*, 226.

49. Schreiner, *Trooper Peter Halket*, 195.

50. Schreiner, *The Story of An African Farm*, 118.

51. Schreiner, *The Story of An African Farm*, 100.

52. Schreiner, *Trooper Peter Halket*, 77.

53. Schreiner, *Trooper Peter Halket*, 249.

54. Schreiner, *Trooper Peter Halket*, 259.

16

WENDY PARKINS

The Art of Extinction

Naturalizing Colonization and Walter Buller's A History of the Birds of New Zealand

Every reader of *Jane Eyre* can recall the power a book of birds has over the forlorn Jane, who seeks refuge in Bewick's *A History of British Birds* in the opening chapter of Charlotte Bronte's novel. Likewise, every reader of nineteenth-century poetry is familiar with the symbolic importance of birds – the skylark, the nightingale, the albatross – in the Romantic imaginary. What Thomas C. Gannon has called "the avian's ubiquity in English literature" may account in part for an overlap of interests between literature and ornithology such as the young Jane Eyre exemplified.[1] The intersection between culture, science, and colonialism, however, raises some disturbing questions about the solace and study of birds in the Victorian period, perhaps best demonstrated by *A History of the Birds of New Zealand*, the result of many years' labor by Walter Buller (1838–1906).

In *The Colonizer and the Colonized* (1957), Albert Memmi argues that the colonizer, in order to transform his usurpation "into legitimacy, ... needs to absolve himself of ... the conditions under which it was obtained." What the usurper ultimately desires in his quest for absolution is "the disappearance of the usurped."[2] Nineteenth-century colonial New Zealand, where the decline and extinction of indigenous species was largely assumed to be inevitable, provides a particularly striking instance of Memmi's argument. According to Buller, the colony's most eminent ornithologist, it was an "almost universal natural law that indigenous forms of animal and vegetable life sooner or later succumb to, and are displaced by, more vigorous types from without."[3] This displacement theory of extinction erased the agency of colonists, allowing them to justify the consequences of violent dispossession as ordained by nature. Such justifications were not confined to the sciences; as Kirstine Moffat has noted, a similar process occurred in early New Zealand fiction where settlement was mythologized "as a noble endeavour [and] Māori [were] eliminated from most of these accounts ... in a way that justifie[d] Pākehā acquisition of land."[4] *Pākehā* is a Māori word, originally applied to English-speaking Europeans who settled in Aotearoa/

New Zealand, now widely used to refer to New Zealanders of European descent. In this chapter, I will explore the politics of extinction in colonial New Zealand through the lens of illustration and scientific rhetoric in which the preservation of specimens was often given precedence over the conservation of species or habitats. With particular attention to *A History of the Birds of New Zealand*, I will suggest that the work of Buller provides an important example of how displacement theory was not confined to the field of natural history. Rather, it allowed a rhetorical slippage that naturalized colonization and legitimized the resulting disempowerment – if not erasure – of the Indigenous peoples of New Zealand.

"Illustrations of Darwinism": From the *Moa* to the Bramble Finch

Across 1872 and 1873, *A History of the Birds of New Zealand* was published in London, the result of many years' labor by Buller, who had studied birds since he was a boy in the far north of New Zealand.[5] In quarto format with thirty-five illustrations, the book was sold by subscription only, for the expensive price of five guineas, but was quickly acclaimed by both the mainstream press and specialist readers. Today, it remains widely known in New Zealand simply as "Buller's Birds" and images from this book continue to feature on posters and household items, just as in earlier generations they appeared on New Zealand stamps and currency. Despite being dubbed the "Audubon of New Zealand," however, Buller was not the source of the book's illustrations. He wrote the text, having previously published a number of significant papers on ornithology, and commissioned a Dutch illustrator, J. G. Keulemans (1842–1912), for the lithograph plates. Keulemans had begun as a taxidermist but his aptitude for natural history and drawing soon saw him turn exclusively to ornithological illustration and lithography, moving to London as his reputation grew. Without the collaboration with Keulemans, it is doubtful that *A History of the Birds of New Zealand* would have achieved the fame and scientific recognition it did. When Keulemans again illustrated the revised and expanded edition in 1888, *The Times* declared his plates "absolutely perfect ... with a truth to nature."[6] Although he had accompanied the German biologist W. L. H. Dohrn on an expedition to West Africa in 1864–5, Keulemans would, for most of his career, complete his illustrations from dead specimens or, less frequently, from captive birds in London. He never visited New Zealand.

Keulemans's important role in *A History* is, then, but one of a number of anomalies in the production and reception of this remarkable book. Painting birds he never saw in their natural habitat, Keulemans showcased the distant colony's avifauna to Europe's scientific establishment. The scale and ambition of *A History* was in part motivated by Buller's desire to prove his ornithological credentials by seeking recognition and endorsement from experts outside New Zealand. Buller believed that the success of his ornithological endeavors depended on his regular presence in scientific circles in Britain and often acted as an agent to assist European collectors to purchase endangered specimens (living or dead) from New Zealand, sometimes flouting new wildlife protection legislation to do so. He would eventually sell his own substantial collection to museums outside his homeland.

Buller, like other ornithologists around the world at this time, believed that the study of specimens was deemed to justify killing birds in the pursuit of knowledge; he later recalled his "delight" when "I shot … my first Piopio, a bird so rare at the far north, even at that time, that it was entirely unknown to the natives of the district."[7] From a twenty-first-century perspective, it seems baffling that a commitment to the conservation of endangered species was not seen as more important than the preservation of specimens (through illustration or taxidermy). What may strike us now as a contradiction between collection and conservation was in large part attributable to the belief that the extinction of native species was an inevitable consequence of colonization, itself an unambiguous embodiment of progress. This view was far from unique to Buller, held also by scientific visitors to New Zealand such as Charles Darwin; in a later essay entitled "Illustrations of Darwinism; Or, the Avifauna of New Zealand," Buller described himself as "a thorough disciple of Darwinism."[8] An evolutionary narrative, then, gave a sense of urgency to Buller's work – as he tirelessly updated, revised, and supplemented *A History* until his death in 1906 – in order that he might leave a thorough scientific record for posterity and secure his place in colonial history as both a man of science and heroic collector.

Displacement theory, however, was not solely associated with Darwin but is also recognizable as a reductive modification of Herbert Spencer's concept of "survival of the fittest." More generally, it provided a benign explanation for the disappearance of native species that acknowledged the impact of colonizers on the environment while also absolving them of blame. In the 1888 edition of *A History*, for instance, Buller declares that "In a newly colonized country, where the old fauna and flora are being invaded by a host of foreign immigrants, various natural agencies are brought into play to check the progress of the indigenous species, and to supplant them by new and more enduring forms."[9] The force of that active verb, *invaded*, is somewhat mitigated by Buller's invocation of "natural agencies" as the origin of change which, by not specifying human intervention, renders the displacement and eventual extinction of indigenous species as something analogous to the ebb and flow of seasons. Blurring nature and history, Buller then affirms the positive outcome of such change through the emergence of what he calls "more enduring forms," with that phrase's implication of vigor and vitality. By extension, the reinvigoration of fauna and flora symbolizes the growing health and strength of New Zealand since the arrival of European settlers.

What then of the fate of the Indigenous people of this "newly colonized country"? Buller, like other colonial commentators, did not hesitate to trace the connection implicit in displacement theory, as evident in an address he gave to the Wellington Philosophical Society in 1884. "The aboriginal race must in time give place to a more highly organised, or, at any rate, a more civilised one," Buller said, "This seems to be one of the inscrutable laws of Nature."[10] He therefore deplored the lack of scholarly attention to the Māori people, because the "race was dying out very rapidly, and … five and twenty years hence there would only be a remnant left." As Buller's biographer, Ross Galbreath, summarized Buller's position: the passing of Māori was not something to be mourned "but a natural phenomenon which the scientist should record."[11]

One notable exception to this view early in the Victorian period is found in *Travels in New Zealand* (1843), a two-volume account by the German naturalist Ernest Dieffenbach. Despite the fact that Dieffenbach was employed by the New Zealand Company on an expedition intended to promote colonization, his *Travels in New Zealand* expressed relatively enlightened views about the place of Māori in the nascent colony. Premised on what the historian Robert Grant has called a "biology of settlement, an order in which humankind was subject to the same natural laws as other species,"[12] Dieffenbach's work understood the laws of nature in somewhat different terms than that of displacement theory, while still accepting the inevitability of colonization, under the right circumstances: "It is with man as with plants and animals; each kind has its natural boundaries, within which it can live, and thrive, and attain its fullest vigour and beauty."[13] While Dieffenbach found New Zealand to be eminently suited – by climate, geography, flora, and fauna – for European settlement, he also urged peaceful coexistence with Māori, rejecting the idea that they were a dying race who could therefore legitimately be marginalized.[14]

It was perhaps not coincidental to the dominance of displacement theory in colonial New Zealand, however, that a precedent for extinction already existed in the giant moa (order Dinornithiformes), a flightless, ostrich-like bird believed to have been wiped out within a hundred years of human settlement, after the arrival of Māori in the thirteenth century.[15] The moa first came to the attention of European scientists through an address to the Zoological Society in London in 1839 by Richard Owen, after he had been sent a moa femur bone. Thereafter the bird became a continuing source of fascination and study throughout the Victorian period. As Geoff Norman notes, however, the existence of moa bones had already been documented by others in New Zealand before this time. Owen would receive further moa material from New Zealand collectors for the next forty years, writing more than thirty papers on the extinct species.[16]

When some of Buller's bird specimens were sent to the 1873 Vienna World's Fair as part of the New Zealand display, they were exhibited alongside moa skeletons, underlining the connection often made between the exotic but precarious wonders of New Zealand, past and present.[17] In New Zealand contexts, an analogy with the *moa* seemed to come readily to mind when discussing the passing of that which once dominated the landscape, a kind of avian Ozymandias. For example, when Anthony Trollope first arrived in the far south of New Zealand in 1872, he wrote: "On landing I immediately asked to be shown some Maoris [sic], but was told that they were very scarce in that part of the country[.] ... [I]t seemed as though I might as well have asked for a moa, – the great bird which used, in former days, to stalk in solitary grandeur about the island."[18] For Buller, then, as for many Victorians, the link between the Indigenous peoples and avifauna of New Zealand was clear and irrefutable, and one he often drew in his writing: just as the Māori was being "rapidly supplanted by his Anglo-Saxon neighbour," Buller wrote, so were the native birds "giving place" to European birds introduced by colonizers from the 1860s.[19] The Encouragement of Acclimatisation Societies in New Zealand Act of 1867 provided public funding to support the importation of animals and birds but local branches of acclimatization societies throughout the colony continued to arrange their own shipments.[20] The Canterbury Society on the South Island, for instance, shipped 444 birds from England in 1866, of which only 166 survived the journey. Undaunted, the Society arranged a further shipment the following year, including "house sparrows, a robin, seventy-seven pairs of blackbirds, twelve pairs of thrushes, seven redpolls, four hedge-sparrows, and one bramble finch."[21]

"Impossible to Preserve": The Last of the *Huia*

Under the guise of a worthy scientific impulse to record and preserve the unique avifauna of the colony before it was too late, Buller's project required not only physical specimens but images as well. In combining accuracy with beauty, however, Keulemans's commissioned illustrations transcended the purely scientific and eventually became a means by which an emerging sentimental attachment to the colony's indigenous avifauna bolstered a counterresponse to displacement theory. There is more than a degree of irony in the fact that it was the scale of Buller's ambition for *A History* that opened up this possibility: sparing no expense in the design and reproduction of ornithological images added considerably to the distinction of the resulting book in bringing these birds to life, as it were.

Keulemans's method was to begin with a sketch for Buller's initial approval, then to complete a finished painting, before the laborious process of reproduction could begin. For the first edition of *A History*, the method of lithography involved drawing the outline on the lithographic stone, followed by hand-coloring. For the second edition, however, chromolithography was used. As Buller's biographer explains:

> Keulemans had to draw a whole series of separate images or patterns [on separate stones] for each basic hue in his original painting. It was a little like copying the painting one colour at a time, with each colour on a new sheet, so that when all were put together they would build up a full-colour facsimile of the original.[22]

While cheaper books might only use two or three colors in such a process, five colors were used in *A History*, plus black to give depth and shading, with perhaps a few highlights touched in by hand.[23]

Artistically, the other notable difference between the first and second editions was the addition of greater detail in the background setting, depicting the habitat in which the bird was typically found, but also rendering the image as far more like a painting than simply a scientific illustration. In the first edition, the images might foreground the bird against a hint of ground vegetation or tree branch, but the emphasis was squarely on the specimen. In the second edition, the bird became part of a more complete, unified composition. For example, Keulemans's lithograph of the huia (*Heteralocha acutirostris*) in the first edition depicted a pair of birds on a short length of unidentifiable branch which does not extend beyond the point where the male bird's claws clutch it, leaving a considerable amount of white space around the image, whereas in the second edition, the two huia are shown among the branches of the *porokaiwhiri* (known as pigeonwood by settlers), with its distinctive scarlet fruit (Figure 16.1). Together, the tree and birds fill the frame more comprehensively than in the earlier version. Keulemans had been able to paint this version from observation of a live specimen that Buller had brought to London in 1886, perhaps in part accounting for the greater artistry of this later rendering. As noted earlier, these enriched depictions were often singled out for praise by reviewers and, ever since, Keulemans's images have taken on a life of their own: the chromolithograph of the huia, for instance, remains the best known representation of this extinct bird.

The power of Keulemans's illustrations to capture the distinctive beauty of New Zealand birds made the images in "Buller's Birds" part of a process

Figure 16.1 John Gerrard Keulemans, Huia (male and female): *Heteralocha acutirostris*. [Plate II. 1888], lithograph, colored 27.3 × 20 cm. *Source*: (Sir) Walter Lawry Buller, *A History of the Birds of New Zealand*, 2nd ed. (London: John van Voorst, 1888). Ref: PUBL-0012-02. Alexander Turnbull Library, Wellington, New Zealand. https://natlib.govt.nz/records/22437196.

by which settlers could increasingly begin to identify emotionally with their new land. No doubt this growing sentimental attachment to the native birds could also be attributed more broadly to a literary and cultural context in which birds were already seen as worthy objects of sentiment for the human observers sharing their environment. As Gannon argues, the avian Other commonly featured in Romantic explorations of beauty and emotional connection gave birds a unique resonance in British and, by extension, colonial culture in the Victorian period.[24] As distinct from the contested human domain that constituted the colonial contact zone, native birds might have seemed a "safe" object of affection and attachment in a new land. At the same time, however, Acclimatisation Societies were also introducing birds from "home," due precisely to those sentimental avian attachments familiar from British literature, thus offering settlers a reassuring point of continuity with the life they had left behind.

If the clash between native and introduced birds was a microcosm of the conflict between Indigenous and settler culture, it was also tragically exemplified in the story of the huia. A native bird highly valued both by Māori and settler communities, the huia disappeared early in the twentieth century and Buller's role in the demise of the species is another instance of his controversial career in public life in New Zealand. The son of missionaries in Hokianga, a remote settlement in northern New Zealand, Buller was fluent in *te reo Māori* from childhood, an uncommon accomplishment at that time, which gave him his start in colonial administration as a Māori interpreter in the Native Department in Wellington. By the early 1860s, he had been appointed a magistrate overseeing Māori land claims (taking the opportunities presented by extensive travel in regional areas to add to his bird collection). Through these colonial posts, as well as his emerging reputation as a man of science from his papers on ornithology, Buller came to the attention of senior government figures in New Zealand, so that he was able to attract generous financial support for his travel to London in the early 1870s to bring his bird book to publication.

Buller thus seems to epitomize the colonial self-made man, benefiting from opportunities presented in New Zealand to open doors for him in the old country, and embodying a blend of European knowledge (in science and law) with a knowledge of the land (*whenua*) and its peoples (*tangata whenua*, the term by which Māori refer to themselves, literally "the people of the land"). While in London awaiting the first publication of *A History*, Buller also took the opportunity to train as a barrister so that, when he returned to New Zealand, he established a law firm devoted to Māori land claims. Through this business he accrued considerable personal wealth, as well as extensive networks of connection not only among Māori landowners and tribal leaders, but also legal and political circles in Wellington. At the same time, though, his sometimes shameless self-promotion made Buller a target for attack in the press and parliament: it was in his interests to cultivate close ties with powerful figures, who might come to his defense when needed.

This was the context in which his friendship with the Governor of New Zealand, Lord Onslow, brought Buller squarely into the cause of the huia. Because of Buller's knowledge of Māori language and culture, Onslow consulted Buller about an appropriate Māori name to give to his son born in 1890. Officially named Victor Alexander Herbert Huia Onslow, the governor's son would always be known in New Zealand as Huia Onslow and at his christening the baby was photographed with huia feathers adorning his head. It was also Buller who, again at Onslow's request, subsequently arranged a meeting of the governor with the Ngāti Huia people, and in September 1891 the Onslow and Buller families travelled to the tribe's *marae* (meeting house) at Ōtaki where, as newspapers subsequently reported, the visitors were welcomed by elders in the following terms:

> You, O Governor ... pay this great compliment to the Māori people – that of
> giving your son a Māori name ... We invoke the spirits of our ancestors to

witness this day that in your son Huia the friendship of the two races becomes cemented. ... There yonder is the snow-clad Ruahine range, the home of our favourite bird! We ask you, O Governor, to restrain the Pākehā from shooting it, that when your boy grows up he may see the beautiful bird which bears his name.[25]

The event also received coverage in England, where the *Daily Telegraph* on November 12, 1891 described the huia as a "rather lugubrious-looking bird ... altogether unsuitable as an ornament for a lady's bonnet" while also noting that "if some measures are not promptly taken for the protection of the huia ... [it] will probably join the moa."[26] The *Daily Telegraph*'s passing reference to the feather trade for millinery marks an acknowledgment of another pressure on endangered exotic birds around the globe, far exceeding the impact of the trade in specimen collection. As Helen Louise Cowie has shown, the craze for bird plumage in the Victorian period had a profound ecological impact in countries that supplied birds (such as Australia, India, the West Indies, and South Africa) but also ultimately led to the founding of wildlife preservation societies like the Society for the Protection of Birds in Britain and the Audubon Society in the USA, which in turn were instrumental in the implementation of protective legislation.[27]

In the New Zealand context, the tribal elders' appeal to Onslow at Ōtaki seems to have galvanized the governor's desire to pursue greater protection of wildlife (specifically, avian). In particular, Onslow supported the idea, first proposed in the early 1870s by T. H. Potts, an MP and amateur naturalist, to establish reserves on remote islands to conserve both native forests and birds, proposing that endangered birds could be caught and relocated to ensure their survival. The need for such measures had increased markedly in the 1880s after ferrets, stoats, and weasels began to be imported in large numbers in a futile attempt to control the colony's rabbit population, but the island reserves, after gaining initial government approval, had never been implemented.[28] Only when Onslow revived Potts's idea in the 1890s did Buller, too, begin to voice support for such reserves, adapting his displacement theory slightly to suggest that an exception to the "law of nature" might be found in insular environments.[29] After a reserve was finally established on Little Barrier Island in 1894, Buller was implicated in allegations of continuing to obtain bird skins from the island; he had appointed the island's custodian, who had previously hunted birds on Buller's behalf elsewhere. The custodian left his post but Buller was officially cleared.[30] As a result of the advocacy of Lord Onslow (formally articulated in a Memorandum written by Buller on Onslow's behalf), in 1892 the New Zealand government added the huia to the Animals Protection Act of 1880.[31] Buller's response to this was shocking, from a twenty-first-century perspective. In a letter to Walter Rothschild, an avid collector to whom Buller had long been sending specimens, Buller wrote:

> Knowing that the proclamation for the strict protection of [the huia] was to appear in a week or two, and that after that, it would be hopeless to get any more specimens, I sent out two parties of Maories [sic] into the woods ... they did not bring in many – only three, all of which I am sending you in spirit ... I have been most anxious to obtain a live pair for you, and another pair for Lady Onslow: but it is too late now.[32]

In fact, Buller continued to hunt for huia and, on his return to England again in 1893, he took a pair of live birds to present to Rothschild.[33]

Buller's capacity to hold apparently contradictory positions – to lament the demise of the huia while continuing to hunt for specimens to capture or kill – goes to the core of the settler colonial experience which, as Lorenzo Veracini has argued, often denied the founding violence of colonization through an insistence on empty landscapes or the inevitability of extinction.[34] If extinction was thus never far from the colonial mind, *A History of the Birds of New Zealand* offered a fantasy of consolation to men like Buller: the losses of extinction might be compensated for if a sufficient memorial in the form of scientific record and exquisite colored plates was preserved.

As Buller approached the end of his own life, he completed his *Supplement to the 'Birds of New Zealand,'* closing with a chapter mostly devoted to the huia, which he now believed to be "hopelessly doomed":

> I know it is the fashion to raise a wail over the disappearance of the New Zealand birds, [but] there are certain species which, from the nature of the case, it is impossible to preserve, and it seems to me that the Huia is one of these ... No one is more in sympathy with protective legislation than myself, that is to say where it can be applied with any success; but here, as in everything else, we must be rational.[35]

Buller may invoke sympathy, but he ends with an insistence on the primacy of the rational over "everything else" – emotions, nature, and, implicitly, *tangata whenua*. This passage is a stark example of what the environmental philosopher Thom van Dooren identifies as "human exceptionalism" which rationalizes extinction by setting *certain* humans apart from the rest of the natural world so that extinction comes to "be regarded as something that happens 'over there' or out in 'nature.'"[36] By contrast, Charles Wentworth Dilke, another Victorian visitor to New Zealand, even as he reiterated displacement theory to account for the incursion and success of new species, outlined a Māori understanding of human–avian relations, one that does not assume the human as exceptional but as entangled. In *Greater Britain*, Dilke recorded a "native saying" that "The birds die because the Maories [sic], their companions, die."[37] Māori valued the huia highly, using all parts of the bird for ornaments but the distinctive tail feathers – black with a striking white edge – were a sign of great *mana* (authority or prestige) and intricately carved containers called *waka huia* were made to hold these feathers.[38] The birds were also a food source so the "companionship" between Māori and huia did not preclude hunting but was nonetheless informed by an understanding of mindful coexistence in a precarious environment.

It is now widely believed that the bird's disappearance was greatly accelerated after a visit by the Duke of York to New Zealand in 1901, when he was publicly presented with a huia feather for his hat. The value of tail feathers increased dramatically, and the last verified sighting of a huia was in 1907.[39] In May 2024, a huia tail feather sold at auction in Auckland for NZD$46,521, "making it by far the world's most expensive feather ever sold at auction," while in 2023, a pair of stuffed huia were sold in Britain for NZD$466,000, "despite public pleas for the New Zealand government to intervene and bring them home."[40] Van Dooren observes that extinction is "never a sharp, singular event" but rather "a slow unravelling of intimately entangled ways of life that begins long before the death of the last individual and continues to ripple forward long afterward, drawing in living beings in a range of different ways."[41] What might it mean to view birds as companions rather than commodities, as grievable losses rather than specimens? As a starting point, it would mean recognizing how the Victorian impulse to locate birds within the domain of science served not only to justify the art of extinction but also to disavow the foundational violence of colonization.

Notes

1. Thomas C. Gannon, *Skylark Meets Meadowlark: Reimagining the Bird in British Romantic and Contemporary Native American Literature* (Lincoln: University of Nebraska Press, 2009), 60.
2. Albert Memmi, *The Colonizer and the Colonized*, trans. Howard Greenfeld (London: Earthscan, 2003), 96, 97.
3. Walter Buller, *A History of the Birds of New Zealand* (London, privately published, 1872–3), 55, see also 81.
4. Kirstine Moffat, "European Myths of Settlement in New Zealand Fiction, 1860–1940," *New Literatures Review* 41 (April 2004), 3–18 at 3. See also Helen Blythe, *The Victorian Colonial Romance with the Antipodes* (Basingstoke: Palgrave Macmillan, 2010), 24–5.
5. Ross Galbreath, *Walter Buller: The Reluctant Conservationist* (Wellington: GP Books, 1989), 108.
6. Quoted in Buller, *A History*, end papers, 2.n.p.
7. Buller, *A History*, 2.340.
8. Galbreath, *Walter Buller*, 247.

9. Buller, *A History*, 1.93.
10. Quoted in Galbreath, *Walter Buller*, 137.
11. Galbreath, *Walter Buller*, 138.
12. Robert Grant, "New Zealand 'Naturally': Ernst [*sic*] Dieffenbach, Environmental Determinism and the Mid Nineteenth-Century British Colonization of New Zealand," *New Zealand Journal of History* 37.1 (2003), 22–37 at 27.
13. Ernest Dieffenbach, *Travels in New Zealand; with Contributions to the Geography, Geology, Botany, and Natural History of that Country*, 2 vols. (London: J. Murray, 1843), 1.1–2.
14. Dieffenbach, *Travels in New Zealand*, 1.19.
15. Geoff Norman, *Birdstories: A History of the Birds of New Zealand* (Nelson: Potton and Burton, 2018), 23.
16. Norman, *Birdstories*, 16–17.
17. Norman, *Birdstories*, 112.
18. Anthony Trollope, *Australia and New Zealand* (London: Chapman and Hall, 1873), 542.
19. Buller, *A History*, 1.55.
20. Dave Hansford, "Hunting Utopia," *New Zealand Geographic* 114 (March–April 2012), www.nzgeo.com/stories/hunting-utopia/.
21. Joan Druett, *Exotic Intruders: The Introduction of Plants and Animals into New Zealand* (Auckland: Heinemann, 1983), 110.
22. Galbreath, *Walter Buller*, 160.
23. Galbreath, *Walter Buller*, 160.
24. Gannon, *Skylark Meets Meadowlark*, 60.
25. *New Zealand Mail* (13 September 1891), 13.
26. Qtd. in Galbreath, *Walter Buller*, 180.
27. Helen Louise Cowie, *Victims of Fashion: Animal Commodities in Victorian Britain* (Cambridge: Cambridge University Press, 2021), 17–54.
28. Galbreath, *Walter Buller*, 125.
29. Galbreath, *Walter Buller*, 182.
30. Galbreath, *Walter Buller*, 212.
31. Galbreath, *Walter Buller*, 182–4.
32. Quoted in Galbreath, *Walter Buller*, 184.
33. Galbreath, *Walter Buller*, 186, 192.
34. Lorenzo Veracini, *Settler Colonialism: A Theoretical Overview* (Basingstoke: Palgrave Macmillan, 2010), 81–2. See also Blythe, *The Victorian Colonial Romance*, 24–5.
35. Walter Buller, *Supplement to 'A History of the Birds of New Zealand,'* 2 vols., (London: Privately published, 1905), 2.157.
36. Thom van Dooren, *Flight Ways: Life and Loss at the Edge of Extinction* (New York: Columbia University Press, 2016), 5.
37. Charles Wentworth Dilke, *Greater Britain*, Vol. 1 (Cambridge: Cambridge University Press, [1868] 2009), 394.
38. Norman, *Birdstories*, 267.
39. Norman, *Birdstories*, 273, 274.
40. Eva Corlett, "More valuable Than Gold: New Zealand Feather Becomes Most Expensive in the World," *The Guardian* (May 21, 2024), https://shorturl.at/LJGkS.
41. Van Dooren, *Flight Ways*, 12.

17

CAROLYN LESJAK

Land Use

The Farm, the Common, and the Wild

There are myriad ways of thinking about the use of land during the long nineteenth century. In this chapter, I focus on three key forms of land use, all of which undergo major transformations over the course of the century: the farm, the common, and the wild. By shifting our attention away from bourgeois subjectivity and the development of the modern individual in literature – the focus of which has been a mainstay of Victorian literary criticism – toward land use, a new view of the environment, in its most capacious sense, and the changes being wrought on it is made available. Specifically, a new narrative about the environment emerges that brings to the fore the integral relations among labor, land, and nature that Victorian literature narrates and that are very much on the agenda today as we grapple with the legacy of these changes and their ongoing consequences for the myriad political-environmental crises we now face. While at first glance, the farm, the common, and the wild might appear to constitute markedly disparate forms of use, they are in fact inextricably connected, often existing in an inverse relationship to one another, as farms replace forests and wetlands, the enclosure of the common by private individuals, state interests, and parliamentary decree appropriates common property and turns that land into private property, and "the improver" or agriculturists – what William Cobbett preferred to call "agriculture-asses" – destroy what were often termed "wastes" or "wilderness."[1] In the process, labor, land, and nature are radically transformed in ways that are detrimental to humans and nonhumans alike and that are, in a word, unsustainable. Moreover, and putting some pressure on Andreas Malm's claim in *Fossil Capital* that "only now is it becoming apparent what it really meant to burn coal and send forth smoke from a stack in Manchester in 1842," I want to suggest that there were plenty of indications that the Victorians and those dispossessed by them could apprehend the at once social and ecological damage at hand.[2] The question is then less whether they knew what was happening and more what they chose to do with that knowledge, a question that is as much ours today – and yet to be answered.

The Rural Landscape

Travelling around the English countryside from 1821 to 1826, Cobbett not only meticulously detailed the range and variety of lands and its uses but also recorded the consequences of the transformations in land use taking place during his lifetime. Illustrative of his eye for detail is an early entry from *Rural Rides* in 1821, where he writes of Faversham Kent: "this is a country of hop-gardens, cherry, apple, pear and filbert orchards, and quickset hedges."[3] Continuing his observations, he notes that:

> I look, *first*, over a large and level field of rich land, in which the drilled wheat is finely come up, and which is surrounded by clipped quickset hedges with a row of apple trees running by the sides of them; *next*, over a long succession of rich meadows, which are here called marshes, the shortest grass upon which will fatten sheep or oxen; *next*, over a little branch of the salt water which runs up to Faversham; *beyond that*, on the Isle of Shepry (or Shepway), which rises a little into a sort of ridge that runs along it; rich fields, pastures and orchards lie all around me.

The richness of the landscape with its fields, orchards, and meadows and Cobbett's appreciation of it is more than merely pastoral, however, as throughout these kinds of descriptions he also intersperses commentary about the land and how one can best live on it. In the midst of this passage, for example, he interjects, "But, alas! what, in point of *beauty*, is a country without woods and lofty trees! And here there are very few indeed." He concludes by declaring that "I a million times to one prefer, as a spot to *live on*, the heaths, the miry coppices, the wild woods and the forests of Sussex and Hampshire."[4]

These wilder places are not simply more aesthetically pleasing for Cobbett, but register as well different ways of living, different "spot[s] to *live on*," especially for the laborers on the land. In Kent in 1823, for example, he writes, "Continual new views strike the eye; but there is little variety in them: all is pretty, but nothing strikingly beautiful. The labouring people look pretty well. They have pigs. They invariably do best in the *woodland* and *forest* and *wild* countries. Where the mighty grasper has *all under his eye*, they can get but little."[5] The "grasper," like the "improver," figures, for Cobbett, the motive force of enclosure, which he witnessed firsthand in his travels and characterized polemically as the "rage for improvements," "the rage for what empty men think was an augmenting of the *capital* of the country."[6] As a farmer himself, Cobbett isn't arguing against farming and agriculture tout court, but rather highlighting the detrimental effects of enclosure, which drives away the *"useful* people," leaves the laborer destitute, and leads to a *"shocking decay"* and ruin in the agricultural villages.[7] The impact permeates not only the land but also the people and the social relations of the countryside, leaving the small farmer and others with smallholdings such as the cottager and landless laborers most affected. In short, land, labor and nature cannot be thought separately: they constitute an interrelated system that, as Cobbett recognizes, is at once fragile, various in its make-up, and at risk from "empty men" driven by the accumulation of capital.

As this record of the countryside shows, thinking the farm, the common, and the wild together allows us to think broadly about land use in the long nineteenth century – not only in terms of the actual changes that were taking place in and on the land that Cobbett documents in such detail, but also in terms of how those changes were being conceptualized, justified, and represented. How, for example, did the enclosure of formerly open fields for the purposes of agriculture impact the day-to-day experiences of the people undergoing such change? What had to happen for wilds to be reconfigured as "useless" or wasteful despite the known advantages they provided on both a social and environmental level? Equally, where can we locate moments of resistance or movements that counter these logics of property and their attendant ideology of possessive individualism? Too often such developments are presented as inevitable. The historical record, however, suggests otherwise – and the literature of the long nineteenth century attests to that "otherwise."

From Family Farms to Capitalist Farms

Much of Victorian literature is set in the countryside, so it should come as no surprise that farms can be found in so many novels throughout the nineteenth century. In George Eliot's *Adam Bede* (1859) and *Middlemarch* (1871), Thomas Hardy's *Far from the Madding Crowd* (1874), William Morris's *News from Nowhere* (1890), and H. G. Wells's *The Time Machine* (1895), to name just a few, farms and husbandry register marked changes in the rural landscape, be it in the degradation of the countryside, the rural reforms taking place over the course of the nineteenth century, or in utopian and dystopian views of land and social relations. While *The Time Machine* may seem like an outlier, the Eloi are "mere fatted cattle, which the ant-like Morlocks preserved and preyed upon – probably saw to the breeding of."[8] Only recently, however, has this environment taken center stage as something like a protagonist in a novel rather than a backdrop or the background for the development of a novel's characters. Although George Eliot described *Adam Bede* as "a country story – full of the breath of cows and the scent of hay," critical work on it has, for the most part, not followed the cows and hay.[9] Instead, as John Rignall's discussion of landscape reflects, we have tended to see in writers like Eliot the use of "nature in the form of landscape to illumine human emotions."[10] This is not to say that Eliot doesn't make those kinds of connections; however, there is a story in the landscape itself that goes missing when we focus primarily on the human side of things. *Adam Bede* is also a "country story" in the sense that it narrates the degradation of the countryside both through the destruction of the common, which has been transformed into impoverished districts like the one where Dinah Morris lives, and through the battle between Mrs. Poyser and her landlord, the old squire Mr. Donnithorne, who wants to enclose the land around the Poysers' farm and shift the entire farm from agricultural to dairy production – the latter a form of specialization that is a key process in the development of a "capitalist agrarian mode of production."[11]

Nowhere are these changes more powerfully represented than in Thomas Hardy's oeuvre, where farming as a set of social and economic relations is represented at both the individual and broader systematic level. It is impossible in such a short space to cover the range and intricacies of Hardy's depictions of farming and how they capture the textures, rhythms and transformations in agricultural production that took place over the course of his lifetime and that formed the basis of his fiction. I offer here, instead, snapshots of the kinds of observations his novels make. In *Far from the Madding Crowd*, the barn as a structure is emblematic of an enduring value: "For once medievalism and modernism had a common standpoint" that neither suffers the fate of an "exploded fortifying art" nor a "worn-out religious creed." As Hardy understands the meaning of the barn, "the defence and salvation of the body by daily bread is still a study, a religion, and a desire."[12] In *Tess of the d'Urbervilles* (1891) and *The Woodlanders* (1887), changes in the scale of production, Anna West argues, represent "mismatches … between systems of production and community," which in turn lead to the tragedies that are the stuff of Hardy's fiction.[13] Moreover, comparing the barn in *Far from the Madding Crowd* to the barn in *Jude the Obscure* (1895) that Jude climbs to get a view of Christminster, West sees a "moving mismatch of functional scale between human and machine, the mechanization of human and animal bodies – and the rendering of the landscape as a resource and product."[14]

Tess narrates that change *within* the novel, showing us a before and after of agricultural practices whose trajectory begins with the older laborers of Flintcomb-Ash remembering a time "when everything, even to winnowing, was effected by hand-labour, which, to their thinking, though slow, produced better results," and then unfolds as Tess moves from her family's farm to Talbothays dairy to the "starve-acre place" of Flintcomb-Ash, where the threshing machine dictates the rhythm and pace of work.[15] Described as the "irresistible swallower" (echoing Cobbett's "grasper"), it is "fed" by Tess and anthropomorphized further as a "raving" and "red tyrant ... which kept up a despotic demand upon the endurance of [the labourers'] muscles and nerves."[16] The thresher is relentless: "It was the ceaselessness of the work which tried [Tess] so severely, and began to make her wish that she had never come to Flintcomb-Ash."[17] In all these instances, the land and agricultural practices are hardly a bit player; they are, as contemporaneous reviewers of *The Woodlanders* said of Egdon Heath, dramatis personae.

When we look at land not as a backdrop but as an integral part of the story, as Hardy prompts us to do, the relations among social, economic, and environmental concerns simply cannot be separated from each other. In the context of farming specifically, his understanding, like other Victorian novelists', of the environment in its most expansive sense highlights how resistance to the mechanization of labor – a tradition that extends back in its most iconic form to the early nineteenth-century Luddites and their practice of machine-breaking – is not about the machines in and of themselves. Instead as Brian Merchant argues in *Blood in the Machine,* a history that connects the Luddites to the contemporary rebellion against big tech, "the machine breakers were not ultimately after the machines themselves but rather the men who were using them to transform social relations and gain power."[18] The aim "was to destroy, specifically, 'machinery hurtful to commonality' – machinery that tore at the social fabric, unduly benefitting a single party at the expense of the rest of the community."[19] The same is true for a range of depictions of the farm and the changes it was undergoing as a result of the shift from family to capitalist farms, which brought with it not only technological change but also the destruction of communal relations or commonality. An increasingly itinerant population – what Hardy refers to as the "landless ones" in *Tess* or the "habitually-removing man" in "The Dorsetshire Labourer," and Eliot refers to as the "man with a bundle on his back and a woman carrying her baby," whom Dorothea sees on the road from her window in *Middlemarch* – is forced to move from town to town and farm to farm in order to find work.[20] This state of landless itinerancy is intimately connected not only to farming and the enclosure of the common, as Cobbett shows, but, as we will see below, also to the destruction of the wild, be it in the form of heaths, forests, coppices, or other lands safe from the "grasper" or "improver."

Emigration Novels and the Colonial Farm

When we shift our focus beyond England to its colonies, the extractive nature of "improvement" and of the regime of private property becomes even more visible, often in excruciating detail. Canadian emigration novels like Susanna Moodie's *Roughing It in the Bush* (1852) and Catharine Parr Traill's *Canadian Crusoes: A Tale of the Rice Lake Plains* (1852), for example, narrate the processes of "development" and, in Moodie's case, the concomitant clearing of the land and the clearing off the land of its Indigenous inhabitants. For our purposes, a key aim of these narratives was essentially to establish the right to ownership based on labor – namely the clearing and ploughing of the land by British settlers. The colonial context highlights a set of relations among labor, land, and nature that are revelatory not only for thinking about representations of land use within the context of the nineteenth century but also today, as the climate crisis looms large.

As Jason R. Rudy argues in his reading of *Little Dorrit* and Charles Dickens's connections to Australia, emigration novels or "outwardly bound narratives ultimately offer little to bourgeois Britons."[21] But they do bring to the fore, in ways that the domestic novels do not, the violence of the British Empire. They also reveal the racialized nature of "improvement" and the logic of and right to private property, as Brenna Bhandar argues: the "notion that land requires improvement because its inhabitants are also in need of civilizational uplift, and vice versa, is no accident of history."[22] Moodie's memoir, like so many emigration narratives, perpetuates numerous myths about the land, property rights, First Nations peoples (the Chippewa and Missasaugas in particular), and the inevitability of "progress." Overtly racist in its characterization of the Anishinaabe, referred to as "these wild people," Moodie's narrative presupposes their genocidal removal.[23] Her final poem includes the following lines: "But soon not a trace/Of the red man's race/Shall be found in the landscape fair."[24] As Moodie reiterates throughout, her memoir is not a work of amusement, but rather a practical guide for those thinking of emigrating to Canada to clear and farm the land. That emigration is a good thing when approached with the proper industry and preparation is never at issue. Even when Moodie reflects on the changes being wrought on the landscape and its peoples, she expresses little more than a passing sigh, at best, moving on always to note the progress being made, the "air of civilization" being given to formerly unspoiled lands and lakes,[25] and the fact that this process necessarily involves destroying Indigenous peoples' livelihoods and lives. On a trip to Stony Lake, for example, Moodie describes how fully the Indians use the islands, gathering everything from berries and onions to "wampum-grass" and birch bark, and then writes: "In short, from the game, fish and fruit which they collect among the islands of this lake, they chiefly depend for their subsistence. They are very jealous of the settlers in the country coming to hunt and fish here."[26] That they are right to be not so much jealous as concerned for their survival is made abundantly clear over and over, and something of which

Moodie is well aware, but not in any way that matters. As she says early on, in one of the most perverse comments of the narrative, "It is a melancholy truth, and deeply to be lamented, that the vicinity of European settlers has always produced a very demoralising effect upon the Indian."[27] In short, the colonial farm entails nothing short of the dispossession and destruction of Indigenous peoples in the name of civilization.

While fictional representations of emigration to and life in other parts of the British Empire may involve less direct representations of land clearing, environmental destruction, and genocidal practices, they perpetuate similar myths about racialized hierarchies of land use and property. In *The Story of an African Farm* (1883), Olive Schreiner's depictions of Native Africans are as problematic as those of other emigration novels, even as her own stance vis-à-vis British colonialism became increasingly critical. Over the course of the period between writing *The Story of an African Farm* and the Jameson Raid of the Transvaal in 1896, Schreiner's views on colonial policy changed dramatically as she moved from an admiration for Cecil B. Rhodes's mission in Africa, captured succinctly in his dictum "You want to annex land rather than natives," to a denunciation of it. But, as M. A. Miller argues, "despite such clear rejection of colonial policies that promoted Native African land theft, Schreiner cannot overcome her own white feminism."[28] Black Native women, as Miller shows, "become proxies who facilitate, through their care labour and servitude, white settler love. In doing so, they become the indentured vehicles that are used to propel the transfer of landowner rights from a white woman to a white man through the language of settler courtship."[29] Likewise, the character Gregory Rose's transness, Miller concludes, in no way jeopardizes his white settler privilege and the land rights and ownership of the farm that go with it.[30]

Schreiner's novel is rife with contradiction, however. Although Native Africans have no voice in the novel, the possibility of an alternative set of relations among land, labor, and nature is gestured toward, in large part through the character of Waldo Farber, the sensitive son of the German farm-keeper. Early in the novel, Waldo muses on the limitations of history books, speculating that, if the kopje and surrounding geography "could talk, if they could tell us now!" then "we would know something."[31] In the same scene, describing the cave paintings in the rocks above where he lies with his sheep, Waldo feels that the "stones are really speaking – speaking of the old times, of the time when the strange fishes and animals lived … and the time when the little Bushmen lived here" and made such paintings, which are "only strange things, that make us laugh; but to him they were very beautiful."[32] This last clause and the history Waldo proceeds to narrate about how the "Boers have shot them all now, so that we never see a yellow face peeping out among the stones" provide a counter-narrative in which the natural environment prevails and the Boers face the same fate as those they have displaced. They, like the Bushmen, will "be gone soon, and only the stones will lie on here, looking at everything like they look now."[33]

This narrative is buttressed as well by a vision of an alternative farming practice, figured in the new sheep-shearing machine of which Waldo creates a wooden model. This tangible model returns him from the inscrutable heights of the infinite to the "renovating relief" of a "simple, feelable, weighable substance; to something which has a smell and a colour, which may be handled and turned over this way and that."[34] The model is a concrete manifestation of the potential connectedness between human and machine, human and animal, that is destroyed by the increasingly abstract relations of production that characterize capitalist land use. The destruction wrought by colonial property relations is figured metaphorically when Bonaparte Blenkins unceremoniously crushes Waldo's model with his foot.

Fittingly, despite the colonial world's best efforts to bend the environment to its will, the nonhuman world has the last word. In the final scene, the naive character Em, thinking Waldo has simply fallen asleep, covers the glass of fresh milk she has brought for him, and assumes he will wake soon to drink it. She couldn't be more wrong though, given the chickens' willingness to rest on Waldo, something which they would not venture to do unless Waldo was dead, for they "knew that men were dangerous; even sleeping they might wake." As Schreiner writes, in one of the best lines ever to conclude a Victorian novel, "But the chickens were wiser."[35]

The Common and an Open-Field Politics

As the family farm became increasingly mechanized and industrial and farming in the colonies denuded and deforested the land, rights to common lands were taken away. What was lost with the destruction of common subsistence rights was not only access to the land but also a communal way of life. Within the colonial context, the Victorians were dispossessing Indigenous peoples of their land and ways of being and knowing; any invocation of the common must therefore be global in scope, as I have argued elsewhere. Within England, the belief in and fight for the common is best understood, to my mind, as an "open field politics"; this would be a way of inhabiting the world that was both real for the Victorians – because present in the unenclosed spaces and common that still remained during the *longue durée* of enclosure – and imagined, as those open spaces became fenced in and enclosed and such a politics necessarily turned to the future. I take the term "open field politics" from Hugh Haughton, who characterizes John

Clare's poetry of protest as an "open field poetics" in which the openness of his poems is analogous to the unenclosed landscape of Clare's early life, to its mobility and its freedom.[36] Clare's own descriptions of his "open-field sense of space" revolve literally around the intimate connections between the social and the environmental and the actual circular organization of open-field parishes.[37]

These kinds of connections are also found in Victorian novels whose subject matter is not explicitly about open fields or spaces free from the processes of enclosure. They find expression through the glimpses of freedom – of movement, of mind – that mark moments when open fields or the common are referenced and traversed. In her industrial novel *North and South* (1855), which takes us far from Clare's fields to the factories of northern England, Elizabeth Gaskell describes Margaret Hale's walks at the beginning of the novel, noting that:

> Margaret used to tramp along by her father's side ... out on the broad commons into the warm scented light, seeing multitudes of wild, free, living creatures, revelling in the sunshine, and the herbs and flowers it called forth. This life – at least these walks – realized all Margaret's anticipations. She took pride in her forest. Its people were her people.[38]

The multiple enclosures that increasingly define so many of Gaskell's characters are the inverse of this freedom. We perceive such unfreedom in the north of *North and South*, as well as in the factory and the industrial strife that fells nearly all of the Barton family in *Mary Barton* (1848) and in the figure of the larch that stands outside the window of the dressmaker's shop in *Ruth* (1853), where the eponymous heroine has been forced to work. This larch, the narrator laments, had once "stood in a pleasant lawn, with the tender grass creeping caressingly up to its very trunk; but now the lawn was divided into yards and squalid back premises, and the larch was pent up and girded about with flag-stones."[39] Just as Cobbett recognized the interconnectedness of the many terrains he traversed, so too did Gaskell, in both the move from south to north and the enclosures that become visible in the traces of the past to be found in a once free larch now "pent up and girded."

Likewise, returns to the past within utopian Victorian fiction have the capacity to reveal alternative ways of reimagining a future common or open-field politics, which neither replicates the lost historical common nor engages in "wooly-headed nostalgia" (to borrow a phrase from Kristin Ross) – a misnomer levelled, for example, at William Morris and his interest in medieval Iceland.[40] But in *News from Nowhere* (1890), a pastoral utopian fiction with its supposed blindness to the realities of industrial society, Morris not only depicts "the concomitant collapse of the extraction economy and the split-level world it created, a world where life above ground was enabled by deposits from below," as Elizabeth C. Miller argues,[41] but also envisions the end of "commercial learning" and a world in which prisons have been abolished.[42] In short, the past is at once a part of history that is gone and a resource for thinking an alternative social and environmentally sustainable future. In *News* the image of the landscape as a garden that has replaced first the "clearings amongst the woods and wastes" in England, and then "the huge and foul workshops" is not a replica of the past but a transformed space defined by its ecological balance and lack of waste.[43] It is not pre- but rather postindustrial. So while the idea of an open field politics may seem antiquated both in the midst of the industrializing long nineteenth century and in our present moment, a return to the land need not equate to nostalgia for a lost past or a turning away from the present. Just as an open field politics was a politics of the future for the Victorians, so, too, can it be for us.

The Wild/Wilderness/Wastes

In his 1881 poem "Inversnaid," Gerard Manley Hopkins writes of a "dark-some burn" (a small river) that "turns and twindles over the broth/Of a pool so pitchblack, féll frówning/It rounds and rounds Despair to drowning." The "groin of the braes" (the hillside along the river) are "wiry heathpacks, flitches of fern/And the beadbonny ash that sits over the burn." Of this landscape, "degged with dew, dappled with dew," Hopkins asks his reader:

> What would the world be, once bereft
> Of wet and of wildness? Let them be left
> O let them be left, wildness and wet;
> Long live the weeds and the wilderness yet.[44]

Again, one needn't fall prey to nostalgia to recognize the beauty in Hopkins's chiasmatic description of "wet and wildness," "wildness and wet"; nor to recognize, beyond the beauty, the usefulness of the wild and "wastes," even as the capitalist logic of John Locke et al. claims such "unused" spaces as useless and hence there for the taking. Such logic links the enclosure movement within England to British expansion abroad and settler colonialism, with its assumption, as Locke would have it, that "as much land as a man tills, plants, improves, cultivates, and can use the product of, so much is his property. He by his labour does, as it were, inclose it from the common."[45]

As we saw above, emigration novels trade in one prevalent and destructive vision of a wild in need of cultivation. In his classic 1995 essay on "The Trouble with Wilderness or, Getting Back to the Wrong Nature," William Cronon troubles another vision of the wild or, in his parlance, "wilderness": that of wilderness as emphatically "natural," disconnected from history and devoid of human influence and shaping. As he writes, "there is nothing natural about the concept of wilderness. It is entirely a creation of the culture that holds it dear, a product of the very history it seeks to deny."[46] He goes on to argue that what is perceived as wild is often the product of a long history of human intervention. It may seem odd to consider the wild in relation to the English countryside, given how unwild it appears in contrast, for example, to the Scottish wilds that Hopkins describes. However, it is in figurations of the wild that various histories – of enclosure, of the development of agrarian capitalism – are documented and made legible in Victorian literature. To return to Hardy, the narrative of *The Return of the Native* (1878) contrasts a plantation of trees unable to withstand a storm to the unenclosed heath, which is perfectly adapted to its environment and hence weathers such turbulations with ease. The unenclosed heath is thus shown to be in no way synonymous with uselessness; nor is it disconnected from a history of land use, of the existence of the common and the wild in which communal values prevailed over individualistic, capitalist ones.

Focusing on land use and the specific connections among land, labor, and nature in Victorian fiction has the capacity to attune us not only to the environment of the nineteenth century, but also to our own. As the range of Victorian literature on the environment, broadly conceived, illustrates, an attentiveness to the land has the capacity to bring to the fore the exploitative and extractive practices that have led to our present climate catastrophe. But equally, and on a more positive note, an attentiveness to the land can, and in fact must, be the ground for a politics of a truly ecological, decolonial future in which, I hazard, the farm, the common, and the wild will play a central role.

Notes

1. William Cobbett, *Rural Rides*, Vol. 1 (London: J.M. Dent & Sons, [1930] 1957), xvii.
2. Andreas Malm, *Fossil Capital: The Rise of Steam Power and the Roots of Global Warming* (New York: Verso, 2016), 4–5.
3. Cobbett, *Rural Rides*, 44.
4. Cobbett, *Rural Rides*, 44.
5. Cobbett, *Rural Rides*, 220.
6. Cobbett, *Rural Rides*, 175, 190.
7. Cobbett, *Rural Rides*, 124, 123.
8. H. G. Wells, *The Time Machine* (Minneapolis: First Avenue Editions, [1895] 2018), 67.
9. George Eliot, *The George Eliot Letters*, ed. Gordon S. Haight, Vol. 2 (New Haven: Yale University Press, 1954), 387.

10. John Rignall, "Landscape," in Margaret Harris, ed., *George Eliot in Context* (Cambridge University Press, 2013), 174.

11. Raymond Williams, *The Country and the City* (New York: Oxford University Press, 1973), 297.

12. Thomas Hardy, *Far from the Madding Crowd* (London: Penguin, 2003), 126.

13. Anna West, "The End of the Farm? Thomas Hardy's Agricultural Vision," *FATHOM* 7 (2022), 9.

14. West, "The End of the Farm?," 2.

15. Thomas Hardy, *Tess of the d'Urbervilles* (London: Penguin, 1985), 406, 360.

16. Hardy, *Tess*, 404.

17. Hardy, *Tess*, 406.

18. Brian Merchant, *Blood in the Machine: The Origins of the Rebellion against Big Tech* (New York: Little Brown and Company, 2023), 62.

19. Merchant, *Blood in the Machine*, 67.

20. Hardy, *Tess*, 342; Thomas Hardy, "The Dorsetshire Labourer," *Longman's Magazine* (July 1883), 252–69 at 259; George Eliot, *Middlemarch* (New York: Penguin, 1994), 788.

21. Jason R. Rudy, "Settled: *Dorrit* Down Under," *Nineteenth-Century Literature* 75.2 (2020), 184–206 at 197.

22. Brenna Bhandar, *Colonial Lives of Property: Law, Land, and Racial Regimes of Ownership* (Durham: Duke University Press, 2018), 181.

23. Susanna Moodie, *Roughing It in the Bush* (New York: W. W. Norton, 2007), 186.

24. Moodie, *Roughing It*, 331.

25. Moodie, *Roughing It*, 222.

26. Moodie, *Roughing It*, 228.

27. Moodie, *Roughing It*, 192.

28. M. A. Miller, "The Costs of Passing in the Transvaal," *Victorian Studies* 64.4 (Summer 2022), 614.

29. Miller, "The Costs of Passing," 615.

30. Miller, "The Costs of Passing," 621.

31. Olive Schreiner, *Story of an African Farm* (New York: Penguin Books, 1979), 48.

32. Schreiner, *Story of an African Farm*, 49.

33. Schreiner, *Story of an African Farm*, 50.

34. Schreiner, *Story of an African Farm*, 105.

35. Schreiner, *Story of an African Farm*, 301.

36. Hugh Haughton, "Progress and Rhyme: The 'Nightingale's Nest' and Romantic Poetry," in Hugh Haughton, Adam Phillips, and Geoffrey Summerfield, eds., *John Clare in Context* (Cambridge: Cambridge University Press, 1994), 66.

37. John Barrell, *The Idea of Landscape and the Sense of Place 1730–1840: An Approach to the Poetry of John Clare* (Cambridge: Cambridge University Press, 2011), 103.

38. Elizabeth Gaskell, *North and South* (New York: Penguin, 2003), 19.

39. Elizabeth Gaskell, *Ruth* (New York: Oxford University Press, 1998), 5.

40. Kristin Ross, "The Meaning of the Paris Commune," Interview by Manu Goswami, *Jacobin*, May 5, 2015.

41. Elizabeth Carolyn Miller, *Extraction Ecologies and the Literature of the Long Exhaustion* (Princeton: Princeton University Press, 2021), 176.

42. William Morris, *News from Nowhere and Other Writings* (London: Routledge and Kegan Paul, [1890] 1970), 59.
43. Morris, *News from Nowhere*, 61.
44. Gerard Manley Hopkins, *The Poetical Works of Gerard Manley Hopkins*, ed. Norman H. Mackenzie, 4th ed. (Oxford: Oxford University Press, 1990), 167–8.
45. John Locke, *Second Treatise of Government*, ed. C. B. Macpherson, Vol. 2 (Indianapolis: Hackett, 1980), 5.31.
46. William Cronon, "The Trouble with Wilderness or, Getting Back to the Wrong Nature," in William Cronon, ed., *Uncommon Ground: Rethinking the Human Place in Nature* (New York: W. W. Norton, 1996), 69–90 at 79.

PART V

Environmentalism

18

ALLEN MACDUFFIE

Pollution

"Pollution" is a quintessentially Victorian term. As Peter Thorsheim argues, the nineteenth century "invented pollution" both materially, through the development of industrial production, rapid, unplanned urbanization, and the creation of a fossil fuel intensive economic infrastructure, and conceptually, through the struggle to understand the social and environmental consequences of all these things.[1] Pressing questions about the effects, the nature, the implications, and the very meaning of pollution affected every discipline and mode of thought imaginable, from economics and public health to architecture and history. The blackened skies and befouled waterways; the rubbish heaps and blighted landscapes; the collapsing slums and raging epidemics – these were, to borrow a phrase from Thomas Carlyle, "signs of the times." Signs of crisis, of a profound breakdown somewhere in the political or economic or social order of English life. But the nature of that crisis, the specific form of the breakdown, the possible means and strategies of redress – these were matters of intense and unresolved contestation throughout the nineteenth century and beyond.

For some, pollution seemed chiefly an engineering problem, remediable through improved infrastructure, more efficient technologies, and better social policy. It is a position often voiced by members of the "sanitary reform" movement, who insisted that much of the waste polluting London and other English population centers was "matter in the wrong place," to quote the famous saying.[2] As the chemist Justus von Liebig argued, what *looks* like pollution is, seen correctly, a valuable resource:

> When we consider the immense value of night-soil [human waste] as a manure, it is quite astounding that so little attention is paid to preserve it. The quantity is immense which is carried down by the drains in London to the River Thames, serving no other purpose than to pollute its waters. A substance, which by its putrefaction generates miasmata, may, by artificial means, be rendered totally inoffensive, inodorous, and transportable, and yet prejudice prevents these means being resorted to.[3]

From this point of view, pollution represents as much a failure of imagination as of material disposal.

But to see pollution as matter in the wrong place implies that there is a right place for it. That implication was, in turn, underwritten by the belief – explicitly declared or tacitly assumed – that nature was a divinely constructed and fundamentally balanced regime, which ultimately had a right place for everything. As Henry Mayhew puts it:

> in Nature everything moves in a circle – perpetually changing, and yet ever returning to the point whence it started[.] … With the same wondrous economy that marks all creation, it has been ordained that what is unfitted for the support of the superior organisms, is of all substances the best adapted to give strength and vigour to the inferior. That which we excrete as pollution to our system, they secrete as nourishment to theirs.[4]

No cheerleader for capitalism, Mayhew nevertheless articulates something of the logic that would inform its apologetics: with proper management and the proper point of view, industrial growth would ultimately be shown to belong to the larger natural harmony.

For others, the appalling state of English cities and other industrial sacrifice zones seemed unmistakable proof that a vast, anti-human, perhaps even planet-killing regime was rising to power, and that the ever-receding promise of the techno-utopia just around the corner was more like a suicide pact with the profit motive. This was the position of Romantic anti-capitalists like Carlyle and John Ruskin for whom pollution was a sign not of imperfect planning, but of a deep spiritual rot at the heart of modernity. Ruskin's dystopian imagination at times makes him sound like he's storyboarding the next *Terminator* film, with depictions of nightmare landscapes ("the whole earth … a globe of black, lifeless, excoriated metal") and an inhuman order programmed to convert people into waste: "the animation of her multitudes is sent like fuel to feed the factory smoke."[5] Pollution for Ruskin is not some mere by-product of capitalism, but its defining feature; by claiming it is not the fires being fed but the *smoke*, he provocatively collapses the metonymic chain of production, suggesting the raison d'être of the industrial system is to manufacture pollution. The smoke spewing from factories and the luxuries gilding English drawing rooms sum to essentially the same thing: signs of a profound transgression against life itself. Industrial England becomes in this view a modern Gomorrah awaiting doom under a pall of its own making.

For socialist critics like Marx and Engels, pollution also looked like a sign that the system was rotten to its core, but in their case the Day of Judgment was coming in revolutionary, rather than biblical, form. Engels's

1845 classic *The Condition of the Working Class in England* describes in often suffocating detail the toxic environments in which the working and non-working poor of "the great towns" were forced to eke out miserable existences. Here is his account of a Manchester neighborhood:

> At the bottom flows, or rather stagnates, the Irk, a narrow, coal-black, foul-smelling stream, full of débris and refuse, which it deposits on the lower right bank. In dry weather, a long string of the most disgusting, blackish-green slime pools are left standing on this bank, from the depths of which bubbles of miasmatic gas constantly arise and give forth a stench unendurable even on the bridge forty or fifty feet above the surface of the stream. But besides this, the stream itself is checked every few paces by high weirs, behind which slime and refuse accumulate and rot in thick masses. Above the bridge are tanneries, bonemills, and gasworks, from which all drains and refuse find their way into the Irk, which receives further the contents of all the neighbouring sewers and privies.[6]

Engels's aim in describing such scenes is to document what Gillen Wood calls the "demographic apartheid" that "separates bourgeois suburbs from the disgusting and deadly working class slums" in nineteenth-century English factory towns.[7] Although pollution is threatening, in part, because of its ability to seep and spill and escape containment, Engels also wants to insist that, in other ways, it is a deliberately localized problem, vented disproportionately onto poor and working-class communities: "these east and north-east sides of Manchester are the only ones on which the bourgeoisie has not built, because ten or eleven months of the year the west and south-west wind drives the smoke of all the factories hither, and that is for the working people alone to breathe."[8] Needless to say, such forms of demographic apartheid persist within wealthy countries – Louisiana's "Cancer Alley" being a prime example in the United States – as well as between wealthy countries and countless regions of the Global South. If Ruskin's essays sometimes scale up to the planetary in ways that seem to anticipate visions of the Anthropocene, Engels's focus on asymmetrical exposure to pollution looks ahead to contemporary discussions of environmental justice.

But "pollution" is also a quintessentially Victorian term in a different way. Along with a number of related words ("corruption," "contamination," "defilement," and the like), "pollution" and its variants were part of a coercive moral vocabulary wielded everywhere for the purposes of social policing. This is most obvious in all matters sexual, where women's bodies especially were subject to a regulatory logic of purity and impurity employed to define their very value as human beings. Such a vocabulary predates the Victorians, of course: Isabella, in Shakespeare's *Measure for Measure*, faced with the offer of sleeping with her brother's captor in exchange for his life, imagines he would rather die "before his sister should her body stoop/To such abhorred pollution."[9] But in the nineteenth century, the moral and material valences of the term become even more complexly interarticulated, so that, for example, promiscuity itself could be described as a kind of contagion generated by new social arrangements and working conditions. The Presbyterian minister Ralph Wardlaw describes *"the corrupting influence of extreme factories,* usually termed *public works*; those especially in which young men and young women, in large numbers, meet and work together ... the diffusive contamination of vice is fearful" (his emphasis).[10] That threat of moral contamination extended to disembodied forms of connection and circulation as well. As Zachary Samalin shows, the Obscene Publications Act of 1857 "sought to regulate the circulation of sexually illicit texts as though they were, in the eyes of the law, public nuisances – akin to chemical poisons, airborne pollutions, and contagious diseases – thus inscribing a sensory discourse of disgust into the juridical as well as the sanitary domain."[11]

This mixing of the moral and material valences of pollution often structured discussions of working-class neighborhoods and city slums. Certain forms of immorality were imagined to spread from person to person, or even from place to person, like a toxic agent or disease, while blighted living conditions were understood as a sign of the degraded moral state of their inhabitants. This was particularly the case when it came to the so-called residuum, the class of casual laborers and non-working poor, which was frequently painted as a threat to the entire project of civilization. In the eyes of many commentators, as Gareth Stedman Jones argues, "its very existence served to contaminate the classes immediately above it."[12] The anxious discourse about the residuum carries complex implications for the period's environmental imaginary. On the one hand, as Jones shows, it helped shift the conversation "from the moral inadequacies of the individual to the deleterious influences of the urban environment" and "prepared the middle-class public to see chronic poverty as an endemic condition of large masses of the population, rather than as the product of exceptional misfortune or improvidence on the part of isolated individuals."[13] Unbreathable air, contaminated water, filthy streets, decaying, overcrowded dwellings: these environments were so overwhelmingly inimical to life that the usual individuating moral categories of personal responsibility and willpower seemed beside the point. On the other hand, approaching the issue through aggregative, population-scaled thinking could lend itself to forms of wholesale dehumanization, where impoverished people are imagined as the *embodiment* of urban pollution rather than those most grievously suffering from it. One can see this in the shocking terms with which the reformer and philanthropist Samuel Smith describes the urban poor: "while the flower of our population emigrate ... the residuum remains behind, corrupting and being corrupted, like the sewage of the metropolis which remained floating at the mouth of the Thames last summer, because there was not scour sufficient to propel it into the sea."[14] Pollution, we might say, gets the poor coming and going: the product of a waste-intensive economic system designed to build wealth for the few and immiserate the many, it was also used, discursively, to shift responsibility away from that process and onto its most despised and powerless victims. In many quarters, then, a moralized discourse of pollution served as a kind of laundering of capitalism itself.

Of course, these issues of class, population, and pollution were (and still are) complexly intertwined with race and empire. Smith's proposed solution was to ship the poorest of the poor off to the colonies, a familiar and still operative logic by which the Global South becomes the dumping ground for whatever the metropolitan power centers of the Global North deem hazardous. Of course, the traffic flowed in the other direction as well, and it should come as no surprise that immigrants from India, Africa, Ireland, Eastern Europe, and many other places were similarly dehumanized as forms of incoming human pollution, contaminating the motherland. The MP George Colomb, for example, complained that London was becoming "a human ash pit for the refuse population of the world."[15] In the later decades of the century, fears that immigrants, non-whites, and the working and non-working poor might pollute the nation and the body politic were intensified through concerns about evolutionary "degeneration" and the loss of the strength and purity of English "blood." Such thinking of course casts its dark shadow across the whole of the twentieth century and beyond, lingering, distressingly, in the contemporary rhetoric of ethnic nationalists and aspiring fascists the world over. As in the present moment, in the nineteenth century the profound cognitive dissonance created by, as William Greenslade puts it, "the rhetoric of progress ... [and] the evidence in front of people's eyes of poverty and degradation at the heart of ever richer empires" made vulnerable populations easy targets for demagogues who wished to conceal the real source – the architects and the beneficiaries – of that poverty and degradation.[16] Pollution was, and is, so difficult to deal with both materially and conceptually because it strikes at the heart of many of the most cherished and unexamined truths of liberal bourgeois ideology: from narratives of historical progress, to the primacy of the autonomous individual subject, to any number of other cultural fictions premised upon binaries of inside and outside, good and evil, human and nonhuman, mind and matter, visible and invisible, us and them. The threat of pollution inheres, in part, in its frighteningly transgressive, boundary-defying, deconstructive quality; no wonder then that oversimplifying narratives that promised to refortify or police those boundaries held such widespread power and appeal then, and continue to do so now.

All of this is to say that the unprecedented material problem of pollution in the nineteenth century raised serious questions about what kind of world this new fossil-fuel intensive economy was creating while also producing a discourse through which those questions were addressed and, often enough, evaded. Both as material problem and protean signifier, pollution lent itself to a Victorian literary imaginary invested in questions of interconnectivity and fragmentation, and struggling to make sense of the disorienting social, existential, and environmental realities coming into being. Although the novel is the place in which such issues received their most sustained treatment, I would submit that a key text here is Robert Browning's endlessly ambiguous narrative poem, "Childe Roland to the Dark Tower Came" (1855). Indeed, the poem's ambiguity, and its intense self-consciousness *about* that ambiguity, in many ways brings us to the heart of the period's epistemological crisis about the semiotics of pollution. While there are no smokestacks or factories to be found in "Childe Roland" and though its courtly trappings on some level suggest a premodern world, its vivid depiction of a thoroughly exhausted and poisoned landscape also evokes a journey through a postindustrial wasteland. The poem's waterways, much like the stretch of Thames that flowed through nineteenth-century London, seem to bob with human discards: "good saints, how I fear'd / To set my foot upon a dead man's cheek," the speaker says about fording a river, "It may have been a water-rat I spear'd / But, ugh! it sounded like a baby's shriek."[17] The speaker here and elsewhere conjures a world in which everything feels inescapably marred and marked by the human. And yet the fact that he dwells in the conjectural and subjunctive, in a backfooted position of retrospective guesswork, raises questions about whether he is responding to a materially humanized world, or projecting his own anthropomorphic constructions upon it. Even he can't be sure, and our awareness of his awareness of his own processes of meaning-making returns us to the kinds of questions facing Victorian observers of toxic landscapes: if these things are signs, what are they signs of? And is the answer to be found in a future state, figured here as the enigmatically beckoning Dark Tower? Or are narratives that are organized around a revelatory or redemptive endpoint simply ways of avoiding the blasted reality of the present? Is Childe Roland's *telos* the solution to the problem, or another expression of it? Browning's poem even considers the way such unsettling indeterminacy produces a compensatory urge to draw lines. Upon encountering a starving horse, the speaker comments: "Seldom went such grotesqueness with such woe; / I never saw a brute I hated so; / He must be wicked to deserve such pain."[18] Obscure as the poem is, what seems clear is that, here, we are being invited to note the speaker's will-to-moralize, and thus at least to wonder about his desire to endow an ambient and impersonal malignancy with more manageable, individualized dimensions.

Browning's poem was written in 1852, just two months before the first serial installment of what is perhaps the central text in any discussion of the representation of pollution in Victorian literature, Charles Dickens's *Bleak House*. Like "Childe Roland," but with a more obvious political axe to grind, *Bleak House* is as much about the epistemological crisis brought about by pollution as it is about the thing itself. As Jesse Oak Taylor puts it in his exemplary reading of the novel: "the principal effect of the climate of smog seems to be a breakdown in both the real and our perception of it."[19] The atmosphere in *Bleak House* has been the subject of so much commentary that one hesitates to set foot again upon such well-trodden ground, but it's worth pointing out the way that the tension between the moral and material valences of pollution that I've been discussing is complexly – and in some cases, incoherently – fused in this novel and indeed in much of Dickens's work. He is at once a keen environmental observer and an arch moralist; a scathing critic of the economic forces deranging the world and a writer whose imagination inclines towards personalization and allegory; a chronicler of modernity sensitive to its wasteful, chaotic, inhuman operations and a narrative architect always looking for ways to bring dispersion and chaos into some kind of resolution. So in *Bleak House*, the pollution engulfing the streets and skies, which initially suggests a systemic, distributed complicity, eventually comes to seem like a problem addressable through individual acts of goodness, self-denial, and loving sacrifice. This is maybe most clearly apparent in the novel's contagion plot, in which an outbreak of smallpox (a direct result, Dickens makes clear, of polluted environmental conditions) is ultimately contained by Esther Summerson's twin heroic acts: exposing herself to the disease to care for a loved one and then isolating herself to prevent further spread. In this way, the character's moral "purity" literally quarantines and symbolically defeats the forces of pollution, scrubbing her corner of the world as clean as her own uncorrupted soul. As I've argued elsewhere, we can see something of the flip side of this dynamic near the end of *David Copperfield*, where the prostitute Martha's putative moral degradation is identified with the contaminated London riverway she gazes into: "As if she were a part of the refuse it had cast out, and left to corruption and decay."[20] Martha is, in this sense, both product and avatar of pollution, just as Esther is both the agent of remediation and the personification of purity itself.

Obviously, such figurations are deeply problematic, not to say pernicious, in terms of both the novels' gender politics and their environmental imaginaries. I would also note, as Marlene Tromp has compellingly argued, that, in his later novels, Dickens played upon widespread xenophobic fears that imagined economic contact with (especially) Eastern countries and regions as a kind of pollution. In his unfinished novel *The Mystery of Edwin Drood*, she argues, this is figured through opium, a foreign commodity "polluting and permeating" not only a given individual body, but the body politic writ large.[21] Thus, the toxic consequences of what would later be termed "globalization" could be set against a mythic domestic purity that was imagined either as still potentially recoverable or else as lamentably consigned to a lost past of stability, order, and hierarchy.

Dickens remains a touchstone in the ecocritical conversation about Victorian literature, as well as in the works of many of our most vital contemporary novelists: Barbara Kingsolver's *Demon Copperhead*, Edward Carey's *Iremonger* series, or any number of China Mieville's novels all testify, in different ways, to the persistent power of Dickens's apocalyptic outrage over a world collapsing under the weight of its own waste. There is, it would seem, something about his visionary representation of pollution that exceeds the tidying up function of his endings or his retrograde hierarchies. It also suggests, as David Kurnick argues in his work on *Middlemarch*, the ways in which our own processes of reading, remembering, and dwelling with fiction often involve a resistance to the organizing drive of the last chapter and the final word.[22] In this case, what lingers from Dickens's depiction of pollution is a powerful vision of impersonal, systemic dysfunction that overwhelms the usual bourgeois assignments of good and evil, or purity and impurity, even if the novelist himself sometimes seems to want to hang onto them. Beyond such pieties, and for long stretches of his novels, Dickens gives voice to a different kind of moral register, an implacable wrath at an inhuman system of waste and exploitation constructed upon the backs of the poor and dragging the entire world down with it.

The tension between, on the one hand, a narrative drive in the direction of increasing clarity and organization and, on the other, pollution's ubiquitous, transgressive material reality is particularly acute in narratives of criminality and detection. The famous "London fog" – a euphemism for what we would today call "smog" – sets the stage not only for many of Dickens's proto-detective narratives like *Bleak House*, but also for the *locus classicus* of the genre, Arthur Conan Doyle's Sherlock Holmes stories.

The "opalescent London reek," as Doyle calls the fog in "The Adventure of the Abbey Grange" (1904), conveys an ambient sense of dread, menace, and uncertainty that indicates the loss of the usual boundaries through which innocence and guilt, true and false, friend and foe, victim and culprit, might be distinguished.[23] Take this stage-setting description of the London streets from an early chapter of *The Sign of Four* (1890): "It was a September evening and not yet seven o'clock, but the day had been a dreary one, and a dense drizzly fog lay low upon the great city. Mud-coloured clouds drooped sadly over the muddy streets. Down the Strand the lamps were but misty splotches of diffused light which threw a feeble circular glimmer upon the slimy pavement."[24] We might notice here Doyle is deodorizing – we might even say dematerializing – city pollution under euphemistic terms like fog and mud and slime. These are imagined primarily as visual impairments, and thereby work to symbolize the moral and epistemological obscurity that requires the detective's penetrative powers. Pollution "makes the case" for him in more ways than one. Much more than in Dickens, pollution in Doyle is imagined less as environmental or somatic threat and more as hermeneutic obstacle, something to be overcome through Holmes's rarefied capacities of detection and ratiocination: "he diagnoses, contains, and neutralizes the noxious agents he investigates," as Susan Cannon Harris puts it.[25]

In *The Sign of Four*, not only does Holmes dispel the moral fog by solving the case, but his blow-dart-wielding, Andaman Islander antagonist embodies the poison and chaos supposedly brought to English shores by the racial other. When that other meets his end by becoming part of the undifferentiated muck of the London waterway – "somewhere in the dark ooze at the bottom of the Thames lie the bones of that strange visitor to our shores" – the racialized symbolic polarities are made as stark as can be.[26] Holmes, avatar and defender of Western civilization, reasserts a regime of order and precisely differentiated forms of knowledge over the entropic forces of "savagery"; the islander, meanwhile, variously described as "misshapen," "dishevelled," "distorted," and "venomous," is the foreign pollutant neutralized by Holmes and the elements into which he can be safely reabsorbed.[27] We see in this a depressingly familiar victim-blaming reversal through which the British Empire, world's leading exporter of waste, lawlessness, and pollution, fashions itself as steward of cleanliness and order. Meanwhile, Indigenous peoples are imagined as the chief source of violence, even though they are overwhelmingly on the receiving end of it. Such a grotesque up-is-down depiction of power differentials remains a staple of imperial and settler colonial rhetoric today, a strategy of occupiers and genocidal regimes the world over.

The detective plot, with its downwards-scaling narrative drive towards individual acts of criminality, and a reassuring *telos* of apprehension and resolution, seems particularly unsuited to representing a problem of such impersonal unruliness and collective complicity as pollution. This also means that subversive variations of the genre, narratives pitched against the established horizon of expectations, can draw even more vividly the mismatch between reassuring fictions of law and order, on the one hand, and the larger, more threatening systemic forces such fictions disguise and enable, on the other. We might think here of a narrative like Joseph Conrad's *The Secret Agent* (1907), which borrows liberally from Dickens and Doyle for its cloak-and-dagger *mis-en-scène*, as in this depiction of the assistant commissioner of police, "enveloped, oppressed, penetrated, choked, and suffocated by the blackness of a wet London night, which is composed of soot and drops of water."[28] Conrad's novel, as much inheritor of Victorian detective fiction as progenitor of the Cold War spy thriller, makes pointed use of nonlinear chronology and anticlimactic narrative structures to suggest that the interplay of crime and detection is a mere sideshow, and that the very agencies tasked with protecting civilization from secret, toxic agents are the ones most actively contributing to its ruin.

In many ways, we are now living among those ruins. It is simply no longer possible, if it ever was, to view the Victorian cityscapes of Dickens or Doyle or Ruskin as belonging to a soiled but soon-to-be-turned page in the history of modernity. Indeed, we now know very well that their wastelands were mere prelude to the more insidious forms of pollution unleashed by a carbonizing modernity. The very concept of pollution itself now also spills beyond the categories the Victorians were familiar with, as today we cope with microplastics and "forever chemicals" circulating invisibly through our water supplies and bloodstreams. We must also now classify a basic molecule like CO_2 as a "pollutant," given the atmosphere-altering scale at which it is being released. We note then a complex relationship between our environmental imaginary and theirs: whereas the nineteenth century often confronted pollution in much more viscerally oppressive forms than many in the Global North do today, they also had more, and more redoubtable, fictions of order at hand with which to downplay, deflect, or defer a full reckoning with pollution's implications. Today, master narratives of inevitable civilizational progress have (thankfully) lost much of their purchase, even if the rhetoric of the polluted "other" remains a staple of revanchist populism. But the reality of pollution has also become, for many in the Global North, a matter of abstraction rather than direct experience. We have become more adept at making pollution disappear, both materially and ideationally, and thus often struggle to remember what the Victorians could not avoid. No wonder then that the century and its literature remain of enduring interest to many struggling to understand, imagine, represent, narrate, and recall the shocking forms of damage we have inflicted, and continue to inflict, upon this planet.

Notes

1. Peter Thorsheim, *Inventing Pollution: Coal, Smoke, and Culture in Britain since 1800* (Athens: Ohio University Press, 2006).
2. The quotation is widely attributed to Lord Palmerston. See, for example, Thomas Hardy, "The Dorsetshire Laborer," *Longman's Magazine* 2 (May to October, 1883), 252–69 at 257.
3. Justus Von Liebig, *Organic Chemistry in Its Application to Agriculture and Physiology*, ed. Lyon Playfair (London: Taylor & Watson, 1842), 184.
4. Henry Mayhew, *London Labour and the London Poor*, Vol. 2 (London: Griffin, Bohn & Company, 1861), 160.
5. John Ruskin, *The Works of John Ruskin*, ed. E. T. Cook and Alexander Wedderburn, 39 vols. (London: George Allen, 1903–12), 16.378, 10.193.
6. Friedrich Engels, *The Condition of the Working Class in England*, ed. Victor Kiernan (New York: Penguin, [1845] 1987), 89.
7. Gillen D'Arcy Wood, "Climate Delusion: Hurricane Sandy, Sea Level Rise, and 1840s Catastrophism," *Humanities* 8.3 (2019), 131 at 131.
8. Wood, "Climate Delusion," 97.
9. William Shakespeare, *Measure for Measure*, ed. A. R. Braunmuller and Robert Watson (London: Arden, 2020), 253.
10. Ralph Wardlaw, *Lectures on Female Prostitution: Its Nature, Effects, Guilt, Causes, and Remedy* (Glasgow: James Maclehose, 1842), 104–5.
11. Zachary Samalin, *The Masses are Revolting: Victorian Culture and the Political Aesthetics of Disgust* (Ithaca: Cornell University Press, 2021), 17.
12. Gareth Stedman Jones, *Outcast London: A Study in the Relationship Between Classes in Victorian Society* (Oxford: Oxford University Press, 1971), 289.
13. Jones, *Outcast London*, 313.
14. Samuel Smith, *The Industrial Training of Destitute Children* (London: Kegan, Paul, Trench & Co., 1885), 11.
15. Quoted in Anne Kershen, *Strangers, Aliens, and Asians: Huguenots, Jews, and Bangladeshis in Spitalfields 1660–2000* (London: Routledge, 2004), 202.
16. William Greenslade, *Degeneration, Culture, and the Novel* (Cambridge: Cambridge University Press, 1994), 15.
17. Robert Browning, "Childe Roland to the Dark Tower Came," *Robert Browning's Poetry*, ed. James Loucks and Andrew Stauffer (New York: Norton, 2007), 181–8 at 185.
18. Browning, "Childe Roland to the Dark Tower Came," in *Robert Browning's Poetry*, 181–8 at 184.
19. Jesse Oak Taylor, *The Sky of Our Manufacture: The London Fog in British Fiction from Dickens to Woolf* (Charlottesville: University of Virginia Press, 2016), 20.

20. Allen MacDuffie, "Dickens and the Environment," in Robert L. Patten, John Jordan, and Catherine Waters (eds.), *The Oxford Handbook of Charles Dickens*. (Oxford: Oxford University Press, 2018), 566–80 at 578–9.

21. Marlene Tromp, "The Pollution of the East," in Marlene Tromp, Maria K. Bachman, and Heidi Kaufman (eds.), *Fear, Loathing, and Victorian Xenophobia*. (Columbus: Ohio State University Press, 2013), 27–55 at 45.

22. David Kurnick, "An Erotics of Detachment: *Middlemarch* and Novel-Reading as Critical Practice," *ELH* 74 (2007), 583–608.

23. Arthur Conan Doyle, *The New Annotated Sherlock Holmes: The Complete Short Stories*, ed. Leslie Klinger (New York: Norton, 2005), 1158.

24. Arthur Conan Doyle, *The Sign of Four* (New York: Penguin, 2001), 21.

25. Susan Cannon Harris, "Pathological Possibilities: Contagion and Empire in Doyle's Sherlock Holmes Stories," *Victorian Literature and Culture* 31.2, 447–66 at 447.

26. Doyle, *The Sign of Four*, 87.

27. Doyle, *The Sign of Four*, 86–7.

28. Joseph Conrad, *The Secret Agent*, ed. Michael Newton (New York: Penguin, 2007), 119.

19

KATE FLINT

Art and Environment

In John Ruskin's 1858 lecture "The Work of Iron," the art critic, social commentator, and pioneer of environmentalist thinking invited his audience to imagine a world in which "all your meadows, instead of grass, grew nothing but iron wire;" and "the whole earth, instead of its green and glowing sphere, rich with forest and flower, showed nothing but the image of the vast furnace of a ghastly engine." A moment later, he suggests that "the most insignificant pebble at your feet" has meaning in it, if rightly read.[1] Ruskin's words here encapsulate the oscillation that environmental attention entails: a continual shift between envisaging changes that take place on a vast scale and the observation of minute detail. Ruskin was intensely and increasingly aware of the shifts to ecological balance that were taking place in nineteenth century Britain. Indeed, by June 1884, the year in which he gave his lectures on *The Storm Cloud of the Nineteenth Century*, he was claiming that "the entire body of English artists, through the space now of some fifteen years" had been "afflicted by the deterioration of climate."[2]

So what might it mean to look at nineteenth-century visual arts with an ecological eye? The answer is multilayered. It starts from the assumption – one that gained in scientific currency during the nineteenth century – that ecosystems are intricately interconnected. It recognizes that what we conventionally call "nature" is not some pristine, God-created state, but is constantly impacted by human activity. It attempts to keep in balance not just the huge shifts in scale that Ruskin suggests, but the combination of pictorial conventions, compositional techniques, close observation, selection, typification, and idealization that inform paintings, drawings, photography, sculpture, and other art forms. It leads us to consider the historical circumstances that result in a landscape looking as it does; how environmental harms, such as pollution and industrial despoliation, come to be represented; the ways in which highly individualized natural forms, such as plants and rocks, are depicted; and how a landscape painting – or, indeed, any painting containing elements of the nonhuman natural world – can contain features interpretable as bearing witness to past, current, and future environmental change. It also acknowledges the interconnectedness not just of ecosystems but also of cultural forms: the images that I discuss here all depend upon, and feed into, the literary production of the period. Many exhibited works gained extra authority through being accompanied by quotations on their first exhibition; actual paintings are referenced in contemporary fiction, and all help the reader create images in their mind's eye as they consume both poetry and novels. The same emphases run through both literature and art: I here single out distance, detail, damage, and denial.

As we will see, some artists from this period directly addressed such change, most obviously through their representation of urban spread and the pollution that came from coal consumption. But adopting an ecological vision also involves reading art with a view to elements that it is easy to take for granted, rather than those that loudly proclaim the industrializing world. Many of the plants growing in prettified cottage gardens, like those painted by Myles Birket Foster and Helen Allingham, or the various species of palms, ficus and fern in James Tissot's conservatories, attest to practices of extractive botanical collecting throughout the British Empire and beyond. The rolling hills of Welsh and Scottish landscapes point to centuries of grazing by close-nibbling sheep, and to an environment maintained for deer and gamebird hunting, all at the expense of native tree growth.

In other words, as Daegan Miller writes: "Every landscape is ultimately symbolic, its outward appearance a jumbled record of particular human ways of living in and making the world, its shards refracting particular ideas about who and what belonged. All landscapes, in other words, are histories, and as histories they can be read, if one can find an introduction."[3]

John Constable's paintings, so frequently approached as though they represent some quintessential, unchanging essence of Englishness, offer a case in point. For a start, their patchwork of fields resulted from the land enclosures that rapidly impacted rural life, helping diminish the rich biodiversity of preindustrial England. Take *View on the Stour Near Dedham* (1822) (Figure 19.1). While undeniably the scene depicts the rural world in which Constable, a miller's son, grew up and which always, as he said, delighted him, it is one shaped by agricultural and industrial economies. The river is much more than a wide curving line leading us into the picture from dark to light, and more than a longstanding food source for locals (there's an eel spear lying in the foreground). The Stour, canalized by Act of Parliament in 1705, was a busy waterway up until the early twentieth century. Around thirty-six barges regularly traveled the waterway in the 1820s, carrying wheat, barley, flour, malt, woolen goods, and bricks down to the coast to be transferred to larger vessels, and bringing back industrial

Figure 19.1 John Constable, *View on the Stour Near Dedham*, 1822,
oil on canvas, 129.5 × 188 cm.
Source: The Huntington Library, Art Museum, and Botanical Gardens.
© Courtesy of the Huntington Art Museum, San Marino, California.

supplies: large quantities of coal; glass, oil, tallow and paper, and iron
and lead. Read in these terms, the painting shows how deeply imbricated
the rural economy is with the economy of the nation as a whole, and how
the demands of this economy impact the land – most notably, in the late
eighteenth and early nineteenth centuries, through the enclosure movement
that took land that had formerly been owned – or at least used – in common, and turned it over to growing food and raising animals for profit.
What looks like a peaceful rural idyll is, in fact, symptomatic of environmental as well as social change.

In what follows, I first focus on two visual properties, drawn from
Ruskin's dueling emphases: distance and detail. I then consider those artists
who directly recorded environmental harm in visual form, whether they
showed industrial processes, modes of extraction, ruined land, or simply
air thick with smoke from domestic and factory chimneys. I conclude by
discussing how over-aestheticization can blind one to the realities of environmental conditions: there can be something alluring and inducive to reverie in a painting of a city half-obscured by pollution. Many, but by no
means all the paintings I discuss loosely fall into the conventional category
of "landscape." But it's worthwhile bearing in mind from the start that

the very term "landscape" is a human-centered one. W. J. T. Mitchell's definition is extremely useful, pointing to the word's unusual doubleness: "Landscape is a medium of exchange between the human and the natural, the self and the other ... Landscape is a natural scene mediated by culture. It is both a represented and a presented space, both a signifier and a signified, both a frame and what a frame contains, both a real place and its simulacrum ..."[4] If landscapes are the products of human impact, an ecological reading might also seek to recalibrate the emphasis. These images can be thought of as "habitat paintings" – inhabited by fish, birds, toads, and humans alike.

Distance

A phrase from Thomas Campbell's poem *The Pleasures of Hope* (1799), "'Tis distance lends enchantment to the view, / And robes the mountain in its azure hue," quickly became a commonplace of art criticism and travel writing.[5] It encapsulates the subjective impact that a particular type of receding view can make, as well as setting down a principle of aesthetic composition in painting. But when one enters deep into nineteenth-century paintings, and considers their horizons, something more troublesome than undiluted immersive pleasure can often be found.

To look into the distance is to be reminded of air – an element often taken for granted in paintings; an invisible medium – but one that can be thickened through water vapor – condensed into clouds or falling as rain; or through smoky emissions. Among the many early nineteenth-century painters who thought attentively about air and atmosphere were Constable, and J. M. W. Turner, both assiduous observers and recorders of skies and clouds. Nicholas Robbins has discussed how Constable's work mediates between the immediate affective properties of weather, and the increasingly scientifically recorded variations in climate, including its changes over time: a foreshadowing of the tension between the extremely local and the vast and impersonal scales that make visual representations of climatic change so problematic.

But other elements come into the equation besides clouds and wind and precipitation. Constable's *The Opening of Waterloo Bridge (Whitehall Stairs, June 18th, 1817)* (1829–32) shows, in the thick grey haze of the horizon, a London seen under the smoky pall of coal-burning fires – both in small workshops and in homes. Turner's view *Leeds* (1816) focuses on the energetic growth of the city spreading up the hill towards us – in the middle and far distance, the whitish smoke from woolen mills blends with the wispy clouds, quietly indicating the source of the capital that is driving this rapid urban expansion. Similarly, the horizon of William Wyld's *Manchester from Kersal Moor* (1852), painted for Queen Victoria when she visited the city, depicts the smoke stacks from a decorous distance, blurring into a pale yellow sunset. The bottom half of the picture is a pastoral scene, complete with goats, suggesting the symbiotic, comfortable existence of town and country: a young couple gaze out over the smoky horizon as they might a landscape of rolling hills. The effects of industrialism certainly exist in these works, but are held at a distance: something to be gazed upon, rather than an enveloping force.

Throughout his career, whether he was painting the thin sunlight of a Leeds day or the blurred onrush of modernity signaled in *Rain, Steam and Speed* (1844), with a tiny hare speeding away from the powerful train, barely visible through the blended haze of downpour and engine emissions, Turner addressed the challenges of painting light mediated by specific atmospheric conditions. This concern with light's optical effects informs his 1823 *Newcastle-on-Tyne*, which not only shows the busy riverside activity of this port, but chimney smoke rendering indistinct the line between hills and sky. Here – as with *Dudley, Worcestershire* (1832) and *An Industrial Town at Sunset* (c. 1830–2) Turner uses a very wet ground and watercolor to blend earth and water and cloud and smoke: a record of what the human eye sees when pollution occludes the specifics of landscape. In other images, especially his later ones, he attended to the physiological effect of looking towards, or directly into the sun: he registered the impact of the environment on the body through the medium of paint.

But if, by the mid century, Turner's sunsets often came to be seen as overly dramatic, as a detail-dominated realist style became more prevalent than his engagement of affect, no one could argue that artists who attempted to paint the skies after the powerful eruption of the Indonesian volcano Krakatoa in 1883 were exaggerating. This eruption led to a huge amount of volcanic ash being released into the atmosphere, resulting in alarmingly fiery skies worldwide – skies that were jokingly compared to those of Turner paintings. Notably, London artist William Ascroft produced over 500 color sketches of the sky above Chelsea during the next few years, recording its startling appearance. Certainly the Krakatoa explosion was not the result of anthropogenic change. But the subsequent ashy diffusion strikingly brought home the global effects of particles emanating from a particular source entering the atmosphere's circulatory systems. This parallel is made, whether deliberately or not, in an 1884 painting by Albert Goodwin, *A Sunset in the Manufacturing Districts* (Figure 19.2). Here, a spectacular orange, crimson, azure, and sullen yellow sky blends with thick

Figure 19.2 Albert Goodwin, *A Sunset in the Manufacturing Districts*, 1884, pencil and watercolor with scratching out on paper, 57.2 × 78.8 cm. *Source*: © 2011 Christie's Images Limited.

grey smoke from the forest of factory chimneys that occupy the horizon. Rather than the smoke signifying a growing, prosperous industrial city, this is pollution reaching up to encircle the globe in its effects.

Detail

John Ruskin insisted that artists needed to observe the natural world with care and attention, learning to understand, as well as represent, the structures of leaves and rocks and, indeed, the shifting appearance of the sky. Young painters, he famously commanded, must "go to Nature."[6] His affirmation of the importance of faithfully recorded detail – whether of pistil and stamen; of feathers or the jagged icy edges of glaciers – was enormously influential. The backgrounds of paintings by the Pre-Raphaelites, like John Everett Millais and Ford Madox Brown, and the many artists stylistically associated with the movement, especially in the 1850s and 1860s (such as John Brett and John Inchbold), are full of lovingly recorded mosses and primroses and ferns and weeds and veined rocks and pebbles, sometimes also honoring the landscapes that Ruskin himself wrote about with a precisely honed vocabulary – the Lake District, the Alps. In turn, Victorian designers, especially William Morris and his circle, developed stylistic abstractions from curving leaves and petals, from vines and hanging fruit, in their patterns for fabrics and wallpapers.

Ruskin's emphasis on detail meshes both with the natural theology that informed many naturalists' celebration of the ordinary and overlooked in the natural world as signs of God's love for even the most apparently insignificant, and with the practices of amateur scientists, finding their subjects in whatever gardens or woods were nearby. But carefully observing and sketching the minutiae of nature also, Ruskin believed, led one to comprehend what we now see as the cornerstone of ecology: the relation of part to whole. For Ruskin, this also pointed towards how humans were ideally holistically and reciprocally connected to the society they inhabited – and to their environment. His sense of nature's interconnectivity parallels the far-reaching reference points in his own prose, in which precisely described architecture and botany and geology swirl associatively around each other and meld with classical and literary references, enacting the impossibility in ecologically aware writing of separating out science, culture, and the connective imagination.

But not all carefully observed paintings of the natural world were directly indebted to Ruskin's precepts. Marianne North produced some of the Victorian period's most spectacular images of plants, trees, flowers and fruit. One of Ruskin's favorite artists, William Henry Hunt, lived, like North, in Hastings, but to her disappointment, he refused to instruct her. However, her paintings proved far more adventurous than Hunt's minutely accurate watercolors of birds' nests and downy fruit grouped on mossy banks. She traveled to Japan and Jamaica, Brazil and India, and many other countries as well. North's works are especially worthy of note since, rather than isolating plants from their surroundings in the manner of botanical illustration (something for which some scientists criticized her), she situates them fully and vividly within a full ecological context. Her plants supply the habitat for butterflies, birds, and insects, which she observes with as much discrimination as she does the shapes of trunks and leaves and petals. She oscillates between the minute and the vast as her eye travels to the horizon and back, again emphasizing the interdependencies of the apparently insignificant and the spectacular wide and deep view. North often painted a close-up of flower or fruit in the foreground, and the entire plant somewhere in the background setting. Through her far-flung travels, she extended her knowledge of the many uses to which plants were put, as well as expanding her botanical expertise, having four species and a whole genus named after her. If she benefited from the connections and networks of the British Empire, her travels are also testimony to the global trade in plant collection, for which the Royal Botanic Gardens in Kew acted as something of a hub. North's paintings now hang at Kew, as she desired, forming a record both of botanical specificity, and of a vulnerability recognized even at the time. The eminent botanical scientist and director of the Botanic Gardens, Sir Joseph Hooker, wrote presciently in the preface to the *Official Guide to the*

North Gallery (1882) that many of the views "are already disappearing, or are doomed shortly to disappear, before the axe and the forest fires, the plough or the flock, of the ever advancing settler or colonist."[7]

Damage

Marianne North observed the impact of industrial modernity at first hand, and globally. Writing of her time in India, she wrote regretfully that she "was sorry to see the number of hideous factory chimneys and coal smoke, which are doing their worst to make Bombay as ugly as Liverpool."[8] Yet in the early decades of the Industrial Revolution, factories and mills, when they were noted at all, were often represented as embedded within rather than obliterating a landscape. For example, Joseph Wright's *Arkwright's Cotton Mill by Night* (c. 1782) shows the world's first water-powered cotton-spinning mill, all its windows illuminated: the source of that cotton, and the status of the enslaved people who harvested it, of course points to a further global context for British industrial development. But, made subservient to the bright silver moonlight, nestling in the Derbyshire hills, it is rendered symbiotic with its surroundings.

Yet artists were soon depicting the technological sublime as infused with terror rather than with pleasurable awe. In Philip de Loutherbourg's *Coalbrookdale by Night* (1801) and Paul Sandby Munn's *Bedlam Furnaces, Madeley Dale* (1803), towering iron foundry flames light up the night sky. William Havell's *Parys Mountain Copper Mine* (c. 1803–4) and Henry Hawkins' *Penrhyn Slate Quarry* (1832) show the ravages made by various forms of extraction. The scale of these enterprises is conveyed by the tininess of the workers themselves, who are simultaneously robbed of individuality. By the time of Henry Warren's engraving *The Black Country Near Bilston* (1869), the landscape is one indecipherable mass of chimneys belching smoke, tangled machinery, flames, some miniaturized people in the middle distance, a foreground of smoking waste and ravaged land (Figure 19.3). The complete dehumanizing desolation of the scene is brought home through the heavy inkiness of Warren's plate, and by the subdued crescent Moon floating in the top left-hand corner, as if irrelevant to the site of environmental destruction below – a complete contrast to Wright's lunar illumination. There is not a blade of grass in Warren's scene. There *is* vegetation in Goodwin's *Sunset*, but it is rough and brown, growing between industrial debris; the trees are starkly dead; the stream that runs through to the foreground seems oily and flecked with polluted foam. On the left, the graffiti on an abandoned house says it all: "TO LET THE HOLE OF THIS PLACE."

Figure 19.3 Henry Warren, *The Black Country Near Bilston, c.* 1869,
steel engraving. Image 14 × 19 cm, sheet 23 × 29 cm.
Source: Published by William Mackenzie, Glasgow, Edinburgh, and London. Science
Museum Group Collection. © The Board of Trustees of the Science Museum, London.

Visual evidence, whether of belching smoke stacks, polluted rivers, or
melting glaciers, was crucial in the nineteenth century when it came both
to publicizing environmental harms and also to bringing home their emotional impact. Much of this evidence took the form of engravings and illustrations: paintings of such scenes were not what most purchasers wanted
in their domestic spaces. By the later Victorian decades, photography also
became a significant tool for recording environmental damage, especially
the blackening effects of pollution. Cartoons, too, like those *Punch* published in the summer of 1858 at the time of the Thames's notorious Great
Stink (such as the image in which Father Thames introduces his children –
Diptheria, Scrofula, and Cholera – to the fair city of London), helped raise
public awareness.

But what seems like incontrovertible evidence of environmental damage
to us now did not always register as such to everyone at the time. There is the
problematic case of American artist Joseph Pennell, friend and biographer

of James McNeill Whistler, who spent twenty years in England in the late nineteenth and early twentieth centuries, producing some of the most shocking depictions of grimy, smoke-choked northern cities, including Bradford, Leeds, and Sheffield. These illustrated articles that appeared in *Harpers' Magazine*. Yet he apparently managed to discount the human and environmental toll of this dark air. The accompanying text deplored "the screen of torpid smoke which obscures [Sheffield's] sky," but Pennell retrospectively celebrated what, for him, was evidence of industrial vigor, collecting a number of etchings, plus similar images of environmental wreckage in North America, in *The Wonder of Work* (1916), in which he extolled these filthy industrial scenes as evidence of laudable productivity and capitalistic growth.[9]

Denial

In *The Wonder of Work*, Pennell quotes Whistler's "Ten O'Clock Lecture," and his famous description of the Thames at dusk, when "the poor buildings lose themselves in the dim sky, and the tall chimneys become campanile, and the warehouses are palaces in the night, and the whole city hangs in the heavens and fairyland is before us."[10] For Pennell, again, these grey and murky paintings are tokens of labor's magnificence, rather than documents of light passing through particulate matter hanging heavy above the river. In many respects Whistler echoes French poet, novelist, and art critic Théophile Gautier, writing in mid century on the visually transformative power of fog and smoke in London. In the midst of a diatribe against its pollution, and after complaining that the city is so filthy that its soot-covered statues of nobility are so black that they look like "negroes or chimney sweeps," Gautier notes that because of the smoky haze, "a factory chimney easily becomes an obelisk, a poorly designed warehouse takes on the appearance of a Babylonian terrace, a gloomy row of columns transforms into the porticos of Palmyra. The symmetrical barrenness of civilization and the vulgarity of forms it employs soften or disappear, thanks to this beneficial veil."[11]

Whistler's Thames paintings, like the foggy river scenes that include Westminster Bridge and the Houses of Parliament that Claude Monet painted a few years later – and like, indeed, a number of Turner's works – pose a particular challenge: how does one weigh up their aesthetic appeal with one's knowledge that they, and the fogs that they show, are beautifying conditions of harm; that we are responding to what Jonathan Ribner has termed the "poetics of pollution;" "enduring art" created "from tainted air"?[12] Furthermore, how deliberate, how tongue-in-cheek, even, was the denial inherent in Whistler's lyricism? Was he, as Monet seems to have been, tone-deaf to environmental harms? Or did he take this aestheticizing position in a provocative stance against his antagonist Ruskin, who four years earlier, in the *Storm-Cloud*, had riled against the "sulphurous chimney-pot vomit" and "devil's darkness" that he saw spewing out of Manchester's chimneys?[13] Most contemporary critics of his work, however, took the painterly obscurities of Whistler's canvases as testimony to his stylistic innovations in painting atmosphere, rather than critiques of the atmospheric conditions themselves.

A completely different type of denial from that found in Whistler's blue-grey Thames scenes is found in the proliferation of rural idylls produced during the closing decades of the nineteenth century. Foster, Allingham, and others painted numerous small watercolors – well within the purchasing reach of the comfortable middle classes – in which rolling farmland and pretty, flower-surrounded cottages offer escapism. In larger paintings, too, fertile fields and the labor sustaining them likewise presents the countryside as something timeless, unchanging, and outside the industrializing processes that had dramatically changed urban conditions – although painters like George Clausen, influenced by French naturalism, did produce far more searching representations of agricultural labor's hardships.

But if one considers the contemporary context of an apparently escapist painting like George Vicat Cole's *At Arundel, Sussex* (1887), something less simple emerges. To be sure, on the left harvesters are binding up stooks of wheat in the golden sun: a scene of plenty. Yet closer to the viewer, sheep stray untended in a lane, and to their right an abandoned plow, an untilled field reverting to its uncultivated state. A period of agricultural depression began in the 1870s, and this painting encapsulates the resulting paradox: what may have been disastrous for laborers and their families unquestionably benefited the countryside's wildlife – even as these displaced laborers simultaneously swelled cities, helping exacerbate already existing urban problems. For a couple of decades, hedgerow uprooting paused, and fallow farmlands allowed birds and insects and mammals to flourish. This was the landscape to which soldiers in World War I looked back with their own particular form of nostalgia: "Loved to the death, inestimably dear."[14]

Conclusion: Looking Back, Looking Forward

Cultural mediation allows spectators to *see* – to become alert to that to which they may have become inured, over-familiarized. Aesthetic abstraction of atmosphere, for example, subtracts noxious smells, tarry taste, stinging eyes, and the soot and grime that settles on one, but it also opens up a space – and not just a space of escapist or nostalgic reverie. It allows one to *think* about what causes the pollution. David Matless's coinage of the "anthroposcenic" is useful here: it describes the conjunction of human-caused environmental change and aesthetics, and is especially pertinent when it comes to investigating site-specific questions about the past and present of nineteenth-century land and city-scapes, and about the futures – whether of environmental degradation or reclamation – that may be latent within them.[15]

One mode of engaging with these paintings in an environmentally conscious way is to ask what is to come for the rural and urban scenes they depict. The coal-driven pollution of London and other urban centers is no more. The industrial effluent that fouled city rivers – from Sheffield's River Don to the Wandle in Surrey, discolored by the dyes released from William Morris's workshops – has been, in very many cases, successfully legislated against. In the Thames, dissolved oxygen concentrations, essential for fish survival, are up; both harbor seals and grey seals are regularly seen. On the other hand, those rivers that flow lazily through many idyllic Victorian landscapes are increasingly contaminated by the run-off from industrial agriculture. The misty horizons of fenland scenes represented an aesthetic effect that has now diminished along with the draining and reclamation of wetlands: reclamation from the point of view of farmers, perhaps, but not of the small invertebrates and insects and migratory birds who relied on these habitats. Flowery meadows of designedly delightful rural scenes have been turned into monocultures by the chemicals used in modern farming.

And anthropogenic climate change has changed familiar features of nineteenth-century paintings in other ways. Constable's landscapes are dominated by leafy elm trees, but well over 90 percent of these are now destroyed by Dutch Elm Disease, flourishing when temperatures warm and water levels drop. The stone pines that signify a generic Italianicity – and, indeed, a continuity with the classical past – in Frederic Leighton's paintings are likewise vulnerable to the aggressive sap-sucking North American pine tortoise scale, itself testimony to the relationship between global trade and the spread of invasive species. The cliffs in many depictions of the seashore, like Charles James Spence's paintings of the Northumbria coast, have often eroded and crumbled.

But we don't need to look solely to large scale changes to consider the futures inherent in nineteenth-century art. The lichen that one sees on a wall or on a boulder may prove to be a significant biomarker of polluted air – as the Victorians themselves came to realize. Such monitoring of local environmental changes was frequently carried out by members of local scientific societies, and correspondents to a range of scientific and nature journals. Their attention to detail, their concern for the ordinary and everyday, and to minute changes in habitat, seasonal patterns, and the variations of even the smallest natural forms, paralleled the emphasis of Ruskin and others. Indeed, this stress on attentiveness to the apparently insignificant connects art of the period not just to developments in scientific scholarship, but to a questioning approach to examining details of paintings that an unattuned spectator might pass over. Our questioning, too, should lead us into other directions with environmental implications, like the sourcing of pigments, dyes and the chemicals used in photography.

Finally, though, it is possible to look at painting from the long nineteenth century with a more optimistic ecological eye – with an eye, for example, to today's rewilding and regeneration projects, whether we're talking about the reclamation of acres of uplands, or local councils planting verges with location-appropriate wildflowers. Closely-cropped moorlands form the backdrop to many of Sir Edwin Landseer's scenes of stag hunting in the Highlands: some of these areas, like his favorite Glenfeshie, are now becoming wooded again. Whether depictions of recognizable locations – at the scale of a view over a growing industrial city or a study of ferns growing alongside a stream – or more selective depictions of natural phenomena, like William Henry Hunt's or Marianne North's; or even more fanciful ones – the daisies and hazelnuts and snails that loom large in Victorian fairy paintings – all demand our own attention, our own close looking. This is attentiveness – and, by extension, reflection – that we would do well to carry into our own daily lives, taking as our jumping-off point the entanglement of art history with environmental change.

Notes

1. John Ruskin, "The Work of Iron," *The Two Paths* (1858–9) *The Complete Works of John Ruskin*, ed. E. T. Cook and Alexander Wedderburn, 39 vols. (London: George Allen, 1903–12), 16.378.
2. Ruskin, Appendix to "The Art of England," *The Two Paths*, 33.404.
3. Daegan Miller, *This Radical Land: A Natural History of American Dissent* (Chicago: University of Chicago Press, 2018), 6.
4. W. J. T. Mitchell, ed., *Landscape and Power* (Chicago: University of Chicago Press, 2002), 5.
5. Thomas Campbell, "The Pleasures of Hope," *The Pleasures of Hope and Other Poems*, 4th ed. (Glasgow: Mundell & Son, 1800), 3.
6. Ruskin, *Modern Painters* 1 (1843), *The Complete Works*, 3.624.
7. Sir Joseph Hooker, "Preface to the First Edition," 1882, Royal Gardens, Kew, *Official Guide to the North Gallery*, 5th ed., rev. and augmented (London: Eyre and Spottiswoode, 1892), iii.
8. Marianne North, *Recollections of a Happy Life*, 2 vols. (London: Macmillan & Co, 1892) 1.336.

9. Unsigned [William R. Bideing], "Sheffield," *Harper's New Monthly Magazine* 69 (June 1884), 67–82 at 67–8. Unsurprisingly Pennell became a great admirer of Mussolini.

10. James McNeill Whistler, *Mr Whistler's "Ten O'Clock"* (London: Chatto and Windus, 1888), 15.

11. Théophile Gauthier, *Caprices et zigzags*, 2nd ed. (Paris: Hachette, 1856), 143, 144–5, my translation.

12. Jonathan Ribner, "The Poetics of Pollution," in Katharine Lochnan, ed., *TurnerWhistlerMonet. Impressionist Visions* (Toronto: Art Gallery of Ontario, 2004), 51–63 at 63.

13. John Ruskin, *The Storm-Cloud of the Nineteenth Century: Two Lectures Delivered at the London Institution* (1884), *The Complete Works*, 34.37, 38. Ruskin, however – even if he's often taken as a proto-environmentalist in making this diatribe – targeted moral decay rather than the deterioration of air quality in these lectures: the pollution was both metaphor and material fact.

14. John Masefield, "August, 1914," in John Lewis-Stempel, *Where Poppies Blow: The British Soldier, Nature, the Great War* (London: Weidenfeld and Nicholson, 2016), xvii.

15. David Matless, "The Anthroposcenic: Landscape in the Anthroposcene," *British Art Journal* 10 (2018), www.britishartstudies.ac.uk/issues/issue-index/issue-10/ landscape-anthroposcene.

20

ADELINE JOHNS-PUTRA

Climate and Empire

Climate is weather aggregated, averaged, and quantified, temporally and spatially. It is an accumulation of measures of everyday or individual meteorological occurrences, such as wind, snow, heat, rain, and so on, flattened, as it were, over time and space to form historical and geographical trends. As an aggregate of recurrences, climate offers a predictable and stable backdrop against which weather events stand out for their very unpredictability.

Yet, climate is not an innocent category. The modes by which weather has come to be understood as climate and the methods by which discrete events have been shaped into climatic data, sequences, and systems are historically (that is to say, politically) contingent. Much of the organization of weather into climate not only coincided with, but was causally related to, national projects of empire in the nineteenth century. The methods of climate quantification were made possible by imperial expansion and how they often justified that expansion in turn.

It was in the literature of empire – particularly, the British Empire – that such justifications were contended, and potentially contested too. Imperial expansion may have enabled science to push at the limits of knowledge, just as science in turn enabled empire to expand its frontiers, but it was also the case that writers were able to question the assumption that this was a simple, centrifugal movement from the seat of empire to its colonial margins. The spaces of empire were not mere sites for the discovery of knowledge (or data) to be analyzed and understood in European metropoles; they were places of an exchange of knowledge, even if the mutuality of that exchange was not always conceded. Similarly, those who wielded both scientific and imperial power together were invariably engaged not in imposing that power but in interaction and experience, again to an extent that they did not always themselves acknowledge.

This chapter discusses, first, how the contours of imperialism – the enlargement of a single country's political jurisdiction and administration across large tracts of land and sea spread out around the globe – made climate science possible. It turns, then, to literary texts that helped to justify colonial expansion under the aegis of scientific expansion, and to proclaim the latter as a function of British power – all this through the persona of the imperial explorer (here, the chapter will focus on the nineteenth-century mania for polar exploration). Remaining with the subject positioning of colonization, the chapter ends with a brief discussion of climate determinism (that is, the idea of climate's agency in shaping physiological and psychological constitutions) in texts that show, wittingly or not, how the colonizing body could not remain untouched by experiences of climate.

The Empire As Natural Laboratory

In general terms, the spatiotemporal quantification of weather into climate occurs as part of the uneven evolution of the scientific method (the practices of empirical observation and measurement to create data upon which hypotheses could be formed) that took place in the age designated in Eurocentric histories as the Enlightenment. However, not only across Europe, but in Qing dynasty China also, the sixteenth to eighteenth centuries saw widespread attempts to document local and daily conditions, including rainfall, temperature, and wind.

Of course, ostensibly isolated records could be more easily collated – and, crucially, data from across different climatic zones could be compared – when geographically distant territories existed within a single jurisdiction, as part, that is, of an empire. One could argue that the expansion of maritime trade meant that climatic records and observations of global weather patterns (most especially, trade winds) could simply be brought back to European centers of commerce.[1] And, as the nineteenth-century pioneer of meteorology and climatology, Alexander von Humboldt (1759–1869), showed, observations could be made in far-flung locations regardless of political boundaries; Humboldt's expeditions and experiments took him from the Baltic to the Mediterranean, from South America to Central Asia. Yet despite this, Humboldt recognized that imperial territories in particular facilitated climatic scientific study and, in 1836, urged the Royal Society to set up research stations across the now widening British empire.[2] At the same time, the growth of mercantile shipping was closely linked to broadening imperial aspirations; for example, the Dutch and the British East India Companies were semigovernmental projects for securing commercial and political expansion together. Certainly, the early nineteenth century saw a series of British meteorological stations set up in colonial jurisdictions, many by the British East India Company. As Katharine Anderson puts it, India, in particular, was "Britain's continent," offering itself up as a "natural laboratory."[3]

Such "natural laboratories" were crucial to the development of concepts that now sit at the heart of climatology. Large, land-based territories allowed for the easy comparison of regional variations. Deborah R. Coen argues that the meteorological field stations of the Austro-Hungarian Empire, under the management of the Hapsburgs' imperial meteorologist Julius Hann, yielded insights about climate interdependencies at micro-, meso-, and macro-scales that were foundational to modern climatology.[4] In the case of the British Empire, India was ideal as its geographical expansiveness and its predictable monsoonal climate created a relatively stable set of parameters.

Not only was it the case that a vast imperial set of "laboratories" might enable the collation and comparison of data; by the mid-nineteenth century, their very existence and thus the potential benefits of such data generated the demand for greater data regulation, bringing about better instrumentation and internationally agreed standards. Thus, when it comes to climatology, not just scientific discovery but the refinement of scientific method were also intricately tied to the workings of empire. In India, in the first half of the century, the quality of these observations was compromised by poorly standardized instruments, unskilled staff, no oversight over observation methods or conditions, and no real coordination of the significance of these observations once dispatched to London. But such trials and errors came to be recognized and redressed over the course of the century, particularly after a failure to predict terrible famines in 1877–8, and were thus transformed into a regulated network of Indian observatories and trained, competent "native" observers. Similarly, the protection of Britain's global maritime interests – commercial and political – meant there was a need for accurate and therefore shareable weather records at sea. The establishment of the British Meteorological Society (now the Royal Meteorological Society) in 1850 and the Meteorological Department of the Board of Trade was followed by the first International Maritime Conference in Brussels in 1853, to ensure the standardization of instrumentation, observations, and logging.[5] Operating in a symbiotic relationship, colonial wealth and trade advantages were protected even as the foundations and methods of modern meteorology were strengthened.

The Imperial Explorer: Arctic Expeditioners

Thus, the forerunners of institutionalized colonial science were "early explorers, soldiers, medics, missionaries and, later, administrators," who took it upon themselves to measure and document the climates to which they traveled, whereas nineteenth-century efforts were part of more formalized, state-sponsored attempts to coordinate weather observations around the globe.[6] By the early nineteenth century, several developments conspired to place the figure of the maritime explorer squarely in the public imagination, and to undergird this with scientific and patriotic credentials. Science as an enterprise had extended beyond the gentlemanly realms of the Royal Society, through the rise of more accessible arts-and-sciences institutions such as the Royal Institution, founded in 1801, and the explosion in the circulation of periodicals such as John Murray's *Quarterly Review*, established in 1809, in which the latest ideas and discoveries could be disseminated.[7] Concurrently, a new geopolitical and scientific frontier had opened up, thanks to advances in navigational technology and propitious climatic conditions (including ice melt as a result of the 1815 Mount Tambora eruption in what is now Indonesia).[8] The Northwest Passage – an Arctic sea lane between the Atlantic and the Pacific oceans – promised greater efficiencies in imperial expansion. The year 1818 saw the first British polar expeditions to set sail since James Cook in 1776, with the link between voyaging and research now greatly enhanced by a more thoroughgoing coordination by the Admiralty with popular avenues for scientific dissemination.

These conditions gave rise to the Arctic explorer as the new standard-bearer for imperial science. What Adriana Craciun calls the "polar print nexus," represented by Murray's and the Admiralty's Arctic exploration narratives, extended from the 1810s well into the mid nineteenth century. As Craciun shows, it includes a raft of *Quarterly* reviews and essays, as well as a book-length history of Arctic exploration, all authored by John Barrow, second secretary of the Admiralty and the chief architect of nineteenth-century British polar exploration.[9] A particular high point is a first-person account by explorer John Franklin in 1823. It ends with the tragic reports around the loss of the ships of Franklin's last, fateful voyage in the 1840s – the Northwest Passage expedition of the *Erebus* and the *Terror*. All this kept the explorer – and a particular Arctic inflection of that type – in the public consciousness for decades.

Perhaps no text in the Murray polar print nexus captures so well the configuration of exploration, science, trade and political interest as Eleanor Anne Porden's poem *The Arctic Expeditions* (1818).[10] From a young age, Porden attended scientific lectures at the Royal Institution and hosted a literary coterie, where she experimented with romances and epics on subjects as diverse as geology, chemistry, and history. She went on, following the popularity of her Arctic poem, to marry Franklin.[11]

Porden's poem was inspired by a Barrow essay in the *Quarterly*.[12] Barrow had celebrated the *Isabella* and the *Alexander*, ships that were preparing to sail under the overall command of John Ross. Barrow used the occasion to argue for a program of Arctic exploration, writing that it would prove or disprove the existence of a Northwest Passage, and enable the reopening of communications with Danish communities in Greenland – so-called lost Greenland.[13] These rousing arguments fired not just Porden's imagination but that of the *Quarterly*'s many readers; the issue containing Barrow's essay sold a staggering 12,000 copies in one day.[14] Yet while the first half of the essay celebrates these humanitarian and scientific objectives, the second half focuses on the gains for Britain if it were to forge a Northwest Passage. The real point, for Barrow, was to argue for government investment and to gain public support, and the payoff was the commercial and political power represented by this new shipping route.

Whereas Barrow discourses broadly on the object of discovery, barely disguising its implications for profit and power, Porden tacks close to the subject of heroism under the banners of scientific and national glory. In doing so, she conceals more effectively than Barrow the workings of power that underpin the imperial project. Running to just over 200 heroic couplets, her poem begins with a send-off for the *Isabella* and *Alexander*:

> Sail, sail, adventurous Barks! go fearless forth,
> Storm on his glacier-seat the misty North,
> Give to mankind the inhospitable zone,
> And Britain's trident plant in seas unknown.[15]

The sailors, launching an assault on a personified Arctic, enact exploration as an invasion of a climatically hostile space – almost of climate itself. It is explicitly the British who spearhead this invasion on behalf of humankind. Britain, when personified as Britannia, wields the trident normally associated with the Greek sea god Poseidon, in a statement of naval supremacy over other nations; Porden's voyagers brandish Britannia's trident in what seems to be a challenge to the power of Poseidon himself, or at least to the ocean and oceanic domains.

The poet then identifies this as not just a rescue operation but a scientific mission. The voyagers go "wherever Science fills the mind / Or grief for man long sever'd from his kind";[16] they "leave, by Science led, [their] native land."[17] The next lines nod, like Barrow's essay, at the promise of discovering the fate of lost Greenland, but primacy is given to the value of scientific knowledge. Indeed, the poem espouses throughout its loyalty to empirical fact over mere imagination. At the outset, it rejects classical muses: "No Muse of all that hymn'd Saturnian Jove / On Pindus' top, or in Hæmonia's grove, / Must prompt the strain."[18] Instead, it favors two scientific sources of navigational knowledge, the North Star – the "star of the Pole!" – and an "unseen Directress!" that turns out to be geomagnetism.[19] And when the poem proceeds to lengthy descriptions of the dangers of Arctic voyaging, it shores these up with citations of journals such as the *Quarterly*. The explorers are exhorted to stay courageous not against the "strange fancies" exaggerated in travelers' tales, but against the "real ills" of extreme cold and snow blindness,[20] debris-ridden icebergs, the effects of the North Magnetic Pole on compasses, and the challenges of telling time from a midnight sun, all of which are clarified in brisk, no-nonsense footnotes. That is to say, the poem works hard to underline the expeditions' contribution to science, providing with its scholarly references a hypothesis to be tested by the discoveries and evidence yielded by the explorers' experiments and observations; the knowledge base at the imperial center is thus refined by data gathered in the world's remote peripheries.

At its conclusion, the poem returns to the opening idea of British power over the elements. It sounds a triumphant note, construing the men as representatives of Britannia, "Queen of the Seas!," and vanquishers of a personified North Pole, the "Genius of the North."[21] The poem ends as it began, uniting the scientist and explorer into a heroic, British conqueror of the natural world. In doing so, Porden's poem contributes to an abiding myth of the explorer as impervious to the lived experience of extreme climates. While she warns of the very real impact of climate on those who would presume to claim empirical and political ownership of geographically distant spaces, she helps to mythologize the explorer's ability to overcome these.

As it happens, both this myth and its fallacy are writ large in the experiences of the man who would become Porden's husband. The expeditions of the *Isabella* and the *Alexander* marked the beginning of Franklin's Arctic career, for when those vessels set sail for the Pole, two others – the *Dorothea* and the *Trent* – voyaged under David Buchan's overall command to the Spitsbergen archipelago (now Svalbard); Franklin captained the *Trent*.[22] It was this connection that prompted his interest in the poem and his request, upon his return, to be introduced to the poet.[23] Soon after that portentous first meeting, Franklin embarked on his second expedition. He was sent by the Admiralty to a port on Hudson Bay in what was then British North America to lead a party north, first overland and then via the Coppermine River, to map the Arctic coast before rendezvousing with an expedition captained by William Edward Parry. But Franklin's Coppermine expedition ended disastrously, with navigational error, the exhaustion of men and supplies, desertion, starvation, and even murder.

When Franklin and other survivors had been rescued and returned, he was charged by Barrow with providing a firsthand account of his experiences. That is, though Franklin had failed in his expeditionary mission, he succeeded in another, arguably more important duty. Barrow, as has been seen, was alive to the importance of not just commercializing and politicizing the efforts of imperial science, but of publicizing them. If Porden's poem was a crucial step, witting or not, in this direction, Franklin's narrative was another, and a more deliberate one. No doubt he had been physically and psychologically battered by his experiences, but his *Narrative of a Journey to the Shores of the Polar Sea* (1823), published by Murray, is a detailed and unemotional description of the trials and tribulations faced by the expedition.[24] Certainly, Franklin was not the first explorer to provide a narrative of the Admiralty's Arctic efforts, for that honor goes to Parry, who had pipped Franklin to a homecoming. Both Parry and Franklin used a dry prosaic style, but, unlike Parry's narrative, Franklin's caused a sensation. His dull prose, contrasted with the high drama of what he had experienced, gave testimonial depth to the climatically invincible scientist-explorer of Porden's imagination. It cemented that figure in the public mind. One could say that the apparent authenticity of its first-person narrative effectively conceals, beneath the veneer of British heroism, the extent of imperial greed and hubris in the face of climatic vicissitude, this in turn buried ever deeper by the narrative's popularity in the cultural imagination.

Twenty years later, Franklin made his final voyage – the last gasp of Barrow's and the Admiralty's attempts to discover the Northwest Passage. In the intervening time, Franklin had returned to the Arctic in 1825. A mere six days after Franklin set sail on this third voyage, Porden died of tuberculosis at the age of just twenty-seven. Upon his return, Franklin published yet another expeditionary account in 1829, remarried, and received a knighthood.

Much was to change in the two decades between Franklin's early Arctic expeditions and his last, both in terms of polar exploration and publication. Several voyages had returned to rapturous celebration in the periodical press, and other publishers jostled to meet public demand for cheaper, abridged versions of the official accounts. Murray responded with new editions of Parry's 1827 and Franklin's 1829 accounts, excising much of their scientific content. With a change of emphasis away from scientific discovery, the now ubiquitous figure of the polar explorer was more popular than ever but necessarily flattened into an enduring hero in the vast theatre of the Arctic icescape. Indeed, when Franklin set sail one last time, Barrow capitalized on this strand of polar-mania in 1845 with a new, synoptic account of the Admiralty's expeditions.

Franklin's Northwest Passage expedition, as is now well known, ended even more tragically than the Coppermine expedition, with the disappearance and death of all, including Franklin himself. Lady Franklin's refusal to countenance this possibility and her tireless championing of a rescue campaign, along with the final, definitive evidence in 1859 of the deaths of the entire expedition, occurred within this new cultural context, in which the explorer had been stripped of his scientific purpose to emerge in a simple contest of courage against climate. It is no wonder that, in the wake of Franklin's disappearance, the explorer figure became more popular than ever, reconstituted for the British public in ballads, dioramas, and even themed dinner parties.[25]

Two textual responses to Franklin's tragic fate and Lady Franklin's just-as-tragic denial are instructive, demonstrating how the cultural imaginary of the loss of Franklin was both shaped by and helped to reshape this focus on the explorer against the elements. The first emerges from among the entrants to an 1860 Oxford University poetry competition, the subject of which was "the Life, the Character, and Death of the Heroic Seaman Sir John Franklin, with special reference to the time, place, and discovery of his death."[26] The very aim of the competition nicely demonstrates the public preoccupation with the explorer's rugged individualism (his "Life" and "Character") pitted against the elements (the "time" and "place" of his death). The competition's advertisement in *The Guardian* emphasizes the epic – that is to say, heroic – potential of such a subject, a generic direction already taken in a poem such as "Arctic Enterprise" (1856) by Chandos H. Abrahall and, indeed, pursued by the winning entry, the unimaginatively titled *Poem Upon the Life, the Character, and Death of Sir John Franklin* (1860) by one Owen Vidal.

Yet, it is not the winning poem, now forgotten, that deserves comment here; it is the piece that came second. Written by a young and yet-unknown Algernon Charles Swinburne (1837–1909), the poem eschews heroic trappings for an elegiac tone.[27] Charlotte Ribeyrol describes how it is "made up of irregular stanzas of varying length and chaotic terza rima," producing an effect of lyrical, even romantic, melancholy.[28] Franklin occurs in the poem not as a man of action but as a defeated figure, the focus not on the explorer but on the majestic landscape in which he now rests and its ability to silence him: "Those gulfs and inlets of the channelled sea / Hide half the witness that should fill with fame / Our common air in England."[29] The result is a lament not for Franklin but for the Victorian ideal of the victorious conqueror of the elements, now overshadowed by the powerful beauty of those elements and futility of that quest.

If Swinburne's poem undercuts explorer heroics by mourning the vanity of his imperious endeavor, the ballad often called "Lady Franklin's Lament for Her Husband," effects a different kind of critique, highlighting those marginalized by such heroics; of the several broadside ballads inspired by Franklin's disappearance in the mid nineteenth century, this, dating from about 1852, is the most popular.[30] As is the case with many such compositions, this ballad reveals, beneath its apparent simplicity, alternative and even inherently contradictory points of view. Only nominally is this a lament by Lady Franklin, for the ballad is sung from the perspective of a sailor, retelling a dream in which he encounters her:

> As homeward bound one night on the deep,
> Slung in my hammock I fell asleep,
> I dream't a dream which I thought was true
> Concerning Franklin and his brave crew.[31]

While the Lady Franklin of the seaman's dream weeps that "Alas! my Franklin is long away," she knows also that "one hundred Seamen with hearts so bold, / ... have perish'd in frost and cold."[32] Indeed, the ballad ends not with Franklin but in memory of "the fate of so many before / Who have left their home to return no more."[33] All this, and particularly the designation of the poetic voice to a poor sailor, suggest that Franklin's heroics, whether fortuitous or fatal, are not the derring-do of one man but the result of the hard work and suffering of those who would have had little say in the decision-making and rationales of such expeditions.

Climate Determinism: Medical Acclimatization and the Colonial Body

The fragility of the myth of the imperial explorer, seen in this nineteenth-century incarnation as the polar explorer, brings us to a familiar topic in studies of imperial climate science, namely, climate determinism – the idea that climates determine the physiological and psychological characteristics of the people who inhabit them. The belief in a European – or even particularly British – climatic invincibility underlies not just Arctic exploration discourse in the nineteenth century but also contemporary discourses around the effects of unfamiliar, colonized spaces on colonizers.

Yet there is an obvious flaw in claims that European physiology is simultaneously formed for climatic endurance by European climates and unaffected by colonial climate. In other words, climate determinism is available as a justification of colonial domination only if it is suitably contorted. Such contortions are readily seen in rationales for indentured labor or slavery. The challenges that long-term settlement posed could betoken weakness, but such weakness could be conveniently ignored and, paradoxically, reshaped into the basis for colonial power in its most brutal form.

Logical fault-lines also run through the discourse of colonial medicine, similarly troubled by how to transform European susceptibility to foreign climates into an apologia for the European's natural fitness to govern. One solution to this contradiction was to attribute to Europeans a superior ability not just to endure but to acclimatize; indeed, acclimatization became an object of intense scrutiny, expressed best in the rise of nineteenth-century acclimatization societies. The idea finds its most potent form in the concept of "seasoning," the idea that a European who survived a local, endemic disease would be hardened to subsequent infections.[34]

The belief in a uniquely British capacity for acclimatization is exemplified by the approach taken by explorer Richard Burton (1821–90). Burton was an avowed climate determinist given to observations on racially derived psychology, once declaring "I believe the European to be the brain, the Asiatic the heart, the American and African the arms, the Australian the feet." In his two-volume *Wanderings in West Africa* (1863), he passes through locations he deems insalubrious and disease-ridden, just as his narrative passes over concerns about miasma and malaria.[35] Indeed, his account of his "discovery" of Lake Tanganyika neglects to mention that he was himself so ill with malaria that he could barely walk without the aid of African helpers; yet, Burton's illness, one could argue, haunts the work, which is constantly preoccupied with climate, race, and disease.[36] Specifically, his illness is the subtext to his anxiety about whether European scientific advances might allow diseases such as malaria to "pass away from the memory of the British public." Moreover, he wonders if not just European science, but European physiology might confer immunity: "It has been a favourite theory that the Jamaican negro and others withstand the heat and miasmata of Africa better than the white man; the contrary is probably the case. The semicivilized African dies of phthisis much more readily than the Englishman; and if exposed to hardship, he becomes ... rotten after the first year."[37] Burton's insistence on white immunity to tropical disease relies on his granting to Europeans an inherent adaptability to disease while denying it to others (here, Africans), even in the face of reports to the contrary and his own inability to acclimatize to malaria.

For a more nuanced argument for acclimatization, medical and cultural, it is worth ending with the example of Rudyard Kipling (1865–1936). As is well known, Kipling's representations of India are not straightforward and his attitude ambivalent at best: the writer was as capable of jingoism as he was of displaying a sensitivity towards India as the country of his birth and young adulthood. Similarly, when it comes to notions of climate determinism and European immunity, Kipling's writing demonstrates both a belief in British physiological supremacy and a sympathetic understanding of the experience of suffering from tropical disease beyond simple notions of seasoning. Such ambiguity may be discerned in his 1901 novel *Kim*. As an impoverished British orphan, Kim occupies a place outside European colonial power; moreover, he takes on a range of identities on a spectrum between colonized and colonizer subjectivities, engaging in espionage for the British but, as a result, appearing as Indian, and throughout remaining a loyal disciple to a Tibetan lama. At the same time, he nurses malarial patients and is one himself. One could argue that

Kim experiences an acclimatization that requires not a resistance to "native" identity but an embrace of it – an adaptability of subjectivity and physiology together. He comes, it would seem, to inhabit his hospital ward nickname of "Little Friend of all the World," acquiring both a familiarity with the disease and an understanding of Indian identity. Yet, equally, one might wonder if Kim is simply displaying a superior form of acclimatization and assimilation befitting the ideal (British) ruler. And, yet again and in the final analysis, one must note that Kim, and Kipling, are here treading a fine line between assimilation and degeneracy – or perhaps provocatively ignoring the line altogether.

The nineteenth century's organization of weather into climate occurred in tandem with the organization of the world into empirical sources and imperial resources. For the collation of meteorological events into so many climate datapoints required access to and the ability to measure such points in various parts of the world. Those who engaged in this activity ventured from European metropoles to "exotic" spaces and were celebrated as scientific and imperial frontiersmen, both inspiring and inspired by myths of the climatic invincibility of the voyaging, exploring, colonizing subject. In literary expressions of empiricism and empire (or empiricism *as* empire), one witnesses the making of those myths as well as the possibility of their undoing.

Notes

1. Martin Mahony and Georgina Endfield, "Climate and Colonialism," *Wiley Interdisciplinary Reviews: Climate Change* 9:e510 (2018), 3.
2. Mahony and Endfield, "Climate and Colonialism," 4.
3. Katharine Anderson, *Predicting the Weather: Victorians and the Science of Meteorology* (Chicago: University of Chicago Press, 2005), 260. Unless otherwise indicated, details of the development of British imperial science in India in the next two paragraphs are derived from Anderson, 250–82.
4. Deborah R. Coen, *Climate in Motion: Science, Empire, and the Problem of Scale* (Chicago: University of Chicago Press, 2018).
5. Catherine Ward and Julian A. Dowdeswell, "On the Meteorological Instruments and Observations Made during the Nineteenth-Century Exploration of the Canadian Northwest Passage," *Arctic, Antarctic, and Alpine Research: An Interdisciplinary Journal* 38.3 (2006), 454–64 at 459.
6. Mahony and Endfield, "Climate and Colonialism," 3.
7. Jon Klancher, *Transfiguring the Arts and Sciences: Knowledge and Cultural Institutions in the Romantic Age* (Cambridge: Cambridge University Press, 2013).
8. Gillen D'Arcy Wood, *Tambora: The Eruption that Changed the World* (Princeton: Princeton University Press, 2014).
9. Adriana Craciun, *Writing Arctic Disaster: Authorship and Exploration* (Cambridge: Cambridge University Press, 2016), 84–6.
10. [Eleanor Anne] Porden, *The Arctic Expeditions: A Poem* (London: John Murray, 1818).

11. Adeline Johns-Putra, "Historicizing the Networks of Ecology and Culture: Eleanor Anne Porden and Nineteenth-Century Climate Change," *ISLE: Interdisciplinary Studies in Literature and Environment* 22.1 (2015), 27–46 at 37–38, 42–3.

12. Porden, *The Arctic Expeditions*, 5–6.

13. [John Barrow], "On the Polar Ice and the Northern Passage into the Pacific," *Quarterly Review*, 18.35 (October 1817), 199–223.

14. Wood, *Tambora*, 129.

15. Porden, *The Arctic Expeditions*, 7.

16. Porden, *The Arctic Expeditions*, 7.

17. Porden, *The Arctic Expeditions*, 8.

18. Porden, *The Arctic Expeditions*, 7–8.

19. Porden, *The Arctic Expeditions*, 8.

20. Porden, *The Arctic Expeditions*, 14.

21. Porden, *The Arctic Expeditions*, 23.

22. Jane Cavell, *Tracing the Connected Narrative: Arctic Exploration in British Print Culture, 1818–1860* (Toronto: University of Toronto Press, 2008), 93. Unless otherwise indicated, details of the polar expeditions and narratives of Franklin and Parry in the next three paragraphs are derived from Cavell, chapter 3 (73–91), chapter 4 (92–116), and chapter 6 (141–66).

23. Johns-Putra, "Historicizing the Networks," 42–3.

24. John Franklin, *Narrative of a Journey to the Shores of the Polar Sea* (London: John Murray, 1823).

25. Francis Spufford, *I May Be Some Time: Ice and the English Imagination* (London: Faber, 1996), 7.

26. Charlotte Ribeyrol, "'Is This the End?' Swinburne's Paradoxical Tribute to Sir John Franklin (1860)," in Frédéric Regard, ed., *Arctic Exploration in the Nineteenth Century: Discovering the Northwest Passage* (London: Routledge, 2013), 155–70 at 155.

27. Algernon Charles Swinburne, "The Death of Sir John Franklin," in Edmund Gosse and Thomas J. Wise, eds., *Posthumous Poems* (London: William Heinemann, 1917), 75–86.

28. Ribeyrol, "'Is This the End?,'" 162.

29. Swinburne, "Death of Sir John Franklin," 76.

30. "Lady Franklin's Lament for Her Husband," Firth c.12 (83), Bodleian Library, Oxford University, rpt. in Michael King Macdona, "Sir John Franklin in Broadside and Oral Tradition," in David Atkinson and Steve Roud, eds., *Printers, Pedlars, Sailors, Nuns: Aspects of Street Literature* (London: Ballad Partners, 2020), 23–36 at 33–4.

31. Macdona, "Sir John Franklin," 33.

32. Macdona, "Sir John Franklin," 34.

33. Macdona, "Sir John Franklin," 34.

34. Jessica Howell, "Climate and Race in the Age of Empire," in Adeline Johns-Putra, ed., *Climate and Literature* (Cambridge: Cambridge University Press, 2019), 163–78 at 168.

35. Richard F. Burton, *Wanderings in West Africa* (New York: Dover, 1991), 175, 145.

36. Jessica Howell, *Malaria and Victorian Fictions of Empire* (Cambridge: Cambridge University Press, 2018), 52–81.

37. Burton, *Wanderings*, 158–9.

21

BARBARA LECKIE

The Uncomfortable Commons in Lewis Carroll and William Morris

In 1880, William Morris gave a lecture on art's failure to meet contemporary political needs. It was a period in which capitalism, with its commitment to economic progress and market economy principles, was on the upswing and Morris and others were frustrated by the seeming incapacity of culture to make any headway against its momentum. "We of the middle classes," Morris proclaimed to his audience, "are the most powerful body of men the world has yet seen."[1] But even with all their power, "a new art" capable of challenging industrial capitalism remained out of reach.

Morris's frustration with the social and political conditions of his period fused the cultural and the environmental. Like many others, he was dismayed by changes in both the natural and the built environment. Through the early 1880s, he introduced environmental and cultural initiatives against air pollution, and he was a persistent advocate for the preservation of buildings as well as the protection of Epping Forest. In the absence of systemic change, however, he realized that piecemeal measures would "do [no] more than scratch the surface" of existing problems.[2] He felt simultaneously encouraged by the rise of protest movements (acknowledging that one person's desire to act reflected "something stirring in the heart of the world") and discouraged by 1882's "summerless season, and famine and war" and the failure, still, for art to catalyze significant political action.[3] "To do nothing but grumble and not to act," Morris wrote to a friend, "that is throwing away one's life."

When I reread these passages recently, I was struck by how closely they echo current responses to the climate crisis. Despite a growing climate movement, international political forums, and incremental policy changes, global carbon emissions continue to rise. What can often look like a great deal of grumbling takes the place of significant action and a "new art" capable of galvanizing action has not yet emerged. The tension Morris identifies between piecemeal change and radical transformation also anticipates a tension in the environmental humanities. What does the environmental turn in Victorian studies and in literary studies in general seek to accomplish? Social and political change? Field-wide change? Or insights that add to the field but leave its political, social, and cultural context intact? I explore these questions by turning to the environment and the commons in Lewis Carroll's *Alice's Adventures in Wonderland* (1865) and William Morris's *New from Nowhere* (1890). Carroll and Morris dramatize the sort of profound systemic unsettling that the latter argues is necessary for real change. In doing so, they stage transformative change through the lens of the commons, what counts as common sense, poetry, and the power, as Carroll puts it, of believing in "impossible things."[4]

The Poetry of the Commons: The Environment and Common Sense

In a highly influential 1968 paper, "The Tragedy of the Commons," Garrett Hardin argues that the commons was a damaging, indeed unsustainable, model of land and environmental management because those working the land would always seek to increase their yields and thus, over time, deplete the land. The paper's thesis built on nineteenth-century thinkers like Jeremy Bentham, Adam Smith, Thomas Malthus, and Charles Darwin and dovetailed with market economy principles and a privileging of the individual that has continued to define not only "common sense" (what goes without saying or is obvious) but also social and political relations in the Global North.[5] The article's title, moreover, directs its reading: after a fall, tragedies have predictable conclusions, and they are not happy ones.

Hardin's ideas did not go unchallenged. Indeed, Elinor Ostrom won the Nobel Prize for illustrating the flaws in Hardin's thinking. She offers myriad examples of historical and contemporary commons in which commoners worked collectively to manage the land rather than in isolation, as Hardin imagined. Even so, Hardin's paper continues to have an outsized influence on thinking about the commons. Indeed, his caricature of the commons is a good example of how an idea – especially an idea that supports mainstream values – can persist long after it has been debunked.

Commons were lands that were privately owned but to which laborers and the working classes had access to hunt, grow food, and graze animals. They were collectively stewarded and, as Ellen Rosenman notes, "*relatively democratic.*"[6] While the commons date back to the medieval period, in the eighteenth and nineteenth centuries, with the rise of steam power and corresponding shift to industrial capitalism, British Parliament passed over 4,000 acts that enabled the enclosure of lands that had previously served as commons. The result was that many of those people who had relied on access to the commons to survive were forced to move to urban areas to seek work. "[T]he destruction of the commons," Carolyn Lesjak writes, generated "profound transformations of a whole social world."[7]

If the "tragedy" of the commons continues to resonate for many critics, in recent years a different tragedy has emerged: the tragedy of the market economy. This tragedy points to a world now marked by resource depletion, rising carbon pollution, and a changing climate on course to surpass the planetary boundaries that sustain life. That is, it is not the commons that should be framed as a tragedy, but industrial and, later, market capitalism. In this context then, I propose the "poetry of the commons" in place of the tragedy of the commons. The poetry of the commons both offers an alternative to the market economy and more accurately captures how the commons traditionally worked: as a collective, land-based, sharing economy. The poetry of the commons – with its focus on the root of *making* in the term "poetry" – contributes to the legibility of the commons as inclusive, interconnected, responsive to changing conditions, oriented toward multiple possibilities, and capable of holding tensions together. While they don't use the phrase "poetry of the commons," many critics are now turning to the variations on the commons as models for political action in the context of intersecting crises that include climate change.

What Carroll and Morris do in their work is gesture toward what this poetry of the commons might look like. However, dislodging prevailing versions of common sense, like the market economy, is not easy. As Gillian Beer notes, "[m]ost major scientific theories rebuff common sense."[8] When shifts in common sense such as Darwin's new ideas are successful, Beer continues, they demand "more than an additive adjustment of theory." They "overturn the observable world" and radically redefine it, a process that involves moving "the status of an 'as if' theory to a 'real description.'"[9] Here Beer nicely captures two things: the difference between ideas that add to existing conceptual models and ideas that transform them; and the role of literary, poetic, and imaginative "as if" thinking in this process. Michael Branch notes that a similar tension between the additive and the transformative attends the role of the environmental humanities. He cautions against using this new field only to add to the array of subjects taught in the humanities instead of transforming them and, potentially, society as a whole.[10]

Carroll and Morris both turn to ideas of the environment to mobilize "as if" thinking – imagining or anticipating a community for their ideas – in the context of common sense. With the rise of industrial capitalism and the market economy, Thijs Lijster writes, the "politics of extraction, exploitation, and inequality" have defined "common sense" rather than "common abundance and mutual care."[11] Lijster also suggests that "acting as if" change is possible has the capacity to interrupt common sense and redefine it. The question then becomes how to generate those shifts in common sense that unsettle unexamined positions and imagine new ones. Can a new poetry of the commons incite the imagination of new possibilities that have the potential to become "real descriptions"?

In his well-known essay "The Climate of History," Dipesh Chakrabarty turns to the nineteenth-century novel to explain what he considers the arbitrariness of the origins of the climate crisis. "[T]he industrial way of life has acted much like the rabbit hole in Alice's story," he writes; "[W]e have slid into a state of things that forces on us a recognition of some of the parametric (that is, boundary) conditions for the existence of institutions central to our idea of modernity and the meanings we derive from them."[12] While many have taken issue with Chakrabarty's claim of the arbitrariness of industrial capitalism, his other point – that this new set of conditions "forces on us a recognition" of climate change – is less often discussed. In particular, the fact that this recognition does not lead to transformative action is passed over.

Alice helps Chakrabarty's reader to imagine the point he wants to make. Alice's world, like ours, confounds "common sense." While Chakrabarty does not address the "acting as if" dimension of literature, in *Alice* and *News from Nowhere*, Carroll and Morris respectively dramatize situations in which the protagonists' "common sense" fails to explain the new environments they encounter, and they must accordingly find new ways to understand what they experience. I want to consider then a poetry of the commons that aligns less with "the fall" of tragedy and more with the "overturn [of] the observable world."[13] Put another way, I want to consider how common sense may be transformed into *commons* sense.

The Fall: *Alice's Adventures in Wonderland*

Alice's Adventures in Wonderland (1865) dramatizes one version of a transformed environment and illustrates how hard it is to find one's bearings when the rules change. In this way, Chakrabarty's "slid[e] into a state of things" above – slow, almost unnoticed – is very different from Alice's fall. In *Alice*, the fall makes vivid to readers how deeply unsettling such an abrupt change is. In the context of Chakrabarty's comparison to current climatic conditions, however, it illuminates the tragedy of market economy models that inform common sense and business-as-usual approaches to the climate crisis. We may recognize the breaking of those parametric boundary conditions that threaten sustained life on the planet, but we continue to use the same Enlightenment tools to address them, doubling down on what is familiar instead of turning to poetry, thinking otherwise, and new possibilities. Our response, in short, is additive rather than transformative.

Alice, however, provides some tools for a different approach: tools for illustrating how language shapes one's perception of what is possible; tools for making sense of what, at first glance, does not make sense; tools for encouraging wonder over instrumental rationality (the word "wonder" and its derivatives are used eight times in the first two-and-half pages of the novel alone); and tools for enabling shifts from recognition to action. In Carroll's nonsense narrative, the practice of believing "impossible things" shades into the recognition "that very few things indeed were really impossible."[14] To be sure, *Alice* addresses the commons neither as a model of land stewardship nor as a conceptual idea of a sharing economy, but it does introduce "nonsense" as a *practice* to dislodge entrenched ideas.

Alice's fall may feel accidental, as Chakrabarty remarks, but it is no ordinary fall, combining as it does falling to sleep, falling down a rabbit hole, and falling from the garden-like river bank to a walled-in garden just beyond her reach. Like those who were eager to benefit from the advantages of industrial capitalism, she "never once considered how in the world she was going to get out again." Instead, she went "Down, down, down," wondering, "Would the fall *never* end?" "Down, down, down" she continued to fall, until "thump! thump! … and the fall was over."[15] Alice, remarkably, is unhurt but finds herself locked in a room from which she cannot easily escape.

There are many aspects of this opening that might call to mind the climate crisis for twenty-first century readers: the helplessness of falling; the inability to make sense of it as one tries to cling to what's familiar (in Alice's case, books and food on shelves as she goes down, down, down); and the feeling that, while one is not hurt, everything is changed. We, like Carroll's Victorian readers, often feel that the old models of common sense no longer apply, while new models are not yet available. The "simple rules" no longer function.[16] In this context, *Alice* stages a collision between the ideas Alice confronts in Wonderland and the ideas that inform her thinking prior to her fall.

Notably, Alice falls *into* the earth. (The original title of this book was *Alice's Adventures Under-Ground*). While the underground is not a commons, she falls into a world richly populated with other living beings from rabbits, caterpillars, dormice, and pigs to serpents, frogs, fish, and lobsters with whom she interacts impartially. She also encounters a cat, a puppy, a dodo (long extinct at the time of writing), a flamingo (not native to England), a gryphon (an imaginary creature), and a mock turtle (a satiric invention). Carroll is making visible, through the extravagant array of Alice's interactions, a world that is unseen by human inhabitants who live for the most part only *on* the earth while also, of course, deeply indebted and tied to it. Despite being underground, moreover, Alice encounters a complex and varied environment filled with trees, grasses, flowers, and mushrooms in lush abundance. And she also encounters a built environment of houses, rooms, doors, and perplexities like croquet games played with living beings, a reminder perhaps that even seemingly inanimate things are alive. When Alice eats a mushroom, her body responds by shrinking or growing; she cannot eat the mushroom without being visibly, radically transformed herself.

The fall's most pronounced departure from Alice's bucolic world on the riverbank is captured in how language works there. To be sure, the underground world of Wonderland approximates a dreamworld, or unconscious, in which recognizable events take on strange and impossible capacities. In the case of Wonderland, animals talk, the sun shines underground, cakes appear out of nowhere, and words, while usually familiar, do not quite make sense. This is also, of course, the world of children's play. It might seem distant from any sort of transformative politics but, by insisting on imagination – thinking "as if" – as a *practice*, Carroll outlines the skills needed for such transformation. As the Queen notes in *Through the Looking-Glass*, she has long practiced believing impossible things: "Why, sometimes I've believed as many as six impossible things before breakfast," she boasts.[17]

Alice quickly realizes that the norms of the familiar world will not help her in Wonderland. She repeatedly tries to draw on what she has learned, imperfectly, in order to make sense of things but finds her skills wanting. Instead of being able to draw on her school "lessons" to navigate this world, lessons lessen, rather than advance, one's knowledge of the world. Words are playfully punned (tortoise/taught us; porpoise/purpose; T/tea), playing cards come to life, and the rules are unknown or unexplained. As Gillian Beer and Tina Choi note, this world also reflects the dizzying shifts to perception introduced by Darwin's ideas in *The Origin of Species* published five years earlier.[18] Similarly, the rise of industrial modernity is knit into a landscape in which sounds in the natural world are compared to the whistle of a steam engine.[19] *Alice*, then, demonstrates how deeply unsettling it can be when one's comfortable world is upended and "additive adjustments" do little to ease this discomfort.

Tina Young Choi notes that the *Alice* books "moved away from the additive, linear logic of traditional children's literature ... and toward the potential for multilinearity and proliferation."[20] When the White Queen asks Alice, "Can you do addition? ... What's one and one and one and one and one and one and one and one and one and one?" she replies that she doesn't know because she "lost count."[21] Carroll, indeed, uses nonsense throughout the text to illustrate the limits of addition. In his privileging of "uncommon nonsense" and departures from "the natural way,"[22] he gestures toward the possibility of a common sense that begins "underground," as only a seed perhaps, but – through forms of cultivation that include not only land but also art (the gardeners in Wonderland, for example, paint the roses red) – makes something new and perhaps even transformative. Thus, while Carroll did not address the enclosure acts or promote the commons, by locating Wonderland in the earth and populating it with talking animals and games – like playing cards – that come to life, he provides his reader with exercises for believing "impossible things" and imagining a different order of relations.

The "Overturn": *News from Nowhere*

Ten years after his disenchanted lecture and subsequent turn to politics, Morris returns again to culture with his novel *News from Nowhere* (1890). In this novel, his protagonist, William Guest, disheartened after a frustrating political meeting, falls asleep in his home by the Thames. Like *Alice*, then, *News* uses the frame of a dream to enable a vision of an alternative world and an alternative idea of common sense. And like *Alice*, in *News* the river-bank is the catalyst for a dream that introduces a departure from established environmental norms. And again like Carroll's heroine, Guest is filled with "measureless wonder" upon reaching Nowhere; indeed, the words "aston-ished" and "bewildered" are used eight times over the space of two pages when he arrives.[23] His wonder is in sharp contrast to the "of course" attitude of Nowhere's inhabitants who, like those Alice encounters in Wonderland, doubt not their own protocols but only those of their interlopers.

Unlike *Alice*, however, *News* revives an idea of the commons that had been eroded by the enclosure acts, as noted above. Indeed, the world of Nowhere is defined by transformative political change, the "overturn" that Guest initially struggles to understand.[24] In Morris's vision, the under-ground – signifying as it does darkness, machinery, and a departure from beauty – is an obstacle to, rather than a vehicle for, transformation. Morris accordingly sets his novel in a future where the railway is replaced by the river and beauty prevails. As Guest observes, the corruption of the late nine-teenth century had "destroyed" the river's "beauty morally, and had almost destroyed it physically."[25] Thus, when he wakes in the new world, he is "astonished" by the lush greenery of the riverbanks and his first instinct is "to take a swim in mid-stream."[26] With his new novel, Morris is ready to think what a "new art" might look like and link it to what I am calling the poetry of the commons.

In nineteenth-century industrial England, land, time, and labor are bought and sold, while leisure, for the majority of the people, is almost unimaginable. The result is a sooty, dark, built-up world of chimneys and factories and clear-cutting in which the rivers are polluted and their banks thick with grime. Guest is graciously introduced to the very different reality of Nowhere by Dick, Dick's partner Clara, Guest's love interest Ellen, and the 102-year-old Hammond who straddles Guest's world and his own.

The world Morris discloses in this poetry of the commons is thoroughly informed by a sense of the commons and what Morris, in other writing, calls the "share-and-share-alike crowd."[27] The river and the land are shared by all, while industrial modernity, with its bottom lines of profits and progress, has been replaced by a sharing economy. Money is only of historical interest. Local communities organize themselves in a world "designed toward the common needs of mankind,"[28] with progress and invention subordinated to leisure and beauty. The natural world itself is thoroughly interwoven with the practices of everyday life. As Hammond explains, the inhabitants appreciate the wildness of nature for itself, feeling no need to improve or transform it: "We like these pieces of wild nature, and can afford them, so we have them; let alone that as to the forests, we need a great deal of timber, and suppose that our sons and sons' sons will do the like."[29] To value the land, Morris suggests, is to value intergenerational sustainability. In the past, Ellen notes, the country was treated as an "ugly characterless waste, with no delicate beauty to be guarded" and with no attention to the changing seasons, weather, and soil. "How could the people be so cruel to themselves?" she asks.[30] Hammond similarly observes the beauty of the untamed over that of the tended garden, and the value of land left to the wiles of sheep over that which had been covered in factories.

If the land can no longer be segmented, owned, and wasted, neither can time. *News* layers and interfuses the past, present, and future in multiple ways: through references to the medieval period that Morris admired; through the dream transportation to an imagined future; through a slowing down of the biological clock which leads to everyone appearing much younger and more vigorous at advanced ages; and through a reimagining of leisure and work. These layers are complicated even further by the novel's subsequent readers, who compare Morris's ideas to their own current experience, as I do here. As Elizabeth Miller puts it, "In *News* Morris effectively takes the historic inversion of the folkloric chronotope and turns it inside out, so the future actually *is* set in the future rather than the past, but is still drawn imaginatively by means of the past."[31] *News* maintains the distinction between 2103 Nowhere and 1880s England for the most part, but as the novel reaches its conclusion, tears in the temporal fabric emerge. Ellen seems to know, for example, that Guest belongs to another time and understands that he will return to that period and not to another country. When Ellen asks what Guest is thinking about, he says, "The past, the present? Should she [Ellen] not have said the contrast of the present with the future: of blind despair with hope?" In that transitional moment, he at once lives, impossibly, in the past (the nineteenth century), the present (Nowhere's utopia), and the future (Nowhere as seen from the nineteenth century).

The novel's environmental and temporal transformations are also reflected in the language. To convey the nonsense of Guest's nineteenth-century common sense, however, the novel resorts not to an amplification of nonsense but to a resignification of terms and contexts, realizing the double negation of Carroll's "uncommon nonsense." Certain words in his new environment attract Guest's attention. The inhabitants of Nowhere, for example, refer to each other as "neighbours" and Guest adopts the terminology himself in an effort to blend in.[32] This technique allows Morris to underscore the ways in which frameworks for knowledge shape what can be seen and understood. The corresponding collisions of meaning, if not as playful as Carroll's in *Alice*, are just as world-jolting. Basic ideas are transfigured and transvalued, with the meaning of familiar words being questioned or given a twist. When Guest asks Dick about school he replies, "School? ... what do you mean by that word?" preferring instead to think of "education" and its root meaning of "lead[ing] out."[33] Factories are called "Banded-workshops[,] ... places where people collect who want to work together."[34] And art "has no name amongst us now," Hammond explains, because it is so thoroughly absorbed into the beauty of labor.[35]

Midway through his extended discussion with Guest, Hammond relates how shifts in language follow from shifts in the conditions of production: "I have been using words and phrases which few people amongst us could understand without long and laborious explanation."[36] One of those words is "nature." Clara, seeking to define the contrast between her world and the previous one she has heard about, notes that, because the previous world made a distinction between animate people and inanimate nature, it "was natural ... that they should try to make 'nature' their slave, since they thought 'nature' was something outside them."[37] This comment anticipates Ellen's oft-cited effusive appreciation of a world without such divisions: "Oh me! Oh me! How I love the earth, and the seasons, and weather, and all things that deal with it, and all that grows out of it."[38] The inhabitants of Nowhere experience the natural world in the tenor of appreciation and sharing rather than exploitation and commodification.

Crucially, Morris also weaves a politics of transformation into his poetry of the commons. In closing the novel, the narrator of *News* notes that "if others can see it as I have seen it, then it may be called a vision rather than a dream."[39] Such visions, or poetry, provide the tools for imagining and believing in what may otherwise seem impossible. Morris's "impossible," unlike Carroll's, is one in which labor, environmental, and personal relations are strengthened by reciprocity and "common abundance and mutual care."[40] As Guest rows down the river with his new friends, the narrator notes that "the folk on the bank talked indeed, mingling their kind voices with the cuckoo's song, the sweet strong whistle of the blackbirds, and the ceaseless note of the corn-crake."[41] Nicholas Frankel, following Arnold Berleant, calls this Morris's "*environmental aestheticism*"; he dissolves "the imagined borders of text and self, to admit the world, and thereby to remind us ... that 'environment is continuous with us, our very condition of being.'"[42] Guest, "stripped bare of every habitual thought and way of acting,"[43] finds his old ideas of common sense increasingly replaced by something more like *commons* sense or a sense of the commons. As Miller puts it, *News* imagines "a new society where feelings of natural interconnection make up the texture of everyday experience rather than a short holiday from smoke and pollution."[44] Commons sense, as formulated by Morris, then, does not add to existing social structures but radically transforms or overturns them.

Conclusion: Commons Sense

When I began this chapter, I had in mind the *uncomfortable* commons as a version of the commons that, through its very unfamiliarity, would create the discomfort and disorientation experienced by Alice and Guest. In Carroll's and Morris's time, as in ours, *any* version of the commons is such a departure from the norm that its idea of common sense – or commons sense – would create unease for many. Today, commons, sometimes called communes, are carved out of business-as-usual economic relations as approximations of the commons – such as community gardens that, while committed to some of the commons' ideals, do not realize their vision of a transformed society. It is more comfortable to fold these experiments into everyday life than to use them to imagine its overturn. Piecemeal changes, in relation to industrial capitalism in the nineteenth century or neoliberalism today, are all too quickly absorbed into existing structures, without changing the frames that define what we have constructed as common sense.

Morris was keenly aware of the ways in which contemporary social and political conditions shaped art and imagination, and vice versa. He recognized, Nikolaus Pevsner writes, "the indissoluble unity of an age and its social system."[45] In this context, I continue to be troubled by academic essays like the one I am writing now that conform to genre expectations and seek to persuade readers through conventional means. I suspect that I am, almost 150 years after Carroll and Morris, continuing to produce not the "new art" – read, new writing – necessary to create transformative change but only that additive writing that is absorbed into the groundswell of what is now so often termed the environmental humanities.

What I seek is the discomfort that makes one look again and pause. And to wonder, as Alice and Guest do in their very different ways, about the world we inhabit. In his Introduction to *News*, Clive Wilmer cites Stephen Coleman as follows: "History can explode. And when it does it is ignited by those who have dared to dream, who have the courage to take on seemingly unbeatable odds, who are brave enough to demand the impossible."[46] Drawing on John Ruskin, Wilmer compares political reform to the building of cathedrals.[47] One labors but one does not always anticipate seeing the results of one's labor in one's lifetime. *Alice* and *News* may not have contributed to the political change that Morris sought. But taking the long view, they can be seen as laying the foundations for something like "*commons* sense" and a practice and poetry of the commons adequate to the demands of the climate crisis that confronts all of us now.

Notes

1. Quoted in E. P. Thompson, *William Morris: Romantic to Revolutionary* (New York: Pantheon, 1955), 244.
2. Thompson, *William Morris*, 257.
3. Cited in Thompson, *William Morris*, 258.
4. Lewis Carroll, *Alice in Wonderland*, Donald J. Gray, ed. (New York: Norton, 1971), 153.
5. Peter Linebaugh, *Stop Thief! The Commons, Enclosures, and Resistance* (Oakland: PM, 2014), 116.
6. Ellen Rosenman, "On Enclosure Acts and the Commons," in Dino Franco Felluga, ed., *BRANCH: Britain, Representation and Nineteenth-Century History*, https://shorturl.at/rMl2Y.
7. Carolyn Lesjak, *The Afterlife of Enclosure: British Realism, Character, and the Commons* (Stanford: Stanford University Press, 2021), 6.
8. Gillian Beer, *Darwin's Plots: Evolutionary Narrative in Darwin, George Eliot, and Nineteenth-Century Fiction* (Cambridge: Cambridge University Press, 2009), 1.
9. Beer, *Darwin's Plots*, 1–2.
10. Michael Branch, "Ecocriticism: Surviving Institutionalization in the Academic Environment," *ISLE: Interdisciplinary Studies in Literature and Environment* 2.1 (Spring 1994), 91–9.
11. Thijs Lijster. "Community, Commons, Common Sense," 10.1 *Social Inclusion* (2022), 152–60 at 159.
12. Dipesh Chakrabarty, "The Climate of History: Four Theses," 35.2 *Critical Inquiry* (Winter 2009), 197–222 at 217.
13. Beer, *Darwin's Plots*, 2.

14. Carroll, *Alice in Wonderland*, 10.
15. Carroll, *Alice in Wonderland*, 8–9.
16. Carroll, *Alice in Wonderland*, 10.
17. Carroll, *Alice in Wonderland*, 153.
18. Beer, *Darwin's Plots*; Tina Young Choi, *Victorian Contingencies: Experiments in Literature, Science, and Play* (Stanford: Stanford University Press, 2022).
19. Carroll, *Alice in Wonderland*, 52, 70.
20. Choi, *Victorian Contingencies*, 119–20.
21. Carroll, *Alice in Wonderland*, 193.
22. Carroll, *Alice in Wonderland*, 82.
23. William Morris, *News from Nowhere and Other Writings* (London: Penguin, 1993), 46–47.
24. Morris, *News from Nowhere*, 126.
25. Morris, *News from Nowhere*, 180.
26. Morris, *News from Nowhere*, 47.
27. Cited in Thompson, *William Morris*, 392.
28. Morris, *News from Nowhere*, 201.
29. Morris, *News from Nowhere*, 106–107.
30. Morris, *News from Nowhere*, 208.
31. Elizabeth Carolyn Miller, "Landscape and Environment," in Marcus Waithe, ed., *The Cambridge Companion to William Morris* (Cambridge: Cambridge University Press, 2024), 245–56 at 248.
32. Morris, *News from Nowhere*, 56.
33. Morris, *News from Nowhere*, 66.
34. Morris, *News from Nowhere*, 81.
35. Morris, *News from Nowhere*, 160.
36. Morris, *News from Nowhere*, 139.
37. Morris, *News from Nowhere*, 200.
38. Morris, *News from Nowhere*, 220.
39. Morris, *News from Nowhere*, 227.
40. Lijster, "Community," 159.
41. Morris, *News from Nowhere*, 218.
42. Nicholas Frankel, "William Morris and the Kelmscott Press," in Florence Boos, ed., *The Routledge Companion to William Morris* (New York: Taylor and Francis, 2021), 501–22 at 518.
43. Morris, *News from Nowhere*, 133.
44. Miller, "Landscape," 246.
45. Cited in Clive Wilmer, "Introduction," Morris, *News from Nowhere*, ix–xli at xxviii.
46. Wilmer, "Introduction," xxxix.
47. Wilmer, "Introduction," xxviii.

22

CAROLINE LEVINE

Form and Activism

Victorian scholars have done crucial work in exposing the ways that nineteenth-century Britain is to blame for the climate crisis unfolding now. Imperial conquest, capitalist economics, and extractivism launched the mass devastation of local economies, ecosystems, and cultures around the world in the name of civilization – and profit. Many Victorians worked to make these practices seem noble, even natural. They told stories about the march of progress and took their own distance from "savagery" as a model for other societies to follow. We are still in the grip of the progress narrative – as many of our own contemporaries put faith in technological advancement, insisting that it will save us from the worst of climate catastrophe. One might argue then that it is crucial to study Victorian culture to understand its devastating legacy. Meanwhile, numerous literary critics have also turned to Victorian works to think about ways to *resist* the drive to ecological destruction, from Charles Darwin's "entangled bank" and John Ruskin's impassioned arguments against the destruction of nature, to critics of the polluted skies, such as Charles Dickens, Robert Louis Stevenson, and Alice Meynell. With these writers in mind, we could equally insist that reading Victorian literature is the best way to critique Britain's role in the ongoing climate catastrophe.

But if we take the second of these paths, we should note that Victorian literature has remarkably little to say about how to go about actually dismantling dominant systems. Dickens expressed perpetual outrage at social ills but offered only scathing accounts of people trying to change them, from the revolutionary Madame Defarge in *Tale of Two Cities* (1859) to philanthropists like Mrs Jellyby in *Bleak House* (1852), Members of Parliament like Mr Gregsbury in *Nicholas Nickelby* (1839), and utilitarian reformers like Josiah Bounderby in *Hard Times* (1854). Dickens "neither created an agenda for reform nor achieved specific legislative change." The hero of George Eliot's *Felix Holt: The Radical* (1866) urges working-class agitators to settle down, since poverty, waste, and ignorance are horrors "which no man can undo." And the author herself famously refused to advocate for women's suffrage, dismissing "overzealous champions of women." Ruskin thundered about industrialization but mostly urged a heightened moral consciousness rather than any particular course of action for change. In both *The Princess Casamassima* (1886) and *The Bostonians* (1886), Henry James's activists are narrow and contemptible. Alfred Tennyson summoned the faint concession that he did "not in the least mind if England, when the people are less ignorant and more experienced in government, eventually *becomes* a democracy." Ruth McAdams makes the powerful case that the Victorian industrial novel pushes anti-union arguments, which have been incorporated into mainstream culture ever since.[1] And even the determinedly political Elizabeth Barrett Browning set about exposing the evils of slavery and child labor in her poetry, yet painted a scorching portrait of the reformer Romney Leigh, whose overconfidence in the work of social improvement must be taken down a peg by the visionary woman artist.

We find a similar refusal to sketch out plans for action in the work of today's literary scholars. We raise awareness and understand historical causes, but few of us imagine that it is the responsibility of literary studies to figure out how to organize social movements. Many in fact insist that practical politics will only reaffirm the dominations of the present. José Esteban Muñoz argues against "gay pragmatism" because it re-entrenches the "corrupt and bankrupt social order," while Karen Pinkus warns environmentalists against the "tyranny of the practical."[2] Other critics insist that if we press literary studies into the service of social programs, we lose the special value of aesthetic experience, which is precisely to resist the pressures of corporate and authoritarian regimes.[3] There are certainly scholar–activists in Victorian studies, and minoritized faculty have undertaken the especially steep uphill struggle to open the field to queer, racialized, and disabled histories and perspectives. But I want to distinguish here between the crucial task of diversifying the literary academy and the project of using literary knowledge to organize for social transformation beyond the university. The latter is rare. While scholars have often understood literature as effective at revealing and exploring social problems, almost all balk at the prospect of using the aesthetic to sketch out pragmatic programs or solutions.

The more I have considered this pattern, the more it has come to seem strange and unconvincing. Why value reading and writing about the horrors of hunger, homelessness, gender inequality, structural racism, enslavement, and environmental destruction, only then to refuse the work of imagining meaningful ways to respond? This is an especially urgent question at this moment of accelerating climate change. While large majorities of the public are convinced that climate change is real, devastating, and human-caused, most people take no action in response. Publics are well aware of the crisis, then, but most of us have no idea what to do. And this is precisely the place where Victorian literature and literary studies live and thrive – in the gap between awareness and action. In this respect, we Victorianists do not challenge dominant ideologies; we play right into a mainstream culture of climate inaction.

A Formalist Approach to Taking Action

As I continue to shift my own work toward the problem of action in the climate crisis, I have been drawing on formalist methods. For literary critics, the word *form* typically refers to the patterns, shapes, and structures that organize texts, like poetic meter or free indirect discourse. In my book *Forms*, I deliberately expanded the definition of form to mean any shape or configuration of materials, any arrangement of elements, any ordering or patterning. This allows me to understand politics as very much a matter of form. Some of the most powerful political battles are waged over spatial arrangements like national borders and incarceration. Societies also depend on temporal orders, from the age of consent to the narrative of civilizational progress. And some of the most terrible causes of suffering take hierarchical forms, like gender and racial inequality.

Since many of these political forms – including racial hierarchies and national borders – are oppressive and violent, lots of politically minded thinkers in the arts and humanities have wanted to say that all forms should be resisted. As Jack Halberstam puts it, "Revolution will come in a form we cannot yet imagine. ... We cannot say what new structures will replace the ones we live with yet, because once we have torn shit down, we will inevitably see more and see differently and feel a new sense of wanting and being and becoming."[4] And so literary critics often turn to breaks in aesthetic form as moments of liberation from the dominant social order. And yet, it is misleading, as Anna Kornbluh argues, to imagine that we can ever free ourselves completely from structuration. All human communities depend on orderings, shapes, and arrangements just for the ordinary project of day-to-day survival. As I have argued in *The Activist Humanist* (2023), it is important not only to break from existing structures but to build forms of collective life that are just, sustainable, and egalitarian, including routines of food and rest, pathways for water and waste, and sheltering enclosures.[5]

I have also been turning to formalist methods to understand more and less effective forms of organizing ourselves for political power. Movements for change can rely on many different forms – elections, committees, unions, marches, boycotts, occupations, petitions, speeches, debates, stories, songs, posters, blockades, mutual aid infrastructure, alliances, coalitions, hierarchies, compromise, consensus, civil disobedience, armed struggle, media campaigns, and social networks, among others. There is no consensus among scholars or activists about which forms work best. For Roger Hallam, it is urgent to engage in mass, nonviolent civil disobedience, while for Andreas Malm, our most effective option is to start blowing up pipelines.[6] It is my own contention that a formalist set of methods can help us to understand which political forms have worked best for achieving genuine social change, and why.

My research suggests that there are three main ingredients to most successful campaigns for change, from labor strikes and AIDS activism to pipeline protests. First, they must draw a broad range of sympathetic supporters. As Erica Chenoweth and Maria J. Stephan argue, the larger and more diverse the campaign in terms of gender, age, religion, class, and ethnicity, the harder it is to isolate and discredit protestors, and the more likely participants are to bring a range of useful skills to the work. As the crowd of protestors grows, the chance of retribution against them declines and momentum intensifies. When police and security forces are connected to protesters through kinship or social networks, they are less likely to commit violence against them. And the more widespread the sympathy and support for the campaign, the more likely those in power are to make concessions or to become divided.[7] The Victorian Anti-Corn Law League, which successfully pushed for free trade and bourgeois manufacturing interests, built a national movement through pamphlets, meetings, and speeches and used economic, political, moral, and religious arguments to try to rally working-class people to their cause, experimenting with strategies for building a mass campaign which many later lobbying and pressure groups would adopt. Parliament was prompted to repeal the Corn Laws, eventually, in part to disrupt a powerful alliance from forming between middle and working classes. Similarly, Gandhi deliberately enlarged his own political movement by recruiting new participants at every village along his famous Salt March and reached out to both domestic and international media to ensure wide coverage. He understood civil disobedience as a good strategy to draw broad-based support because the spectacle of peaceful protestors being violently repressed by state forces can move even casual observers to sympathy. Most effective movements also draw on existing groups to create coalitions. Interestingly, different organizations within a movement do not have to agree on strategies or values to succeed. In fact, in what is called the "radical flank effect," activists who undertake extremist tactics increase support for more moderate positions within the same movement.[8]

The second formal ingredient for success is sustained pressure over time. One big march or media sensation drive can spark a burst of excitement, but the energy can also just as quickly fizzle without having realized any meaningful goals. Daniel Hunter argues that politicians often simply "wait until the heat blows over."[9] The Chartists certainly suffered from the struggle to maintain momentum. In 1842, their leadership splintered, and one of the movement's most impressive offshoots, the short-lived Miners' Association of Great Britain and Ireland, collapsed with the failure of the General Strike in 1844.

Third, successful activists organize around clear goals. It is not enough to critique the status quo; movements must spell out a path forward. For Marx and Engels, Critical-Utopian Socialism – the Owenites and the Fourierists – failed on exactly these grounds, creating communities that considered themselves superior to the larger society without building toward a larger revolution.[10] More recently, Occupy Wall Street dissolved without realizing material change in part because of the main form it took – the occupation of a bounded public space. Enough people must simply continue to occupy Zuccotti Park indefinitely, withstanding forces of deterioration – including activist exhaustion, a lack of sympathy from a broad public, and dwindling media interest – with no opportunity to declare or negotiate a victory. For many, this freedom from linear temporality was the movement's special strength. But its commitment to the proliferation of many equally valid goals meant that there was no shared purpose to keep the movement going. The fact that it did not have "a natural end point" meant that it had little option but to peter out without realizing any specific demands.[11]

While many revolutionary thinkers have argued against practical goals because these tend to be coopted by powerful interests, others, including Rosa Luxemburg and Angela Davis, have made the case that organizing for near-term goals can be a crucial step in a larger revolutionary struggle. Since people are most inclined to mobilize around immediate causes of suffering and concrete demands, it is a mistake not to recognize the revolutionary potential in any campaign that draws large numbers of people even if the demands are not themselves revolutionary. Women's suffrage was for Luxemburg a crucial example.[12]

These three ingredients – large sympathetic publics, sustained pressure, and shared goals – have allowed comparatively powerless groups to win meaningful victories. For example, the tiny Kenyan town of Lamu successfully opposed the building of a $2 billion coal-fired power plant. Coordinating protests, letter-writing campaigns, a poetry competition, a lawsuit, and frequent invitations to the media, local groups worked together with national and global environmental and human rights organizations, all in the interests of the same clear goal: to prevent the building of the plant. In June 2019, they won. A town of 25,000 people had successfully "stopped a giant in its tracks."[13]

Literature and Activism

How important was poetry to the successful campaign in Lamu? Many nineteenth-century thinkers asserted that literary writing was itself an effective form of activism. George Eliot said that she was "teaching the world through books."[14] I want to probe this claim here, arguing that unless large public support, sustained pressure, and clear goals are also at work, literature often raises awareness without prompting meaningful change.

Two Victorian examples will help to make this clear. Let's first take Thomas Hood's "The Song of the Shirt" (1843). This is a poem about a seamstress working long hours merely to survive. The poem was a huge hit: it quadrupled the sales of *Punch* magazine, where it was first published, and was quoted in every other major newspaper, set to music, printed on handkerchiefs, and rendered in numerous paintings. But while Hood successfully inspired broad public support, his readers did not organize around clear, shared goals. Some thought that inspectors should go into women's homes to regulate conditions, but to others that seemed like an unacceptable intrusion into the sanctity of domestic spaces. Henry Mayhew recommended tariffs and unionization, while Charles Kingsley proposed emigration to Australia for redundant women. It was not until organized labor pushed to pass the Trade Boards Act in 1909 – sixty-six years after Hood's popular poem – that home garment workers started to feel the benefits of a legally binding minimum wage.[15]

Elizabeth Barrett Browning's poem, "The Cry of the Children," played a role in a more immediately successful movement for change. Drawing attention to the suffering of children working in factories, the poem first appeared in August 1843. Although Barrett Browning herself was associated with the Whigs, she published the poem in *Blackwood's Edinburgh Magazine*, a Tory publication that had been quite critical of her work, perhaps deliberately broadening her readership across party lines.

The poem appeared in the middle of a political struggle that had been going on for years. The "Poor Man's Earl," Anthony Ashley-Cooper, 7th Earl of Shaftesbury, had spent more than a decade pushing for a ten-hour workday to replace laboring routines in mines and factories that stretched to twelve or even sixteen hours. Parliament had been debating these changes almost every session since the Factory Act of 1833. At the moment Barrett Browning's poem appeared, some MPs were advocating for the repeal of all regulations, others for their expansion.

What exactly did "The Cry of the Children" contribute to the cause? It did not stimulate the passage of any specific law, but it carried a strong affective force on the side of further legislative reform. *The Dublin University Magazine* said: "as your indignation kindles against their oppressors, you love the noble womanly soul that has made you feel so well what is just and human." *Tait's Edinburgh Magazine* put it this way: "The 'cry of the factory children' moves you, because it is no poem at all – it is just a long sob, veiled and stifled as it ascends through the hoarse voices of the poor beings themselves." W. J. Fox, an orator, minister, and Member of Parliament, quoted "The Cry of the Children" at length in an 1846 lecture to a Working Men's Association, claiming that the poem lends working-class children "its own voice to claim their rights, to describe their wrongs and their sufferings."[16] The poem pulled on public heartstrings, deepening sympathy for the oppressed child workers.

But it would not be right to conclude that only the skilled poet could move people in this way. Barrett Browning herself was inspired to compose "The Cry of the Children" in horrified response to a more prosaic piece of writing: the report of the Royal Commission on Children's Employment. Running to hundreds of pages, the Commission's accounts include interviews with employers, managers, and children working in mines, collieries, ironworks, and mills. Children as young as five worked long hours and suffered from terrible injuries, hunger, and fatigue. Esther Craven worked as a "hurrier" in the coal mines from the age of nine. "I get all the skin off my leg sometimes by the stones in the gate … a pick struck me once and broke my finger." John Nurse, a twelve-year-old in the Treforest Tin Works in Wales, "goes to work at half past four in the morning and leaves at seven at night." "'In truth,'" he says, "'it is very hard.'"[17]

These reports caused a sensation. *The Times* was "revolted" by accounts of "indecencies amounting to barbarism." *The Christian Lady's Magazine* hoped that "the unanimous voice of England will proclaim" that the horrors of children's labor "shall exist no longer." Dickens urged reform in a letter to the *Morning Chronicle* in 1842. Soon after the first report appeared, Lord Ashley wrote in his diary: "the feeling in my favour has become quite enthusiastic; the Press on all sides is working most vigorously."[18] The Mines and Collieries Bill successfully passed in July 1842, prohibiting women and girls, as well as boys under ten, from working underground. In other words, poetry was not the only kind of writing to draw broad sympathy and stimulate public outcry: the dreary accounts of inspectors also had substantial affective power.

Barrett Browning's poem did have one demonstrable advantage over the Commission's prose. "The Cry of the Children" had a surprisingly long activist afterlife, invoked for decades after its first publication in a range of labor reform contexts. In the 1870s, for example, George Smith led a campaign to alleviate the horrors of children's work in the brick-making business. His 1871 book, *Cry of the Children from the Brickyards of England*, is explicit about its debt to Barrett Browning.[19] Once again, however, this was a case where writing formed only one piece of a larger campaign. Smith convinced one factory inspector, Robert Baker, to take up his cause. He then persuaded Liberal reformer A. J. Mundella to push for the successful passage of the Brick and Tile Yards Act of 1871 in the House of Commons.[20]

Almost seventy years after the poem was published, the American company Thanhouser Films drew on "The Cry of the Children" to rouse sympathy for workers in the aftermath of the "Bread and Roses" strike, led by immigrant laborers and the Industrial Workers of the World. In his silent film version (available through various sources online), director George O. Nichols used not only Barrett Browning's title but also her poetic lines as intertitles between gritty images of child laborers in a Massachusetts mill town. He then unfolded his own tragic story of "little Alice" – inspired by the character in the poem but set in his own contemporary context. More than a thousand people crowded into a showing of the film version of *The Cry of the Children* organized by socialists in the Bronx in 1912, and Woodrow Wilson invoked Thanhouser's film in his campaign against Taft's ineffectiveness on child labor.[21]

Why did "The Cry of the Children" endure? Here, poetic form worked in its favor. Unlike the Commission's reports, the poem's account of the suffering of working children was general enough to be portable to all industrial contexts, and short excerpts could travel without needing elaborate explanation. But Barrett Browning's art was only ever effective as one piece of prolonged, organized collective protests waged in lots of places: in the pages of newspapers and novels, in streets and squares, and on the floor of Parliament. A single work of art, then as now, does not accomplish social change on its own: it can have meaningful effects only when it forms part of a large chorus of voices that sustains pressure over time to achieve specific goals.

Organized Collective Action

Why has literary studies focused so little attention on the nuts and bolts of organized collective action? It is in part because we have eschewed organizing forms in favor of textual ruptures and openings. It is in part because of the atomizing forms our own labor takes, as MacAdams argues.[22] And it is in part because we still live in a culture obsessed with individuals. In the classroom we tend to focus on specific writers and texts, reading them closely for their uniqueness. Many nineteenth-century middle-class social movements, including abolitionist sugar and cotton boycotts and temperance campaigns, also emphasized individual choice and consumption. Working-class movements were more inclined toward collectivist tactics, including mass petitions and demonstrations, general strikes, and violent uprisings. Canonical literature, however, tends to draw us back toward individual spheres of action. The most monumental social novels, *Middlemarch* and *Bleak House*, end by contracting to the domestic scale. It is a heavy lift, in this context, to shift our literary energies toward building and organizing sustained collective campaigns. As the long life of "The Cry of the Children" demonstrates, however, it is precisely the embeddedness of aesthetic objects in collective campaigns for change that maximizes their impacts across demographics and time.

It is especially important to focus on collective action when it comes to climate change. Most of us do not realize that the fossil fuel companies have thrown millions of dollars behind canny and effective campaigns to get us to focus on individual actions instead of building a mass environmental movement. It was British Petroleum that invented the very idea of the "carbon footprint" to make us ordinary people take responsibility for the climate crisis. Big Oil knew that if they got us to embrace individual actions like recycling our plastics and eating plant-based diets we would be likely to succumb to what social scientists call the "single action bias"; that is, doing one environmentally friendly action makes us feel that we have done our part. Larry Thomas, former President of the Society of the Plastics Industry, predicted that a recycling campaign would distract us from what the fossil fuel companies were doing. "If the public thinks recycling is working, then they are not going to be as concerned about the environment."[23] These campaigns have successfully diverted attention toward our own small actions and away from these companies' ongoing push to build new pipelines, oil rigs, and coal mines right now, against every warning from the Intergovernmental Panel on Climate Change. The accumulation of individual actions has been ineffective – recycling plastics does not get at the causes of climate change – and too sluggish to draw down emissions at large enough scales to prevent planetary systems from reaching the tipping points that will trigger irreversible warming feedback loops.

Instead of focusing on single actions, whether a text or a purchase, I am suggesting that all of us can – and should – be putting our energies into organizing large-scale, sustained campaigns that have clear goals. Instead of feeling guilty (or self-righteous) about our own individual actions, we would do better to come together in groups to put pressure on the small number of companies that are actually driving the climate crisis, including ExxonMobil, Chevron, BP, Shell, Gazprom, Halliburton, and ConocoPhillips. We do not have to start from nothing or make huge sacrifices. We can join existing organizations that are working to stop fossil fuel subsidies and permits to build new pipelines, such as the Climate Reality Project and Stop the East African Crude Oil Pipeline.[24] We can enter the global struggle to divest institutions, banks, and pension funds to restrict the financing of fossil fuels, including 350.org, TIAA-Divest,[25] Vanguard S.O.S.,[26] and Stop the Money Pipeline.[27] We can engage in direct actions, such as Extinction Rebellion's disruptions of sports events and public gatherings.[28] We can connect environmental concerns to unionization through Labor for Sustainability,[29] or the Blue Green Alliance.[30] The more introverted among us can download the Climate Action Now app and do a short action on our phones every day.

We should also keep studying literature. But let's do so in ways that move beyond the usual literary focus on heightened awareness to explicit questions about effective strategies for change. Do different literary forms – poetry, drama, fiction – have distinctive roles to play in social movements? What combinations of aesthetic and non-aesthetic forms have advanced the struggle for social transformation in the past, and what forms should guide action in the climate crisis? Environmentalists know that we need to move away from ideologies of human individualism. One path is to embed the study of literature in large collective action campaigns to bring down Big Oil – before it is too late.

Notes

1. On Dickens, see David Vincent, "Social Reform," in Robert L. Patten, John O. Jordan, and Catherine Waters, eds., *The Oxford Handbook of Charles Dickens* (Oxford: Oxford University Press, 2018), 420–35. George Eliot, "Address to Working Men, by Felix Holt," *Blackwood's Magazine* 103 (January 1868), 2; and see June Skye Szirotny, "Why George Eliot Was Not a Political Activist," *Journal of International Women's Studies* 13.3 (July 2012), 184–93. John Ruskin, *The Complete Works of John Ruskin*, ed. E. T. Cook and Alexander Wedderburn, 39 vols. (London: George Allen, 1904), 10.197. Ruth McAdams, "'Three Cheers for the United Aggregate Tribunal!': Confronting Anti-union Discourse, Then and Now," *Victorian Literature and Culture* 51 (January 2024), 555–67. Tennyson, qtd. in Cornelia Pearsall, *Tennyson's Rapture* (Oxford: Oxford University Press, 2008), 41.

2. José Esteban Muñoz, *Cruising Utopia* (New York: New York University Press, 2009), 20; Karen Pinkus, *Fuel: A Speculative Dictionary* (Minneapolis: University of Minnesota Press, 2016), 4.

3. For example, Jonathan Kramnick, *Paper Minds* (Chicago: University of Chicago Press, 2018).

4. Jack Halberstam, "The Wild Beyond: With and for the Undercommons," in Stefano Harney and Fred Moten, eds., *The Undercommons: Fugitive Planning and Black Study* (Brooklyn: Minor Compositions, 2013), 5.

5. Anna Kornbluh, *The Order of Forms* (Chicago: University of Chicago Press, 2019); Caroline Levine, *The Activist Humanist: Form and Method in the Climate Crisis* (Princeton: Princeton University Press, 2023).

6. Roger Hallam, *Common Sense for the 21st Century* (New York: Chelsea Green, 2019); Andreas Malm, *How to Blow Up a Pipeline* (London: Verso, 2021).

7. Erica Chenoweth and Maria J. Stephan, *Why Civil Resistance Works* (New York: Columbia University Press, 2012), 41.

8. Brent Simpson, Robb Willer, and Matthew Feinberg, "Radical Flanks of Social Movements Can Increase Support for Moderate Factions," *PNAS Nexus* 1.3 (July 2022), 1–11.

9. Daniel Hunter, *Climate Resistance Handbook* (350.org, 2019), 47–8, https://shorturl.at/5RYcz.

10. Karl Marx and Friedrich Engels, *The Communist Manifesto*, ed. Gareth Stedman Jones (Harmondsworth: Penguin, 1967), 255–6.

11. Craig Calhoun, "Occupy Wall Street in Perspective," *British Journal of Sociology* 64.1 (March 2013), 31.

12. Rosa Luxemburg, *The Rosa Luxemburg Reader*, eds. Kevin B. Anderson and Peter Hudis (New York: Monthly Review, 2004), 129.

13. Otsieno Namwaya, "Tribunal Stops Kenya's Coal Plant Plans," *Human Rights Watch* (July 1, 2019), www.hrw.org/news/2019/07/01/tribunal-stops-kenyas-coal-plant-plans.

14. George Eliot, *The George Eliot Letters*, ed. Gordon S. Haight, Vol. 6 (New Haven: Yale University Press, 1954–5), 405.

15. Sheila Blackburn, *A Fair Day's Wage for a Fair Day's Work? Sweated Labour and the Origins of Minimum Wage Legislation in Britain* (Aldershot: Ashgate, 2007), 245–6.

16. "Miss Barrett's Poems," *Dublin University Magazine* (February 1845), 144; George Gilfillan, "Female Authors No. II: Mrs. Elizabeth Barrett Browning," *Tait's Edinburgh Magazine* (September 1847), 623; W. J. Fox, "Reports of Lectures Addressed Chiefly to the Working Classes," *People's Journal* 1 (1846), 136.

17. Children's Employment Commission, *First Report of the Commissioners: Mines* (London: Clowes, 1842), 80; Commissioners for Inquiring into the Employment and Condition of Children in Mines and Manufactories, *Appendix to First Report of Commissioners (Mines)*, facsimile ed. (Shannon: Irish University Press, 1968), 515.

18. *The Times*, qtd. in Peaches Henry, "The Sentimental Artistry of Barrett Browning's 'The Cry of the Children,'" *Victorian Poetry* 49.4 (2011), 543; "The Factories," *Christian Lady's Magazine* (June 1842), 566; Dickens, in Carolyn Berman, *Dickens and Democracy in the Age of Paper: Representing the People* (Oxford: Oxford University Press, 2022), 183–84. Lord Ashley, in Edwin Hodder, *The Life and Work of the Seventh Earl of Shaftesbury* (London: Cassell, 1886), 418.

19. George Smith, *Cry of the Children from the Brickyards of England* (London: Haughton and Co., 1879), 3. Joseph Cook also used the poem to advocate for child labor reform in Massachusetts, see *Boston Monday Lectures* (London: R. D. Dickinson, 1879), 42–56.

20. Susan Lammin, "George Smith of Coalville (the Children's Friend)," in Jill Stewart, ed., *Pioneers in Public Health* (London: Routledge, 2017), 46–55.

21. Richard Abel, "1912: Innovative Nostalgia, and Real-Life Threats," in Charles Kiel and Ben Singer, eds., *American Cinema in the 1910s* (New Brunswick: Rutgers University Press, 2009), 81–2.

22. Ruth McAdams, "'Three Cheers for the United Aggregate Tribunal!,' Confronting Anti-union Discourse, Then and Now," *Victorian Literature and Culture* (15 January 2024), 566.

23. Rebecca Solnit, "Big Oil Coined 'Carbon Footprints' to Blame Us for Their Greed," *The Guardian* (August 23, 2021), https://shorturl.at/dIb5R; George Monbiot, "The Big Polluters' Masterstroke Was to Blame the Climate Crisis on You and Me," *The Guardian* (October 9, 2019), https://shorturl.at/rkX3l; Center for Research on Environmental Decisions, "The Psychology of Climate Communication," 21–2, cred.columbia.edu/guide; Larry Thomas, qtd. in Laura Sullivan, "How Big Oil Misled the Public into Believing Plastic Would Be Recycled," *Morning Edition* (September 11, 2020), https://shorturl.at/nvtt1.

24. At: climaterealityproject.org; stopeacop.net.

25. At: tiaa-divest.org.

26. At: vanguard-sos.com.

27. At: stopthemoneypipeline.com.

28. At: rebellion.global.

29. At: labor4sustainability.org.

30. At: bluegreenalliance.org.

FURTHER READING

This selective guide to further readings focusses on influential and recent approaches to key topics discussed in the collection, as recommended by its contributors. It is separated into the five subcategories of the chapter collection itself. By clustering these recommendations in this fashion, the larger scholarly contexts for the ideas that weave across chapters are emphasized, while avoiding steering readers toward only one or two approaches to exploring the topics of any one chapter.

The Global Imaginary

David E. Allen, *The Naturalist in Britain: A Social History* (London: Allen Lane, 1976).

Adelene Buckland, *Novel Science: Fiction and the Invention of Nineteenth-Century Geology* (Chicago: University of Chicago Press, 2013).

Bruce Clarke, *Energy Forms: Allegory and Science in the Era of Classical Thermodynamics* (Ann Arbor: University of Michigan Press, 2001).

Margaret Cohen, *The Novel and the Sea* (Princeton: Princeton University Press, 2010).

Margaret Cohen, ed., *A Cultural History of the Sea in the Age of Empire* (London: Bloomsbury Academic, 2021).

Dennis Denisoff, *Decadent Ecology in British Literature and Art, 1860–1910: Decay, Desire, and the Pagan Revival* (Cambridge: Cambridge University Press, 2022).

Ian Duncan, *Human Forms: The Novel in the Age of Evolution* (Princeton: Princeton University Press, 2019).

Justin D. Edwards, Rune Graulund, and Johan Höglund, eds., *Dark Scenes from Damaged Earth: The Gothic Anthropocene* (Minneapolis: University of Minnesota Press, 2022).

Nathan K. Hensley and Philip Steer, eds., *Ecological Form: System and Aesthetics in the Age of Empire* (New York: Fordham University Press, 2018).

Joris-Karl Huysmans, *Against Nature*. Translated by Margaret Mauldon (Oxford: Oxford University Press, 1998).

William Stanley Jevons, *The Coal Question: An Enquiry Concerning the Progress of the Nation, and the Probable Exhaustion of Our Coal-Mines* (London: Macmillan, 1865).

Edwin Ray Lankester, *Degeneration: A Chapter in Darwinism* (London: Macmillan and Company, 1880).

Barbara Leckie, *Climate Change, Interrupted: Representation and the Remaking of Time* (Stanford: Stanford University Press, 2022).

Carolyn Lesjak, *The Afterlife of Enclosure: British Realism, Character, and the Commons* (Stanford: Stanford University Press, 2021).

Dana Luciano, *How the Earth Feels: Geological Fantasy in the Nineteenth Century United States* (Durham: Duke University Press, 2024).

Tobias Menely and Jesse Oak Taylor, eds., *Anthropocene Reading: Literary History in Geologic Times* (State College: Pennsylvania State University Press, 2017).

Elizabeth Carolyn Miller, *Extraction Ecologies and the Literature of the Long Exhaustion* (Princeton: Princeton University Press, 2021).

Timothy Morton, *Hyperobjects: Philosophy and Ecology after the End of the World* (Minneapolis: University of Minnesota Press, 2013).

Andrew Porter, ed., *The Oxford History of the British Empire: The Nineteenth Century* (Oxford: Oxford University Press, 1999).

Michael S. Reidy, *Tides of History: Ocean Science and Her Majesty's Navy* (Chicago: University of Chicago Press, 2008).

Helen M. Rozwadowski, *Vast Expanses: A History of the Oceans* (London: Reaktion Books, 2018).

Cannon Schmitt, "Imaginary Worlds: Sea of Ink," in Margaret Cohen, ed., *A Cultural History of the Sea in the Age of Empire* (London: Bloomsbury Academic, 2021), 203–28.

Cannon Schmitt, "Technical Maturity in Robert Louis Stevenson," *Representations* 125.1 (Winter 2014), 54–79.

Cannon Schmitt, "Tidal Conrad (Literally)," *Victorian Studies* 55.1 (Autumn 2012), 8–29.

Andrew Smith and William Hughes, eds., *EcoGothic* (Manchester: Manchester University Press, 2013).

Neferti X. M. Tadiar, *Remaindered Life* (Durham: Duke University Press, 2022).

Anna Tsing, Heather Swanson, Elaine Gan, and Nils Buband, eds., *The Arts of Living on a Damaged Planet: Ghosts/Monsters* (Minneapolis: University of Minnesota Press, 2017).

Imperialism and Colonialism

D. M. R. Bentley, "The Romantic Aesthetics of Settlement in 19th Century Canada," *Literature Compass* 9 (2012), 66–79.

Debjani Bhattacharya, *Empire and Ecology in the Bengal Delta: The Making of Calcutta* (Cambridge: Cambridge University Press, 2018).

Tim Bonyhady, *The Colonial Earth* (Melbourne: Melbourne University Press, 2002).

C. A. Cranston and Robert Zeller, eds., *The Littoral Zone: Australian Contexts and Their Writers* (Amsterdam: Rodopi, 2007).

Alfred W. Crosby, *Ecological Imperialism: The Biological Expansion of Europe, 900–1900*, 2nd ed. (Cambridge: Cambridge University Press, 2004).

Helen Anne Curry et al., eds., *Worlds of Natural History* (Cambridge: Cambridge University Press, 2018).

Tony Hughes d'Aeth, *Like Nothing on this Earth: A Literary History of the Wheat Belt* (Crawley: University of Western Australia, 2017).

Elizabeth DeLoughrey and George Handley, *Postcolonial Ecologies: Literatures of the Environment* (Oxford: Oxford University Press, 2011).

Felix Driver and Luciana Martins, eds., *Tropical Visions in an Age of Empire* (Chicago: University of Chicago Press, 2005).

Ken Gelder and Rachael Weaver, *The Colonial Kangaroo Hunt* (Melbourne: Melbourne University Press, 2020).

Radhika Govindarajan, *Animal Intimacies: Interspecies Relatedness in India's Central Himalayas* (Chicago: University of Chicago Press, 2018).

Richard H. Grove, *Green Imperialism: Colonial Expansion, Tropical Island Edens and the Origins of Environmentalism, 1600–1860* (Cambridge: Cambridge University Press, 1995).

Ramachandra Guha and Madhav Gadgil, eds., *This Fissured Land: An Ecological History of India* (Berkeley: University of California Press, 1993).

Graham Huggan and Helen Tiffin, eds., *Postcolonial Ecocriticism* (New York: Routledge, 2010).

Nicholas Jardine, J. A. Secord, and E. C. Spary, eds., *Cultures of Natural History* (Cambridge: Cambridge University Press, 1996).

Susan K. Martin, "'Tragic ring-barked forests,' and the 'Wicked Wood': Haunting Environmental Anxiety in Late Nineteenth-Century Australian Literature," in Laurence W. Mazzeno and Ronald D. Morrison, eds., *Victorian Environmental Nightmares* (Chamonix: Palgrave Macmillan, 2019), 121–43.

David Philip Miller and Peter Hanns Reill, eds., *Visions of Empire: Voyages, Botany, and Representations of Nature* (Cambridge: Cambridge University Press, 1996).

Grace Moore, "'So wild and beautiful a world around him': Trollope and Antipodean Ecology," in Deborah Denenholz Morse, Margaret Markwick, and Mark W. Turner, eds., *The Routledge Companion to Anthony Trollope* (New York: Routledge, 2014), 399–411.

Beate Neumeier and Helen Tiffin, eds., *Ecocritical Concerns and the Australian Continent* (Lanham, MD: Lexington Books, 2019).

Geoff Park, *Ngā Uruora: The Groves of Life: Ecology & History in a New Zealand Landscape*, (Wellington: Victoria University Press, 2018).

Bruce Pascoe, *Dark Emu: Aboriginal Australia and the Birth of Agriculture* (Brunswick, Victoria: Scribe, 2018).

Kavita Philip, *Civilizing Natures: Race, Resources, and Modernity in Colonial South India* (New Brunswick: Rutgers University Press, 2004).

Deborah Bird Rose, *Nourishing Terrains: Australian Aboriginal Views of Landscape and Wilderness* (Canberra: Australian Heritage Commission, 1996).

Kyle Whyte, "Settler Colonialism, Ecology, and Environmental Injustice," *Environment and Society* 9 (2018), 125–44.

Vegetal and Animal Correlations

Sarah Amato, *Beastly Possessions: Animals in Victorian Consumer Culture* (Toronto: University of Toronto Press, 2015).

Mary Bowden, "Vegetal Being in Samuel Butler's *Erewhon*: The Narrative Challenge of Nineteenth-Century Plant Science," *ISLE: Interdisciplinary Studies in Literature and Environment* 28.3 (Autumn 2021), 966–85.

Elizabeth Hope Chang, *Novel Cultivations: Plants in British Literature of the Global Nineteenth Century* (Charlottesville: University of Virginia Press, 2019).

Cameron Clark and E. L. McCallum, "Nature Bites Back: The Anti-pastoral Thesis in Queer and Trans Studies," Special Issue: *Regeneration: Environment, Art, Culture* 1.1 (2024), 1–20.

Dennis Denisoff, *Decadent Ecology in British Literature and Art, 1860–1910: Decay, Desire, and the Pagan Revival* (Cambridge: Cambridge University Press, 2021).

Jacques Derrida, *The Animal that Therefore I Am* (New York: Fordham University Press, 2008).

Jane Desmarais, *Monsters Under Glass: A Cultural History of Hothouse Flowers from 1850 to the Present* (London: Reaktion Books, 2018).

Emily Dickinson, *Emily Dickinson's Herbarium: A Facsimile Addition* (Cambridge, MA: Belknap, 2006).

Ivan Kreilkamp, *Minor Creatures: Persons, Animals, and the Victorian Novel* (Chicago: University of Chicago Press, 2018).

M. M. Mahood, *The Poet As Botanist* (Cambridge: Cambridge University Press, 2008).

Michael Marder, *The Philosopher's Plant: An Intellectual Herbarium* (New York: Columbia University Press, 2014).

Michael Marder, *Plant-Thinking: A Philosophy of Vegetal Life* (New York: Columbia University Press, 2013).

Catherine Maxwell, "Cultivating the Imagination: Plants and Flowers in Later Victorian Poetry," in Grażyna Bystydzieńska and Emma Harris, eds., *From Queen Anne to Queen Victoria: Readings in 18th and 19th Century British Literature and Culture* (Warsaw: University of Warsaw Press, 2021), 113–38.

Catherine Maxwell, *Scents and Sensibility: Perfume in Victorian Literary Culture* (Oxford: Oxford University Press, 2017).

Elaine P. Miller, *The Vegetative Soul: From Philosophy of Nature to Subjectivity in the Feminine* (Albany, NY: State University of New York Press, 2002).

Fabienne Moine, *Women Poets in the Victorian Era: Cultural Practices and Nature Poetry* (New York: Routledge, 2016).

Timothy Morton, *Ecology Without Nature: Rethinking Environmental Aesthetics* (Cambridge, MA: Harvard University Press, 2007).

Catriona Mortimer-Sandilands and Bruce Erickson, *Queer Ecologies: Sex, Nature, Politics, Desire* (Bloomington: Indiana University Press, 2010).

Dahlia Porter, "Specimen Poetics, Botany, Reanimation and the Romantic Collection," *Representations* 139 (2017), 60–94.

Beverly Seaton, *The Language of Flowers: A History* (Charlottesville, VA: University of Virginia Press, 1995).

Catriona Sandilands, "Fear of a Queer Plant?" *GLQ: A Journal of Lesbian and Gay Studies* 23.3 (May 25, 2017), 419–29.

Anna Tsing, *The Mushroom at the End of the World: On the Possibility of Life in Capitalist Ruins* (Princeton: Princeton University Press, 2015).

Lynn Voskuil, "Victorian Plants: Cosmopolitan and Invasive," *Victorian Literature and Culture* 49.1 (2021), 27–53.

Cary Wolfe, *Animal Rites: American Culture, the Discourse of Species, and Posthumanist Theory* (Chicago: University of Chicago Press, 2003).

Cary Wolfe, *Before the Law: Humans and Other Animals in a Biopolitical Frame* (Chicago: University of Chicago Press, 2012).

Environmental Uses and Abuses

Brenna Bhandar, *Colonial Lives of Property: Law, Land, and Racial Regimes of Ownership* (Durham, NC: Duke University Press, 2018).

Helen Blythe, *The Victorian Colonial Romance with the Antipodes* (Basingstoke: Palgrave Macmillan, 2010).

William Cobbett, *Rural Rides*, Vol. 1, 1830 (London: J.M. Dent & Sons, 1957).

Helen Louise Cowie, *Victims of Fashion: Animal Commodities in Victorian Britain* (Cambridge: Cambridge University Press, 2021).

William Cronon, *Uncommon Ground: Rethinking the Human Place in Nature* (New York: W. W. Norton, 1996).

Cara Daggett, *The Birth of Energy: Fossil Fuels, Thermodynamics, and the Politics of Work* (Durham: Duke University Press, 2019).

John Bellamy Foster, *Capitalism in the Anthropocene: Ecological Ruin or Ecological Revolution* (New York: Monthly Review, 2022).

Donna Haraway, "Anthropocene, Capitalocene, Plantationocene, Chthulucene: Making Kin," *Environmental Humanities* 6.1 (2015), 159–65.

Naomi Klein, *This Changes Everything: Capitalism vs. the Climate* (London: Penguin, 2015).

Carolyn Lesjak, *The Afterlife of Enclosure: British Realism, Character, and the Commons* (Stanford: Stanford University Press, 2021).

Allen MacDuffie, *Climate of Denial: Darwin, Climate Change, and the Literature of the Long Nineteenth Century* (Redwood City: Stanford University Press, 2024).

Allen MacDuffie, *Victorian Literature, Energy, and the Ecological Imagination* (Cambridge: Cambridge University Press, 2014).

Andreas Malm, *Fossil Capital: The Rise of Steam-Power and the Roots of Global Warming* (London: Verso, 2016).

Laurence W. Mazzeno and Ronald D. Morrison, *Victorian Writers and the Environment: Ecocritical Perspectives* (New York: Routledge, 2016).

Elizabeth Carolyn Miller, *Extraction Ecologies and the Literature of the Long Exhaustion* (Princeton: Princeton University Press, 2021).

Jason W. Moore, *Anthropocene or Capitalocene?: Nature, History, and the Crisis of Capitalism* (Oakland, CA: PM Press, 2016).

Jason W. Moore, *Capitalism in the Web of Life: Ecology and the Accumulation of Capital* (London: Verso, 2015).

Wendy Parkins, ed., *Victorian Sustainability in Literature and Culture* (New York: Routledge 2017).

Heidi C. M. Scott, *Fuel: An Ecocritical History* (London: Bloomsbury, 2018).

Philip Steer, *Settler Colonialism in Victorian Literature: Economics and Political Identity in the Networks of Empire* (Cambridge: Cambridge University Press, 2020).

Jesse Oak Taylor, *The Sky of Our Manufacture: The London Fog in British Fiction from Dickens to Woolf* (Charlottesville: University of Virginia Press, 2016).

Anthony Trollope, *Australia and New Zealand* (London: Chapman & Hall, 1873).

Environmentalism

Katherine Anderson, *Predicting the Weather: Victorians and the Science of Meteorology* (Chicago: University of Chicago Press, 2005).

Deepak Bhargava and Stephanie Luce, *Practical Radicals: Seven Strategies to Change the World* (New York: The New Press, 2023).

Deborah R. Coen, *Climate in Motion: Science, Empire, and the Problem of Scale* (Chicago: University of Chicago Press, 2018).

Christine Corton, *London Fog, the Biography* (Cambridge, MA: Belknap, 2015).

Devin M. Garofalo, "Lyric Geology: Anthropomorphosis, White Supremacy, and Genres of the Human," *Diacritics* 50.1 (2022), 32–61.

Devin Griffiths and Deanna Kreisel, "Special Issue: 'Open Ecologies,'" *Victorian Literature and Culture* 48.1 (Spring 2020), 1–28.

Dewey W. Hall, ed., *Victorian Ecocriticism: The Politics of Place and Early Environmental Justice* (Lanham, MD: Lexington Books, 2017).

Mark Harrison, *Climates and Constitutions: Health, Race, Environment and British Imperialism in India, 1600–1850* (New Delhi: Oxford University Press, 2002).

Carolyn Lesjak, *The Afterlife of Enclosure: British Realism, Character, and the Commons* (Stanford: Stanford University Press, 2021).

Caroline Levine, *The Activist Humanist: Form and Method in the Climate Crisis* (Princeton: Princeton University Press, 2023).

Thijs Lijster, "Community, Commons, Common Sense," *Social Inclusion* 10.1 (2022), 152–60.

Peter Linebaugh, *Stop Thief! The Commons, Enclosures, and Resistance* (Oakland, CA: PM Press, 2014).

Allen MacDuffie, *Victorian Literature, Energy, and the Ecological Imagination* (Cambridge: Cambridge University Press, 2014).

Martin Mahony, "Meteorology, Climate Science, and Empire: Histories and Legacies," in Zeke Baker, Tamar Lar, Mark Vardy, and Stephen Zehr, eds., *Climate, Science and Society: A Primer* (London, Routledge, 2023), 11–18.

Martin Mahony and Georgina Endfield, "Climate and Colonialism," *Wiley Interdisciplinary Reviews: Climate Change* 9 (2018), e510.

Andres Malm, *Fossil Capital: The Rise of Steam Power and the Roots of Global Warming* (London: Verso, 2016).

Ruth McAdams, "'Three Cheers for the United Aggregate Tribunal!': Confronting Anti-Union Discourse, Then and Now," *Victorian Literature and Culture* 51.4 (Winter 2023), 555–67.

Elizabeth Carolyn Miller, *Extraction Ecologies and the Literature of the Long Exhaustion* (Princeton: Princeton University Press, 2021).

Wendy Parkins, ed., *Victorian Sustainability in Literature and Culture* (New York: Routledge, 2017).

James Phillips, "Beauty Is a Fact under Siege," *Journal of Victorian Culture* 25.1 (Winter 2020), 63–76.

Ellen Rosenman, "On Enclosure Acts and the Commons," in Dino Franco Felluga, ed., *BRANCH: Britain, Representation and Nineteenth-Century History*, https://branchcollective.org/?ps_articles=ellen-rosenman-on-enclosure-acts-and-the-commons.

Zachary Samalin, *The Masses are Revolting: Victorian Culture and the Political Aesthetics of Disgust* (Ithaca, NY: Cornell University Press, 2021).

Heidi C. M. Scott, *Chaos and Cosmos: Literary Roots of Modern Ecology in the British Nineteenth Century* (University Park: Pennsylvania State University Press, 2014).

Jesse Oak Taylor, *The Sky of Our Manufacture* (Charlottesville, VA: University of Virginia Press, 2016).

E. P. Thompson, *William Morris: Romantic to Revolutionary* (New York: Pantheon, 1955).

INDEX

Cambridge Companions to ...

AUTHORS

Edward Albee edited by Stephen J. Bottoms

Margaret Atwood edited by Coral Ann Howells (second edition)

W. H. Auden edited by Stan Smith

Jane Austen edited by Edward Copeland and Juliet McMaster (second edition)

James Baldwin edited by Michele Elam

Balzac edited by Owen Heathcote and Andrew Watts

Beckett edited by John Pilling

Bede edited by Scott DeGregorio

Aphra Behn edited by Derek Hughes and Janet Todd

Saul Bellow edited by Victoria Aarons

Walter Benjamin edited by David S. Ferris

William Blake edited by Morris Eaves

Boccaccio edited by Guyda Armstrong, Rhiannon Daniels, and Stephen J. Milner

Jorge Luis Borges edited by Edwin Williamson

Brecht edited by Peter Thomson and Glendyr Sacks (second edition)

The Brontës edited by Heather Glen

Bunyan edited by Anne Dunan-Page

Frances Burney edited by Peter Sabor

Byron edited by Drummond Bone (second edition)

Albert Camus edited by Edward J. Hughes

Willa Cather edited by Marilee Lindemann

Catullus edited by Ian Du Quesnay and Tony Woodman

Cervantes edited by Anthony J. Cascardi

Chaucer edited by Piero Boitani and Jill Mann (second edition)

Chekhov edited by Vera Gottlieb and Paul Allain

Kate Chopin edited by Janet Beer

Caryl Churchill edited by Elaine Aston and Elin Diamond

Cicero edited by Catherine Steel

John Clare edited by Sarah Houghton-Walker

J. M. Coetzee edited by Jarad Zimbler

Coleridge edited by Lucy Newlyn

Coleridge edited by Tim Fulford (new edition)

Wilkie Collins edited by Jenny Bourne Taylor

Joseph Conrad edited by J. H. Stape

H. D. edited by Nephie J. Christodoulides and Polina Mackay

Dante edited by Rachel Jacoff (second edition)

Daniel Defoe edited by John Richetti

Don DeLillo edited by John N. Duvall

Charles Dickens edited by John O. Jordan

Emily Dickinson edited by Wendy Martin

John Donne edited by Achsah Guibbory

Dostoevskii edited by W. J. Leatherbarrow

Theodore Dreiser edited by Leonard Cassuto and Claire Virginia Eby

John Dryden edited by Steven N. Zwicker

W. E. B. Du Bois edited by Shamoon Zamir

George Eliot edited by George Levine and Nancy Henry (second edition)

T. S. Eliot edited by A. David Moody

Ralph Ellison edited by Ross Posnock

Ralph Waldo Emerson edited by Joel Porte and Saundra Morris

William Faulkner edited by Philip M. Weinstein

Henry Fielding edited by Claude Rawson

F. Scott Fitzgerald edited by Ruth Prigozy

F. Scott Fitzgerald edited by Michael Nowlin (second edition)

Flaubert edited by Timothy Unwin

E. M. Forster edited by David Bradshaw

Benjamin Franklin edited by Carla Mulford

Brian Friel edited by Anthony Roche

Robert Frost edited by Robert Faggen

Gabriel García Márquez edited by Philip Swanson

Elizabeth Gaskell edited by Jill L. Matus

Edward Gibbon edited by Karen O'Brien and Brian Young

Goethe edited by Lesley Sharpe

Günter Grass edited by Stuart Taberner

Thomas Hardy edited by Dale Kramer

David Hare edited by Richard Boon

Nathaniel Hawthorne edited by Richard Millington

Seamus Heaney edited by Bernard O'Donoghue

Ernest Hemingway edited by Scott Donaldson

Hildegard of Bingen edited by Jennifer Bain

Homer edited by Robert Fowler

TOPICS

For EU product safety concerns, contact us at Calle de José Abascal, 56–1°, 28003 Madrid, Spain or eugpsr@cambridge.org.

www.ingramcontent.com/pod-product-compliance
Ingram Content Group UK Ltd.
Pitfield, Milton Keynes, MK11 3LW, UK
UKHW021920280426
470499UK00017B/332